China's Death Penalty

Routledge Advances in Criminology

1. Family Life and Youth Offending
Home Is Where the Hurt Is
Raymond Arthur

2. China's Death Penalty
History, Law, and Contemporary Practices
Hong Lu and Terance D. Miethe

China's Death Penalty

History, Law, and Contemporary Practices

Hong Lu and Terance D. Miethe

Routledge
Taylor & Francis Group
New York London

Routledge
Taylor & Francis Group
270 Madison Avenue
New York, NY 10016

Routledge
Taylor & Francis Group
2 Park Square
Milton Park, Abingdon
Oxon OX14 4RN

Routledge is an imprint of Taylor & Francis Group, an Informa business

Transferred to Digital Printing 2009

International Standard Book Number-10: 0-415-95569-6 (Hardcover)
International Standard Book Number-13: 978-0-415-95569-0 (Hardcover)

Library of Congress Cataloging-in-Publication Data

Lu, Hong, 1966-
China's death penalty : history, law, and contemporary practices / Hong Lu and Terance D. Miethe.
p. cm. -- (Routledge advances in criminology ; 2)
Includes bibliographical references and index.

ISBN10: 0-415-95569-6 (hbk)
ISBN10: 0-415-80396-9 (pbk)

ISBN13: 978-0-415-95569-0 (hbk)
ISBN13: 978-0-415-80396-0 (pbk)

1. Capital punishment--China. 2. Capital punishment--China--History. I. Miethe, Terance D. II. Title.

HV8699.C6L8 2007
364.660951--dc22 2006034687

Visit the Taylor & Francis Web site at
http://www.taylorandfrancis.com

and the Routledge Web site at
http://www.routledge-ny.com

Contents

	Tables	vii
	Preface and Acknowledgments	ix
1	**Introduction**	**1**
2	**Death penalty as law and punishment**	**11**
3	**Historical and legal development of the death penalty**	**27**
4	**Contemporary substantive and procedural criminal law on the death penalty**	**49**
5	**The application of the death penalty**	**69**
6	**The process of death sentence and execution**	**89**
7	**Reforms and the future prospects of the death penalty**	**121**
	Appendix: Judicial judgment documents for a sample of capital cases	141
	Notes	187
	Bibliography	237
	Index	249

Tables

1.1	Status of the death penalty in twenty-first century countries and territories	5
3.1	Sentences in courts of more than twenty counties in the Shan-Gan-Ning Border Region controlled by the Communist Party	44
4.1	Capital offenses under PRC's criminal law (1979)	51
4.2	Supplemental capital offenses by decrees between 1979 and 1997 (forty-seven new capital offenses)	52
4.3	Capital offenses stipulated in the 1997 Criminal Law	54
4.4	Review procedure for capital punishment as stipulated in the 1996 Criminal Procedure Law	59
4.5	Selected crimes with definition, aggravating factors and sentencing range in the 1997 criminal law	62
5.1	International pattern of death sentence and execution over time	74
5.2	Number of known executions in China for select years	75
5.3	Offender's age in capital and non-capital cases	78
5.4	Percentage distribution of male offenders in capital and non-capital cases	79
5.5	Percentage distribution of low occupational status of offenders in capital and non-capital cases	80
5.6	Percentage distribution of transient offenders in capital and non-capital cases	81
5.7	Percentage distribution of recidivist offenders in capital and non-capital cases	82
5.8	Percentage distribution of offenders who "voluntary surrendered" or "confessed" in capital and non-capital cases	83
5.9	Percentage distribution of death and monetary consequences in cases with capital and non-capital sentences	86
6.1	Average days between arrest and end of first trial	108
6.2	Average days between first trial and second trial/ first review	108
6.3	Average days between first review and final review/approval of the death sentence by the Supreme Court	109

6.4 Average days for capital cases to conclude with or without the final review and approval by the Supreme Court 111

Endnotes

4.1 Selected review procedure for capital punishment amended in the interpretations by the Supreme People's Court 213
5.1 Reversion rate in the Appellate Court and the Supreme Court 217

Preface and Acknowledgments

Recent decades have witnessed dramatic changes in the abolition of the death penalty movement internationally. By 2005, more countries have abolished the death penalty in law or in practice than countries that have retained the death penalty. Even among the retentionist countries, significant legal reforms have been undertaken to ensure its humane and fair imposition. For example, in the United States, the Supreme Court in 2005 issued a ruling that prohibited execution of individuals younger than eighteen years old. In China, a series of legal reforms have been taking place to conform to international standards. Most notably, these legal reforms in China's death penalty include restricting the application of death sentences and executions to adults older than eighteen years of age, mandatory legal representation for all death penalty cases, reduction of judicial discretion in commutation decisions for offenders completing the suspended death sentence, and the Supreme Court's initiatives to take back review and approval authority for all death penalty cases.

Using documentary and observational data, this book provides systematic descriptions and analyses of the death penalty theory, law and practice in China. The focus of this book is the past two decades since the economic reforms. The book discusses the major changes in the substantive (e.g., scope of capital punishment) and procedural laws (e.g., mandatory legal representation, mandatory review process) regarding the death sentence and execution in China, and how these changes affect the actual practice (e.g., average time it takes for a capital case to move from one stage to the next in the criminal justice system). Drawing upon Western literatures on this issue, this book also discusses various sociological factors (e.g., public opinion, offender's and victim's status), both internal (e.g., maintaining governmental legitimacy and social order) and external (e.g., increasing pressure to abolish and/or restrict the use of the death penalty), and their impact on the current death penalty law and practice, and its future prospects in China.

This book is written for graduate students, undergraduate students, social legal scholars, and policy makers who are interested in law, crime and punishment, and the current debate and future prospects of the death penalty in the global context. We hope this book on the current developments of the death penalty law and practice in China will increase their substantive interest in the future study of these issues of law and society.

Compared to the abundance of death penalty literature available in other parts of the world, particularly in the United States, published research on the death penalty in China is relatively scarce. This is due to several factors. China has not published systematic national data on death sentences and executions, which prevented any accurate description of the scope of the death sentences and executions in this nation. The relatively slow development in social science research also prevented scholars from drawing any meaningful conclusions about the demographic distributions of death sentences and executions and the public opinions related to this issue.

Under these conditions, the current study would not have been possible if not for the dramatic changes in China in the recent decades. The changes are mostly manifested in the blossoming Internet industry that facilitates speedy dissemination of information. During the course of this research, we benefited from numerous Web sites (e.g., the Supreme Court [http://www.chinacourt.org], the National People's Congress News Center for providing the Searching Index of China's Laws and Regulations [http://202.99.23.199/home/begin1.cbs], China Daily, People's Daily, Legal Daily, and Xinhua News Agency [http://www.xinhuanet.com]) for their timely dissemination of new laws, regulations, interpretations, and news regarding the death sentences and executions in China. We also benefited from the online public opinions polls on the death penalty conducted from time to time on the Web sites of Xin Lang (http://www.sina.com), Yi Jing (http://www.163.com), and Sou Hu (http://www.sohu.com). We admire and appreciate the editors of these Web sites for their courage and insights in providing the cutting-edge information that was not available and considered politically sensitive two decades ago.

We were also pleasantly surprised with the professionalism and openmindedness of some of the Chinese legal professionals and officials. During the course of this research, the first author conducted numerous interviews and observed court trials and mediation sessions in several courts in China. We are grateful for the accommodation and assistance provided to the author by those legal professionals and officials.

We would also like to express our sincere thanks to our colleagues and research collaborators, Professor Lening Zhang of St. Francis College, Professor Jianhong Liu of Rhode Island College, and Professor Bin Liang of Oklahoma State University, Tulson, for their friendship, support, and insights in China's law and social control. We have benefited tremendously from working with them on other related projects that ultimately led to the publication of this book. We owe special debts to our research assistants (Xiaojun Liang, Alicia Boots, Hua Li, and Peng Deng) for their devotion and tireless efforts in library research, data transcription, and data coding.

We would also like to thank our editor at Routledge, Benjamin Holtzman, for his patience and support throughout the editorial process.

In addition, much of the research was conducted during the sabbatical leave awarded to the first author by the University of Nevada, Las Vegas (UNLV). We would also like to acknowledge the generous financial support of the UNLV SITE (Stimulation, Implementation, Transition and Enhancement) grant, New Investigator's award, and the Faculty Travel Award.

Finally, we would like to express our deepest gratitude to our spouses, Jason and Nancy. They have been friends, companions, and more importantly, our emotional and intellectual sounding boards that helped us through difficult times when working on this project. Our deepest gratitude also goes to our children, Shannon, Selina, Alex, and Zachary, for their understanding, patience, and unwavering support. This book is dedicated to them.

1 Introduction

The world came to know about China's death penalty practices mostly through research and media reports from Western countries. Biased or not, its death penalty practices are frequently vilified in both substance and procedures. In fact, the common stereotypical image is that China uses the death penalty to suppress minority threats in questionable legal proceedings that lack basic procedural safeguards, force confessions, and provide little access to legal representation. The presumed application of capital punishment to a wide array of criminal misconduct, its execution by a single-bullet shot to the back of the head, the quick and immediate imposition of the punishment after conviction, and the harvesting of the person's organs for transplant purposes are other salient elements of the Western image of China.

As is true of all stereotypes, there may be some element of truth in all of these portrayals. However, Western research and media rarely captured the complex procedural requirements and the rapidly changing law and practices surrounding the death penalty in China.[1] To illustrate this neglect, consider the following recent developments in death sentences and executions in China:

- Four peasants convicted of murder in Hebei province finally had their death sentences reversed by a higher court in 2004, nearly ten years after their convictions. They were tried on four different occasions for these charges in a lower court.[2]
- An offender convicted of murder and sentenced to death was allowed to meet with his parents and wife after sentencing in Guilin, Yunnan province.[3]
- After being legalized in criminal law, lethal injection was first used in criminal executions in Kunming, Yunnan province in 1997.[4]
- In Sichuan Deyang Intermediate People's Court, six defendants were convicted of a series of murders, robberies and rapes without confessing to these crimes. These defendants were given the death penalty and suspended death sentences. These convictions were the first cases in the PRC history in which the death penalty was imposed by solely

relying on the DNA evidence without the corroboration of the defendants' confession.[5]
- A serial rapist in Henan province had his death sentence reduced to a suspended death sentence because of his meritorious service in helping the law enforcement authority solve a murder case.[6]
- An indigent peasant in Anhui province was sentenced to death with two year suspension for robbery and murder. However, he was exonerated by an appeals court with the assistance of a legal aid defense attorney.[7]

The absence of discussions of the complex procedural requirements and most recent developments of the Chinese death penalty practice in Western studies is primarily due to limited access to data. To date, China has not published systematic national data on death sentence and execution. Though most trials are public, the public has also little access to complete court transcripts. Under these conditions, it is somewhat easy to see why there is a certain level of mystic and vagueness surrounding lethal executions in China.

The closest estimate of the annual number of death sentences and executions in China is probably provided by Amnesty International's Death Penalty Logs.[8] These counts are derived from Chinese media reports of such events. Unfortunately, this source offers at best a snapshot of selective aspects of the death penalty in China. As is true in other areas of research that use media accounts for developing samples, lethal executions that are covered in Chinese media reports are probably qualitatively different in the terms of the offender (e.g., their rank, social position) or their crimes (e.g., its seriousness, novelty) than death sentences that were not considered "newsworthy" enough to be covered in media outlets.

Using these media accounts and published judicial documents of selected capital cases, the current research attempts to describe and analyze the theory, law, and practice of the death penalty in China. While historical and comparative data are drawn for this analysis, the primary focus of this book is on the substantive and procedural issues surrounding the use of the death penalty since China's economic reforms starting in 1978. This inquiry into China's death penalty will focus on its application in both theory and practice.

Empirical research on the nature and extent of capital punishment in modern China would not have been possible ten years ago because the data for such analyses were simply not available. However, within the past decade, legal reforms in China have intensified with the revision of Criminal Law and Criminal Procedure Law in 1997 and 1996. As a consequence of these legal changes, Chinese courts of various levels and major universities and research institutions have started to publish criminal court case collections that contain judicial judgments in actual criminal cases, including the death penalty cases. Various official Web sites (e.g., Web sites of the Supreme Court, Superior Court, and some local courts) and other Web sites (e.g., http://www.chinacourt.org,http://www.law-star.com) have also developed only recently as a forum for providing valuable information on legal resources, analyses of complex cases, research articles, and criminal court case judgments. These data sources, in conjunction with traditional academic sources (e.g., research articles, books, yearbooks, and encyclopedias published in Chinese and English; the authors' own fieldwork), will serve as the basis for the current research.

THE VALUE OF COMPARATIVE RESEARCH AND CASE STUDIES

By all accounts, the modern world is an increasingly global and international one. The language of world markets, multi-national penetration, international councils, and concerns about global issues (e.g., global warming, war, disaster relief efforts) remind us of this wider global perspective. Within this international context, an examination of China's death penalty provides a basis for understanding the sources of social change and their impact on legal policies and practices in China and elsewhere. This understanding becomes even more important as China asserts its dominance as an economic superpower in the twenty-first century.

Despite our emphasis on a case study of China, comparative methodologies, particularly methodological relativism, will be employed in describing and analyzing China's death penalty law and practices. Methodological relativism refers to a research strategy that allows an observer to "devise cross-cultural generalizations" while maintaining "respect for cultural diversity."[9] The present study attempts to achieve this goal in several ways. First, the analysis of China's contemporary death penalty practices is situated in the context of international practices. Second, the evaluation of these practices is placed within an evolving historical context. Third, the analysis is embedded in the current political, economic, social, and legal context. By conducting this type of comparative case study, we hope to minimize ethnocentrism and develop a greater understanding of the rationale and practices surrounding the death penalty within this context.

INTERNATIONAL TREND ON THE DEATH PENALTY

All societies have mechanisms for maintaining social order and punishing wrongdoers. Not all societies, however, utilize the death penalty, particularly a state-sponsored death penalty for these purposes. Traditional societies, for example, often rely heavily on clan laws, not the state law, in punishing the wrongdoers. The tribe/village council, clan leader, and household head had the authority to put their members to death if they deemed that the members' action violated particular customs. The death penalty was largely an extra-legal punishment in these homogenous, traditional societies characterized by direct and intimate social relations. However, changes in these traditional societies also brought about the use of the death penalty as a state punishment that was almost exclusively regulated by state domestic laws.

As societies became more complex and technologically advanced, heterogeneity and pluralism gradually replaced homogeneity of values and beliefs. With the further globalization movement in recent decades, international organizations have increasingly exerted their influence and value in arenas that were traditionally dictated by domestic laws, particularly in aspects regarding human rights. Sovereign states have also increased their compliance with international norms in an effort to be integrated in the world system.

Human rights norms and the death penalty

There are two fundamental human rights principles central to the death penalty debate: the right to life and the protection against cruel, inhuman, and degrading punishments.[10] Both of these normative principles can trace their roots to aspects of Anglo-American constitutional law.

The principle of right to life was made famous by the Declaration of Independence of 1776, referring to the right not to be deprived of life without due process of law. The protection against cruel, inhuman, and degrading punishments originated in the English Bill of Rights of 1689. The specific aims of this law were to safeguard individuals from barbaric treatment as prisoners and exceptionally cruel and painful methods of lethal execution such as drawing and quartering, and disemboweling.[11] Though no explicit fundamental opposition to the death penalty can be derived from these norms, these principles contributed to the death penalty abolition movement in recent decades.

Several international organizations have influenced the nature and scope of domestic laws and practices on the death penalty in modern times. Most notable is the United Nations (UN). As early as 1966, the UN adopted the *International Covenant on Civil and Political Rights* (ICCPR) stating that "every human being has the right to life" and that "no one shall be arbitrarily deprived of his life." It further restricted the use of death penalty to the most serious crimes. The specific resolution entitled *Safeguards Guaranteeing Protection of the Rights of those Facing the Death Penalty*, drafted in 1984 and endorsed in 1985 by several bodies of the UN,[12] represented the most comprehensive and explicit restriction of the death penalty in the history of this organization.[13] Since the passage of the *Safeguards*, the official stand of the UN on the death penalty includes the following:

- The use of the death penalty must be restricted to "intentional crime with lethal or other extremely grave consequences;"
- Offender categories excluded from the death penalty included juveniles, pregnant women, new mothers, and the insane; and
- Offenders sentenced to death must be based on "clear and convincing evidence leaving no room for an alternative explanation of the facts."[14]

Aside from the UN, several other international organizations have also issued mandates and resolutions that focus on the death penalty. For example, the European Union proclaimed the abolition of the death penalty in 1989.[15] The *American Convention on Human Rights*, effective in 1978, tightened the restrictions on the use of the death penalty and affirmed that once nations abolished the death penalty, they may not reintroduce it.[16] Other regional treaties such as the *African Charter of Human and People's Rights* and the *Arab Charter of Human Rights* were less aggressive on the abolition of the death penalty. In fact, the African Charter did not explicitly mention the death penalty. While the Arab Charter did not prohibit the death penalty, it proclaims the right to life and excluded the imposition of the death penalty for certain types of person and crime.[17]

Global abolitionist movement

Recent developments in international tribunals and international judicial cooperation have also been directed primarily toward the legal abolitionist of the death penalty. For example, the 1993 Statute of the International Tribunal for the former Yugoslavia stipulated that the maximum sentence for crimes tried in the international criminal court shall be life imprisonment.[18] Sovereign states, relying on one another in international judicial cooperation in areas of extradition, have also increasingly insisted upon treaty provisions that permit them to refuse the extradition request if the accused faced the possibility of the death penlty.[19]

Internationally, a growing number of nations have been moving toward abolishing the death penalty, either in law or in practice (see Table 1.1). By

Table 1.1 Status of the death penalty in twenty-first century countries and territories

Status	*Number*
Abolished, law or practice	120
For all crimes	(85)
For common crimes	(11)
No executions in past ten yrs.	(24)
Detained and use death penalty	76
Total countries/territories	196

Source: Amnesty International (2005).

June 2005, a total of 120 countries and territories have either abolished the death penalty in law or in practice. Among them, eighty-five countries and territories have abolished the death penalty for all crimes; eleven countries have abolished the death penalty for all common crimes but reserved the death penalty for wartime crimes; twenty-four countries retain the death penalty in law but have not carried out any executions for the past ten years or more. A total of seventy-six other countries and territories retain and use the death penalty.

Although seventy-six countries and territories have used the death penalty in the twenty-first century, the vast majority of known executions took place in only a few countries. For example, about 97 percent of all known executions in 2004 were carried out in a total of four countries: China (3,400 executions), Iran (159 executions), Viet Nam (64 executions), and the United States (59 executions).[20]

The global distribution of the abolitionists and retentionist countries varies dramatically across world regions. Most countries within the Middle East, the Caribbean, Asia, and Africa have retained the death penalty, whereas most countries in Europe, Oceania, and the Americas (e.g., North, Central, and South America) have abolished the death penalty.[21]

Regarding the scope of the death penalty, the *Safeguards* adopted by the Economic and Social Council of the United Nations specifies that capital punishment may be imposed only for the most serious crimes (i.e., intentional acts with lethal or other extremely grave consequences). Given that countries vary widely in their social, political, cultural, religious, and legal contexts, this restriction of the scope of the death penalty is bound to be interpreted differently. In an attempt to provide some uniform definitions of serious crimes, the American Convention on Human Rights states that political offenses or related common crimes shall not be capital offenses.[22] The UN Commission on Human Rights urged in its various documents that the death penalty shall not be imposed on nonviolent financial crimes, nonviolent religious practice, other expressions of conscience, sexual relations between consenting adults, evading military service, abetting suicide, drug related offense, corruption, apostasy, illicit sex, terrorism, and aggravated robbery with the use of firearms that did not result in death or injury.[23] Currently, retentionist countries have widely applied the death penalty to a variety of nonviolent and non-lethal offenses, including offenses against the state and public order,[24] drug trafficking,[25] economic and property offenses,[26] sexual offenses,[27] and religious crimes.[28]

The severity of punishment in law for some countries does not necessarily translate into heavy reliance on the death penalty in practice. However, in other countries, the legal theory and the reality of imposition of capital punishment are more closely related.

According to annual reports compiled by Amnesty International (e.g., AI 2004, 2005), the number of abolitionist countries have increased over time but the number of death sentences and executions have not steadily declined as a consequence. In fact, the most recent data shows that 7,395 death sentences were imposed in sixty-four countries and 3,797 executions were carried out in twenty-five countries in 2004. These are the highest numbers in the recorded history of the death penalty,[29] and they suggest that abolitionist practices in many countries are being overshadowed by the continued and even increased use of capital punishment in China and other retentionist countries with relatively large numbers of executions.

Previous research and public commentaries also highlight the wide variability in methods of execution over geographical and historical contexts.[30] Up until the last quarter of the twentieth century, hanging and shooting were the most common method of execution. Other methods included stoning, beheading, electric chair, and gas chamber.[31] Since the introduction of lethal injection in the United States in 1977, most executions in the United States and a growing number of those in other countries have involved this particular method. Its popularity is often attributed to its more humane imposition and the lower degree of physical disfigurement during the execution.[32]

Aside from the calls for its total abolition by anti-death penalty groups on various moral grounds, most academic interest in the death penalty from Western scholars has focused on various issues about its fair, impartial, and humane imposition. The possibility of racial discrimination in the imposition of death sentences and, more recently, issues surrounding its use on other populations (e.g., juveniles, the mentally ill) and DNA exonerations of dubious convictions of innocent people are the major concerns in the death penalty debates in the United States.[33]

The prior empirical research in the United States suggests that death sentences have been (1) imposed on vulnerable populations (e.g., juvenile, the mentally insane), (2) meted out arbitrarily, (3) highly selective and discriminatory against marginalized groups, and (4) often erroneous in its imposition.[34] Contrary to the general belief that the government and the public share similar views about the death penalty, public opinion surveys often show that citizens in abolitionist countries do not necessarily have a strong opposition to the death penalty.[35] For example, most citizens in Great Britain appear to support the death penalty, although this punishment was abolished there over thirty years ago.[36]

THE DEATH PENALTY IN CHINA

The use and development of the death penalty in China has profound implications in the world for several reasons. The most obvious implication derives from the fact that China is the world's leader in the imposition of death sentences and executions in modern times. It has been estimated that China consistently accounts for at least 70 percent of recorded death sentences and executions in the world.[37] Any changes in policies regarding the death penalty in China would certainly have a significant impact on international trends and the perceptions about capital punishment across the world.

From a sociological perspective, the importance of China's death penalty lies in its historical secular tradition, particular economic structure, and legal traditions. China has a long history of state-sponsored lethal punishments and this punishment seems to have little religious underpinnings. Its long history as an agrarian-based economic society, strengthened by the state's collectivist responsibility system in both the ancient times and the earlier period of the socialist China (1949–1978), have been major contributory factors in its culture of collectivism and intolerance of deviance and crime. Furthermore, the patriarchal sociopolitical system during the imperial rule and the Communist ideology in the first thirty years of the PRC served as a catalyst for the inquisitorial legal system in which defendant's rights were subject to the interest of the state and the collective good. Under these conditions, pro-death penalty policies seemed to be a natural consequence.[38]

Although these sociopolitical conditions are important for understanding capital punishment in China and other countries, none of these structural factors alone could account for the legal status and prevalence of the death penalty in China. For example, the death penalty has been abolished for all crimes in some agrarian societies (e.g., Cambodia, Costa Rica) and it has been abolished in practice in another agrarian society (e.g., Mexico).[39] Similarly, being a secular state is not necessarily a good predictor for pro-death penalty policy and the inquisitorial legal system has no clear linkage with the use of the death penalty either.[40]

The ultimate question becomes "what socioeconomic, political, and other forces operate in ancient and modern China that continue its use of the death penalty as the most severe and indispensable means to maintain order and reinforce norms?" As a research pathway to seek answers to this question, the current study draws upon the historical and current sociopolitical and legal factors that contribute to the use of capital punishment, with particular emphasis on the major socio-economic changes associated with its economic reforms. In this way, we will be able to address more fully the rationale, theory, and conditions under which the death penalty can continue to sustain itself in contemporary China and other countries as a method of state-sponsored social control.

THE CURRENT APPROACH AND ORGANIZATION OF THE REMAINING CHAPTERS

As a state-sponsored sanction, the death penalty as an ultimate punishment must be stipulated in and carried out in accordance to law in China. These substantive and procedural laws are a product of historical forces and the prevailing social, political, and economic context. This interplay between law and society will be a dominant theme throughout this book. The general orientation of the remaining chapters is summarized below.

Chapter 2 focuses on the theoretical aspect of the Chinese death penalty both as law and punishment. Drawing upon several Western frameworks on the study of law (e.g., legal formalism, sociological jurisprudence, legal realism), this chapter discusses the rationale, theory, and context of the death penalty in China. By discussing the Chinese official depiction of law and punishment and current sociopolitical and legal conditions, we attempt to lay the necessary foundation for readers to better understand the functional and symbolic meaning of the death penalty law and its actual effects.

The understanding of the contemporary Chinese death penalty law and practice must also be grounded in its historical context. Accordingly, chapter 3 describes the legal development of the death penalty throughout three major historical eras in Chinese civilization (i.e., the ancient time [imperial era: 221 B.C–1911], a brief Republican era [1912–1949], and its pre-reform period of socialist China [1949–1978]). For each of these historical periods, sociopolitical conditions and particular views on punishment are first delineated, followed by a discussion of the prevailing death penalty laws and practices.

Chapter 4 takes the "law-on-the-book" approach with descriptions of the substantive and procedural laws regarding the death penalty in contemporary China, particularly developments since 1978. More specifically, it describes legal definitions of various capital offenses, the wide variety of punishments for a particular offense type, procedural requirements for capital offenses (e.g., appeals and review) and other unique characteristics of the law related to the death penalty (e.g., exempt populations, confession, legal representation, and the suspended death sentence).

Chapter 5 provides an empirical analysis of the death penalty "in action." Using secondary sources and court documents, it examines the prevalence of death sentences and executions, and the particular offense (e.g., violent, property, economic, corruption, public order, and public safety offenses) and offender characteristics (e.g., age, gender, occupation, residency status, criminal history, attitude, and confessions) associated with them. In addition, it examines the scope and severity of the imposition of the death penalty when compared with the law and other types of criminal sanctions (e.g., life and long-term fixed sentence).

Chapter 6 describes the legal process involved in the imposition of death sentences and executions in China. It first describes the general processes underlying death sentences and executions, followed by a description of courtroom dynamics and the sentencing rally. The discussion of the usual review process for complex capital cases sheds light on the evolving Chinese criminal process that embodies elements of both the internal struggle within China and the external influences. As timing is critical in criminal cases, particularly capital cases (both in terms of ensuring the defendant a fair trial and a speedy trial), this chapter also provides analyses of the lengths of criminal processing for capital and non-capital offenses. Lastly, the process of execution by shooting and lethal injection is described.

The concluding chapter summarizes the theoretical and practical aspects of the death penalty in China. It addresses the likely consequences of rapid social changes on death penalty practices, particularly the death penalty debate, and the ongoing reforms in the areas of confessions, legal representation, and procedural safeguards (e.g., Supreme Court's final review and approval authority). Citing a controversial capital trial, it further discusses the practical difficulties of imposing the death sentence when confronted with contradictory goals of upholding the law (e.g., law's supremacy and objectivity) and respecting social norms (e.g., systematic discriminatory practice towards the marginalized migrant population). This chapter concludes with discussions of the implications of this research for understanding capital punishment and other forms of state-sponsored social control in an increasingly global and international world.

2 Death penalty as law and punishment

To understand the death penalty in contemporary Chinese society, a broader approach to the study of the death penalty as law and punishment is beneficial. This chapter begins with an examination of the legal aspect of the death penalty. Drawing upon several Western perspectives on the study of law (e.g., legal formalism, sociological jurisprudence, and legal realism), it describes the Chinese rationale and conception of law, and the unique sociopolitical and legal conditions that may facilitate or hinder the actual operation of the law on the death penalty. The chapter concludes with a discussion of Chinese theories on punishment that focus on reintegrative shaming and moral education, and its justification and policies on the death penalty.

THE DEATH PENALTY AS LAW

Scholars define law in various terms depending on their discipline (e.g., jurists, sociologists, anthropologists) and perspective (e.g., comparative, capitalist democratic, critical). From a sociological perspective, Weber considers the following three conditions essential in defining state law: (1) external pressure in the form of actions or threats of action by others to comply with the law; (2) the actions or threats of action always involve coercion or force; and (3) those who implement the external threat are public officials.[1] Besides coercion, Black contends that law has other styles of social control, including compensatory, therapeutic and conciliatory.[2] Despite these different approaches in defining law, it is generally believed that state law is qualitatively different from other forms of social control (e.g., customary law). Because of its coercive nature, state law is often viewed as a last resort, a preferred remedy only after all other social control mechanisms have failed.

Law has various functions. Its function of social control has become increasingly important in a modern, complex, and heterogeneous society (e.g., the United States), as informal social control tends to weaken in these types of social conditions. Law also serves the function of dispute resolution and social engineering through promulgation and legislation of the intended social change.[3]

Western approaches to the study of law

There are several approaches to the study of law in Western societies. Earlier legal scholars were preoccupied with laws' perfection, that all laws should be logical and consistent. Law was considered as a science, having inherent logic, and largely independent of, if not superior to, other elements (e.g., politics, economy) of a society. This strand of legal study, most popular in the nineteenth century, is called legal formalism.[4]

With rapidly changing social conditions in the early twentieth century due to the industrialization movement, legal scholars became increasingly concerned with the adaptability of law to the changing social reality. They believed that laws were urgently needed to deal with emerging social relations in the family, religion, politics, and the economy. This type of scholarship that emphasizes the importance of social context and sociological information to lawmaking is called sociological jurisprudence. This perspective was immortalized by the classic works of Roscoe Pound.[5]

Within the broad spectrum of sociological jurisprudence, most scholars take the functionalist approach to the study of law. Functionalist scholars generally believe that law is based on consensus. They are interested in analyzing societies with a holistic approach, seeing the system as integrated through shared values and in a state of dynamic equilibrium, and regarding social relations as multiple and reciprocal. For example, Durkheim argued that even deviance could serve certain functions in a society by reaffirming the boundary of propriety.[6]

In contrast, the Marxian conflict approach challenges this consensus view of society by arguing that law is a product of tension and conflict between groups and individuals. Law is an instrument of domination and control used by the ruling classes over the less powerful ones. Law represents the interests of the ruling class, rather than serving as a compromise between various interest groups. For example, Quinney argued that the underclass will continue to be the object of criminal law as the law is increasingly used to maintain the social order that is set forth by the ruling class.[7]

The Soviets took the Marxian critical theory a step further by stressing law's function of achieving socialist transformation and protecting the dictatorship of the proletariat. The most representative was Leninism, which regarded law as an instrument, a necessary educative tool in promoting the socialist program. This instrumentalist view of law was primarily precipitated by the Marxist-Leninist fundamental understanding of law and legal institutions as only being necessitated by the existence of classes and social inequality and will eventually wither away once these social conditions are eliminated. Socialist legality, according to Leninists, should thus be marked by "informality, flexibility, and the explicit dominance of political objectives" with popular mobilization, which was the complete antithesis of the function of bourgeois law.[8] Consistent with this view, the renowned Soviet legal scholar Vyshinsky stressed the coercive and instrumental aspect of law, which should be used by the ruling class to suppress antagonistic forces.[9]

If sociological jurisprudence is more concerned with issues of lawmaking (e.g., the content of law must be socially embedded to be able to improve social reality), legal realism focuses on the implication of the law by questioning its actual effect and implementation.[10] For example, sociological jurisprudence would be more interested in whether death penalty laws are necessary in a particular social context and how it is spelled out, whereas legal realists would look at the actual imposition of the death penalty. To the realists, the content of the law is insignificant (e.g., first degree murder is subject to the death penalty) if the process is tainted during the actual enforcement of the laws (e.g., when only African American defendants convicted of first degree murder are sentenced to death). Influenced by legal realism, the critical legal studies movement further asserts that law cannot operate independently of the social context in which lawyers and judges are acting on their particular personal experiences and biases they bring into their legal decisions.[11]

Although different in their primary focus (e.g., a focus on the content of law versus the impact of law), sociological jurisprudence and legal realism are both representative of a more practical approach to law. This sociological approach to the study of law represented a significant movement away from the nineteenth century legal formalism. For the legal formalist, law was a supreme and value neutral institute that was independent of politics, economics and culture.

Drawing upon these Western perspectives, the following section examines these basic questions about the legal aspect of the death penalty in China:

- What is the Chinese view on law — is it a result of consensus of the people and various interest groups, or merely a tool used by the ruling class? Does law have supreme power, or is it subject to changes in political and economic structures?
- Can legal ideals and ideas (e.g., equality, fairness and justice) be implemented in accordance to the "original intent" of the law?

Answers to these questions are essential for a fuller understanding of the current status of death penalty laws and practice. This is of particular importance when attempting to speculation about the future of the death penalty in China.

Sociopolitical conditions in China

According to proponents of sociological jurisprudence, the establishment of good laws is not possible without knowledge of the social context in which they operate. We take this assumption to be true and begin our analysis of the social context of contemporary China in order to understand its law. This contemporary era in China refers to the reform period from 1978 to 2005.

After the death of Mao Zedong, the Chinese political leadership under Deng Xiaoping started the economic reforms. The initial goals of the reforms were to transform China from a backward agricultural-based society into a modernized country in the areas of industry, agriculture, technology, and national defense.[12] The reform has revolved around the transformation of the socialist state-planned economy to a market economy. This was attempted in both the rural and urban areas.

In the agricultural sector, for example, early reforms focused on maximizing production with de-collectivization, introduction of the household responsibility system, and adjustments in state procurement price. The more recent agricultural reforms have been concerned with increasing farmers' incomes, improving product quality, and absorbing excess rural laborers with the development of small townships.[13] In the urban economy, privatization and reorganization of state-owned enterprises, along with a series of reforms involving housing, pension, finance, medical reforms, and reemployment were initiated, designed to improve economic productivity, stabilize the market order, boost consumer confidence, and provide social protections for workers.[14]

These reform efforts have thus far made China one of the fastest growing and most robust economies in the world.[15] The reform achievements amazed many China observers, who variously called the reform as "the China miracle," "dramatic," "remarkable," and "unprecedented." China, as some scholars have claimed, will soon become "the next economic powerhouse."[16]

Compared to the economic reforms, the political reforms are lagging behind. China has remained a one-party system with the Communist Party dominating the political landscape. Deng and his successor Jiang Zemin repeatedly stressed the reform policies of "one center (economic development), two basic points (reform and opening policy), and four principles (the way of socialism, people's democratic dictatorship, guidance of the Chinese Communist Party, and adherence to Marxism and Leninism and Mao's ideology)," which ensured the Party leadership over governmental and economic affairs.[17] Some progress in political reforms has been made during this time period, including direct and competitive election of governmental and Party leaders at certain levels, separation of the party and political functions, making the political process public and transparent, and reducing media censorship.[18] None of these political reforms, however, have been able to provide effective oversight and checks and balances of the Party's power.

Economic reforms have dramatically impacted societal structure and the way of life in China. The most significant change was the weakening of the traditional urban household registration system. In the past, the registration system effectively linked urbanites to jobs, schooling, food rations, welfare, and medical care under the planned economy. Market economy demands that people freely choose their jobs and other social programs. The convergence of people from different walks of life inevitably brought different ideas, life styles, values, and beliefs into the same community. Technological advances and globalization further precipitated the rise in diverse social and cultural beliefs, particularly in urban coastal areas.[19]

There is little doubt that these reform efforts have affected the Chinese society in numerous positive ways. Some of these positive influences include the shifting focus from the political and ideological struggle to economic development, an improved living standard, greater individual freedom to pursue economic success and personal pleasure, and wider tolerance and gradual acceptance of plural cultures and values, particularly those of Western countries.[20]

The dramatic transformation brought by the economic reforms, however, also created conflicts and problems. The most acute problems were (1) the increasing urban-rural gap in resource allocation and income,[21] (2) the influx of the "floating population,"[22] and (3) the glorification of materialism and individual success that has lead to the subsequent erosion of communitarian ideas of personal sacrifice.[23]

One major manifestation of these conflicts was the skyrocketing crime rates in China. These increasing crime rates not only included the traditional violent crimes and property crimes, but it also involved corruption and other illicit crimes (e.g., prostitution, drug use) that were once eliminated during the Mao era.[24]

The main challenge faced by the current Chinese political leadership is the "balancing act" between social stability and growth. In other words, how can political leaders effectively maintain political, economic, and social stability and order, and continuously sustain economic growth and secure its political identity at the same time?

As a means of achieving this balancing act, law has become a major instrument for social order. In fact, after experiencing the lawless and tumultuous period of the Cultural Revolution (1966–76), Chinese political leaders became increasingly aware of costs of "rule of man" and appreciated the prospect of stability brought by written laws. As legal scholars have long recognized, law can simultaneously be both a facilitator of change and a product of political, economic, and social conditions. What is important is how law is viewed and defined in this particular social context.

Chinese contemporary view on law

The Chinese view on law has evolved over various historical periods. Ancient China during the imperial era (221 BC–1911 AD) was characterized by the debate and harmonization of Confucianism and Legalism, resulting in China's long history of legal codification, particularly in the areas of penal laws. The brief Republican period (1912–49) was marked with attempts at legal reforms through the application of legal principles and the borrowing of legal documents from Western countries. The founding of the People's Republic of China in 1949 set forth the beginning of the Marxian influence on the mainstream view of law and politics. Mao effectively integrated Marxism with China's revolutionary experience, using law as an instrument of class struggle, and subjected it to politics and the economy.

Despite different political systems and eras, the Chinese law has historically emphasized "the state, not the society; authority, not rights; rule of man, not rule of law; concentration of power, not separation of power; collectivism, not individualism; substantive issues, not procedural issues."[25] The historical legacy of some of the fundamental features of traditional Chinese law such as "law as a political tool," "law as an administrative tool," "law as a supplementary/secondary tool," and "law as a tool for social stability," may inevitably influence and help shape contemporary Chinese law.[26] We will discuss these evolving historical views on law in detail in chapter 3.

China was at a major cross-road in the late 1970s after the death of the greatest political and military leaders in the Communist revolution in 1976: Mao Zedong and Zhou Enlai.[27] Having experienced three decades of class struggle, major political and ideological campaigns, and planned economy, socialism did not seem to bring benefits to ordinary citizens, particularly peasants, as it was promised. Citizens were also terrified with the lawlessness brought by political movements that could subject anyone, including governmental officials, to torture and labor camps. The nation was looking for its direction and future.[28]

Deng's rise to power marked the beginning of the economic reforms. Deng and his successor Jiang proposed legal reforms that helped shape the legal system in the 1980s and the 1990s, respectively. While both claimed to follow strictly Marxist, Leninist and Maoist thought, and to insist upon building the socialist legal system, the focus of their proposals diverged somewhat from these systems of thought. Deng's views on law are reflected in the following three summary statements.

First, Deng believed that the central principle of the Communist Party was to develop democracy and consolidate the system of "rule by law." He thought that these principles were necessary conditions for the successful enforcement of other party policies (e.g., developing the market economy and the open-door policy).[29] He pointed out that democracy must be formalized and legalized. Socialist democracy, including its content and process, must be written into rules and laws, and should not be altered by the will of any political leaders.[30] He recognized the severe shortage of laws at the time, and urged the lawmakers to "focus on promulgating criminal law, civil law, procedure law and other necessary laws..." to adjust social conflicts.[31] He was also a chief proponent of the streamlining of lawmaking, calling for the quicker passage of laws. Instead of waiting for "the complete package," he said that "legal articles could be rough at the beginning and be gradually amended."[32]

Second, following Maoism, Deng insisted on a people's proletariat dictatorship that treated the people (e.g., the proletariat class such as workers, peasants) with the democratic process and the enemy (e.g., the bourgeois class) with a dictatorship. He further stated that those who threaten the political and economic order or commit serious violent, property and economic crimes should be severely and swiftly punished. In particular, Deng stressed the law's importance in cleansing the corrupt elements in the Party and the government. He believed that "education" and "law" were two effective ways to control corruption. Cautious about the disastrous consequence brought by political struggles in the past, Deng stressed that the only reliable method in dealing with corruption as the last resort was law.[33] Aside from warning public officials to abide by the laws, Deng also urged them not to interfere with law enforcement. He pointed out the importance of "judicial independence" and "equality before law" in safeguarding the integrity of the legal system.[34]

Third, Deng placed great importance on the people's representative system as an oversight body. Deng rejected Western multi-party political system, but recognized the importance of checks and balances. He asserted that the Chinese system of multiparty cooperation led by the Communist Party was the most efficient way in dealing with the Chinese affairs and suitable for the Chinese social conditions.[35]

These views on law laid the foundation for China's unprecedented growth in lawmaking in the 1980s. Along with the 1982 Constitution that stipulated the principles of the supremacy of the Constitution and the protection of citizens' basic rights of politics, economy, culture and society, other areas of laws including Organization Law, Criminal Law and Criminal Procedure Law, and China-Foreign Equity Joint Venture Law were drafted and passed.[36] These laws were used to formalize and legalize political, economic and social order, and as a political instrument to express the party policy. Nevertheless, these laws largely inherited the political and ideological overtone of the Mao era.[37]

As an example of its consistency with Maoist principles, the Constitution stressed the proletariat dictatorship and the criminal law stipulated a number of anti-revolutionary crimes. The laws remained punitive and duty oriented. For example, the Constitution mainly emphasized the need to protect socialist political and economic structure, whereas criminal laws focused very much on crime and punishment, rather than on the process of ensuring the rights of the defendant. In addition, the content of the law was very abstract and brief. Despite these caveats in laws, the relative proliferation of laws during the 1980s represented a significant movement away from the "rule of man" era during Mao, and one step closer to the ideas of "rule by law."

The Jiang era started in 1989 and marked the deepening of the economic reforms. With dramatic economic growth and a decade of lessons and experiences in the economic arena, China started to reevaluate the relationship between law, politics, and economy. Jiang's perspective on law was expressed in four Chinese words *yi fa zhi guo*, meaning "manage the country with law."[38] Chinese scholars interpreted this idea as the "rule of law"[39] based on the following reasons. First, Jiang repeatedly stressed that law was superior to party and politics, thus asserting law's supremacy. Second, law was no longer viewed primarily as a political weapon to oppress and punish, but rather as a way to manage relations and affairs in all spheres of political, economic, and social lives.[40]

In accordance with this idea of "rule of law," written laws must be available and publicized. Following these ideas, another wave of lawmaking was launched in the early 1990s, focusing mostly on the economic front.[41] Important administrative and penal laws were also promulgated or revised, such as *Administrative Procedure Law*, *Lawyer's Law*, *Judge's Law*, *Law on Public Security Organ*, and both the substantive and procedural criminal laws.

The content of law in this period became much more encompassing and sophisticated than previous legal reforms. For example, compared to the 1979 Criminal Law that contained only 192 articles, the 1997 Criminal Law had 451 articles. The new legal code also covered several emergent forms of criminal behavior (e.g., drug trafficking, prostitution, and credit card fraud). Even for some traditional crimes, the definitions were expanded. Corruption, for example, was classified in the general category of "encroaching on property" in the 1979 code, but it was redefined in the 1997 code as a separate crime category containing three different crimes: graft, bribery, and embezzlement. Similarly, the 1996 Criminal Procedure Law significantly improved lawyer's involvement in criminal investigations. Their involvement now extends from pretrial investigation (e.g., bail) to cross-examination at trial, and post trial appeals. These revisions of China's laws on criminal procedures are much closer to current international standards on procedural safeguards (e.g., mandatory legal representation in specified case types, rules on the appeal and review).[42]

Law enforcement was also strengthened under Jiang's leadership as it was viewed critical in the "rule of law" framework. Besides stressing the principles of "protecting the integrity of Constitution and laws and the equality before law," Jiang pointed out that it was important to establish effective mechanisms to ensure strict enforcement. The following three steps have been taken in this regard:

- The establishment of an inspection system for law enforcement agencies for purposes of allocating responsibilities and ensuring efficiency in law enforcement activities.
- The establishment of judicial accountability and independence to make sure that erroneous and wrongful enforcement of law is avoided and corrected.
- The refinement of the system of judicial oversight to ensure that judicial power not to exceed the legal limit.[43]

Within this context of strengthening the enforcement of the law, these legal changes also required more legal experts and professionals. Consequently, educational and training programs for judges and lawyers grew rapidly, a State Judicial Exam was established, law firms started to privatize, and legal aid programs proliferated.[44]

Improving citizens' legal consciousness was also an integral part of Jiang's idea of "rule of law." Because of the lack of a formal tradition within this new legal system, the formation of citizens' legal consciousness required some degree of mass education and training. In fact, to cultivate citizens' sense of law (i.e., to abide by the law and to use the law to protect one's own rights), Jiang stressed that the state and political officials must play a major role in leading by example, advocating the law's importance, and disseminating legal knowledge to ordinary citizens.[45]

Overall, Jiang's view on law appeared to be a continuation of Deng's approach, only more systemized and comprehensive. Both views were expressed within the framework of Marxist, Leninist, and Maoist thought, the proletariat dictatorship, and the socialist democracy and legal system. Both were also pragmatic and instrumental,[46] relying on laws to carry out the party's reform policies. Both Deng and Jiang recognized the importance of law in maintaining order and represented a movement away from rule by man.

Within this Chinese framework of "rule by law" and "rule of law," Jiang's view appeared to be closer to Western ideas about these principles. The Western "rule of law" primarily refers to law's supremacy and independence. Law in this context is not merely an instrument, but embodies the core values and beliefs of the society.[47] However, from the perspectives of sociological jurisprudence and legal realism, law's supremacy does not mean that law can be completely above and separated from social reality, nor can it remain constant without changes.

Within this context of competing theoretical views about the nature of law and society, Jiang's proposal to strengthen law, law enforcement, and legal consciousness, in theory, represented a more holistic approach to achieving law's supremacy and independence. Whether or not his efforts to build a sound legal structure and culture actually translated into the ideals of the "rule of law", however, remains an open question. How legal realists would evaluate China's legal reform efforts and the ideals of the "rule of law" are described below.

Chinese legal structure

The existence of an adequate legal structure is one of the basic necessary elements to ensure that laws are enforced according to their original intent. The Chinese legal system has a four-tiered organizational structure. These include (1) the district courts (equivalent to municipal courts of limited jurisdiction in the United States), (2) municipal-level intermediate courts (equivalent to the state superior courts in the United States), (3) provincial-level superior courts (equivalent to the State Supreme Court in the United States), and (4) a national-level Supreme Court. With this legal system, all criminal cases involve one trial and one judicial review. However, death penalty cases are an exception in that they must also receive a final review by the Supreme Court under provisions of the 1997 Criminal Law.

The Chinese judicial system had traditionally employed an inquisitorial model of justice. Compared to adversarial system, the Chinese system has some unique features such as the belief in the absolute truth,[48] the presumption of guilt, an emphasis of crime control and the overwhelming power vested to the state, particularly the procuratorate,[49] in achieving the goal. Historically, these structural features of China's inquisitorial model put the defendant and the defense attorney in a subordinate and disadvantaged position.[50]

The legal reforms have been directed at changing some of these structural features through the introduction of judicial independence, a judicial responsibility system, legal representation, legal training, and legal access via legal aid programs. Following the views of Deng and Jiang, these efforts focused on the establishment of professionalism and accountability within the judicial system for purposes of making the legal system more effective and efficient.[51]

Regardless of the specific intentions of the reform efforts, however, several problems associated with the current legal structure may hinder the realization of its legal objectives. These problems are examined below.

First, judicial independence has not been fully realized because of the continuation of past legacies. Courts of various levels remain affected by local politics and party intervention, resulting in local protectionism.[52] The judicial oversight committee within the court, set up to ensure the quality of judicial decisions, may also serve as a way to interfere with judicial decisions as the committee is mainly comprised of party members. Judicial corruption has also become rampant as judges bend the rule for political, economic, and social relational inducement.[53] In addition, tensions between the lower court and the higher court have intensified, partly due to the demands of different political constituencies.

Second, in the attempt to transform the legal system from an inquisitorial to an adversarial system, judges are now removed from evidence gathering. However, defense attorneys' access to evidence and ability to gather evidence and cross-examine witnesses has not been fully established. These two factors have resulted in an even more imbalanced power between the state and the defendant, tipping heavily in favor of the procuratorate. For example, when a police agency is accused of torture by a defendant, both the presiding judge and procuratorate in the previous inquisitional system had the authority and duty to investigate the accusations. Under the current system, however, only the procuratorate have the responsibility to conduct the investigation. The fact that defense attorneys rarely gain access and cooperation from Chinese police agencies also limits the utility of legal representation for solving this problem. Under these conditions, serious questions of procedural fairness arise because of the potential conflict of interest and lack of adequate adversarial voice.

Third, with the adoption of the semi-adversarial system, parties involved in the case should, in theory, be similar in resources and qualifications in order to compete with each other. However, most defendants in China have little financial resources to compete with the state. While lawyers in China possess the best educational qualifications among all legal practitioners (e.g., judges, procuratorates, police officers), it is also true that judges and prosecutors (and the police) remain the dominant players in the criminal justice system. Because of previous operating norms and the low educational qualifications of judges and prosecutors, it may take a considerable amount of time before laws are carried out in China in accordance with the prescribed legal procedures.[54]

Fourth, the new criminal procedure laws greatly strengthened the protection of defendants' rights (e.g., right to defense attorney, access to bail, mandatory legal representation, and free from coerced confession). However, the structural layout of a typical Chinese courtroom clearly reveals the secondary status of criminal defendants even in the context of this revised legal structure. In most Western developed countries (e.g., United States, England, France, and Germany) and regardless of their legal traditions (e.g., common law, civil law), the defendant is invariably placed with the defense on the same side of the courtroom.[55] In contrast, the Chinese defendant is placed in the center of the courtroom, looked down upon by a panel of judges, and with the defense attorney on one side of the courtroom and the procurator and the victim on the other side of the room. From a practical standpoint, this makes it difficult for the defense team to communicate with the defendant during trial. Psychologically, it makes the defendant feel isolated and become an alienated, detached object within the trial.[56] The decreased likelihood of receiving a fair trial within this structural context is also compounded by other issues surrounding criminal prosecution in China (e.g., the legalization of criminal confession,[57] limited access to legal representation).

If the legal structure provides the basic machinery and tools for institutionalization of legal rules, legal culture, if adequate, serves as the lubricant to ensure the smooth operation of these laws. While legal structures may be altered dramatically in a short period of time, it is widely recognized that legal culture takes a long time to cultivate. The following characterizes the unique features of the legal culture in contemporary China.

Chinese legal culture

A deeply rooted aspect of Chinese culture is the general lack of concerns for individual rights. The long imperial tradition of Chinese society revolved around family, the clan, and the emperor. This interdependence fostered the emergence of a political and legal thought of collectivism and rule of man.[58] Within this context of centralized political power and group orientation, both the Chinese government and its people have had a strong desire for peace and stability, and been particularly fearful of disorder and chaos.

Although clearly aware of the possible arbitrariness and cruelty of the criminal justice system, fundamental aspects of China's collective culture has long established a tradition of tolerance toward particular abuses. In particular, the cultural legacy of collectivism (i.e., the willingness to sacrifice a few for the interest of a whole community) and other cultural beliefs (e.g., punitive attitudes toward crime, the lack of sympathy toward criminal defendant) has allowed the Chinese to consider the lawless behavior of the government acceptable.[59]

These particular aspects of Chinese legal culture have been repeatedly demonstrated in major events throughout its history. Particular examples include (1) the massive executions following a failed peasant uprising during the Ming Dynasty (e.g., the Taiping Rebellion [1851–56]), (2) the heavy reliance on harsh punishments immediately after the takeover of the Communists in 1949 for order maintenance purposes,[60] and (3) the current "strike-hard" campaigns against crime and civil unrest caused by the economic reforms. As the "strike-hard" campaigns illustrate, the general punitive attitude toward crime in the pre-reform socialist period has remained largely intact in contemporary China.[61]

Over the last quarter century, "crime fighting" efforts on the part of the Chinese government has become highly politicized. During the 1980s and 1990s, China has been at the proverbial crossroad between "rule of man" and the "rule of law." On the one hand, the Chinese government seems resolute in its further construction of the socialist legal system with unprecedented legal promulgation. However, its newly established legal procedures have been routinely violated, as is evident by the temporary suspension of the mandatory review of the death penalty cases by the Supreme Court in order to meet the needs of the "strike hard" campaign against criminal activities. This type of contradiction between legal theory and reality demonstrates both the fragility and instrumental nature of the Chinese law.

As another aspect of Chinese legal culture, the recent development of the legal profession has suffered because of the penal nature of the law and traditional lack of emphasis of individual rights. Traditionally, law in China has been an instrument for the ruling class to advance their interest. Rarely, it served the interest of the people. The distaste of law and litigation resulted in a very slow growth of the legal profession and the general tendency of shunning away from using legal professionals to assert one's rights. This cultural legacy may severely impede the actual development of an adversarial legal system.

A final component of the legal culture involves the role of science and technology. Within the Chinese context, the relatively low development of legal innovations is also tied to limited educational opportunities and the slow growth of social science research. Even within contemporary China, empirical research and public opinion surveys are limited and discourse about legal issues is often driven by political or ideological considerations rather than empirical evidence.

THE DEATH PENALTY AS PUNISHMENT

Based on the Western literature, there are five basic justifications for punishment within state-sponsored criminal justice systems: retribution, deterrence, incapacitation, rehabilitation, and restoration.

Retribution represents one of the oldest justifications for punishment. It reflects the principle of "just deserts" by assuming offenders' blameworthiness and requiring that punishment be proportional to the crime.[62]

Deterrence is based on the utilitarian doctrine and represents the "preventive model." From the deterrence perspective, punishment can prevent future crime through the threat or actual imposition of punishment. Both the general deterrence and specific deterrence can be best achieved with swift, certain, and severe application of punishment.[63]

Incapacitation represents the "predictive model." Punishment is meted out not based on the particular offense committed, but based on the future likelihood of recidivating. The justification for incapacitative punishment is to reduce the offender's physical capability to recidivate by the physical means of imprisonment, electronic monitoring, and the death sentence.[64]

Rehabilitation underlies the "medical model" with the focus on offender's treatment and reform. Contrary to the retributive idea that "punishment must fit the crime," the rehabilitative idea requires that punishment fit the individual.[65]

Restoration focuses on reconciliation and has its current roots in the victims' rights movement revived in many Western countries in the 1980s. This "justice model" emphasizes not only procedural justice, but also the end result of a just society through participation of all parties involved in the dispute — offender, victim, and their family and community.[66]

These main purposes of punishment are not completely independent and exclusive of one another. In fact, a particular punishment may serve different, yet multiple, purposes. For example, the death penalty could simultaneously serve purposes of retribution, deterrence, and incapacitation. When the suspended death sentence is imposed, it may serve an additional goal of rehabilitation.

Chinese perspectives on punishment

There is little doubt that the long history of the death penalty in China is grounded in the moral justification of retribution. The old saying of "a life for a life" has been deeply rooted in the Chinese culture for thousands of years. Contemporary examples such as the execution of a Red Army leader who shot a female volunteer to death because of her refusal of his marriage proposal during the Yanan era (the 1930s),[67] the execution of the landlords who had "blood debts" during the 1950s, and the execution of gangsters who robbed and murdered along the railways in the 1990s, all were justified because of their heinous acts and the need to appease the public's indignation.

The death penalty can also be justified on the grounds of deterrence and education. The Chinese have several popular proverbs (e.g., "killing one to warn a hundred," "killing a chicken before a monkey") that are suggestive of the deterrent effect of the death penalty. Many Chinese political leaders have also expressed their supportive views of the death penalty for this reason. For example, notice the use of these justifications in the following accounts:

- Mao in 1952 insisted upon executing two offenders involved in the biggest corruption case since the establishment of the PRC (People's Republic of China). He explicitly mentioned that this punishment would curb corruption, cleanse the party and the government, educate the party members and public officials, and renew the relationship between the party, the government, and the general public.[68]
- During the reform era, Deng initiated the strike-hard campaign in light of the surging crime rates. On numerous occasions, he pointed out that "the death penalty cannot be abolished. Some criminals must be given the death sentence... we cannot be soft on crimes... in this critical time, we must deal with crime with swift and severe punishment... for those who committed violent and economic crimes, the imposition of the death sentence on a few most serious ones is a necessary educative tool."[69]
- In the face of rampant corruption and crimes committed by offspring of public officials and celebrities, Deng said that "these crimes must be investigated and severely punished because of their bad social effects and influence."[70]

- Professor Chen, one of the most prominent Chinese legal scholars on the death penalty, also pointed out that "the abolition of the death penalty in the current socio-political time is not warranted for its value of deterrence and social defense."[71]

Due to the general lack of development in social science research in China, little empirical research has been done to evaluate the actual deterrent and educative effects of the death penalty. However, based on the utilitarian doctrine, the death penalty may serve a better deterrence in the Chinese context where it can be implemented with swiftness, certainty and severity.[72]

Chinese policy on the imposition of death sentence and execution

Throughout history, severe punishments combined with moral education have been at the center of all ancient and contemporary Chinese governments. While leniency was advocated during the peaceful and prosperous times, lethal punishments by incredibly cruel methods of execution (e.g., slicing, garroting) were especially common during tumultuous times.

The historical contexts for the use of death penalty have been wide and varied. For example, during the Communist revolution (e.g., the 1930s and 1940s), the death penalty was used to suppress counterrevolutionaries, the corrupt elements, and criminals. It was used to unite the ideological and political fronts of the Communist Party. After the establishment of the PRC, the death penalty was used to reinforce the community ideology of proletariat dictatorship. Within the current reform era, the death penalty has served as a mechanism to consolidate the economic reform and maintain social order.

The Chinese legal system in the last half of the twentieth century was often characterized by its grass-roots basis and its delivery of popular justice. Its application of the death penalty was no exception. In sentencing rallies and political campaigns, the public's emotions may run high. Judicial decisions in this context may be rendered not by law, but by the overzealous public opinion. To prevent excessive and erroneous killings, Mao in the early 1950s pointed out the need to establish the system of the death sentence with suspended execution. He said "those, who did not have 'blood debt,' had not caused grand public indignation, and their act was not the most severe to warrant an immediate execution, should all be given the death sentence with a two-year stay, forced to engage in labor reform, and be observed of future behavior."[73] This policy of "kill fewer, kill carefully" has continued to be the official policy on the death penalty throughout the socialist era.

The current death penalty policy in China can be summarized with reference to three basic principles: (1) it cannot be without the death penalty; (2) it cannot be with the excessive use of the death penalty; and (3) it must prevent erroneous killing.[74] This policy stresses the importance of the death penalty to the total scheme of punishment in socialist China.

This overwhelming dominance of the retentionist view on the death penalty, as reflected in the official policy, is largely grounded in the contemporary sociopolitical environment of instability, historically higher crime rates and class conflicts, the deep-seeded retributive ideas, and the relatively weak consciousness of individual and human rights among the general public.[75] The prevention of excessive and erroneous killings seems to be primarily derived from external pressures (e.g., the international abolition movement and human rights advocacy) and internal demands (e.g., rule of law, governmental legitimacy).

SUMMARY

This chapter provided the theoretical framework for studying the death penalty both as law and as punishment. As it revealed, the approaches to the study of law involved legal formalism, sociological jurisprudence, and legal realism. Taken together, these perspectives permit the discovery of the basic essence of the death penalty law and its impact on society.

A variety of purposes provide justification for punishment, including retribution, deterrence, incapacitation, rehabilitation and restoration. By linking the Chinese death penalty policy with the punishment perspectives of retribution and deterrence, this chapter further laid the necessary foundation for the study of the death penalty system in China.

3 Historical and legal development of the death penalty

The long history of China has been accompanied by a persistent reliance on the death penalty. Despite sporadic periods of abolition[1] and strong philosophical opposition by Confucians in ancient times,[2] the death penalty has been widely used throughout Chinese history for purposes of social control, order maintenance, and regulation of individuals and private groups. Its use in these areas has varied depending on the prevailing social, political, and economic conditions of the particular time.

This chapter provides a general overview of the historical and legal development of the death penalty in China. For purposes of description, we classify the history of China into three periods: (1) Imperial China (from the earliest Chinese civilization to the Qing dynasty),[3] (2) the Republican era (1911–49),[4] and (3) the first thirty years of socialist China (1949–78).[5] Below we discuss the particular sociopolitical context, views on punishment and the death penalty, relevant stipulations in substantive and procedural laws, and unique execution practices within each of these historical periods.

IMPERIAL CHINA

As one of the earliest civilizations in the world, China has several distinct periods in its early historical evolution. From a Marxist interpretative framework, China's early historical development is depicted as primarily a primitive commune (pre-1700 BC), followed by a slave period (1700–221 BC) and centuries as a feudal society (221 BC–1911 AD). As an alternative framework, this historical period is said to have begun with the archaic monarchy (until 221 BC) and then developed into a centralized state governed by emperors and the authoritarian paternalism (221 BC–1911 AD).[6] Our discussion in this section encompasses the vast period between the first dynasty with written records in 1700 BC and the last imperial dynasty ending in 1911.

Sociopolitical context of Imperial China

China's early written history of the first four thousand years was widely characterized by war, civil unrest, massive struggle for political and economic power, and numerous reform efforts. The earliest available written records depicted the Shang (1700–1027 BC) and Western Zhou Dynasty (1027–771 BC) as an archaic monarchy with patriarchal and aristocratic characteristics.[7] This period of time and the next few centuries leading to the unification of China (211 BC) were a period of economic upsurge and innovation while simultaneously a time of social upheavals. The economic upsurge accentuated inequalities. While creating a small class of merchant entrepreneurs and large landed proprietors, it also drove poor peasants from their land resulting in a growing number of tenant farmers, agricultural laborers, and people enslaved for debt. These economic changes, along with the changing political structure in the old aristocratic society where the upper ranks of the nobility were declining and the new heads of state seeking monopolized power, caused wars and reforms that represented most parts of the spring-autumn period (770–476 BC) and the Warring States period (475–221 BC), and gave birth to the centralized state.[8]

One of the most influential rulers in Chinese history was Shi Huangdi. He conquered the independent kingdoms to end the Warring States period, established the first centralized country in China and became the first emperor of the Qin dynasty in 221 BC. Though the Qin dynasty was short lived, lasting only until 210 BC, this centralized sociopolitical structure would last for roughly the next two thousand years.

As emperor of this new country, Shi Huangdi implemented sweeping land and agrarian reforms to pacify the landlords while at the same time trying to maintain strict control of the populace and reinforce the political dominance in the fragile union. Shi Huangdi's rule was considered extremely repressive, and included such practices as taking away weapons from the populace, heavy taxes and forced labor of peasants, imposing severe punishment on those who disobeyed orders, and burning books that were thought to promote old aristocratic culture.[9] Subsequent dynasties such as the Western Han (206 BC–24 AD) and the Sui dynasty (581–618 AD) also were characterized by conflicts between the landlords and peasants and the ongoing struggle to maintain a unified China.[10]

The Tang dynasty (618–907 AD) marked the onset of the most prosperous and powerful period in Imperial China. Many technological advances were made in areas of production such as ship-building, the manufacture of bronze mirrors, brocade weavings, porcelain, brass work, and mining.[11] China's political and cultural influence and power in this period also extended over many parts of Asia including northern Vietnam, southern Manchuria and Korea, and central and west Asia.[12] However, internal struggles and conflicts over land, heavy taxation, and social unrests led to the overturn of the Tang Dynasty.[13]

After the disintegration of the Tang Dynasty, China's sociopolitical history was characterized by several periods of relatively short duration (e.g., the Five Dynasties [907–960] and Ten States [902–979], followed by more prolonged periods of rule (e.g., Song [960–1279], Yuan [1279–1368], and Ming [1368–1644] dynasties). These post-Tang dynasties further developed technical and production skills that sustained Imperial China's position as a world power.

The last imperial dynasty, the Qing Dynasty (1644–1911), was plagued with civil riots, peasant uprisings, foreign invasions, and wars, particularly since the last half of the nineteenth century. The lack of technological advances in both agriculture and industry, compounded with heavy taxation, official corruption, population increase, and sporadic occurrence of flood and drought, placed inexorable pressure on the already fragile economy.[14] Banditry, riots, and social unrests followed with uprisings in North China (e.g., the Nien War in 1868) and other parts of China (e.g., the Muslim Rebellions in Yunnan [1856–73], Shensi and Kansu [1862–73]).[15] The Boxer Rebellion (1899–1901), growing out of the anti-foreign and anti-Christianity sentiment among the Chinese populace as a result of the increasing presence of foreign ministers and consuls in China and decades of foreign humiliations from defeated wars and unfair treaties, inadvertently weakened the power of the Qing dynasty.[16]

Internationally, the Qing government suffered several defeats in wars against the British government (e.g., the Opium War in 1840) and subsequent military losses with the French (1884–85) and Japanese (1894–95) governments.[17] These losses have been attributed to the weak Qing administration and its isolationism in foreign policy, gross incompetence in governance and military operation, and basic corruption. The series of internal and external struggles in the late Qing Dynasty led to its collapse in 1911.[18]

View of punishment and the death penalty in Imperial China

During this long historical period of ancient China, Confucianism played an indispensable role in shaping the Chinese view on law and public morality. Along with Legalism, it helped conceptualize and rationalize punishment and the use of the death penalty. Confucianism emphasized the educational function of morality in governing a state. Essential to understanding Confucianism are the concepts of *xiao, zhong,* and *ren.*[19]

Xiao (filial piety) emphasizes one's sense of love from his/her most basic and closest human relationships — one's parents, grandparents, elderly in one's clan, and siblings. For preserving these special relationships, Confucius encouraged various rituals (e.g., marriage, funeral) and rules (e.g., a son should not travel far away while his elderly parents were alive) in accordance with one's social relations and status.[20]

The idea of *zhong* expands one's love, loyalty, and uprightness to the family and clan to one's country and emperor. Being loyal, respectful, and obedient to the emperor was one's obligation and, in turn, the emperor would love and protect his subjects. Here, differentiation and hierarchy found within the family and clan structure was transformed and duplicated in the larger society.[21]

The Confucian principle of *ren* involves benevolence or humaneness. *Ren* was believed to be crucial to an orderly and virtuous society. This teaching of *ren*, "to love all devotedly,"[22] was especially revolutionary in 551 BC, when one's love was narrowly depicted only in the context of family and clan. In fact, the antithesis of *ren* (i.e., private revenge, self-interests, and rivalry among clans) was the primary norm during this tumultuous period. To change the normative context, Confucius advocated universal love (i.e., love without the boundary of group identity) through the teaching of philosophical ideas such as "do not do to others as you would not wish done to yourself."[23]

As the means for achieving an orderly and virtuous society, Confucius placed far more importance on his basic principles (i.e., *xiauo, zhong, ren*) than the rule of law and punishment. By setting the moral or ethical tone of piety and benevolence, Confucius believed that exemplary conduct of the leader would produce voluntary conformity by the people. People also submit to rules by fear of punishment, but Confucius argued that such punishment has less potential to bring about an orderly and virtuous society because it does not develop in the wrongdoer a proper sense of shame.[24] Accordingly, Confucianism refuted the effect of punishment on human behavior and denounced the role of law in maintaining social order.[25]

When times were relatively peaceful and orderly, emperors throughout Imperial China understood the power of Confucian principles for ruling their country. For example, in the aftermath of the fall of the repressive Qin regime, Emperor Wen of Western Han Dynasty abolished all mutilating punishments in 167 BC by remarking that "once a limb was cut off, it could not grow again."[26] During the most prosperous period in imperial China, the Tang Dynasty, emperors were particularly receptive to lenient punishment. Emperor Gaozu, for example, restricted the death penalty to only murder, robbery, desertion from the army, and treason. This legal change was probably invoked to gain support from the populace by reversing the harshness of punishment under the previous Sui Dynasty. Similarly, about five thousand persons charged with assisting a Tang prince to overthrow Empress Wu, a capital crime, were spared of the death penalty due to a "humane" governor's plea to the empress.[27]

Although the previous examples suggest some periods of relative benevolence, the available historical records indicate that harsh punishment and the widespread use of the death penalty were dominant themes throughout Imperial China. In fact, the Legalists' advocacy of stern punishments was widely accepted by most emperors as necessary to rule effectively, particularly during tumultuous and rebellious times.[28]

Legalism, primarily derived from the beliefs of Shang Yang (390–338 BC), stressed rigid application of law and harsh punishment. Shang Yang argued the importance of applying punishment "equally" by subjecting all peoples (commoners and the aristocrats and the military officials) to punishment in an effort to strengthen and maintain state control during the time of war and acute class conflicts.[29] The expressions of "the most enlightened way of governing is to trust measures, not men," and "punish severely the light crime," manifested the core principles of Legalism.[30] The *Book of Lord Shang,* the most representative writing of Legalism, highlighted two major features of legalists' views on law and punishment. It states that in a well-governed society, "punishments are many and rewards are few," and people should be compelled under heavy penalties to "spy upon and inform against their relatives and neighbors." With harsh laws and group responsibility, being filial to one's family and kinship, core of Confucianism, was no longer important so long as one was an upright subject of the ruler.[31]

Specific times of harsh punishment within China's imperial history include the following:

- Extremely severe and cruel punishments were widely applied in Shi Huangdi's conquest of other independent states and his unification of China in the early Imperial period.[32] Harsh laws also propelled rebellions during this period of time.[33] More than a million laborers (e.g., especially convicts and other disliked groups) were sent to their death in enormous construction projects like the "Great Wall".[34]
- In the aftermath of almost every peasant uprising throughout this period of history, massive executions were administered by the surviving government to maintain control. The *Taiping Rebellion* (1851–64) is especially infamous for its various types of death and carnage (e.g., suicides, executions, killings in conflict).[35]
- Offenders of looting and banditry, particularly against foreign merchants toward the late Qing Dynasty, were frequently given the death sentence to pacify the populace and foreign governments. For example, sixteen offenders were sentenced to immediate decapitation and exposure of the head for murdering thirteen French sailors and looting their cargo in 1828.[36]

Historical accounts suggest that the death penalty in Imperial China was applied primarily to persons of lower socioeconomic status.[37] However, especially during war times and other periods of acute internal and external threats, capital punishment was also used to gain compliance from persons of higher ranking (e.g., military officials, the privileged class). Examples of death sentences for persons of higher status include the following accounts:

- King Wu of the Western Zhou Dynasty declared that officials who did not follow the king's regulations were to be put to death without pardon. He also mandated death sentences for persons who promulgated innovations or failed to perform their prescribed duties.[38]
- After a peasant uprising in the Tang Dynasty, thirty-nine military officials who switched allegiance with the enemy were executed.[39]
- Six reformers of the elitist group who tried to introduce major social and institutional changes at the end of the Qin Dynasty were executed as dissidents.[40]

Substantive criminal law on the death penalty in Imperial China

China has had a long history of codification, particularly in its penal codes. The earliest available record from the Shang dynasty (1700–1027 BC) contained Five Punishments (*wu xing*) for wrongdoing. These punishments included *mo* (permanent branding on the offender's face), *yi* (amputation of the offender's nose), *fei* (feet amputation), *gong* (amputation of a male's reproductive organ or locking a woman up for life), and *da pi* (the death penalty).[41]

Although there is some variation across the historical period, physical amputation and the death penalty were the dominant forms among the five punishments in the early period of ancient China.[42] However, since the Han dynasty (206 BC–24 AD), beatings and wearing of foot irons gradually replaced bodily amputation. The Sui Code (581 AD) officially abolished physical mutilation with the exception of capital punishment.[43] Under the Sui Code, the "new" Five Punishments included beating with a light stick, beating with a heavy stick, penal servitude, exile for life, and the death penalty. Subsequent penal codes in Imperial China (e.g., the Tang Code, the Qing Code) had similar provisions and, for the most part, abolished physical amputation but preserved corporal punishment and the death penalty.

There is enormous variability in the number of capital offenses stipulated in laws throughout this period of Chinese history. For example, in Punishments of *Lu* (*Lu Xing*), written approximately during the Warring States (475–221 BC), the death penalty was applicable to 200 offenses.[44] The Tang Code (653 AD) included a total of 233 capital offenses. The Song Dynasty (960–1279) retained all capital offenses from the Tang Dynasty and gradually added sixty other offenses, making a total of 293 capital offenses.[45] The number of separate capital provisions then dropped dramatically to a low of 135 offenses in the Yuan Dynasty (1279–1368).[46] The number of separate capital codes increased again, including 282 capital offenses during the Ming Dynasty (1368–1644) and then skyrocketed to over 800 separate offenses in the Qing Dynasty (1644–1911).[47]

Capital offenses have encompassed a variety of behaviors in China's imperial history. The death penalty was often meted out for unfilial and unbrotherly conduct,[48] drinking alcohol, betraying the state, stealing, and murder in earlier period of ancient China. The Tang Code (653) provides some idea of the type of offenses punishable by death in later dynasties. These offenses included crimes against the emperor (e.g., failure of a physician or chef to follow proper formulas in preparing the emperor's medicine or meals), the state (e.g., treason), the family (e.g., beating, murdering, or lodging accusations against elderly family members, failure to provide elders with adequate support, and incest),[49] violent offenses (e.g., murder, robbery, rape), property crimes (e.g., theft, arson), offenses of morality (e.g., corruption), and economic offenses (e.g., illicit manufacturing and selling of governmentally controlled goods).[50] In addition, "depraved crimes" such as killing three or more members of a household, disfiguring or burning a body in the process of murder, witchcraft,[51] and sorcery with special reference to *gu* poison[52] and other black magic[53] were also punishable by death.

When deciding on the appropriate punishment, Confucian teachings of *xiao*, *zhong*, and *ren* were often given special considerations during this period of time. In fact, Confucianization of the Legalists' principles highlighted the consistent theme of penal codes throughout Imperial China.[54]

Under the idea of filial piety (*xiao*), for example, a son may receive a death sentence for beating his father, but the reverse situation (i.e., a father beating his son) may go unsanctioned as one's parental duty to discipline children.[55] Similarly, a son who committed a capital offense may have his sentence reduced if he were the only heir to care for his elderly parents. The idea of *xiao* also allowed and encouraged a younger family member to assume a legal punishment imposed upon an older member of the family, in some cases, even the death penalty.[56]

Under the Confucian principle of *zhong* (i.e., respect for master, governmental officials, and ultimately the emperor), public officials enjoyed privileged status in ancient China. This privileged status, in some instances, allowed public officials to redeem their punishment with money and reduction of their ranks. Redemption was even possible in cases with a potential death sentence. However, due to Confucian beliefs that public officials should lead by exemplary behaviors, officials were also subject to heavier punishment than commoners for certain types of crimes.[57] Particularly when officials were involved in treason, the punishment could be execution of one's kindred to the third degree including the offender's parents, brothers, spouse and children.[58]

The Confucian idea of *ren* (i.e., benevolence and humanness) requires special considerations for weaker individuals in society. Consistent with this principle, the Tang Code and the subsequent penal codes stipulated that the young (fifteen and younger), the old (seventy and older), women (particularly pregnant women), and the mentally or physically infirmed should be given lenient sentences.[59] Confucius's *ren* also captures the belief in the basic goodness of human nature and the ability of human transformation through thought reform. Under the Tang Code and subsequent penal laws, the reduction of punishment for those who voluntarily confess to misconduct is consistent with this basic tenet.[60] The strong emphasis placed on one's criminal intent and prior criminal record in sentencing decisions is also tied to the Confucian notion of *ren*.[61]

Procedural criminal law on the death penalty in Imperial China

Throughout the written history of ancient China, the penal code has dealt primarily with crime definitions and punishments. There was no separate code of criminal procedures. Although some procedural safeguards were impeded in these early penal codes, the basic content of criminal law in Imperial China was almost exclusively substantive rather than procedural.

No separate criminal justice system existed in ancient China.[62] At the local district (*xian*) level, judicial and administrative powers were vested in the local magistrate. The legal process followed closely an inquisitorial approach. For example, a typical trial conducted at the local level involved a complaint filed by the victim and/or the family.[63] The magistrate played all major official roles. He was the judge, the prosecutor and the defense lawyer, rendering a decision after questioning all parties involved in the case (i.e., the offender, victim, and any witnesses).[64]

Due to the lack of investigative technology and skills, material evidence was rarely available or used by the local magistrate. Instead, confession was crucial for a conviction.[65] If defendants refused to cooperate or admit their crime, the magistrate could order beating to "force" a confession. This practice of physical torture for confession was legal throughout Imperial China.[66] Once conviction was obtained, the sentence was immediately carried out for lighter punishment (e.g., less than one hundred blows in a Song court).

During the Song dynasty and subsequent periods, criminal offenses involving more severe punishment were forwarded to the prefecture for review. Both the facts and the law were reviewed at the prefecture level and the defendant was asked to repeat his/her earlier confession to make certain that the confession was reliable.[67] The presiding prefecture official could release the accused, modify the sentence, or sustain the previous sentence. Again, if the sentence was lighter (e.g., no more than penal servitude in a Song court), the case would not go beyond the prefecture level; but if it was exile or the death penalty, the case must be forwarded to circuit supervisor for review.

In the Song Dynasty, the review process for the death penalty cases differed depending upon both the facts and the law. If the facts and the law were clear, execution could be carried out at the prefecture level upon the approval of the circuit supervisor. However, if there were doubts about the facts or the laws, the case must then be forwarded to the emperor.[68] In the Ming and Qing Dynasty, all death penalty cases were forwarded to the Board of Punishment in the capital city for review and then ratified by the emperor.[69]

Emperors in various imperial periods could offer exemptions and amnesties for death penalty cases.[70] In the Ming Code, for example, 185 offenses out of the 282 capital offenses required execution after assizes.[71] The Tang Code and its subsequent revisions in later dynasties specified that offenders could be exempted from the death penalty because of their age (e.g., too young or too old), health condition (both physical and mental), official rank, and/or family obligation (e.g., sole male heirs in the family who commit capital offenses would be allowed to stay home to care for their elderly parents and perform other duties as required by the Confucian principle of filial piety).[72] Amnesties were also granted by emperors to either free entirely the death row inmate or commute the death sentence to a lighter one. Under the penal codes of the Ming and Qing dynasties, several capital offenses under a category called "miscellaneous" were primarily symbolic sanctions that were commonly commuted to a lesser, non-capital penalty.[73]

Even though death penalty cases were expected to move from one level to another in accordance to the law in the imperial system, the defendant and the family could bypass the jurisdiction and file petition to a higher authority if they believed that the local official was corrupt. Defendants also had a final chance to plea for innocence at the market place moments before public execution. Upon proclamation of innocence in this setting, a retrial was required on the facts of the particular case.[74]

During this period of Chinese history, no advocates or lawyers were permitted in courts. There were, however, three types of individuals with some legal training and knowledge involved in the administration of justice. The first group were officials (e.g., local magistrate) who achieved their position through literary (not law) examination for academic degrees. As part of their examination, "judgment writing" skills (focusing more on literary rather than judicial skills) were tested. Once appointed, these officials served as interrogators and adjudicators. The second group involved clerks who were more familiar with the legal system and were in charge of managing the litigation process. The third group consisted of commoners who were educated and possessed legal knowledge to aid litigation. They were labeled as "litigation tricksters," and their role most resembled that of private attorneys in the current context.[75]

Defense assistance by third parties has been largely prohibited throughout China's history.[76] A primary reason for this prohibition is that such practices were regarded as inciting the populace to challenge the small elitist establishment and represented "rebelliousness and disrespect for the paternalistic bureaucracy."[77] These "litigation tricksters" also enjoyed very low prestige in ancient China, defamed as malicious and greedy "loafing pettifoggers," treated as illicit, and often persecuted for performing legal services.[78] This was primarily because their activity was inconsistent with Confucian teaching (e.g., their activities were viewed as entrapping people for the sake of profit, stirring up disputes and corrupting the system).[79]

Overall, the imperial period in China's history was not a receptive socio-political context for issues of procedural justice or reform. Rather than being a "lawless" times, detailed procedural requirements were often stipulated in penal codes, particularly with regard to death penalty cases. However, basic functional needs of the prevailing rulers to maintain and/or enhance their hierarchical authority resulted in a criminal process that was highly disciplinary and repressive throughout the ancient history.[80]

Execution practices in Imperial China

Numerous legal and extralegal methods of execution were used throughout the history of Imperial China. The most widely recognized methods included beating to death,[81] decapitation, chopping the body into pieces, drowning, being torn apart by carriages, slicing of the body, burning, hanging, and strangulation.[82] Death was also the unintended consequence of some non-lethal punishments such as beatings, severe bodily mutilation, and harsh conditions of hard labor. In the post-Tang dynasties, the standard execution methods involved decapitation, strangulation, and slicing.[83]

During this entire period of Chinese history, decapitation was the most common form of execution. It was often done in a swift and ritualistic manner. In particular, the offender's head was quickly severed with a sharp sword or knife by an executioner standing on the left-hand side of the criminal. The criminal was kneeling with face down, and hands crossed and bound behind the back and grasped by another executioner standing behind the criminal.[84] This practice was called "casting away in the marketplace," with the beheading often followed by the public exposure of the corpse and/or the mounting of the head on a pole. Decapitation could be applied to many types of criminal offenses including murder, banditry and stealing.[85]

As a method of execution, strangulation was often accomplished by tying the criminal to a post while two executioners slowly turned a rope twisted about the criminal's neck.[86] In the Tang Code, strangulation was applied to wide range of crimes such as logging a complaint against grandparents or parents with a magistrate, scheming to kidnap and sell a person into slavery, and opening a coffin while desecrating a tomb.[87] Although more painful in its infliction, strangulation was widely considered a less severe punishment than decapitation because of the Chinese belief that it would be disrespectful to the ancestors if a person died without having his/her body intact.

Slicing was the most severe and painful method of execution in this era. The technique varied in its administration, but it typically involved numerous cuts (ranging from eight to 120 cuts) of particular body parts, including cuts to the face, hands, feet, breast, stomach, and head while alive. The subject of this punishment slowly dies from the loss of blood.[88] Death by slicing was applied to crimes such as treason, parricide, mutilation of a living person for purposes of witchcraft, murder of three or more people from the same family, and other offenses known as "Ten Abominations," such as practiced in the Qing Dynasty.[89] Slicing was extremely brutal not only because of the physical suffering while the condemned alive, but also because of its religious significance to deprive the condemned of any coherent existence in the next world as the condemned no longer had his/her full flesh intact.

Execution in early Chinese history was mostly carried out in public. Public display of those executed may be interpreted as serving various functions such as reinforcing collective values through the visible demonstration of the evil of certain conduct, reaffirming the power of the prevailing political authority, and the deterrence of others from the commission of similar acts of misconduct.

Records from the year 1060 of the Song Dynasty indicate that a total of 2,560 offenders were sentenced to death. About one-half of these cases involved premeditated homicide or those during fights (1,300 cases), another 5 percent were homicide between relatives (e.g., those who killed their mothers, fathers, uncles, brothers, and husbands), nearly forty percent involved cases of forceful robbery (970 cases), and the remaining cases involved sexual crimes resulting in death.[90] Literature from the late period of the Qing Dynasty suggests that there were massive executions among those who took part in peasant uprisings.[91] Depending upon how such offenses are counted in available records (e.g., are particular offenses within a peasant uprising classified as treason, murder, looting, banditry), conclusions about the most prevalent executable offenses could change dramatically.

It is difficult to develop a social profile of persons executed during this period because of the lack of comprehensive data. However, given the extreme sensitivity to the growth of any "organized centers of resistance" to the governmental power, dynasties for centuries had levied stiff penalties on those large organized groups engaging in banditry, smuggling, and religious cult practices.[92] For the specific offenses of murder and robbery, it seems that persons who are young, male, peasants and lower class members, and dissenters and deserters were the groups that were most commonly executed.

The existing data on death sentences during the Song and Yuan Dynasties shows great volatility in the numbers over time and a dramatic decrease since the early 1100s. The number of recorded executions peaked around 3,400 cases in the late 1000s and dropped to less than fifty cases by the beginning of the 1300s. Unfortunately, it is unknown how representative these numbers of executions were for each historical period.[93] Summary, extrajudicial executions during periods of internal conflict among warring groups are not included in any data source and even official counts of legal executions in this period are problematic because of the lack of comprehensive court records. However, even if the available information provides a gross underestimation of death penalty practices, it still suggests that capital punishment was a relatively common response to perceived threat and misconduct at the end the eleventh century.

The available data for this period indicates a sizeable gap between those given a death sentence and those actually executed. For example, only twelve persons were executed among the 132 capital crimes in 1116 and 1117.[94] During another year in the twelfth century, only 181 of 1,811 persons of capital crimes were executed.[95] Similarly, only twenty-five persons out of 264 capital cases forwarded for review in 1085 were approved for execution.[96] An imperial order in 1131 stated that all men subject to the death penalty would only be exiled.[97] Overall, the vast majority of criminals in the Tang Dynasty could expect their sentences reduced by pardon or commutation if their offense was not particularly heinous or political.[98] Heavy criticisms were often leveled against the lenient tendency of the review of the death sentence in the Yuan Dynasty.[99]

In contrast, executions of large number of offenders were common occurrence in the Qing Dynasty, especially during and after the Taiping Rebellion (1850–64).[100] As another example of executions during this historical period, Bodde and Morris vividly described an execution of thirty-four bandits in Canton in 1851, with decapitation of thirty-three men and slicing of the ring leader, all completed in less than five minutes, at a public market.[101]

REPUBLICAN CHINA AND THE EARLY COMMUNIST MOVEMENT (1911–49)

After the collapse of the last imperial dynasty, the Qing Dynasty, China experienced a brief Republican period controlled primarily by the Nationalists (1911–49). The Communist Party collaborated with the Nationalist government in various wars such as the North Expedition War and the war against the Japanese invasion (1937–45). They also fought against the Nationalists' cracking down on the Communist's increasing expansion both in territory and in military force. In this section, contrasts and comparisons are made between the two drastically different perspectives and approaches on the death penalty in urban areas controlled primarily by the Nationalists and in the countryside, particularly in the western region of China, occupied mainly by the Communist Party led by Mao.

Sociopolitical context

The brief Republican period between 1911 and 1949 was characterized by two major developments: civil wars[102] and an intellectual revolution.[103] The early decades of the Republic era (roughly between 1911 and 1930) ended with a successful war of the Northern Expedition (1926–28) waged against the Northern warlords by the National Revolutionary Army, the joint forces of the Nationalist Party and the Communist Party.[104] The period of the 1930s and the 1940s was marked by constant internal strife between the Communist Party led by Mao and the Nationalist Party led by Jiang for territory and military control and their united efforts in fighting the Japanese aggression.[105]

Despite the tumultuous civil wars and wars against Japanese invasion, the Republican period was also an era of intellectual development, particularly in the realm of political thought. The collapse of the imperial regime that controlled China for thousands of years led to the rethinking of the traditional Confucian ideology.[106] Chinese intellectuals looked increasingly for new liberal Western strains of political thought for government and some turned their attention to Communism.[107] The May Fourth Movement in 1919 led by student protesters against the provisions in the Treaty of Versailles after World War I sparked political debates on the direction of China, the introduction of Marxism and Leninism, and the founding of the Chinese Communist Party in 1921.[108] Following a series of victories and setbacks in the fight with the Nationalist Army and the Japanese, the Communist Red Army finally found its roots in the countryside and rallied the populous support in the fight against the Japanese and overturning the Nationalist government in 1949.[109]

View of punishment and the death penalty

During the Republic period, the Nationalist government and Communist Party had two qualitatively different perspectives on punishment and the death penalty. The Nationalist government tried to reform the legal system by inserting basic Western legal principles of rationality, humanness and justice into the punishment system. These efforts included the abolition of forced confession and the elimination of some cruel form of execution (e.g., death by slicing).[110] Ancient penal practices such as tattooing, body amputation, beheading of the corpse, and the public display of heads were also prohibited in this period. Other reforms under the Nationalist government involved attempts to modernize China's prison system through staff training, education and rehabilitation of prisoners, and the implementation of prison rules and a reward system for the inmates.[111]

As a result of these reforms, the only methods of punishment stipulated in the criminal law of 1908 were fines, incarceration and the death penalty.[112]

However, despite these ambitious ideas, unique political and social conditions of the time (e.g., the war against Japan and the Chinese civil war, political and judicial corruption, and poverty) prevented the actual realization of many of these reforms.[113]

As true in other historical periods, the death penalty remained a strong legal punishment in jurisdictions controlled by the Nationalist government. During this time, there was some opposition groups that voiced concerns about the death penalty, among them, legal experts and governmental officials. Their major arguments for the abolition of the death penalty involved issues of human rights, the spirit of humanism, the lack of evidence of its assumed crime reduction effect, its contradiction with the reform ideals, and the international abolition movement of the death penalty.[114] However, this opposition was clearly the exceptional pattern. Instead, the death penalty remained a powerful tool in suppressing political opposition and maintaining order even within the relatively more formalized and modernized legal system envisioned by the Nationalist government.

While the Nationalist government tried to formalize and humanize the process of justice, at least in its formality, the Communist Party employed largely ad hoc tribunals and followed a more "popular justice" approach in their territorial base, independent of the Nationalist Government. For example, during the early years of the Communist development (1924–33), the Peasant Association controlled all rural affairs, including spouse disputes, gambling, opium possession, embezzlement, and counterrevolutionary activities on the Communist base.[115] The association had full authority in imposing fines, sentencing offenders to hard labor,[116] imprisonment, banishment, and the death penalty.[117] Public rally, mass struggle meetings, and indiscriminate killings and lootings of the gentries were common occurrence.

Despite accusations of terror and chaos from both the "law-abiding" gentry class and the Russian Soviet consultant to the Chinese Communist Party, Mao insisted that peasants were the best judge in rural affairs. He asserted that "to correct wrongs one must go to the other extreme, without which they cannot be righted."[118] Clearly, punishment and the death penalty in this period were regarded as necessary tools in class struggle, eliminating the danger, and enforcing the communist rule. As one official put it, "do not unnecessarily kill anyone, yet do not permit any counterrevolutionary activity in the Soviet area."[119] This popular approach to criminal justice in the early Communist movement was derived from Mao's political thought on the people's democratic dictatorship as exhibited in Mao's early writings.[120]

Substantive criminal law on the death penalty

The Nationalist government's attempt to create a modern legal system resulted in a series of laws known as the Six Codes (Constitution, Civil

Code, Commercial Code, Civil Procedural Code, Criminal Procedural Code, and Criminal Code).[121] The substantive criminal law primarily regulated and penalized counterrevolutionaries (e.g., Communist Party members), violent crimes (e.g., murder, robbery), property crimes (e.g., theft), marriage-related offense (e.g., adultery), public order crime (e.g., prostitution, gambling), drugs (e.g., possession of opium), and economic crimes (e.g., swindling, misappropriation).[122] Capital punishment was applied to the most serious crimes such as counterrevolutionary offenses.[123] Although capital punishment was no longer able to extend to other family members (i.e., collective capital punishment of family members was abolished), other disciplinary sanctions for failure to perform one's duties in the local social control networks (e.g., the system of *baojia*) could extend to other family and clan members and even the neighbors.[124]

Several statutes passed during the early era of the Communist movement stipulated capital punishment for most counterrevolutionary offenses[125] such as attempts to overthrow the government, sabotage, armed riots, espionage, assassination, desertion with weapons, and obstructing trade, as enacted in 1933.[126] Statutes in later times expanded the capital offenses by including acts endangering the Republic, traitors and war criminals.[127]

Within jurisdictions of the Nationalist government, offenders were processed differentially based on their socioeconomic status (e.g., income, occupation, employment, property ownership) and education background. Low education was considered a prime cause of crime in this period so individuals with this characteristic were punished more severely.[128] Similar punishments were also common among other disadvantaged groups (e.g., the unemployed, low income, property-less class).

Differential treatment of offenders was also a requirement in the Communist controlled territories. However, within this context, offenders with more privileged class positions (e.g., individuals of landlord-gentry, rich peasant, and capitalist backgrounds) were more likely to receive severe punishment. Other social characteristics of offenders also influenced punishment decisions, including the offenders' age (e.g., persons under sixteen years old received lesser punishment), past contribution to the communist movement (e.g., individuals having provided services for the revolution and/or having been wounded or crippled while fighting for revolutionary causes should receive more lenient punishment), and attitude (e.g., those who voluntarily confessed[129] and showed sincerity and remorse received lighter punishment).[130]

Procedural criminal law on the death penalty

Laws during the Republican era were greatly influenced by Western legal ideologies. This was especially true within jurisdictions of the Shanghai Mixed Court presided by Chinese magistrates and foreign assessors who handled cases involving extra-judicial territories (e.g., disputes between

Chinese and foreigners).[131] Legal counsel was permitted in the courtroom, torture to extract confession was abolished, and evidence was allowed to be presented and argued in similar fashions to the adversarial process in many Western legal systems. In addition, it was required that death sentences be confirmed by the Ministry of Justice, regardless whether the verdict was rendered in a traditional Chinese court or the Mixed Court.

In contrast, the process of capital offenses was more informal in the Communist jurisdictions. Local non-judicial units (e.g., Committees for the Suppression of Counterrevolutionaries) were given authorities to arrest, try, and execute counterrevolutionaries. This power, however, became more restricted later in the 1930s and the 1940s. No formal procedural laws and policies existed on how to conduct a trial in the Communist territorial base, particularly in early years (1924–33).

Even after the procedural laws were established later in this historical era, criminal procedures were not necessarily strictly followed. Judicial cadres neither recorded trial proceedings nor rulings, suspects were often tortured until confession was made, and executions were sometimes quickly conducted without higher-level authorization.[132] For example, several procedural requirements involving the length and availability of judicial review were bypassed in the early 1930s, presumably to keep the masses' interest high in counterrevolutionary cases.[133] Only after the Communist Party expanded its base and reinforced its control from 1935 to 1944 did it start to issue directives requiring that no other organizational unit other than the judicial and public security units could carry out the legal responsibilities for imposing popular justice.[134] Legal counsel had little place in the communist legal ideology as lawyers were perceived as cynical, mercenary, dishonest, and merely a tool of the bourgeois class.[135]

The prevailing forum for criminal trials in the Communist jurisdiction during this period involved mass trials. Mass trials were designed to mobilize the people (using advertising such as billboards, banners, and slogans), encourage their participation (by providing additional evidence, describing personal experience, and expressing their sentiment and judgment about the case), and serve as a function of public condemnation and degradation.[136]

Execution practices in the Republican era (1911–49)

Official documents kept by the Nationalist government indicated an attempt to use a more cautious and humane approach to execution. Science and technology that may result in a more "impartial and clinical death" (e.g., the preference of the gallows for conducting executions) was given more emphasis than prior manual executions that unnecessarily prolonged suffering and pain during execution (e.g., slicing).[137]

Despite its attempts to minimize the suffering during the execution, the Republic era did not eliminate the rather gruesome methods of execution.

In fact, various methods of execution remained in practice, including hanging,[138] decapitation with a sword, shooting through the back of the head, and beheading with the exposure of head in public.[139] Execution continued to serve as a public display and potential deterrent to others during this period.

The prevalence of death sentences in actual court practices is difficult to determine due to the absence of systematic national data in this period. However, scattered reports during this period provide a general idea of the use of death sentences.

Crime statistics on over 9,000 cases in Beijing reported in the Ministry of Justice Yearbook in 1918 indicated six persons were sentenced to death while 2,153 were given a prison sentence, 1,963 were sentenced to a short-term detention, and 1,932 were fined.[140] Based on national Judicial Statistics for the year of 1931, 188 offenders were sentenced to death, with 53,812 sentenced to imprisonment and 16,000 received fines. For the year of 1933, 122 offenders were sentenced to death, with 56,000 sentenced to imprisonment and 30,000 sentenced to a fine.[141]

Although official records rarely showed executions for counterrevolutionary offenses, most Chinese historians contend that executions of Communist Party members were common, particularly during the crackdowns on the Communists in the 1920s.[142]

Similarly, in territories controlled by the Communist Party, peasants were allowed to mistreat and execute counterrevolutionaries at will, particularly during early years of the Communist movements.[143] Public sentiment was often the dominating force for criminal sentences and executions. Executing counterrevolutionaries and the gentry class was regarded as a means to mobilize the Communist base.[144] The normal method of execution in the Communist territory was shooting. However, in some instances, beheading was also employed.[145]

Compared to the recorded death sentences in jurisdictions of the Nationalist government during similar periods of time, and relative to other sentences granted in the Communist territorial base, death sentences were very frequently used by the Communists. For example, available documents on a total of 1,641 cases tried by all levels of the People's Commissariate of Justice during a three-month period in 1932 revealed 271 death sentences, 349 sentences of imprisonment, 399 sentence to hard labor, and 141 sentences involving fines.[146] Data from later years (see Table 3.1) indicated fewer death sentences, but the proportion of capital sentences among the total sentenced cases remained very high.[147]

THE FIRST THIRTY YEARS OF SOCIALIST CHINA

Mao and his comrades established the People's Republic of China (PRC) in 1949. The first thirty years of Socialist China (1949–78) were punctuated

Table 3.1 Sentences in courts of more than twenty counties in the Shan-Gan-Ning border region controlled by the Communist Party*

	Year of Sentence			
Type of Sentence	*1939*	*1940*	*1941***	*Total*
Death Sentence	49	91	6	146
Education/Criticism	414	407	213	1,034
Exiled	0	12	8	20
Fines	69	119	122	31
Confiscated	34	63	15	112
Imprisonment	781	1,446	701	2,928
Other	0	0	6	6
Total	1,304	2,106	1,143	4,553

* The data was first presented in a newspaper, Liberation Daily, October 13, 1941. Numerous crime types were involved including traitor, banditry, corruption, opium, gambling, larceny, fraud, neglect of duty, looting, interfering with marriage and family, damaging public mores, disturbing public order, deserting.
** 1941 data based on only six months from January to June.
Source: Patricia E. Griffin. The Chinese Communist Treatment of Counterrevolutionaries: 1924–1949 (Princeton, NJ: Princeton University Press, 1976, 87).

by intense factional struggles. We describe below the socioeconomic conditions, substantive and procedural laws, and the death penalty and execution practices during this early period of Socialist China.

Sociopolitical context (1949–78)

In the first thirty years of socialist construction, China's sociopolitical environment was characterized by continuing revolution and class struggle with a series of political and economic campaigns that at times served as a catalyst for legal construction,[148] yet mostly were destructive to law and order.[149] The proletarian dictatorship was designed to suppress political enemies including the bourgeois class (e.g., capitalists, landlords) and the counterrevolutionaries (e.g., former officials and military personnel of the Nationalist government).[150] The goal was to unite and encourage peasants and workers to fully participate in the socialist political process.

Mao was determined to eliminate all forms of differentiation left over from the long ancient tradition in Chinese society: those differentiations between classes, sexes, urbanites and peasants, and the intellectuals and the laborers. Instead of hierarchy and rank, the communist virtue of self-sacrifice for the good of the collectives was promoted.[151]

Under the leadership of Mao, other major transformations took place in Chinese society. Economically, the state-planned economy became the single dominant economic form.[152] Fundamental living necessities were rationed on the basis of the number of people in the household. Housing, medical care, and children's education were distributed through the workplace in urban areas and the communes and/or the production brigade in the countryside. Peasants were allowed little mobility because they were tied to their allotted collective land. Urbanites were effectively managed and controlled within the community through the household registration system and at work by their dependencies on the government for jobs and basic benefits.[153] Under these sociopolitical conditions, China was a highly regulated and virtually crime-free society.

View of punishment and the death penalty (1949–78)

The legal system and ideology of the PRC were based on the pre-1949 experience of communist justice and the Soviet model. An important component in China's socialist construction was the integration of Mao's ideology of "living law" into the political climate of class struggle. Mao believed that the "living law" should supplant the rigid law of small elites and that law should be flexible to meet the needs of changing social conditions, particularly in the process of the continuing revolution.[154] He championed a relativistic approach to crime and punishment based on the nature of contradictions — the contradiction between "the enemy and us," and the contradiction "among the people."[155] Popular participation was also regarded as crucial in achieving socialist justice. In the spirit of popular justice, no formal body of law was codified,[156] few legal professionals were trained, and legally prescribed procedures were virtually nonexistent.[157] Ad hoc people's tribunals, summary justice, and punishment reflective of political and popular sentiment at the time were the primary means of rendering justice during this time period.[158]

It is important to note, however, that the implementation of Mao's ideology of informalism and popular justice was not without any resistance. In fact, Conservative Party members led by Liu Shaoqi, with the backing of the Soviet consultants, attempted to adopt the Soviet legal model with a more formal, bureaucratic, and codified legal framework during the 1950s. For example, drafts of criminal law and criminal procedure law were produced in the 1950s and continued being revised later in the 1960s.[159] This conception of a legal system called for more written, fixed laws, predictable outcomes with the certainty of legal procedures, and cases handled by trained legal professionals.[160] As a result, functions of the various justice agencies were defined along with the rights of the citizens.[161]

The relative emphasis on formal and informal elements in the Chinese justice system in the mid-twentieth century was in constant flux, depending upon the political climate of the time.[162] Ultimately, however, it was Mao's idea of the "living law" and popular justice that prevailed. Given the goal of the Communist Party was to bring about rapid political, economic, and social change (i.e., to change both physical conditions and human nature), Mao's ideas of popular justice and a living law that emanated from the common people fit especially well in this revolutionary environment.[163]

Under the sociopolitical conditions of early socialism, China was considered a largely lawless and chaotic country with harsh and arbitrary punishments. Despite Mao's rhetoric on restricting the scope of the death penalty and gradually abolishing the death penalty in Socialist China, the death penalty continued to be a primary tool for the suppression of criminal activities, particularly counterrevolutionary offenses.

Substantive criminal law on the death penalty (1949–78)

During this early period of Socialist China, only a handful of penal statutes were enacted and no legislatively promulgated penal code existed. Based on these penal statutes, counterrevolutionary offenses, corruption, crimes undermining the state monetary system, consumption and production of opium and other narcotics, and issues regarding labor re-education were the major concerns for criminal matters.[164] Capital offenses stipulated in these legal statutes/directives included three major types of offenses: counterrevolutionary offenses, corruption, and economic crimes.

Capital offenses for counter-revolutionary activities included (1) maintaining a link with the imperialist and betraying the motherland; (2) inciting government workers and soldiers to insurrection; (3) espionage (e.g., directing enemy airplanes and ships to bombardment targets); (4) criminal activities for counterrevolutionary objectives (e.g., destroying or plundering military installations, factories, mines, forests, farms, dams, jetties, communication lines, transport systems, banks, warehouses, safety devises; using poison, spreading bacteria or excitants of infectious diseases to harm people, livestock, and crops; counterfeiting official documents; impairing the market or monetary system at the order of internal or external enemies); (5) undermining the unity of the people and the government; (6) engaging in counterrevolutionary agitation and spreading rumors; (7) secretly crossing the boarder for counterrevolutionary purposes; and (8) organizing mass flight of prisoners.[165]

Corruption was defined as "the seizure, theft, or appropriation of state property by deception or substitution, the appropriation by extortion of the property of other persons, bribery and other illegal acts committed by workers in state institutions, enterprises, schools and the agencies under their jurisdiction in the guise of taking care of the public interest."[166] The statute specified that "if the sum appropriated exceeds 100,000,000 yuan" punishment should be imprisonment for a term of more than ten years or life imprisonment. A death penalty was mandated if the circumstances of the crime are "unusually serious." Additional aggravating circumstances were stipulated such as slandering to cover up corruption, damaging public property to destroy evidence, refusing to confess or offering an incomplete confession, bribery, theft or sale of state economic information. Sentences for other types of corruption (e.g., bribery, theft) shall follow the principle of analogy.[167]

Economic offenses subject to the death penalty included counterfeiting state bank notes for counterrevolutionary purposes or financial purposes.[168] Here, the capital economic offenses mainly concerned the interests of the state financial institutions as they were regarded vital in the socialist state-planned economy.

Other types of criminals such as "local despots," "bandits," and "secret agents" were also subject to the death penalty.[169] Surprisingly, some common violent crimes such as murder and rape were not stipulated in the decrees for punishment.

Procedural criminal law on the death penalty (1949–78)

During the "golden age"[170] of law in the early period of the PRC, a few decrees stipulated in the 1950s, such as the Act of the PRC for the Organization of Public Security Stations, Act of the PRC for the Organization of People's Courts, Law of the PRC for the Organization of People's Procuracies, codified the formality and the procedure of criminal investigation and trial.[171] For example, the police's authority in detention, arrest and search was defined and restricted. Under these procedural laws, a mixed bench consisted of one professional judge and two lay judges (people's assessors) in first instance and three judges in appeals were also required for a trial. Trials, in most instances, were public and the defendant was entitled to legal representation.[172]

Even under the legal framework spelled out by these laws and decrees, however, a Western perspective on procedural justice would find serious limitations in their form and content. For example, contrary to independent judiciaries in most Western countries, Chinese judges did not enjoy independent authority, but were subject to supervision and interference by the Communist Party. Defense attorneys were restricted to act only on behalf of the state and the people, not for the defendant. In fact, they were obliged to report privileged information disclosed by their client to aid the state's criminal investigation. Procurator possessed much greater power than the defendant because one represented the state and the other was perceived as "enemies" to be condemned. In addition, the trial was conducted in an inquisitorial setting where the court worked cooperatively with the police and the procurator as the accuser and the defendant was expected to be submissive and repentant about his/her guilt.[173] All of these conditions are contrary to procedural practices found within most adversarial legal systems of the Western world.

Under the conditions of an extremely hostile political climate during the beginning of the PRC and the Communist ideology of continuing revolution in the subsequent decades, judicial and extrajudicial punishment were utilized to eliminate all sources of political oppositions and antisocial elements. The police had virtually unlimited power in investigating, detaining, prosecuting and convicting criminal suspects[174] Criminal punishment was frequently administered outside the regular criminal justice system where no record was kept and no counsel was present. Mass campaigns were effectively used in channeling the public sentiment against the "bad elements" of the society and uniting the public for the Communist cause.

While legal representation in capital cases was not mandatory, confession was almost a requirement for offenders during this period of time. To meet the political and social demands, procedural safeguards were often bypassed.

Because of the lack of regard for legal procedure and law, the number of judicial death sentences and executions during this period of time was largely unknown. However, extrajudicial killings during political campaigns and famines in the early 1960s reportedly involved millions of deaths.

CONCLUSION

This chapter provided a historical overview of the death penalty law and practice during the Imperial, the Republican, and the early Socialist China, spanning several thousand years. It revealed the constant debate and struggle between ideas of formal law and informal justice, the persistent official reliance on the death penalty in order maintenance, and the widely neglected official recording of death sentences and executions during these historical times.

Despite the deeply rooted Confucian ideology of benevolence and propriety, and the attempted legal reforms at the turn of the twentieth century, it appeared that the Chinese laws have continued to focus on punishment, not rights, and collectivity, not the individual. Its use of the death penalty had steadfastly served the functions of social control and order maintenance.

4 Contemporary substantive and procedural criminal law on the death penalty

This chapter provides a detailed description and analysis of the laws and regulations on the death penalty in contemporary China. All major laws, governmental decrees, and judicial interpretations related to the death penalty passed after 1978 were included in the analysis. This chapter first describes the substantive issues involving the death penalty law, followed by the procedural legal issues. It then examines the various aspects of the death penalty laws unique to Chinese practices, including the exempt population, aggravating/mitigating circumstances, and the suspended execution.

SUBSTANTIVE CRIMINAL LAW ON THE DEATH PENALTY

The People's Republic of China (PRC) did not have a codified criminal law approved and passed by the legislative body until 1979, at the beginning of the economic reforms, even though decrees and statutes issued by various executive or judicial branches existed. Following Deng's call for building the socialist legal system, criminal law along with other laws were promulgated. In contrast to laws regulating economic activities (e.g., China-Foreign Equity Joint Venture Law) that anticipated and facilitated possible changes in the economic arena, the criminal law borrowed heavily from drafts of the 1950s and the 1960s, thus reflecting primarily the political and ideological thought on crime and punishment during the Mao era.

China's criminal code (1979)

Compared to some of its Imperial counterparts and the current law (1997) in the PRC, the first Criminal Law (1979) under the PRC overemphasized the political nature of crime and lacked clarity in defining both the substantive and procedural issues involving crime and punishment. The law covered eight broad crime types with a total of 192 separate articles.[1] Among these eight general crime types, twenty-eight specific offenses were punishable with the death penalty.[2]

The largest category of capital offenses was found within the general category of counterrevolutionary offenses. A total of fifteen capital offenses were contained in this category, including overthrowing the political power of the dictatorship of the proletariat and the socialist system (1979 CL, Article 103). Capital offenses within other general offense categories include endangering public security (with eight capital offenses such as arson in Article 106), infringing upon personal rights (with three capital offenses such as murder in Article 132 and rape in Article 139), and infringing upon property rights (with two capital offenses such as robbery in Article 150 and corruption in Articles 155).[3] Table 4.1 summarizes all capital offenses that are specified under the original PRC's criminal law of 1979.

Supplementary governmental regulations between 1979 and 1997

The original PRC's criminal law in 1979 was concerned primarily with regulating criminal activities (especially violent crime and political offenses) that were prevalent during the Mao era when class struggle and planned economy dominated the political and economic structure. However, this criminal code became quickly outdated because it did not anticipate the changes in crime during the economic reforms. As discussed in the previous chapter, these economic reforms brought significant changes in all spheres of politics, the economy and the wider society, resulting in a dramatic rise of crime rates, particularly for economic crimes and public order crimes.

As a response to the surging crime rates, a series of decrees were issued by the Standing Committee of the National People's Congress (NPC) to supplement the 1979 Criminal Law. The major governmental decrees included:

- the 1982 Decree on Severely Punishing Those Who Disturb the Economic Order
- the 1983 Decree on Severely Punishing Those Who Threaten Public Security
- the 1990 Decree on Prohibiting Narcotics
- the 1991 Resolution on Prohibiting Prostitution and Pimping

Along with other statutes, the decrees expanded the scope and the number of capital offenses significantly, from the previous twenty-eight offense types to seventy-five offense types before the revision of the criminal law in 1997. These decrees and their respective capital offenses are presented in Table 4.2.

China's criminal code (1997)

The criminal law undertook major revisions in 1997 as the economic reforms deepened. Compared to the 1979 law, the revised code of 1997 was

Table 4.1 Capital offenses under PRC's criminal law (1979)

Counterrevolutionary Offense (Fifteen Capital Offenses):

Article 91: colluding with foreign states in plotting to harm the country.
Article 92: conspiring to subvert the government or dismember the state.
Article 93: encouraging members of the armed forces, the police, or militia to defect to the enemy.
Article 94: defecting to the enemy.
Article 95: participating in armed mass rebellion.
Article 96: organizing a jailbreak.
Article 97: espionage or aiding the enemy:
(1) Stealing, secretly gathering or supplying intelligence for the enemy;
(2) Supplying arms and ammunition or other military materials to the enemy;
(3) Joining a secret service or espionage organization or accepting a mission assigned by the enemy.
Article 100: carrying out acts of sabotage to promote counterrevolution such as hijacking aircraft, causing explosions, stealing state secret, manufacturing arms:
(1) causing explosions, setting fires, breaching dikes and using technical or other means to sabotage military equipment, production facilities, communications or transportation equipment, construction projects danger prevention equipment or other public structures or public property;
(2) stealing state records or military materials or plundering industrial or mining enterprises, banks, shops, warehouses or other public property;
(3) hijacking ships, naval vessels, aircraft, trains, trams or motor vehicles;
(4) directing the enemy to any bombing or shelling target; and
(5) manufacturing, forcibly seizing or stealing guns or ammunition.
Article 101: mass poisoning or spreading infectious diseases to promote counterrevolution.

Endangering Public Security (Eight Capital Offenses):

Article 106: setting fires, breaching dikes, causing explosions, spreading poisons.
Article 110: sabotaging a means of transport, transportation facilities, electric power or gas facilities, or inflammable or explosive equipment.

Infringing upon Personal Rights (Three Capital Offenses):

Article 132: murder.
Article 139: rape and rape involving a minor.

Infringing upon Property Rights (Two Capital Offenses):

Article 150: robbery.
Article 155: graft.

Source: *The 1979 Criminal Law of the People's Republic of China*. Website of Zhongguo Falu Fagui Jiansuo (Searching Index of Chinese Law and Regulation) at http://202.99.23.199/home/begin.cbs.

much more comprehensive and substantial, encompassing ten broad crime categories with 451 Articles. They included (1) endangering national security; (2) endangering public security; (3) undermining the socialist market economic order; (4) infringing upon the rights of the person and the demo-

Table 4.2 Supplemental capital offenses by decrees between 1979 and 1997 (forty-seven new capital offenses)

1981 Decree on Punishing Military Personnel Who Derelicts Military Duty (Articles 4, 10, 11, 12, 14, 16, 17, 18, 19, and 20; Thirteen New Capital Offenses)

- stealing, secretly gathering or unlawfully providing military secrets for the enemy or foreign agencies
- employing violent or threatening means to obstruct commanding officers or on-duty servicemen from carrying out their duties
- stealing or robbing military equipment
- stealing or robbing military materials
- sabotaging major military equipment
- sabotaging major military facility
- fabricating rumors to mislead people thereby undermining the morale of the army during wartime
- deserting on the eve of a battle resulting in a great loss in combat or in a battle
- refusing to carry out an order in wartime resulting in major losses
- intentionally providing false military information leading to major losses
- intentionally delivering false military order
- mortally afraid of death, laying down his weapons and voluntarily surrendering to the enemy
- looting and torturing innocent civilians during a war

1982 Decree on Severely Punishing Those Who Disturb the Economic Order (Article 1; Seven New Capital Offenses)

- smuggling
- racketeering
- theft
- habitual theft
- stealing and illegally exporting precious cultural relics
- drug trafficking*
- bribe-taking

1983 Decree on Severely Punishing Those Who Threaten Public Security (Articles 1 and 2; Ten New Capital Offenses)

- hooliganism
- intentional assault
- abducting and selling human beings
- illegally manufacturing, selling, and transporting weapons, ammunitions bombing materials or explosives
- stealing, robbing weapons, ammunitions or explosives
- organizing or utilizing a cult organization to engage in counterrevolutionary activities
- utilizing superstitions to engage in counterrevolutionary activities
- forcing women into prostitution
- inducing or sheltering women to engage in prostitution
- teaching others with criminal techniques

1988 Supplementary Regulation on Punishing Those Who Leak National Secrets (One New Capital Offense)

- stealing, secretly gathering, purchasing by bribery or illegally proving the national secrets or intelligence for foreign institutions

1990 Decree on Prohibiting Narcotics (One New Capital Offense)

- transporting and manufacturing illicit drugs

1991 Supplementary Regulation on Punishing Illegally Digging and Robbing Ancient Remains or Tombs (One new Capital Offense)
- illegally digging and robbing ancient remains or tombs

1991 Resolution on Severely Punishing Those Who Abduct and Sell Women and Children (Three New capital Offenses)
- smuggling of women and children
- abduction of women and children
- kidnapping and extortion

1991 Resolution on Prohibiting Prostitution and Pimping (Two New Capital Offenses)
- organizing others in prostitution
- forcing others into prostitution

1992 Decree on Punishing Those who Hijack an Aircraft (One New Capital Offense)
- hijacking

1993 Resolution on Punishing Those Who Produce and Sell Fake and Shoddy Products (Two New Capital Offenses)
- manufacturing and selling fake medicine
- manufacturing and selling poisonous foods

1995 Resolution on Punishing Those Who Disturb the Financial Order (Four New Capital Offenses)
- currency counterfeiting
- illegal and fund-raising fraud
- financial instrument fraud
- credit-card fraud

1995 Resolution on Punishing Those Who Issue, Counterfeit or Sell Special Value-Added Tax Invoices (Two new Capital Offenses)
- illegally issuing value-added tax invoices
- counterfeiting or selling counterfeited value-added tax invoices

---

Source: The number of capital offenses derived from these decrees was based on Chen's (2002) accounting (Xingliang Chen. *The New Horizon of Contemporary Criminal Law in China*, Beijing: The Chinese University of Politics and Law Publishing House, 2002, 540–57). These Decrees and Resolutions can be found on the Web site of *Zhongguo Falu Fagui Jiansuo* (Searching Index of Chinese Law and Regulation) at http://www.novexcn.com/china_law_contents.html.

cratic rights; (5) encroaching on property; (6) disrupting the order of social administration; (7) endangering the national defense interest; (8) crimes of graft and bribery; (9) dereliction of duty; and (10) violating duties by military servicemen. The only crime category that does not carry a capital penalty involves dereliction of duty (chapter 9).[4] Table 4.3 presents all capital offenses stipulated in China's criminal law of 1997.

This revision widened the scope of capital offenses from murder, rape, and robbery to newly emergent offenses such as drug trafficking, terrorism, producing or distributing poisonous, harmful, or shoddy goods or medicines, forcing others into prostitution, and financial instrument and/

Table 4.3 Capital offenses stipulated in the 1997 criminal law

Crimes of Endangering National Security (Article 113; Seven Capital Offenses)

- Plotting to jeopardize the sovereignty, territorial integrity and security of the country
- Instigating to split the country
- Organizing, plotting, or carrying out armed rebellions, or armed riots
- Organizing, plotting or acting to subvert the political power of the State
- Espionage
- Stealing, secretly gathering, purchasing by bribery or illegally providing the national secrets or intelligence for foreign institutions
- Providing the enemy with armed equipment or military materials

Crimes of Endangering Public Security (Articles 115, 119, 121, 125, 127; Fourteen Capital Offenses):

- Arson
- Breaching dikes
- Causing explosions
- Poisoning
- Threatening public security with dangerous methods
- Sabotaging transportation instruments
- Sabotaging transportation infrastructures
- Sabotaging electric power
- Sabotaging inflammable or explosive facilities
- Hijacking an aircraft
- Illegal manufacturing, trading, transporting, and mailing guns, ammunition or explosives
- Illegally trading or transporting nuclear materials
- Stealing or snatching guns, ammunition or explosive materials
- Forcibly seizing guns, ammunition or explosive materials

Crimes of Undermining the Socialist Market Economic Order (Articles 141, 144, 151, 157, 170, 199, 205, and 206; Fifteen Capital Offenses):

- Producing or distributing bogus medicines
- Producing or distributing poisonous or harmful foods
- Smuggling weapons and ammunitions
- Smuggling nuclear materials
- Smuggling counterfeited currencies
- Smuggling cultural relics
- Smuggling precious metals
- Smuggling rare plants and their products
- Counterfeiting currency
- Illegal fund-raising fraud
- Financial instrument fraud
- Letter of credit fraud
- Credit-card fraud
- Illegally issuing value-added tax invoices
- Counterfeiting or selling counterfeited value-added tax invoices

Crimes of Infringing upon the Rights of the Person and the Democratic Rights (Articles 232, 236, 239, and 240; Five Capital Offenses)

- Murder
- Rape
- Statutory rape
- Kidnapping
- Abducting women and children

Crimes of Encroaching on Property (Articles 263 and 264; Two Capital Offenses):
- Robbery
- Theft

Crimes of Disrupting the Order of Social Administration (Articles 295, 317, 328, 347, and 358; Eight Capital Offenses):
- Imparting criminal methods
- Organizing a jail break
- Prison riots using weapons
- Illegally digging and robbing ancient remains or tombs
- Illegally digging or robbing fossils of ancient human beings or fossils of ancient vertebrate animals
- Smuggling, trafficking, transporting or manufacturing narcotics
- Organizing another person to engage in prostitution
- Forcing another person to engage in prostitution

Crimes of Endangering the National Defense Interest: (Articles 69 and 370; Two Capital Offenses):
- Sabotaging military weapons, military installations or military communications
- Knowingly providing unqualified weapons or military installations to the armed forces

Crimes of Graft and Bribery: (Article 383; Two Capital Offenses):
- Graft
- Bribe-taking

Crimes of Violating Duties by Military Servicemen: (Articles 421, 422, 423, 424, 426, 430, 431, 433, 438, 439, and 446; Thirteen Capital Offenses):
- Refusing to carry out an order in wartime
- Deliberately concealing military intelligence, furnishing falsified intelligence
- Refusing to disseminate military orders, or falsely disseminated military orders
- Surrendering to the enemy
- Deserting on the eve of a battle
- Obstructing commanding officers or on-duty servicemen from carrying out their duties
- Defecting to a foreign country
- Illegally obtaining military secrets
- Illegally providing military secrets to foreign organs
- Fabricating rumors to mislead people during wartime
- Stealing or robbing weapons or military materials
- Unlawfully selling or transferring military weaponry
- Injuring or killing innocent residents or looting property from innocent residents during wartime

Source: Wei Luo. The 1997 Criminal Code of the People's Republic of China (Buffalo, NY: William S. Hein & Co., Inc., 1998).

or credit card fraud. The stipulation of these new capital offenses clearly indicates a shift of the Chinese government's focal concerns from political interests in the past to economic and social issues in the present.

There are several clear illustrations of the use of new capital codes to address evolving social and economic conditions in contemporary China. For example, in the "getting rich is glorious" atmosphere[5] under China's new free market economy, numerous incidents of people producing and selling harmful, fake, and/or shoddy products to make a profit occurred that directly threatened the economic order and public health. The death penalty was used as one measure to deter and punish these offenses. In one particular case in 1997 where nine people engaged in producing and selling liquors with substitute materials and without a license that caused thirty-two deaths and three injuries, five offenders were sentenced to death, three offenders were sentenced to death with a two year suspension of execution and one was sentenced to life imprisonment.[6] The most recent expansion of capital offenses involves another contemporary health issue in China, the intentional spread of the SARS disease.[7]

Explanations for the increasing number of capital offenses derive primarily from the economic reforms and the consequential changes in political, social, and cultural institutions. For example, the promotion of the market economy and the open-door policy by the economic reforms facilitates a host of new activities, including criminal ones. While the old value system of communitarian and collectivism was abandoned, a new value system associated with individualism and economic entrepreneurship along with its control mechanisms has not yet been fully established. This state of anomie in the post-reform era created both opportunities and confusions.[8] With the increasing crime rates and the lack of internal control in many regulatory agencies (e.g., financial institutions in preventing financial fraud, government agencies in prohibiting corruption, and business bureaus in regulating fraudulent business practices and preventing hazardous products), stiff legal sanctions, including the use of the death penalty, were considered one of the only viable methods of social control.[9]

PROCEDURAL CRIMINAL LAW ON THE DEATH PENALTY

For the most part of socialist China, the terms of "criminal procedure" and "due process rights" remained largely absent. It was only until the passage of the criminal procedure law in 1979 and its revision in 1996 that certain rights and procedures similar to their Western counterparts were codified and made available to criminal suspects in China.

China's criminal procedure law (1996)

The content of China's criminal procedures in 1996 continued to affirm the traditional four-tired court system, involving the *Basic Level People's Court*, *Intermediate People's Court*, *Higher People's Court* and the *Supreme People's Court*. Under this system, capital cases are typically first tried at the intermediate criminal court, then reviewed by the superior court, and finally ratified by the Supreme Court.

The contemporary Chinese criminal justice system is indicative of a semi-inquisitorial and semi-adversarial legal system. Under this legal model and resulting from the legal reforms in the 1990s, the judge's role in criminal investigation is gradually withering away and the criminal defense attorney's role has increased in all phases of criminal proceedings (e.g., the pre-trial investigation, trial and post-trial appeals). The People's Procuratorate, however, remains a powerful state agency in charge of criminal prosecution.[10]

As true in most other countries, a criminal trial in contemporary China is conducted in a courtroom, mostly open to public.[11] A trial is typically presided by a panel of judges with a chief judge and two deputy judges (or lay judges). The chief judge controls the tempo and order of the courtroom by following the detailed rules of judicial proceeding prescribed in the criminal procedure law. These rules of procedures cover opening statements, presentation of the case, cross-examination, debate, and closing statements. The judge can directly question the defendant, though the prosecution and the defense now bear the responsibility of presenting the evidence, including questioning the defendant in the courtroom. The defendant is allowed to defend for him/herself in the courtroom and is given an opportunity to read his/her own statement.

Accompanying the changing dynamics within the criminal justice system was the increasing emphasis on procedural justice. Comparing these two procedure codes of 1979 and 1996, even the harsh critics of the Chinese human rights records regarded the 1996 law "likely to result in better protection of defendants' rights."[12] The major improvements in procedural safeguards in the legal code of 1996 compared to the procedural practices under the 1979 law include the following:[13]

- No conviction to be made without court trials. This breaks the long historical tradition of little separation between the administrative and judicial systems. Individuals could be easily found guilty without judicial proceedings in the past. This new stipulation represents a significant improvement toward the rule of law.[14]
- Abolishing the system of exemption from prosecution. In the past, individuals could be found "guilty" by the procuratorate with its grant of exemption from prosecution without a criminal trial. The abolition of this practice signifies the formalization and legalization of the criminal process that ensures individuals' rights for a judicial hearing before being found guilty. For minor criminal cases where the facts are clear, simplified procedure is introduced into the law to enhance judicial efficiency.[15]
- Earlier and greater access to criminal proceedings by defense attorney. A defense attorney under the new law is allowed to provide legal services for criminal suspects during the phase of criminal investigation

by the police. They now have more rights in evidence gathering and cross-examination. More importantly, legal representation is now mandatory for death penalty cases, which is further ensured with the establishment of a legal aid program.[16]

- Shifting of judges' role of criminal investigation during the pre-trial phase to conducting courtroom hearings. The hands-off approach similar to judges in an adversarial system presumably enables the Chinese judges to concentrate on adjudication rather than investigation, presumably helping improve judicial efficiency and professionalism, and reduce potential biases and corruption.[17]
- Abolishing the administrative compulsory measure of custody-for-investigation and restricting the scope of investigation by procuratorates. These new stipulations attempt to restrict the state power represented by the police and the procuratorates, and protect the rights of the individuals from the undue interference of the state. In the meanwhile, the scope of private prosecution is expanded that grants more protections to the victim of a crime.[18]

Review process for the death penalty cases

The new criminal procedure law also stipulated an elaborate review process for capital punishment. The process of review conducted by the superior court could be initiated by an appeal of either the defendant or the procurator.[19] The original sentence could not be increased if the defendant appeals but could be increased if the procurator appeals. The review would be automatically conducted even if there was no appeal because the Chinese law requires a mandatory review of all capital offenses, including a death sentence with a two-year suspension of execution, by the superior court. All death penalty cases must then be ratified by the Supreme Court except in cases where the superior court is authorized to conduct the final review. Table 4.4 provides the detailed review procedure for capital punishment as stipulated in the 1996 Criminal Procedue Law.[20]

The Supreme Court's mandatory final approval authority for capital punishment was waived several times in the past twenty years or so due to the demand of the "strike-hard" campaigns. The death sentence imposed on the following crimes can now be finally reviewed and approved by the superior court of each jurisdiction: murder, robbery, rape, explosion, arson, poisoning, damaging the damn, sabotaging major transportation and electrical equipment.[21]

To prevent the further expansion of the final review authority in capital cases, the Standing Committee of the NPC issued a Decision Regarding the Approval of Cases Involving Death Sentences in 1981. This decision stressed that capital cases for counterrevolutionary offense, corruption and bribery, smuggling, and drug trafficking must still be ratified by the Supreme Court.[22] In 1991, due to the high number of capital sentences imposed on

Table 4.4 Review procedure for capital punishment as stipulated in the 1996 criminal procedure law

Article 199. Approval of the Supreme People's Court Death sentences shall be verified and approved by the Supreme People's Court.
Article 200. Review of Higher People's Courts Cases of first instance where an immediate people's court imposes a death sentence and the accused does not wish to appeal shall be reviewed and verified by the higher people's court first, and then submitted to the Supreme People's Court for verification and approval. If the higher people's court does not agree with the death sentence, it may bring the case up and try it or remand the case back to the intermediate people's court for a new trial. Cases of the first instance where a higher people's court imposes a death sentence and the accused does not wish to appeal, and cases of the second instance where a death sentence is imposed, shall be submitted to the Supreme People's Court for verification and approval.
Article 201. Approval of Higher People's Courts Cases where an intermediate people's court imposes a death sentence with a two-year suspension of execution shall be verified and approved by the higher people's court.
Article 202. Formation of a Collegiate Bench of Three Judges The verification and approval of a death sentence by the Supreme People's Court and the verification and approval of a death sentence with a two-year suspension of execution shall be conducted by a collegiate bench composed of three judges.

Source: "The 1996 Criminal Procedure Law." In *The Amended Criminal Procedure Law and the Criminal Court Rules of the People's Republic of China: with English Translation, Introduction and Annotation*, ed. and trans. Wei Luo (Buffalo, New York: William S. Hein & Co., Inc., 2000), 111.

drug trafficking in the southern region of China, the Supreme Court issued a decision to authorize the superior courts of Yunan and Guangdong provinces the final authority to ratify the death penalty for narcotics trafficking cases. The exception was that narcotics trafficking cases first tried in the superior court or cases involving foreign countries must still be reviewed and approved by the Supreme Court.[23]

Besides these regular adjudicative proceedings, cases may be reviewed under a special procedure of supervising adjudication. This process may be initiated by the defendant, close relatives or legal representatives through a petition to challenge the legal ruling of the death penalty after it has been ratified. If the court finds any of the following conditions exists, a retrial should be conducted. These special conditions include that (1) new evidence emerged; (2) uncertain and insufficient evidence was used for a conviction; (3) there was an error in the application of the law; and (4) judicial corruption was involved.[24] The process of supervising adjudication may also be initiated by courts at any levels and the procuratorates at any levels.[25] The court shall form a new collegiate bench to conduct retrial of these cases. The new trial shall be concluded within three months after the initiation of the supervising adjudication process and when needed, may be extended to the maximum of six months.[26]

The process of supervising adjudication is not part of the normal judicial proceeding. Therefore, the initiation of this special process does not suspend the enforcement of legal rulings that have already become effective. The only exception is for the death penalty cases. The court shall suspend the execution and make a report to the Supreme Court upon discovery of any of the following circumstances in a death penalty case (1) erroneous judgment; (2) disclosure of major criminal facts or performance of substantial meritorious service by the offender; and (3) the offender is pregnant.[27]

In addition to the above described judicial proceedings, defendants and their family members could also resort to administrative avenues to appeal their case at any time — before, during, or after the trial. This system of administrative intervention or oversight of judicial matters derives from a deeply rooted distrust in law within Chinese culture. In ancient times, Chinese citizens, when wronged by local officials, tended to bring their case to circuit officials, and sometimes all the way to the capital city of Beijing due to concerns of local protectionism and corruption. In the current time, *xin fang,* the Office of Letters and Calls, set up in every municipality and province, primarily serves as an outlet for citizens to protest public officials' misconduct and gross negligence of their duty. With regard to capital cases, citizens could use *xin fang* to protest a wrongful conviction resulted from judicial corruption.[28]

Legal process of execution

The law of criminal procedure also stipulates detailed rules on carrying out the death sentence. Under this law of criminal procedure (see Articles 210 thru 213), once the death sentence ruling is finalized and becomes legally effective, the President of the Supreme Court shall issue and sign the order to carry out the death penalty. In cases where the superior court is granted the final approval authority of the death sentence, the President of the high court shall issue and sign the order to carry out the death penalty. After receiving the order, a court at the lower level shall carry out the execution within seven days. The court shall notify the procuratorate at the same level to oversee the execution.[29]

The death penalty may be carried out by shooting, injection or other means, and on an execution ground or in a place within a designated detention center. Before execution, the offender's identity is verified, and his/her last words are recorded or letters collected. Execution shall be publicly announced but not shown to the public. After the execution, the court clerk on the spot shall make a written record of the execution, submit the report to the Supreme Court, and notify the offender's family. For offenders who are sentenced to the death penalty with two-year suspension of execution, the public security agency shall hand them over to the prisons to serve the sentence.[30]

CHARACTERISTICS OF THE DEATH PENALTY LAW

As discussed in the previous chapters, Chinese socialist law is a fusion of Confucian philosophy, Marxist ideology, Western capitalistic democratic influence and the unique Chinese socialist experience. In the following section, major characteristics of the substantive and procedural criminal laws related to the death penalty are discussed.

Wide range of sentencing options and judicial discretion

A wide range of sentencing options are available in the Chinese criminal law, including public surveillance, criminal detention, fixed-term imprisonment, life imprisonment, and the death penalty, with additional supplementary penalties of fines, deprival of political rights, and confiscation of property.[31] A capital offense is typically subject to more than one of these sentencing options as few crimes carry a mandatory death sentence. In addition, most capital offenses will only result in the death sentence when involving aggravating circumstances. These special circumstances are nevertheless not sufficient conditions for the death sentence. Table 4.5 presents selected crimes with definition, aggravating factors and their respective sentencing range stipulated in the 1997 criminal law.

To reduce sentencing discretion and enhance its uniformity particularly in the death penalty cases, criminal laws also have stipulations of minimum criteria for the death sentence. For example, Article 43 of the criminal law of 1979 stipulated that the death sentence shall only be applied to criminals who have committed the most heinous crimes with the most evil intent (*zuida erji*). Article 48 of the criminal law of 1997 changed this stipulation slightly, replacing it with "the most heinous crime (*zuixing jiqi yanzhong*)." Both requirements showed that not only the dangerousness of the offense but also the dangerousness of the offender were critical in sentencing decisions of death vs. non-death.[32]

Other institutions that have law making authority such as the NPC, Supreme Court and Supreme Procuratorate have also issued interpretations to guide sentencing decisions. For example, a 2002 Interpretation issued by the Standing Committee of the NPC stipulated that individuals who are convicted of accepting bribery (Article 385) have the ability to carry out the judgment (e.g., confiscating property) but refuse to do so, or interfere with the enforcement of the judicial ruling with the abuse of power, "shall be given a heavy sentence within the legal limit."[33] The "heavy sentence" for this crime is the death penalty.

Table 4.5 Selected crimes with definition, aggravating factors and sentencing range in the 1997 criminal law

Murder	*Sentence Range*
Legal definition (Article 232)	
Anyone who intentionally commits homicide	> 10 yrs, life, death
Rape	
Legal definition:	
Rape (Article 236 Section 1)	
Anyone who rapes a woman by violence, coercion or other means;	3–10 yrs.
Statutory Rape (Article 236 Section 2)	
Anyone who has a [sic] sexual relations with a minor girl under the age of fourteen;	
Aggravating Factors (Article 236 Section 3)	> 10 yrs., life, death
(1) raping a woman or having sexual relations with a minor girl in a disgusting way;	
(2) raping many women or having sexual relations with many minor girls;	
(3) raping a woman before many people in a public place;	
(4) raping a woman in turn with another man or other men;	
(5) causing a severe injury, death or other serious consequence to the victim.	
Abduction of Women	
Legal definition	
Abduction of Women (Article 240 Section 2)	5–10 yrs. and fines
[Anyone] abducting, kidnapping, buying, selling, delivering, receiving or transferring a woman ... for the purpose of selling them	
Aggravating Factors (Article 240 Section 1)	> 10 yrs., life, death
(1) a ringleader of a gang engaged in abducting and selling women;	
(2) abducting and selling more than three women;	
(3) raping an abducted woman;	
(4) inducing or forcing an abducted woman to engage in prostitution or selling an abducted woman to another person who would force her to engage in prostitution;	
(5) kidnapping women by using violent force, threats or anaesthetic drugs for the purposes of selling the women;	
(6) causing severe bodily injury, death or other serious consequences to an abducted woman;	
(7) selling a woman outside of China.	
Forcing Women into Prostitution	
Legal definition	
Organizing and Forcing Prostitution (Article 358 Section 1)	5–10 yrs.
Anyone who organizes or forces another person to engage in prostitution;	
Inducing or Sheltering Prostitution (Article 359 Section 1)	< 5 yrs.
Anyone who induces other people to engage in prostitution, shelters other people to engage in prostitution or introduces other people to the practice of prostitution;	

	Sentence Range
Aggravating Factors (Article 358 Section 2 & 3) (1) arranging for people to engage in prostitution, where serious circumstances are involved; (2) forcing a minor girl under the age of 14 to engage in prostitution; (3) forcing more than one person to engage in prostitution or repeatedly forcing others to engage in prostitution; (4) forcing another person to engage in prostitution after raping her; (5) causing serious injuries, death or some other serious consequences to the person who is forced to engage in prostitution.	> 10 yrs., life, death
Drug trafficking Legal Definition (Article 347) Anyone who engaged in smuggling, trafficking, transporting or manufacturing narcotics shall be investigated for criminal responsibility and given criminal punishment no matter how small or large the quantity of narcotics is.	
Sentencing guide (1) Anyone who engaged in smuggling, trafficking, transporting or manufacturing narcotics in any of the following situations: (a) more than 1,000 grams of opium or more than 50 grams of heroin or methamphetamine or other narcotics with a large quantity; (b) the ringleaders of narcotics smuggling, trafficking, transporting or manufacturing narcotics; (c) providing armed protection for those smuggling, trafficking, transporting or manufacturing narcotics; (d) using violent forces to resist inspection, detention or arrest under serious circumstances, or (e) participating in international organized narcotics transportation and distribution.	> 15yrs., life, death
(2) > 200 & < 1,000 grams of opium or > 10 & < 50 grams of heroin or methaphetamine	> 7 yrs. + fine
(3) < 200 grams of opium or < 10 grams of heroin or methamphetamine.	3–7 yrs. + fine
Graft Legal Definition (Article 382) The crime of graft occurs when any state functionary takes advantage of his office to illegally possess, isappropriate, deceptively obtain or use other means to illegally acquire public property. Any person, who is entrusted by a state organ, state-owned company, state-owned enterprise, state institution or a people's organization to handle state deceptively obtain or uses othe means to illegally acquire public property have committed the crime of graft.	

(*Continued*)

Table 4.5 Continued

Anyone who conspires with persons described in the preceding two paragraphs to engage in graft shall be treated as joint criminals.	
Sentencing guide	
(1) Where the value of an individual graft is not more than 5,000 yuan:	
(a) where serious circumstances are not involved;	Administrative Sanction
(b) where serious circumstances are involved	< 2 years
(2) Where the value of an individual graft is not less than 5,000 yuan nor more than 50,000 yuan:	1–7 years
(a) serious circumstances are involved;	7–10 years
(b) where the offender committed graft valued between 5,000 and 10,000 yuan, has repented after committing the crime and actively returned the illegally obtained money and property	lighter or exempt sentence; administrative sanction
(3) Where the value of an individual graft is not less than 50,000 nor more than 100,000 yuan:	> 5, confiscation of property
(a) exceptionally serious circumstances are involved	Life, confis. of property
(4) Where the value of an individual graft is more than 100,000 yuan:	> 10, life, confis. of property
(a) exceptionally serious circumstances are involved	Death + confis. of property

Source: Wei Luo. *The 1997 Criminal Code of the People's Republic of China; With English Translation and Introduction.* Buffalo, New York: William S. Hein & Co., Inc., 1998.

Exempt population/special treatment

Consistent with Confucian ideas of benevolence and propriety and in line with global trends, the Chinese death penalty law protects various special populations from its imposition. These special populations involve minors and pregnant women.

Minors are exempted from the death penalty because of their unique intellectual, mental and psychological development. The criminal law of 1979 stipulated that (1) only offenders of eighteen years or older could be sentenced with the death penalty; and (2) in cases involving particular grave circumstances, offenders of sixteen or seventeen years old could receive the death penalty with a two-year suspension of execution.[34] The 1997 Criminal Law complied with the international standard by making it a firm minimum age requirement of eighteen years old for the death penalty (Article 49).[35]

Pregnant women have continued to be exempted from the death penalty in China (Article 49).[36] Besides these particular stipulations for the capital cases, other demographic characteristics such as offenders' physical and mental disabilities (Article 18 & 19) are all mitigating circumstances in judicial sentencing.[37]

Attitude and confessions

Rooted in Confucian ideology, offenders' attitude has long been institutionalized and codified in the penal codes throughout Chinese history. Defendants' confession was first recognized as a mitigating factor in criminal adjudication in the Qin Code (221–207 BC),[38] and then elaborated and improved in the Tang Code (625 AD).[39] After the establishment of the PRC, the 1952 Statutes on Penalties for Corruption stipulated that offenders shall be treated leniently if he/she confessed to the crime before its discovery and/or the confession was full and frank.[40] Similarly, the 1979 and 1997 Criminal Laws both stipulated a possible lighter (within the sentence range) and/or mitigated (lower than the sentence range) sentence for voluntary confessions. A voluntary confession occurs when offenders voluntarily turn themselves in before the officials have discovered their wrongdoings (1979 CL Article 63; 1997 CL Article 67).[41]

The institutionalization of confessions in the Chinese criminal justice system was further precipitated by other requirements of the law. For example, there has no law equivalent to the U.S. Fifth Amendment that protects against self-incrimination. In contrast, Chinese defendants are expected to be honest in answering questions from the legal authorities even though they cannot be coerced into admitting guilt (CPL Article 93). In addition, with the general lack of rigorous legal representation and a culture of repentance, submission and cooperation, confession is likely to be continuously regarded for its probative and corrective value.[42]

Legal representation

By any measure, criminal defense has been improved dramatically in contemporary China. The 1996 Criminal Procedure Law granted the defense attorney unprecedented access and authority in various areas ranging from bail, pre-trial criminal investigation, and cross-examination. The most significant development was the mandatory requirement of legal representation for capital cases. As the 1996 Criminal Procedure Law stipulates," in cases where the accused may be sentenced to capital punishment and he does not retain any defenders, the people's court shall appoint a lawyer, who voluntarily is undertaking a legal aid obligation, to defend him."[43]

Criminal defense was made possible not only due to the stipulation of the criminal procedure law, but also due to developments in other areas such as education and training,[44] the establishment of the Chinese Bar Association and the Legal Aid programs,[45] and the legal reforms that transformed the inquisitorial system to the adversarial system.

Death sentence with a two-year suspension of execution

Death sentences with a two-year suspension of execution are part of the death sentence in the Chinese sentencing structure. It is one of the most unique features of the Chinese death penalty practice.[46] The current 1997 criminal law stipulated that the suspended death sentence may be applied when an offender "should be sentenced to death," but "the immediate execution is not essential."[47] The law, however, did not specify the conditions under which "the immediate execution is not essential."

The following factors are some of the exceptional circumstances in practice that may lead to a two-year suspension of the death sentence. First, the offender voluntarily submitted to authority and performed meritorious services. Second, the offender was the gang member, but not the gang leader. Third, the victim was partially blamed for the crime. Fourth, the offender could serve as live evidence. And lastly, the offender has overseas connections (e.g., the offender's immediate family members were a foreign national).[48]

The earliest form of a suspended death sentence could be traced to the Han Dynasty (206 BC–25 AD), when death row inmates were allowed a chance to spare their lives for meritorious service.[49] This practice was followed by the subsequent dynasties. Immediately upon its establishment, the PRC institutionalized the death sentence with a two-year stay of execution to deal with counterrevolutionaries. It was later expanded to offenses such as robbery, abduction, and corruption in the 1950s.[50] During this early period of socialist China, records showed that death row offenders placed on the suspended sentence typically were sent to labor camps or prisons to engage in labor reform. Upon successful evaluation by the correctional agencies after two years, the original death sentence was reduced; if the evaluation was unsatisfactory, the original sentence was carried out.[51]

The first PRC criminal law in 1979 formalized such practice and specified that if the offender showed remorse after the two year stay, the death sentence should be commuted to life imprisonment. If the offender had meritorious services, the sentence should be further reduced to fifteen to twenty years of incarceration.[52] All capital offenses were eligible for the suspended death sentence.

The criminal law of 1997 further affirmed the practice but it made the sentencing decision at the end of the two year stay more objective. Instead of focusing on offenders' remorseful attitude based on the old law, the new law focused on whether the offender intentionally committed a crime during the period of the stay. If no intentional crime is committed, the sentence "shall be commuted to life imprisonment upon the expiration of the two-year period; if he performs substantial meritorious service, his punishment shall be commuted to fixed-term imprisonment of not less than 15 years and no more than 20 years (Article 50)."[53]

CONCLUSION

This chapter presents the death penalty law on the book. It first described related substantive and procedural criminal laws and various governmental decrees in contemporary China. It then discussed major features of the death penalty system including the wide sentencing range, exempt population, criminal confession, legal representation, and the suspended execution as stipulated in these laws.

From the perspective of the law, there have been significant improvements in both the substantive and procedural criminal laws in terms of the clarity of crime definition and punishment, as well as procedural protections for individual defendants. There are, of course, problems with the law. Some problems involve the inherent logic of the law (e.g., the simplicity of crime definition and wide range of sentencing options). Others have to do with the operability and feasibility of the law such as confession and legal representation because of the inherent contradiction between the public interests and the rights of the individual defendants in the Chinese context. From a global perspective, current Chinese laws reflect another type of contradiction that is represented by the dramatic increase in the number of capital offenses, and at the same time, increasing procedural protection of the defendants' rights.

5 The application of the death penalty

After the review of the substantive and procedural laws on the death penalty, this chapter examines how these laws are applied in the actual legal process. The description of this "law-in-action" aspect of the death penalty focuses on the actual use of the death sentence and executions, and the offender and offense characteristics associated with them.

This chapter examines three related questions about the death penalty. First, to what extent is the death sentence imposed and execution carried out in China? Second, what types of criminal offenders (e.g., differences by age, gender, occupation, criminal history) are most likely to be subject to the death penalty? Third, what types of criminal offenses (e.g., differences between violent, property, and economic offenses) and specific elements of them (e.g., differences in offense severity) are most likely subject to the death penalty? The data sources used to address these questions are also discussed.

DATA SOURCES ON CHINA'S DEATH SENTENCES AND EXECUTIONS

No published national data on the number of death sentences and executions exists in China. Data used in the analyses of this chapter and the following chapters of this book are drawn from several secondary sources. They include Amnesty International's Death Penalty Log (China) and Annual Reports, Law Yearbook of China (1987–2005), various criminal case collections published in Chinese from 1994 to 2004, and related websites. The nature, characteristics, and caveats of the data derived from these sources are summarized below.

Amnesty International's death penalty log (China) and annual reports

The organization of Amnesty International (AI) was launched in 1961. Its primary mission has been to promote general awareness of human rights and oppose specific abuses of human rights, including the death penalty imposed by sovereign governments.[1] The *Amnesty International's Death Penalty Log* on China provides data on the number of known death sentences and executions. We analyzed data contained in these AI summaries for the years of 1996, 1998, and 2000.

The primary sources for the death penalty logs included publications and broadcasts from foreign and Chinese state news agencies. For example, the 1996 death penalty log relied on sources such as Agence France Presse, The Associated Press, Agencia EFE (National Spanish news agency), Foreign Broadcast Information Service (U.S. publication), People's Broadcasting Station (Chinese State Radio Service), BBC Summary of World Broadcasts, *South China Morning Post* (Hong Kong's English language newspaper), and New China News Agency (Chinese State News Agency).[2]

Based on these sources, the 1996 death penalty log from Amnesty International reported a total of 6101 death sentences (including suspended death sentences), 4,367 executions, and 424 death sentences with a two year reprieve. To minimize errors, Amnesty International adopted the following methods in recording the number of death sentences and executions in China: (1) when in doubt of accuracy or certainty, the figures were not included; (2) where two conflicting reports existed, the lower figure was used; (3) when a combined figure of death sentences and prison sentences were given, only one death sentence was recorded; and (4) when a group was sentenced to death, only one sentence was entered.

Given these counting rules, the number of death sentences and executions in China reported by the AI death penalty log constituted a conservative estimate of the actual number of death sentences and executions imposed in that particular year. The AI reports also underestimate the number of death sentences and executions because it is restricted to those offenses that have been reported in published news reports.[3] Even with these limitations, however, the death penalty log compiled by Amnesty International is the most comprehensive data available on death penalty practices in China. Amnesty International has provided annual counts of the number of death sentences and executions worldwide since 1980. Data on capital punishment is available in various reports on Amnesty International's Web site (http://www.amnesty.org.).

Law Yearbook of China — 1987–2004

The *Law Yearbook of China* is an annual official publication of the Chinese Society of Legal Study, published by the Law Yearbook of China Press. Its inaugural issue came out in 1987. It aims to provide domestic and international readers with comprehensive and authoritative coverage of the up-to-date lawmaking, law enforcement, the dissemination of legal knowledge, legal education, and legal research activities. Reports contained in every issue are provided by the related departments of the central and local governments and organizations, thus representing the official account of these legal developments.[4]

The latest (2004) issue of the *Law Yearbook of China* contained fifteen parts.[5] Part 12 of this issue presented statistics involving the activities of the judiciary, procuratorate, public security, justice department, administrative review and the civil administration in 2003. The death penalty data was primarily derived from the judiciary section of these statistics. More specifically, the judiciary section of Part 12 presented the number of cases tried in 2003, organized in three categories based on their legal dispositions: (1) not guilty; (2) guilty but exempt of criminal punishment; (3) guilty with criminal punishment.

Among the category of guilty with criminal punishment, cases were further divided into several categories: (1) detention, probation, and supervision; (2) less than five years of incarceration; and (3) more than five years of incarceration, life, and the death sentence. As the number of cases involving the death sentence was lumped together with the number of cases involving other fixed-prison sentences and life imprisonment, it is difficult to gauge the exact number of death sentences and executions each year based on this data source. Nevertheless, because it is the only Chinese official crime data, and one of the few sources providing data related to the death penalty, a review of the general trend of these serious crimes may help provide an alternative estimate the use of the death penalty in China.

The *Law Yearbook of China* also includes a section on selected judicial judgment documents that contains cases tried in the previous year. A judicial judgment document is a legal document prepared by the chief judge after discussions with the panel of judges presiding over the criminal case. It is a legal document that contains legal rulings of a trial court that could either be appealed by the defendant, protested by the procuratorate, reviewed by the higher court, or enforced by the respective legal authority (e.g., the corrections agency, the public security agency), depending upon the nature of the ruling and the stage of the criminal process (e.g., whether it was in the trial of first instance, second instance, or the process of review). This legal document typically is several pages in length, containing essential information such as offender attributes (e.g., age, gender, education, occupation, criminal history), offense characteristics (e.g., time, location, weapon use, motive, offender-victim relation, cooffending pattern, offense severity), criminal proceeding (e.g., legal representation, time of the arrest, detention), evidence and arguments presented by the prosecutor and the defense (e.g., physical evidence, witnesses testimony, offender's confession and/or admission), and the court's reasoning (e.g., citing relevant laws, presenting mitigating and aggravating facts) and ruling (e.g., guilty or not guilty decision). These documents related to capital cases were also included in our analysis.

Various courts (e.g., the Supreme Court, Chengde Intermediate Court) also periodically publish judicial judgment documents of major cases tried in their jurisdiction. These periodic reports were also used as supplemental data for this study.

Criminal case collections

In addition to Amnesty International reports and the *Law Yearbook of China*, another data source for studying capital punishment include criminal court case collections published in Chinese between 1994 and 2004.[6] These national (published by the Supreme Court and universities) and regional publications (published by the respective provincial superior court) encompassed judicial judgment documents of all major types of violent, property, economic, corruption, public safety and public order crimes tried and reviewed in the basic courts, intermediate courts, superior courts and/or Supreme Court.

These publications were designed to showcase "carefully selected" criminal cases "typical" of each type of the crime and reflect emerging and changing crime patterns and behaviors.[7] The purpose of putting together these case collections, according to the editors of these various publications, was to facilitate legal research, provide guidance for legal enforcement, and educate the general public.[8] Because of these purposes, the cases included in these collections are a nonrandom subset of criminal cases in China. Under these conditions, cases in these publications give a general idea of the nature of serious crimes in China, but they have limited value for inferring the prevalence of capital punishment in this country.

As a source of information for understanding the nature and processing of capital and non-capital cases across China, the criminal case collections are useful because they provide details about a relatively large number of these cases. By providing a showcase for the development of judicial work and exerting influence and guidance for future judicial practices and legal research, criminal cases included in these collections are assumed to represent a wide variety of serious offenses that address a diverse array of substantive and procedural issues (e.g., what constitutes a voluntary surrender, how aggravating and mitigating factors play out in capital cases). When supplemented with other sources, the criminal case collections provide a basis for understanding substantive and procedural issues in the imposition of capital and non-capital sentences across a wide range of criminal offenses.

Related Web Sites

As the development of the death penalty in China is rapidly unfolding, gaining insight into these legal and practical developments of recent years from published scholarly research (e.g., books and journal articles) can be augmented with more current information that is provided in various national and international websites. In fact, Internet sources in China and elsewhere have increasingly become a primary means for the timely dissemination of laws, policies, reforms, practices and opinions.

To ensure that data from internet sources is reliable, websites sponsored by reputable news agencies of the state and local governments (e.g., *New China News Agency* [xinhuanet], *CCTV*, *China Daily*, *Legal Daily*, *People's Daily*) and courts (e.g., the Supreme Court Web site [http://www.chinacourt.org]) were the primary Web sites used in this study. Additional reliability assessments of information from other websites involved checks of their original references before being cited in this study. Whenever there is doubt about the reliability of the data reports, the information was cross-checked with at least two reputable website sources to further confirm its accuracy.[9]

Caveats about the data

Although we have compiled various data sources, one major obstacle for studying the death penalty in China is the lack of systematic and comprehensive data. As we previously discussed, neither the Chinese domestic sources nor international sources provide the specific number of death sentences and executions in China, let alone systematic and detailed data on the sentencing process.[10] Even among the sources that provide some information on death sentences and executions in China (e.g., the judicial judgment document), it is difficult to gauge the true extent and nature of the death sentence and execution in China due to the nonrandom nature of the samples.

Nevertheless, an assessment of the general trends and patterns of the death sentence could still be made with careful comparisons of the information provided by Amnesty International and the *Law Yearbook of China*. In particular, characteristics of the offender and the offense, and factors involved in the death sentence rulings, may be identified through the coding and analysis of the judicial judgment documents contained in various sources.

THE PREVALENCE OF DEATH SENTENCES AND EXECUTIONS

Death sentence and execution in the global context

As discussed in chapter 1, seventy-six countries in the world retain and use capital punishment as of June of 2005. Further data by Amnesty International in the past twenty-five years reveals wide fluctuations in the total number of death sentences and executions over this time period (see Table 5.1). Although many countries of the world have retained capital punishment, the majority of death sentences and executions were carried out by only

Table 5.1 International pattern of death sentence and execution over time

Year	*# of Death Sentences*	*# of Executions*
2005	5,186	2,148
2004	7,395	3,797
2003	2,756	1,146
2002	3,248	1,526
2001	5,265	3,048
2000	3,058	1,457
1999	3,857	1,813
1998	3,899	2,258
1997	3,707	2,607
1996	7,101	4,272
1995	4,165	3,276
1994	4,032	2,331
1993	3,760	1,831
1992	2,697	1,708
1991	2,703	2,086
1990	2,005	2,029
1989	2,826	2,229
1988	1,240	1,903
1987	1,185	796
1986	1,272	743
1985	1,435	1,125
1984	2,068	1,513
1983	1,160	1,399
1982	1,435	1,609
1981	3,209	3,278
1980	1,295	1,229

Source: Amnesty International Annual Reports 1993–2005; Hood, 2002, 89.

a handful of nations. Countries such as China, Iran, Saudi Arabia, and the United States have consistently and actively resorted to death sentences and executions to punish its offenders. According to data from Amnesty International, 97 percent of all known executions in 2004 took place in China, Iran, Viet Nam, and the United States. During 2001, the combined number of executions in China, Iran, Saudi Arabia, and the United States accounted for 90 percent of the total executions in the world. Similarly, 85 percent of known executions in 1999 took place in China, Iran, Saudi Arabia, Democratic Republic of Congo, and the United States.

A closer examination of the distribution of the number of executions in the world shows that China is, by far, the leading nation in execution. For example, China accounted for approximately 90 percent of the known executions in the world in 2004, far outnumbering the executions that occurred in all other countries combined during this period. The predominance of China as the undisputed world leader in the imposition of the death penalty is found in other years as well.

Death sentence and execution in contemporary China

According to the *Law Yearbook of China*, criminals convicted and sentenced to more than five years of incarceration, life and death sentence constituted slightly over 20 percent of the total number of criminals convicted and given a sentence. This percent remained relatively stable over the past few years. For example, out of a total of 690,506 criminals convicted and given a criminal sentence in the year 2002, 160,324 criminals were given a fixed prison sentence of at least over five years in length, a life imprisonment or the death penalty.[11] Similarly, 158,562 criminals in 2003 were given the severe penalty of more than five years in prison, a life or the death sentence out of a total of 730,355 criminals convicted and given a criminal penalty.[12]

Anecdotal evidence provides somewhat mixed results about general trends in death sentences and executions in China. For example, the dramatic expansion of the scope of capital punishment in the revised criminal law and the continuous waiver of the Supreme Court's final review and approval authority in capital cases seemed to indicate the increasing use of the death sentences and executions in China in recent years. However, a study conducted by Chinese scholars revealed that the current number of death sentences is only about 50 percent of that prior to 1997. These scholars attributed this decline to the more careful imposition of death sentences (e.g., it is now extremely rare for the procuratorate to protest a ruling of death with suspended execution to the high court for a heavier sentence) and the tendency for more cases to receive the suspended death sentence in recent years than in the past.[13]

Further evidence of a decline in executions is found in another report that suggests that the Supreme Court since 2003 has modified more than 20 percent of the death sentences with immediate execution to death with a two-year suspension or life imprisonment in its final review. It has also been

Table 5.2 Number of known execution in China for select years

Year	*# of Execution*
2004	3,400
2003	726
2002	1,921
2001	2,468
2000	>1,000
1999	1,077
1998	1,067
1997	1,876
1996	6,100
1995	2,190
1994	1,791

Source: Amnesty International (2005)

reported that in 2003 a substantial number of death sentences were either reduced to suspended death or life imprisonment (38 percent) or returned for a retrial (4 percent) by superior courts of provinces and autonomous municipalities.[14]

Amnesty International provides more specific assessments of the number of death sentences and executions in China. According to Amnesty International, the number of death sentences in China has ranged between one thousand and six thousand per year over the past decade.[15] There is no uniform pattern in these executions over time. For example, Amnesty International documents 1,791 executions in 1994, 6,100 executions in 1996, and 1,921 executions in 2002.

The huge fluctuation in the number of death sentences, if close to the actual pattern of death sentences, might be the result of the "strike-hard" campaigns that target certain groups of people and/or offenses in a specific time frame. For example, offenses such as train robbery, murder, causing explosions, drug trafficking, corruption, and religious cult practices have been at varying times the target of government crack downs over the years, and their numbers in the death penalty cases should be expected to increase in this time period. The fluctuation in the number of death sentences and executions could also be an artifact of the reporting of these events. Given the demand of the strike-hard campaign, media outlets should be expected to report more death sentence and execution cases, resulting in crime waves and death sentence waves that would not have existed.

If we compare the number of executions with the number of death sentences over the years, we find that there had been at least a 30 percent difference between these two numbers in any given year (in some years, the gap was much wider, at 50 percent). However, this gap between death sentences and actual executions is probably much narrower considering the following factors. First, a unique category, the death sentence with a two year stay of execution (referred to as Death2 in the following tables), is considered as part of the death sentence when in theory and by law, there is a very little chance that execution will be carried out on these offenders. If these cases are excluded from the overall number of death sentences, the gap between the number of death sentences and executions will be reduced.[16] Second, our assessment of death sentences and executions is based on data from AI that is initially derived from news reports. Missing data could easily account for some of the death sentences not resulting in execution. For example, according to AI reports, in the *Ganxu Daily*, on May 28, 1996, six offenders were sentenced to death (among them, one received a two-year stay of execution) for holding up cars with weapons on twenty-four occasions and injuring twenty-five people, but no execution information was given. It is very unlikely that all six offenders had their death sentences reversed on appeals because the reversal rate is generally low in Chinese courts.[17] Under these conditions, more complete data would further reduce the gap between capital convictions and actual executions.[18]

OFFENDER CHARACTERISTICS OF THE DEATH PENALTY CASES

In the following sections on the offender and offense characteristics, data used for the analysis was drawn from judicial judgment documents contained in the criminal case collections published between 1994 and 2004, *Law Yearbook of China*, and several court official Web sites. A review of these cases revealed that a total of six crime categories (e.g., violent, property, economic, public safety, public order, and corruption) had cases that carried the death sentence. Thus, all cases of these six crime categories that received a sentence greater than ten years, life, and death were included in the analysis. This case selection criterion yielded a total of 1,010 cases.

The selected cases were classified into three groups for the purpose of analysis in this study: (1) death sentence with immediate execution (544 cases), (2) suspended death sentence (128 cases) and life imprisonment (96 cases),[19] and (3) fixed-prison sentence of greater than ten years (242 cases). Given that a variety of criminal offenses are subject to the death penalty, offenses within each of the three categories of death, life and long-term prison sentence were further broken down to six offense categories of violent (e.g., murder, assault, rape, kidnapping), property (e.g., robbery, theft, fraud), economic (e.g., credit-card fraud, manufacturing and selling fake products), public safety (e.g., explosion, arson), public order (e.g., drug trafficking, forcing prostitution) and corruption (e.g., graft and bribery) under the 1997 criminal law.[20]

Studies of the social profile of those executed indicate that capital punishment is not uniform across social groups. The following analysis attempts to construct the offender's profile in capital and non-capital cases. These offender profiles are based on their typical age, gender, occupation, residency status, criminal history, and the recorded attitude of the offender in the case descriptions.

Age

Western sociolegal studies revealed that capital offenders typically involve persons who are disproportionately young adults when they commit their capital crimes.[21] Studies on the death penalty in China suggest that older teenagers and young adults are disproportionately more likely to be given the death penalty. It was estimated that at least 50 percent of offenders executed in recent years had been between eighteen and twenty-five years old.[22]

Our current analysis revealed that the mean age of all the death penalty cases was 32.4 years old. The youngest offender sentenced to death was seventeen years old,[23] whereas the oldest offender sentenced to death with immediate execution was sixty-seven years old.[24] Among 456 offenders who were sentenced to death with immediate execution and whose age was identified in the document, more than one-fourth of them were younger than twenty-five years old; and slightly over two-thirds were younger than thirty-five years old. When considering only the violent crime category, the average age of capital offenders became much younger (e.g., about one-third of capital offenses were committed by offenders of twenty-five years old or younger and over three-fourths of violent capital crimes were committed by offenders of thirty-five years or younger).

The offender's age diverged dramatically by the type of convicted offense. Of the six different crime categories, offenders' average age was the oldest in the corruption category (about forty-three years old) and the youngest for property offenses and violent offenses at twenty-eight and thirty years old, respectively[25] (see Table 5.3).

Across offenses with different degrees of severity, the overall average age for offenders in capital vs. non-capital cases did not diverge significantly. There were no clear patterns in the average age of offenders involved in capital vs. non-capital offenses across the six offense categories, except that offenders involved in economic offenses and offenses against public order appeared to be much younger in capital cases than in non-capital cases (see Table 5.3).

Gender

Both men and women are subject to the death penalty with the only exception being pregnant women. Across the spectrum of both Eastern and Western cultures, criminal offending is often found to be disproportionately a male phenomenon. Even when women are engaged in crime, the traditional patriarchal ideas tend to regard women as being less evil and in need of protection. Under these conditions, we might expect that women are far less likely to be sentenced to death than men.[26]

Table 5.3 Offender's age in capital and non-capital cases (R = Range; $\bar{x}$ = Mean; n = Sample Size)

Sentence	*Violent*	*Property*	*Economic*	*Corruption*	*Public safety*	*Public order*	*All cases*
Death	R: 18–61 $\bar{x}$ = 30.3 n = 148)	R: 17–47 $\bar{x}$ = 28.0 (n = 132)	R: 24–54 $\bar{x}$ = 30.1 (n = 35)	R: 22–67 $\bar{x}$ = 42.7 (n = 65)	R: 20–58 $\bar{x}$ = 33.2 (n = 24)	R: 21–61 $\bar{x}$ = 32.6 (n = 52)	R: 17–67 $\bar{x}$ = 32.4 (n = 456)
Death2 & Life	R: 15–58 $\bar{x}$ = 28.3 (n = 56)	R: 16–62 $\bar{x}$ = 31.3 (n = 58)	R: 24–62 $\bar{x}$ = 40.8 (n = 20)	R: 20–62 $\bar{x}$ = 40.0 (n = 29)	R: 20–47 $\bar{x}$ = 29.9 (n = 10)	R: 17–60 $\bar{x}$ = 36.9 (n = 30)	R: 15–62 $\bar{x}$ = 33.40 (n = 203)
> 10 yrs.	R: 14–48 $\bar{x}$ = 29.9 (n = 48)	R: 18–58 $\bar{x}$ = 31.2 (n = 107)	R: 27–55 $\bar{x}$ = 39.1 (n = 22)	R: 21–63 $\bar{x}$ = 40.8 (n = 29)	R: 22–53 $\bar{x}$ = 31.7 (n = 16)	R: 25–63 $\bar{x}$ = 39.2 (n = 19)	R: 14–63 $\bar{x}$ = 33.5 (n = 241)

Table 5.4 Percentage distribution of male offenders in capital and non-capital cases

Sentence	*Violent*	*Property*	*Economic*	*Corruption*	*Public safety*	*Public order*	*All cases*
Death	91% (n = 189)	98% (n = 145)	95% (n = 38)	84% (n = 73)	95% (n = 38)	93% (n = 73)	93% (n = 544)
Death2 & Life	91% (n = 64)	98% (n = 61)	95% (n = 20)	82% (n = 34)	100% (n = 10)	82% (n = 34)	91% (n = 223)
> 10 yrs.	94% (n = 48)	98% (n = 107)	96% (n = 22)	87% (n = 30)	100% (n = 16)	84% (n = 19)	95% (n = 242)

Our analysis showed that overall the vast majority of capital offenses were committed by men with only a small percent (7.5 percent) of capital offenses committed by women (see Table 5.4). Women were responsible for a small proportion of total capital offenses in China, but their contribution to capital offenses is still significantly large when compared to the 1.5 percent of female death row inmates in the United States.[27]

An analysis of gender differences in capital sentences by crime categories showed several patterns about women's differential involvement in particular types of capital offenses (see Table 5.4). First, women represented the highest proportion of offenders in corruption cases (e.g., about 16 percent of these cases involved female offenders), but capital sentences were just as likely as non-capital sentences for women convicted of these crimes.[28] Second, public order offenses are the only potential capital crimes in which gender differences existed in the type of sentence. For these crimes, males represented 93 percent of offenders who received an immediate death sentence, whereas males accounted for a smaller proportion (i.e., 83 percent) of those given a suspended death sentence or lesser penalty. Overall, males predominate as the convicted offenders of potential capital cases and there is little substantial difference in their relative prevalence as offenders who received capital and non-capital sentences among these different types of criminal offenses.

Occupation

Western research on capital crimes typically suggests that these offenders are unemployed or held a job of low status prior to their arrests. Only a few studies have explored the occupational status of criminal offenders in China. For example, one study of murder and robbery offenses in cities of Beijing and Shenzhen found that rural residents, unemployed and workers committed nearly 80 percent of these crimes.[29] Another study of 237 minor theft cases revealed that the majority of theft offenders (63 percent) were unemployed at the time of crime commission.[30] The link between occupational status and criminal offending was also observed in a study of self-report data in Tianjin that revealed a high correlation between offending and low job satisfaction.[31]

Among the cases where offenders' employment and occupation status were known (36 percent), our analysis of these capital cases indicated that the majority of capital offenders (62 percent) were either unemployed or rural residents. For those who were employed, nearly 70 percent held a low status job (e.g., worker, clerk, self-employed) whereas approximately 30 percent held a high status job (e.g., manager, governmental official).

It is important to note that the opportunity to commit particular offenses (e.g., economic violations, corruption, threats to public safety) in China are associated with one's socioeconomic status. Accordingly, it should not be surprising to find occupational differences in involvement in potential capital offenses. As shown by the sample sizes in Table 5.5, persons of low occupational status (e.g., laborers, unemployed) are rarely involved in serious cases of economic crime, corruption, or public safety violations. However, while less than one-third of persons given the death penalty for corruption offenses held low status jobs, the vast majority of capital offenders convicted of common street crimes (e.g., violent [85.7 percent] and property [100 percent]) were involved in low status occupations.

A comparison across offenses of different severity (e.g., capital vs. non-capital offenses) indicated consistent patterns of offenders' occupational status and offense type. For example, the majority of offenders in serious violent and property offenses were of low status regardless of whether they were given capital or non-capital sentences (see Table 5.5). The same was true of the proportion of offenders involved in crimes against public order. A total of 60 percent (3 of 5) of these offenders given ten years or more of imprisonment had low occupational status compared to a slightly higher proportion of 75 percent for those who received an immediate or deferred death sentence.

Residency status

Just as race is one of the critical factors in sociological analyses of the Western sociological research, residency status is the product of China's political

Table 5.5 Percentage distribution of low occupational status of offenders in capital and non-capital cases

Sentence	*Violent*	*Property*	*Economic*	*Corruption*	*Public safety*	*Public order*	*All cases*
Death	85.7% (n = 21)	100% (n = 18)	— (n = 0)	28.6% (n = 28)	— (n = 0)	75.0% (n = 4)	67.1% (n = 76)
Death2 & Life	70.0% (n = 10)	66.6% (n = 27)	11.1% (n = 9)	35.3% (n = 17)	100% (n = 3)	75.0% (n = 4)	61.4% (n = 70)
> 10 yrs.	91.7% (n = 12)	69.8% (n = 43)	26.7% (n = 15)	37.0% (n = 27)	85.7% (n = 7)	60.0% (n = 5)	58.7% (n = 109)

and economic structure that defines individuals' life style and social status. Residency status has two underlying dimensions: (1) urbanites vs. rural residents, and (2) locals vs. transients.

In official and scholarly publications, transients, "the floating population," have been invariably portrayed as one of the major sources of social unrest and disorder. They are particularly blamed for contributing to crimes in large urban areas where the employment opportunities and wealth is most concentrated.[32] Similarly, rural residents, constituting a large proportion of the transient population, had been blamed for their contribution to crime and disorder.[33] A study examining whether offender's low social status affects sentencing decisions found that while Chinese offenders' transient status did not have a direct impact on final sentencing dispositions, it did have a conditional effect on the final sentencing dispositions, depending upon their pretrial detention arrangements.[34]

Because many judicial judgment documents did not identify offenders' residency status, nor their rural origin (e.g., when a rural migrant worker in a city committed a crime, his/her current employment was most likely to be listed, rather than his rural residential status), this posed coding problems for this variable. To be consistent, a coding scheme was developed that classified offenders into either the "transient" category or the "local resident" category depending on their listed place of origin, jurisdiction of the case, and their current employment.[35] According to this coding scheme, transients were defined as individuals who committed a crime in a location other than their hometown, and though may have lived and worked in the place other than their hometown for a period of time, they did not have the same privileges as did the local residents (e.g., rural migrant worker).

As Table 5.6 indicates, most crimes (capital and non-capital offenses) were committed by local residents, even though transients contributed a substantial amount of serious crimes in China. Proportionately, slightly more transients committed capital offenses (42 percent) than non-capital offenses (38 percent). However, the pattern of their distribution among the six crime categories for capital and non-capital offenses seem unclear. While transients committed more capital offenses than non-capital offenses

Table 5.6 Percentage distribution of transient offenders in capital and non-capital cases

Sentence	*Violent*	*Property*	*Economic*	*Corruption*	*Public safety*	*Public order*	*All cases*
Death	38.1% (n = 189)	44.8% (n = 143)	36.8% (n = 17)	15.1% (n = 73)	36.8% (n = 17)	72.3% (n = 65)	41.9% (n = 534)
Death2 & Life	28.6% (n = 63)	49.2% (n = 61)	33.3% (n = 14)	17.6% (n = 34)	50.0% (n = 10)	58.8% (n = 34)	38.6% (n = 223)
> 10 yrs.	31.3% (n = 48)	48.6% (n = 107)	18.2% (n = 22)	26.7% (n = 30)	25.0% (n = 16)	47.4% (n = 19)	38.0% (n = 242)

in some crime categories (e.g., violent, economic, and public order crimes), in other crime categories (e.g., corruption), transients' contribution to capital offenses was less than was true of non-capital offenses.

Criminal history

China is well known for its low recidivism rates due to its comprehensive social defense and informal social control system that successfully integrates the offender back into the community, and its severe punishment.[36] Based on the Chinese criminal law that recidivists shall receive heavier punishment, we predicted that capital offenders are disproportionately more likely to encompass offenders with a criminal history.

National reporting on recidivism rates had been largely absent until 1992 when a nation-wide study on recidivism reported an 8 percent recidivism rate in China.[37] There has been no follow up study and national reporting on recidivism rates since then. This is primarily due to difficulties in gaining access to the national prison records and the complex arrays of correctional programs in China.

The judicial judgment document reports the offender's prior history of criminal arrests, convictions and sentences served, if any. Based on this information, we determined that overall a small proportion of capital offenders (14 percent) had a criminal history of at least one arrest. Among them, offenders involved in crimes against public order[38] and property offenses[39] tended to show the highest recidivist rate at 23 percent whereas offenders involved in corruption and offenses against public safety tended to exhibit the lowest recidivism rate (4 percent) (see Table 5.7).

Consistent with our prediction, proportionally fewer non-capital offenders had a criminal history than capital offenders, with only one exception involving offenses against public safety (see Table 5.7). A further analysis of cases involving public safety revealed that the only capital offender and the two non-capital offenders convicted for public safety-related offense who had a criminal record involved the theft and smuggling of firearms.

Table 5.7 Percentage distribution of recidivist offenders in capital and non-capital cases

Sentence	*Violent*	*Property*	*Economic*	*Corruption*	*Public safety*	*Public order*	*All cases*
Death	10.1% (n = 189)	22.8% (n = 145)	10.5% (n = 38)	4.1% (n = 73)	3.8% (n = 26)	23.6% (n = 72)	14.2% (n = 543)
Death2 & Life	7.8% (n = 64)	11.5% (n = 61)	0.0% (n = 21)	2.9% (n = 34)	0.0% (n = 10)	11.8% (n = 34)	7.6% (n = 224)
> 10 yrs.	0.0% (n = 48)	12.3% (n = 106)	0.0% (n = 22)	0.0% (n = 30)	12.5% (n = 16)	10.5% (n = 19)	7.1% (n = 241)

Attitude and confessions

Confessions are expected and/or required for Chinese offenders suspected of a crime both for probative reasons and correctional values.[40] As described in chapter 4, Chinese law prohibits confessions extracted with coercion and physical torture, but the cultural expectation and potential legal reward are a great attraction for criminal offenders to confess.

Prior studies examining the extent and impact of confession in contemporary China revealed that the Chinese judiciary classified offenders' attitude into four categories: (1) refusal of admission of guilt, (2) admission of guilt, (3) confession, and (4) voluntary submission.[41] In theory, sentencing disposition should vary by offenders' confessing attitudes. More specifically, those who refused to admit guilt may be given a heavier sentence; and those who confessed, showed repentance, and voluntarily surrendered to the authority may be granted judicial leniency.[42]

In capital cases, two competing theories about the likelihood of confession may be formulated. First, because of the grave nature of the offense and possible application of the death penalty, offenders may be unwilling to risk their lives to confess to the crime. Second, the serious nature of the offense may also lead capital offenders to hope that by confessing to the crime, their life could be spared if judicial leniency is granted.

Given that all criminal offenses in the current analysis involve serious cases that carry a sentence of at least ten years, offenders' attitude may be considered for leniency only under extraordinary circumstances.[43] Due to this focus, our study explores only the percent of court-recognized remorseful confession and voluntary surrenders in capital and non-capital offenses.[44]

Based on the data presented in Table 5.8, offenders in capital cases were much less likely to be recognized by court as having a "good attitude" that deserved judicial leniency than in offenders in non-capital offenses. In a few capital cases (e.g., seven violent crimes and four property crimes) where offenders' confessions were recognized by courts, judicial leniency was ultimately not granted because of the grave consequences of their crimes.

Table 5.8 Percentage distribution of offenders who "voluntary surrendered" or "confessed" in capital and non-capital cases

Sentence	*Violent*	*Property*	*Economic*	*Corruption*	*Public safety*	*Public order*	All cases
Death	19.4% (n = 36)	14.8% (n = 27)	— (n = 0)	0.0% (n = 6)	0.0% (n = 6)	0.0% (n = 6)	14.6% (n = 82)
Death2 & Life	36.4% (n = 22)	53.3% (n = 3 0)	50.0% (n = 4)	45.5% (n = 11)	42.9% (n = 7)	25.0% (n = 4)	44.9% (n = 78)
> 10 yrs.	30.8% (n = 26)	35.7% (n = 42)	40.0% (n = 5)	35.5% (n = 20)	33.3% (n = 3)	50.0% (n = 4)	35.0% (n = 100)

Many other crimes of grave consequences, however, appeared to have received judicial leniency. This was supported by a comparatively higher proportion of cases (44.9 percent) involving confessions and voluntary surrender in suspended death and life imprisonment cases. Uniformly across the six offense categories, there were far more cases involving offenders' confessions that resulted in suspended death and life imprisonment than was true of those who received a death sentence with immediate execution (see Table 5.8).

Determining the particular circumstances in which one crime with grave consequences deserves leniency under offender remorse and/or voluntary surrender, and another crime with similar circumstances does not deserve leniency, is more art than science. However, it is clear that both judicial discretion and jurisdictional disparities in culture and community norms affect the ultimate impact of confessions on sentencing dispositions in the Chinese courts. For example, in a recent capital case of robbery-rape-murder by two teenagers in Guizhou province, one nineteen-year-old offender was sentenced to death with immediate execution and the seventeen-year-old offender was sentenced to life imprisonment by Anshun Intermediate Court. The appeals court, Guizhou Superior Court, reduced the death sentence to suspended death citing that the nineteen year old confessed to the crime and showed good attitude. Many questioned the superior court's discretion, arguing that the offender's "good attitude" was not a legal mitigating factor, and even if it were a mitigating factor (e.g., voluntary confession), the court must also consider other facts in the case to determine whether a judicial leniency should be granted. In this case, it involved two separate robberies, two separate rape incidents against the same victim, and the use of brutal methods killing the teenage victim. According to the prosecutor in this case, "the superior court simply went too far with its consideration of offenders' attitude in this case!"[45]

OFFENSE CHARACTERISTICS OF THE DEATH PENALTY CASES

As discussed in chapter 4, the current Chinese criminal law stipulated a total of nine broad categories of offenses and sixty-eight separate offenses as punishable by the death penalty. Whether, and to what extent, the death sentence has been imposed on these capital offenses is an important question as it may reveal the symbolic (e.g., declare and uphold sociopolitical beliefs and values) or functional (e.g., serve as a threat or maintain order) nature of the criminal law in a particular sociopolitical context. The law is largely symbolic if the death penalty has rarely been imposed on capital offenses. In contrast, it has functional values of deterrence and incapacitation when the death penalty has been imposed and with relatively high frequency.

Because capital offenses involve a variety of offenses in China, an examination of its symbolic or functional nature of the capital punishment law should be approached with two research questions: (1) whether the death penalty has been imposed on offenses in a particular offense category; and (2) to what extent the death penalty has been used in these offenses.

Scope of capital offenses

Available records indicate that in the past decade or so, the majority of death sentences involved violent offenses such as robbery, murder, and rape.[46] Economic offenses and offenses of corruption have increasingly become the target of the death penalty,[47] even though their percentage among death penalty cases remains small. For example, based on Amnesty International's log of death sentences,[48] out of 4,490 death sentences in 1996 for which the convicted offenses were known, 66 percent involved violent offenses (i.e., robbery, murder, rape, abduction of children and women), 3 percent involved economic and corruption related offenses (e.g., corruption, embezzlement, fraud, and tax), and about 13 percent involved drug trafficking.[49] Similarly, out of a total of 1,411 death sentences in the year 2000 for which the convicted offenses were known, 67 percent were violent offenses, 9 percent were economic and/or corruption cases, and 14 percent were drug offenses.

Our review of all cases of death sentences with immediate executions that are included in the judicial judgment documents indicated that only six of the nine broad crime categories of capital offenses contained an actual capital case in these samples. More specifically, the capital offenses in these documents involved 26 incidents of offenses against public safety,[50] 38 economic crimes,[51] 189 violent offenses,[52] 145 property offenses,[53] 73 offenses against public order,[54] and 73 corruption cases.[55]

No death penalty cases in our sample dealt with the three categories of offenses endangering national security (e.g., espionage), offenses endangering the national defense interest (e.g., sabotaging military weapons, installations or communications), and offenses violating duties by military servicemen.[56] This serves in sharp contrast to the pre-reform socialist era where a significant number of capital offenders were considered counterrevolunationaries.[57]

The noninclusion of the death penalty cases involved in the three political-military offense categories could mean one of the followings: (1) no death sentence was imposed on these offenses in the reform era; (2) death sentence was imposed very rarely on these offenses that did not deserve attention; or (3) the death sentences were imposed on these offenses as frequently as those offenses included in the case collections, but they were not reported for reasons of political sensitivity, military secrecy, or less relevance to the purpose and objectives of the case collections.

As illustrated by these sample cases, the death penalty has been quite frequently imposed for many different types of ordinary offenses, as stipulated by law. The most commonly included cases in these judicial documents involve violent offenses and property crimes.

Severity of capital offenses

The nature of criminal incidents may diverge dramatically depending upon various factors such as offender-victim relationship, the number of offenders, type of weapon use, the nature and magnitude of substance/alcohol use, the location of the offense, the level of offense planning, and damage/outcome of the criminal act.

The Chinese criminal law stipulated that the death sentence should be only imposed on criminals "who have committed the most heinous crimes (CL, Article 48)," where there is the presence of evil intent, vicious and cruel methods, and extremely grave consequences.[58] Particular qualifications were stipulated for offenses such as theft (e.g., the death penalty can be imposed only when (1) financial institutions and the amount is extraordinarily large, or (2) precious cultural relics under serious circumstances were involved [Article 264 1&2]) and intentional assault (e.g., the law stipulated that the death penalty can be imposed only when the intentional assault caused a person's death, or severe bodily injury and disability using especially vicious means).

One of the most basic ways to explore offense severity involves comparisons of violent offenses according to their consequences (i.e., death vs. physical injury). In a similar manner, the severity of property offenses can be explored by their economic consequences (i.e., amount of monetary damage). As summarized in Table 5.9, more than 80 percent of violent capital offenses involved at least one death, which was significantly greater than offenses that received suspended death sentence or life imprisonment (66 percent), and offenses of fixed long term prison sentences (33 percent).

Table 5.9 Percentage distribution of death and monetary consequences in cases with capital and non-capital sentences

Sentence	*Violent offenses*	*Corruption cases*
Death	81% with death (n = 189)	Range: 230,000–33.6 million Mean = 10.3 million yuan (n = 22)
Death2 & Life	66% with death (n = 64	Range: 96,742–1.1 million Mean= 432,538 yuan (n = *15)*
> 10 yrs.	33% with death (n = 48)	Range:58,650–33.4 million Mean = 3.73 million (n = 27)

Similarly, corruption related capital offenses had resulted in far greater economic costs (at an average of 10.3 million yuan) than their non-capital counterparts.

SUMMARY

Using a variety of data sources, this chapter described the extent and pattern of death sentences and executions internationally and in the specific case of China. Overall, despite a major shift toward a global abolitionist movement in the past few decades, the number of death sentences and executions has not declined worldwide.

In the absence of national data on the death sentences and executions in China, the estimate based on AI's reports of the published capital cases by the Chinese news media and anecdotal evidence in the literature revealed no clear patterns for either the number of death sentences or executions in China. However, there seemed little doubt that China has continued to contribute to the majority of the world's death sentences and executions.

The examination of the sociodemographic profile of capital offenders is helpful for the comprehensive understanding of the death penalty practices in China. Our analysis revealed that capital offenders were disproportionately young, particularly in violent offenses, where young offenders (thirty-five years or younger) were responsible for nearly 80 percent of violent capital offenses. Female involvement in capital offenses varied dramatically across crime categories. While they were most likely to be involved in corruption cases (16 percent), women were least likely to be involved in property offenses, particularly due to crimes of robbery where less than 1 percent of these cases were committed by a female offender.

Consistent with their relatively low social status in China, most capital offenders were either rural residents or unemployed (62 percent). Among those who were employed, their occupational status exhibited an almost inverse pattern with most corruption offenders (more than 70 percent) holding a high status job and other street criminals holding a low status job (ranging from 75 percent and 100 percent).

As mobility has become a unique characteristic in the reform-era China, transient population has been increasingly blamed for major crimes in urban areas. Our analysis showed that a substantial amount of capital offenses (42 percent) were committed by transients. Although its variation in some crime categories (e.g., violent, property, economic, public safety) is rather consistent, transients were least likely to commit corruption offenses (15 percent) and most likely to commit public order offenses (72 percent), particularly in cases of drug trafficking. Our data further revealed that recidivism rate among capital offenders was at an approximately 15 percent, with higher than average recidivism rates in some crime categories of property offenses (e.g., 21 percent of offenders involved in robbery and 29 percent in theft had a criminal history) and public order offenses (e.g., 20 percent of drug offenders had at least one prior arrest).

A criminal confession is one of the hallmarks of the Chinese criminal justice system. Compared to non-capital offenses, offenders' confession attitudes were least likely to be noted by courts of various levels in capital offenses (e.g., 15 percent in capital offenses as compared to 35–45 percent in non-capital offenses). Even when their confessing attitudes were noted, no leniency was granted to capital offenders due to the grave nature of their crimes.

Despite the broad scope of capital offenses (a total of nine crime categories) stipulated in the Chinese law, death sentences were primarily meted out to offenders in six categories (e.g., violent, property, economic, corruption, public safety, public order). The disparity in the imposition of death sentence on some but not other capital offenses seemed to reflect the state crime control policies that emphasize the maintenance of economic and social order, but not targeting the counterrevolutionaries as in the pre-reform era. Lastly, our analysis showed that capital offenses indeed involved crimes with grave personal and monetary consequences as most violent capital crimes (81 percent) involved at least one death and an average cost for corruption was at approximately 10 million yuan.

This preliminary analysis of the sociodemographic profile of capital offenders and offenses suggests a need for further study of the offense-specific characteristics in the Chinese context, both between the offense categories (e.g., violent, property) and within the offense categories (e.g., murder, rape, kidnapping within the violent offense category) due to the dramatic differences among these different crime types. Future research should also examine the situational dynamics of capital offenses to discern convergent and divergent patterns of offender-victim relations, location of offense, and weapon use. This would not only be useful for crime prevention, but also provide important information on sentencing patterns involving capital offenses. Finally, with more systematic and representative data, future research should also examine the impact of legal and extralegal factors on sentencing dispositions involving capital and non-capital offenses using multivariate analysis techniques.

6 The process of death sentence and execution

Few issues in China and elsewhere warrant more attention to the principles of procedural justice than the application of the death penalty. This chapter explores the actual process underlying the imposition of the death sentences and executions in China. Published documents and actual case narratives are used to illustrate both typical and the unusual processes.

THE GENERAL LEGAL PROCESS IN CAPITAL CASES

The movement of a criminal case in the current Chinese criminal justice system typically has two routes depending on its severity, clarity of facts, and adequacy of evidence. In cases of a relatively minor nature involving clear and simple facts and evidence, the case goes through a speedy route of "simplified procedure."[1] When criminal cases may result in more than three years of incarceration, where the facts are not clear, or the evidence is not sufficient, the case must go through the full trial process.

The full trial process involves a trial of first instance, presided by a collegiate bench composed of a chief judge and two deputy judges or lay judges. The trial generally follows the procedural formality stipulated in the criminal procedure law, including elements such as the presentation by the prosecutor, reading aloud indictment and questioning the accused, the introduction of physical evidence, the presentation of opinions and rebuttals, the final statement by the defendant, deliberation of a verdict, and public announcement of judgments and the delivery of judgments.[2]

All judicial judgments issued by courts that conducted the first trial may be either appealed by the defendant or protested by the procuratorate within ten days. Once the appeals (protesting) process is initiated, the appellate court typically reviews the files and questions the parties to determine the facts identified and the law applied by the first court. The appeals court may or may not commence a court session to try a case appealed by the defendant, but must hold a trial for cases protested by the procuratorate.

The court of second instance is mandated to conclude the new trial within one and half months, except in special circumstances where the length of the trial could be extended.[3] The possible outcomes of an appeal include: (1) to reject the appeal or protest and sustain the original judgment; (2) to alter the original judgment; or (3) to remand the case back to the original court for a retrial.[4] This trial/review conducted by an appellate court is considered a final process for most cases in the Chinese system, except for the death penalty cases.

A capital case goes through the same process as other serious criminal cases until the end of the second trial/first review. Death penalty cases require an additional, final review and approval by the Supreme Court. This review is automatic and mandatory for all death penalty cases except for cases (e.g., violent offenses) where the superior court of each province and autonomous municipality and region is granted the final review and approval authority. The Supreme Court may sustain the lower court's ruling, make changes to the previous rulings, or send the case back for a retrial. In extraordinary circumstances, the Court may conduct a trial itself. Narratives of judicial judgment documents involving capital cases are provided below to help illustrate the actual normal process in death penalty cases.

Case of Sun Aijun

Defendant Sun Aijun was detained by the police for his suspected involvement in an intentional assault and rape case on November 24, 2000, and was subsequently arrested on December 1, 2000. Huian Intermediate People's Court of Jiangsu province received the case and conducted the trial (the specific date of the commencement of the trial was not available). The court examined both evidence and arguments presented by the prosecutor (e.g., evidence from sources such as the defendant's confessions, eyewitness testimony, the police record, and forensic evidence) and the defense (e.g., the defendant had performed major meritorious service by providing truthful leads for other crimes) and concluded the trial on August 14, 2001. The judicial judgment for both the charges of intentional assault and rape was

Case #1 Timeline for the case of Sun Aijun

- November 24, 2000: Sun was detained for suspected intentional assault.
- December 1, 2000: Sun was arrested and charged with intentional assault and rape.
- August 14, 2001: Sun was tried by Huian Intermediate Court and sentenced to death and the deprival of political rights for life.
- September 6, 2001: Jiangsu Superior Court retried the case and sustained the original sentence. The case was not submitted to the Supreme Court for final review and approval because death sentences in violent crimes may be reviewed and finally approved by the superior court.

Source: Mingshan Zhu (ed.). Selected Chinese Criminal Court Cases — 2002 (Beijing: Chinese People's University Publishing House, 2003), 242–246.

guilty. Sun Aijun was given a death sentence and the deprival of political rights for life.

The defendant and his court-appointed defense attorney appealed the judgment to the Superior People's Court of Jiangsu Province, claiming that the sentence was too severe and requested a lighter sentence. Their main contention for the reduced sentence was that the defendant confessed to the crime and voluntarily provided leads for other crimes that resulted in other arrests. After conducting a review of the facts and evidence presented in the case, the Superior Court reasoned that even though the defendant performed major meritorious service, no leniency shall be granted because of his past criminal history and grave consequences involved in the current case (violently raping and assaulting multiple victims, involving two minors).

The Superior Court on September 6, 2001 issued the judicial judgment that rejected the defense's appeal, sustained the original death sentence, and finally approved that death sentence for immediate execution.[5] In sum, it took less than 10 months starting from the initial police detention for this defendant to be investigated, prosecuted, tried at the court of first instance and the appellate court, and finally approved and executed for his crime.

Case of Fang Yong

On January 7, 2000, defendant Fang Yong was arrested by the police for his suspected involvement in embezzling funds as an accountant in a bank. Ningbo Intermediate People's Court (Zhejiang province) conducted the first trial on June 6, 2000 and issued a judgment that Fang be sentenced to death.

The defense appealed by arguing that the application of the law was wrong in this case, that counterfeiting financial instruments to get cash should not be rendered as graft, but fraud. The Superior Court of Zhejiang province accepted the case, reviewed the documents, questioned the defendant, and heard from both sides (i.e., the prosecutor and the defense), and decided not to conduct a public trial. The court on December 8, 2000,

Case #2 Timeline for the case of Fang Yong

- January 7, 2000: Fang was arrested and charged with graft. He embezzled funds from the bank where he was employed as the accountant.
- June 6, 2000: Fang was tried by Ningbo Intermediate Court and sentenced to death and the deprival of political rights for life.
- December 8, 2000: Fang was retried by Zhejiang Superior Court and had his original sentenced reduced to life imprisonment and the deprival of political rights for life. The Supreme Court was not involved because a non-death sentence rendered by the Court of Appeals is considered the final proceeding.

Source: Qimei Zhang (ed.) Judicial Document Selections of the People's Court — Zhejiang 2000 (Beijing: Law Press, 2001), 161–163.

Case #3 Timeline for the case of Xiang Yanrong

- April 23, 2000: Xiang was detained.
- May 31, 2000: Xiang was arrested and charged with selling narcotics.
- April 4, 2001: Xiang was tried by Kunming Intermediate Court and was sentenced to death with a two year suspension of execution and the deprival of political rights for life.
- July 25, 2001: Yunnan Superior Court sustained the original sentence. The Supreme Court was not involved in this case because the death sentence with a two year suspension of execution issued by the court of appeals is considered the final ruling.

Source: Mingshan Zhu (ed.) *Selected Chinese Criminal Court Cases — 2002* (Beijing: Chinese People's University Publishing House, 2003), 480–484.

issued the judgment to reduce the original death sentence to life imprisonment. The new ruling was primarily based on an erroneous application of the law, that a portion of funds identified as money embezzled by the defendant in the original ruling, was ruled as misappropriation (i.e., it should not be recognized as graft).[6]

This modified ruling of life imprisonment by the superior court was final because non-capital cases are not reviewed and approved by the Supreme Court.

Case of Xiang Yanrong

Defendant Xiang Yanrong was detained by the police for her suspected involvement in selling narcotics to an undercover police officer on April 23, 2000, and was subsequently arrested on May 31. Kunming Intermediate People's Court (Yunna province) tried the case. Based on the facts corroborated by multiple witnesses that the defendant sold heroin in the amount of 245 grams to an undercover police officer in a hotel room, the court issued on April 4, 2001, the judicial judgment of the death sentence with a two year suspension of execution. The defendant appealed with main arguments that the evidence used in convicting her was not sufficient.

After reviewing the evidence, the Superior Court of Yunnan province on July 25, 2001, ruled that the facts were clear and the evidence was sufficient, and the original ruling should be sustained.[7] The ruling was final because a suspended death sentence does not require the Supreme Court's final approval.

Case of Ma Bijuan

Defendant Ma Bijuan was arrested for selling narcotics on February 23, 2001, and was subsequently arrested again on May 31. Dali Baizu Autonomous Regional Intermediate Court (Yunnan province) tried the case and issued on April 19, 2001, the judicial judgment of the death sentence with

Case #4 Timeline for the case of Ma Bijuan

- February 23, 2001: Ma was arrested and charged with selling narcotics.
- April 19, 2001: Ma was tried by Dali Baizu Autonomous Regional Intermediate Court and sentenced to death with a two year suspension of execution, confiscation of the house owned by the family, and the deprival of political rights for life.
- February 22, 2002: Ma was retried by the Yunnan Superior Court and sentenced to death with immediate execution, confiscation of the house, and the deprival of political rights for life.
- June 4, 2002: The case was reviewed by the Supreme Court. The Court sustained the superior court's rulings on the death sentence with immediate execution, and the deprival of political rights for life, but changed the ruling on the confiscation of the family house to confiscation of defendant's personal property.

Source: "The Case of Selling Narcotics by Ma Bijuan." The Supreme Court Web site at http://www.court.gov.cn/study/penal/200401120019.htm (accessed 1/12/2004).

a two year suspension of execution and confiscation of the house owned by the defendant's family.

The defendant did not appeal. The procuratorate protested. The Superior Court of Yunnan province on February 22, 2002, ruled to increase the original sentence to death with immediate execution and confiscate the house owned by the family.

As required by law, the case was subsequently sent to the Supreme Court for review and final approval. The Supreme Court reviewed the documents in this case and ruled on June 4, 2000, that the facts are clear and the evidence is sufficient. Due to the extremely huge amount of heroin involved (598 grams) in the case, the Supreme Court ruled that the defendant should be sentenced to death with immediate execution. However, the Court overturned the lower courts' ruling on the confiscation of the defendant's house owned by the family, and changed it to the confiscation of the defendant's personal property.[8]

Case of Deng Chenhui

Defendant Deng Chenhui was arrested on May 15, 2002, as a criminal suspect for graft and had remained in detention throughout the trials. Tianjin No. 2 Intermediate Court sentenced the defendant to death with immediate execution on June 13, 2001. The judgment was appealed by the defendant. The Superior Court of Tianjin reviewed the case and rejected the defendant's appeal on December 5, 2001.

In accordance to the criminal procedure law, the case was forwarded to the Supreme Court for final review and approval. Based on the extremely large amount of funds embezzled by the defendant (in a total of 4.4 million Chinese yuan; approximately $550,000), the Supreme Court issued

Case #5 Timeline for the case of Deng Chenhui

- May 15, 2000: Deng was arrested and charged with graft, the embezzlement of a large amount of funds (4 million Chinese yuan).
- June 13, 2001: Deng was tried by Tianjin No. 2 Intermediate Court and sentenced to death, confiscation of all personal property, and the deprival of political rights for life.
- December 5, 2001: Deng was retried by Tianjin Superior Court and the original sentence was sustained.
- August 12, 2002: The Supreme Court sustained the original sentence and finally approved the death sentence.

Source: "The Case of Graft by Deng Chenhui." The Supreme Court's Web site at http://www.court.gov.cn/study/penal/200401120020.htm (accessed 1/12/2004).

the judgment on August 12, 2002, by sustaining and finally approving the original sentence. The ruling went into effect immediately. No information was given on the exact date of execution. In accordance to the Chinese criminal procedure law, however, the offender would have been executed within seven days after the sentence was finally approved.[9]

COURTROOM DYNAMICS

As part of an evolving legal system, Chinese courts are now promoting a new culture in judicial work. The new culture involves the imbuement of a social morality in the rule of law (e.g., judicial fairness, judicial efficiency, judicial independence, and judicial supremacy and democracy) that resonates in the Chinese public consciousness.[10] This has been attempted through the development of an authoritative persona, via a newly established ethos of procedural propriety, procedural regularity, and the design of a new judicial uniform. Sentencing rallies are still held regularly as forums for raising public consciousness. However, public executions in the aftermath of these sentencing rallies have been banned since the economic reforms.

Courts in China vary in sizes, physical conditions, staffing, and professional quality. These differences are reflective of their geographic location (e.g., urban vs. countryside) and administrative rank (e.g., municipal courts vs. superior courts). Courtroom dynamics also diverge depending upon the type and nature of the cases (e.g., petty crime vs. capital offenses) and the amount of political and media attention (e.g., defendant who is an ordinary rural resident vs. a high ranking public official involved in the case).

Using data from personal observations and secondary accounts, the following sections illustrate the courtroom atmosphere and sentencing rallies, typically occurring in urban areas. It is within these contexts that death penalty decisions are made and their effects become manifested in the behavior of individuals and the wider society.

Courtroom atmosphere

By any indication, Chinese courtrooms are intimate, yet solemn and formal. The courtroom typically has the national emblem hung on the wall above the judicial bench. At the center of the courtroom are the key judicial officers and the court clerk. The station where the defendant stands behind is positioned in front of the bench. To the right of the bench is the prosecution's table and to the left is the defense table. The defendant is typically escorted by several judicial police into the courtroom, standing behind the station or at the center of the courtroom facing the judges in some basic-level courts, where there is no station for defendants to stand behind. The judicial police may stand at either side of the bench, or sit in one of the seats in the audience or separate seats provided for them. Depending on the size of the courtroom, audience seats range from as few as less than ten seats to as many as a few dozens.

Chinese judges are now wearing a new type of judicial uniform, with a black rope symbolizing the solemnity of the position, and the red stole and gold toggle representing the national colors. The new uniform projects a nonmilitary, more civilian-like appearance that symbolizes the separation between the judiciary and the state, and exerts a professional and authoritative appearance.

Prosecutors and the judicial police in this courtroom environment are dressed in a more traditional military-style uniform. Defense attorneys typically wear Western-style civilian clothing or business suits (e.g., shirt and tie for male attorneys and shirt or dress for female attorneys). Defendants wear the jail uniform of various kinds (e.g., a vest, a jacket with the jail's name printed on the clothes), with or without handcuffs and/or foot chains when in the courtroom.[11]

Following the inquisitorial tradition that emphasizes truth finding, the trial is only one of the many hearings throughout the process of criminal investigation in China. Even in the current context where the trial is moving away from the inquisitorial style and more toward an adversarial system, adjudication decisions remain primarily based on documents (e.g., police interrogation records signed by the defendant, witnesses; forensic evidence) prepared by the procuratorate, the police, and the defense attorney prior to the trial, rather than evidence presented, examined, and admitted during the trial in court. The outcome of the trial, therefore, is typically determined before the trial starts.

Compared to trials in an adversarial system, the Chinese trial is brief, routinized, and predictable. Spontaneous and dramatic moments, such as a surprising witness showing up in court and the prosecution and defense rebutting each others' witnesses, are rare events in Chinese courtrooms. In fact, the opportunity for these dramatic moments is also limited because Chinese law does not require that witnesses personally testify in court.

The brief nature of Chinese trials is clearly illustrated by the capital murder case of Dong Wei (see Case #6 below). In this particular case, the entire first trial took about two hours; no witnesses testified in court. The swiftness of trials is attributed to the particular goals of these legal proceedings. As a Chinese legal scholar put it, the trial is more of a process that affirms and reviews the police and the prosecutor's activities rather than adjudicates.[12]

The Chinese trial, however, is not without its signature events. One such event is that after the defendant reads his/her final statement, typically prepared in advance, the prosecutor gives a lecture directly to the defendant appealing to their moral and legal consciousness. For example, in a case involving theft, after the completion of judicial questioning, the prosecutor turned to the defendant who was in his twenties and said in a fatherly and authoritative tone:

> just because you needed money to play video games, you stole from others. Do you know that the money you stole may be someone's sweat and blood money, may be in need for a sick family member, or an elder. It was not easy for your parents to raise you until this day, how are you going to face them and repay them with your behavior? Do you want your parents to live with the guilt and shame for the rest of their lives?[13]

In another case involving manslaughter in a DUI case, the lead prosecutor turned to the defendant, pointed at the defendant's direction with a pen in his right hand, and lectured in a high-pitched voice:

> You took away a life! Hadn't you thought about the consequences of your behavior? Don't you know that you not only took away one person's life, but also someone's mother, sister, daughter and a good worker? How could you sleep at night? If everybody acted like you irresponsibly in our society, how can this society be functional?[14]

Perhaps the most dramatic event occurs when the defendant overturns his/her previous testimony and claims being tortured and coerced into confession in an open court. In some of the recent high profile cases, it was reported that defendants, to varying degrees, claimed that they were forced into confessing their "crimes." For example, Chen Guoqing and three other co-defendants bared their scares to open court during their first trial claiming that they were beaten and physically tortured by the police interrogator and forced into confessions.[15]

In another high-profile case, defendant Cheng Kejie, the highest ranking governmental official in China ever charged with a capital crime (bribery) in the history of the PRC, changed his testimony in court, denying everything he admitted to the investigator. It was reported that Cheng appeared very sincere and remorseful and was fully cooperative with the investigator before the trial. Even though the investigators knew that corrupt officials were more likely to deny their confessions than not during a trial, Cheng's complete denial in court still took everyone by surprise.[16]

According to various judicial documents and reports, the Chinese judiciary responded to these types of incidents by establishing a set procedure. Judges would typically order the procuratorate to conduct investigations about the truthfulness of the claims. The procuratorate would conduct interviews, obtain signed affidavits from involved police officers and jail guards, and medical reports of the defendant by the government designated hospitals, and submit a written report of their findings to the court. The findings of the report are then used in the court's ruling. In most cases, the judge rules "no clear evidence indicates that the defense's claim of torture existed," or "the defendant's confessions were corroborated with other evidence, thus could be used as evidence in this judgment." In other cases, the court indicated that "the investigation of the allegation of the police abuse is not conclusive."[17]

The sentencing rally

Sentencing rallies are one of the hallmarks of socialist law. Embedded in the ideas of popular justice, a sentencing rally provides an important platform for the judiciary to disseminate law, the public to express indignation and moral outrage, and for the defendant to be shamed and condemned. It serves as an effective way to educate the public, restore community sense of justice, and reinforce the ideas of rule of law. Its impact is likely to multiply as television coverage of trials and sentencing rallies have become increasingly popular in China in recent years.[18]

Currently, sentencing rallies have been frequently used by Chinese courts as a legal ritual to publicly announce important judicial sentences involving major criminal offenses of the time. It is typically held in a stadium, housing hundreds of thousands of people, with an audience organized by the work units, the street committees, and various branches of local governments (e.g., women's federation, labor department).

A rally usually starts with "a group of convicted criminals brought out on stage, handcuffed and under the guard of a line of court police. The criminals may have placards around their necks and tied to their backs, which detail the criminal's name, the nature of the offense and the sentence given and they usually stand at the front of the stage under guard, in front of a group of legal and political officials."[19] The rally then proceeds with public officials' speeches, judicial announce of sentences, and the public parade of the offenders.[20] Afterwards, the offenders will be either taken back to the prison or taken to the execution ground.

As a forum for public humiliation and moral indignation, sentencing rallies are also extremely important in the reform era because they reaffirm the authority relations between the state and the people.[21] The goals of these activities are in contrast to the "accusation rallies" in the Mao-era where the mass-line justice and class struggle took priority over law and permitted violent acts and insulting words towards defendants by the masses. Current sentencing rallies emphasize legal education and deterrence by focusing on the announcement of judicial decisions by a judicial officer.

Sentencing rallies have been particularly mobilized during the "strike-hard" campaigns in the recent two decades to demonstrate the government's effectiveness in their control over the surging crime rates. In a 2004 report from the City of Shijiazhuang, a "hundred day campaign" led to the arrest of 2,576 criminals, 516 of which were involved in serious crimes. A public sentencing rally was held in the City's Intermediate People's Court for those who were sentenced to death. After the sentence was read by the chief judge, the crowd erupted and shouted: "these bastards should have been shot to death a long time ago!"[22]

To mark the World Anti-Drug Day, courts of various jurisdictions in Guangdong province held a total of 73 sentencing rallies announcing sentences for 773 offenders involved in drug trafficking in the first half year of 2005.[23] Similarly, a group of offenders involved in drug trafficking heard their sentences of life imprisonment or death in a sentencing rally held in a stadium in Shanghai on June 26, 2005. Offenders sentenced to death were immediately taken to the execution ground immediately after the rally.[24]

With the aid of television and Internet coverage, sentencing rallies and public parades of major offenders will likely to continue. The visual image of an offender handcuffed with placards hung around the neck and held down by the authority transmits a powerful message of state control and the rule of law.

USUAL REVIEW PROCESS INVOLVING COMPLEX CASES

As described previously, most capital cases go through a trial by the court of first instance (typically an intermediate people's court of a municipality), reviewed by an appeals court (typically the superior court of a province or the autonomous municipality and region), and finally reviewed and approved by the Supreme Court. In rare cases, however, a case may be tried and retried multiple times due to the complex facts and laws involved, different opinions held by different judicial entities, or concerns about the political impact of a particular outcome of the case.[25] A review of several high-profile capital cases in recent years may help shed further light on the inner workings of the Chinese judiciaries in these unusual or exceptional cases.

Case #6 Timeline for the case of Liu Yong

- July 7, 2000: Liu was detained by the Public Security of Shenyang City.
- August 10, 2000: Liu's arrest was approved by Shenyang People's Procuratorate. He was prosecuted by Liaoning Tieling People's Procuratorate.
- April 17, 2002: Tieling Intermediate People's Court of Liaoning Province sentenced the defendant to death with immediate execution.
- August 15, 2003: Liaoning Superior People's Court changed the verdict and sentenced the defendant to death with a two-year reprieve.
- October, 2003: The notice of a new trial was served on Liu Yong.
- December 18, 2003: The Supreme Court commenced the new trial at Jin Zhou city, Liaoning Province.
- December 22, 2003: The Supreme Court rendered a judgment sentencing Liu Yong to death and issued an order to execute the death sentence immediately. Liu Yong was executed on the same day.

Source: "Supreme Court Retries Shenyang Gang Leader." On the Web site of *People's Daily* (English edition) at http://english.people.com.cn/200312/19/eng20031219_130753.shtml (accessed 12/19/2003).

Case of Liu Yong — convicted of organized crime

The case of Liu Yong was one of the most significant capital cases in the history of the PRC. Its notoriety is due to the fact that it was one of the few ordinary criminal cases retried by the Supreme Court after its judicial decision was finalized.

Liu Yong was allegedly a gang leader in Shenyang, the capital city of Liaoning Province in Northeast China. As a former board chairman of Shenyang Jiayang Group, Liu Yong was charged for "organizing, leading and actively participating in a mafia-style group, willful and malicious injury, pillage and illegal business operations." He was also charged with murder, smuggling, drug dealing, gambling, tax evasion, extortion, illegally holding or hiding a firearm or ammunition, disrupting public services, intentional destroying or damaging public or private property, theft and bribery.[26]

With offenses involving thirty-four people and the longest indictment in Chinese legal history, Liu Yong was sentenced to death with immediate execution by Tieling Intermediate Court of Liaoning Province on April 17, 2002. However, the Liaoning Superior Court on August 15, 2003, modified the lower court's penalty and sentenced Liu to death with a two-year suspension for execution, using virtually the same charges, and attributed the alteration to "specific circumstances relevant to this case."

This modification of the sentence ruling sparked great controversy in both the public and legal circles. A popular Web site in China (http://wwww.sohu.com) has recorded more than 80,000 comments on the case posted by Internet users, setting a record in Chinese Internet history. One Internet user commented that "if someone like Liu Yong who committed so many vicious crimes does not deserve the death sentence, who does?" The public was particularly outraged by the possible judicial corruption that Liu's political and financial influence may have affected the superior court's decision in this case.[27] Legal officials were especially concerned about Liu's attorney paying fourteen top legal experts in the country to sign an affidavit expressing unanimous views that torture and coercion into confession could not be completely ruled out in this case, and that the original verdict against Liu had been heavy-handed.[28]

Consequentially, the Supreme Court ordered an unprecedented retrial for the case.[29] On December 18, 2003, a retrial was commenced in the Jinzhou Intermediate Court. To prevent further obstruction and undue influence, all the judges and judicial police of the Jinzhou Court were replaced with officers sent by the Supreme Court in the retrial.[30] On the fifth day of the trial, the Supreme Court announced its final ruling of death with immediate execution, and ordered Liu to be executed immediately following the trial.

Case of Dong Wei — convicted of murder

The capital case of Dong Wei was a dramatic and unusual event in the recent history of the Chinese criminal justice system. This ordinary assault-turned into-murder case, like many other assault cases, initially started from a trivial altercation, and quickly escalated into a violent fatal incident, ultimately claiming two people's lives (i.e., the victim and the defendant). This case would have gone unnoticed if not for the extraordinary efforts taken by the defense attorney who went beyond the legal limit to seek the Supreme Court's help. In particular, the defense attorney had the process halted on the day when the execution was scheduled, obtained a retrial, but he ultimately failed to save his client's life. This case sparked a new wave of debates on the death penalty, its review process, and the judicial reform.

Dong Wei, a twenty-five-year-old peasant, was detained and arrested under the suspicion of "intentional assault" for allegedly assaulting and wounding a man with whom he had a fight outside a dance hall in Yanan city, Shaanxi province. The police transferred the case to the prosecution after completing the investigation, but their case was returned for further investigation due to insufficient evidence. Without additional new evidence, the case was again forwarded from the police to the procuratorate office. On November 26, 2001, the Yanan Intermediate Procuratorate brought the charge of murder instead of intentional assault (the victim died a few days after being hospitalized) against Dong Wei to the court.[31]

Yanan Intermediate Court in Shaanxi Province conducted the trial for this case. The defense argued that the facts were unclear, the evidence was insufficient, and the defendant acted in self-defense because the crime was precipitated by the victim. The attorney further requested an important witness to testify in court as his testimony was not included in the police

Case #7 Timeline for the case of Dong Wei

- May 2, 2001: Crime occurred. Dong Wei was allegedly hitting the victim on his head with a brick repeatedly, causing him to be severely wounded. The victim later died from these injuries.
- May 4, 2001: Dong was detained for intentional assault.
- June 5, 2001: Dong was arrested for intentional assault.
- November 26, 2001: Yanan Intermediate Procuratorate (Shaanxi province) charged the defendant with murder and brought the case to the Yanan Intermediate Court for adjudication. Prior to the prosecution, the Procuratorate Office returned the case to the Public Security's office due to insufficient evidence; without any additional evidence, the case was forwarded to the Procuratorate Office.
- December 21, 2001: Yanan Intermediate Court sentenced the defendant to death with immediate execution and deprival of political rights for life.
- December 25, 2001: The defense appealed the case to the Superior Court of Shaanxi province.
- April 22, 2002: The Shaanxi Superior Court sustained the original sentence of the lower court. The judgment became effective immediately as the Court had the final authority to approve the death sentence in certain violent crimes (including murder).
- April 27, 2002: The defense attorney was notified of the ruling of the Superior Court, and brought an emergency petition to the Supreme Court.
- April 29, 2002: The execution was scheduled, but it was ordered to be temporarily halted by the Supreme Court via a telephone call minutes before the execution was scheduled to start.
- August 26, 2002: The Shaanxi Superior Court Issued the second judgment, sentencing the defendant to death with immediate execution.
- September 5, 2002: Dong was executed.

Source: "The Judicial Judgment Document of the Case of Dong Wei." In An Examination of the Death Penalty System in China, ed. Xingliang Chen (Beijing: China Procuratorial Publishing House, 2003), 308–311.

record. The attorney's arguments were rejected and request was denied. On December 21, 2001, the Court sentenced the defendant to death with immediate execution.[32]

The defendant appealed. His lawyer argued that (1) the criminal incident was precipitated by the victim, that the victim was the first who verbally and physically assaulted the offender and that the offender acted as self-defense; (2) there was a gross lack of evidence in determining the circumstances under which the offender attacked the victim with the final blow on his head; and (3) the only eyewitness who gave the testimony to the police offered contradictory testimonies. He also requested another eyewitness to testify in court. The Superior Court of Shaanxi Province reviewed the case in a "closed session" without hearing from the defendant or any of the witnesses, sustained the lower court's ruling on April 22, 2002, and scheduled the execution date on April 29.[33]

Only two days before the execution was to be carried out, the defendant's attorney and family were notified. In an attempt to halt the chain of events leading to execution, the defense attorney went to Beijing, the capital city of China, to personally appeal the case at the Supreme Court. It was reported that he was turned away at the front gate. On the morning of the execution (April 29, 2002), the lawyer managed to gain access to the Supreme Court under false pretences, and persuade the Deputy Judge Li Wuqing to review the case file. In the petition, he wrote:

> As a defense attorney for Dong Wei, I truly believe that sentencing Dong to death was flawed. In this life-death moment, I had to hastily come to Beijing to appeal to the Supreme Court for Dong. Please order the Shaanxi Court to halt the execution and designate new officers to review the case... The victim in this case was someone who insulted women in public and first initiated the fight. Dong hit him on the head with a brick out of desperation and self-defense. If Dong was given the death sentence, it would be an erroneous ruling! I am pleading the Supreme Court to review the case in order to protect the integrity of the law.[34]

According to reports, Judge Li Wuqing heard defense attorney Zhu Zhanping's briefing on the case at 9:55 a.m. on April 29 and called other judges of the Supreme Court who were in charge of the Western region to review the case file. Upon reviewing the documents, the judge agreed with the lawyer that Dong's case needed a more thorough review. He immediately drafted a request to the President of the Supreme Court to halt the execution while trying to contact judges at both courts in Shaanxi. At 10:18 a.m., he reached a vice-president's phone of the Shaanxi Superior Court and obtained the phone number of the executing officer. He called the executing officer at 10:24 a.m. by asking: "Was the shot fired?" Upon hearing that the execution was not carried out, he ordered: "I am from the No.1 Criminal Court of the Supreme Court, I am now ordering you to postpone the execution until 3:00 p.m. this afternoon. During this time period, we will contact you for further instructions." Soon after, the Supreme Court's "Order to Temporarily Suspend the Execution" was issued.[35]

Before the further "review" process started, the defense attorney sent in two requests via a telegraph to the Supreme Court: (1) requesting judge Zhang Congli, involved in the first hearing, to be excused from the second review; (2) requesting the case to be reviewed in a different jurisdiction. Both requests were denied. Upon the Supreme Court's order to re-form the collegiate bench to review the case, the Shaanxi Superior Court formed a new committee of five members with three members were from the previous review committee. It again held a "closed hearing"[36] to review the case. The death sentence with immediate execution was once again sustained

Case #8 Timeline for the case of Chen Guoqing and Associates

- November, 1994: Suspects detained on suspicion of murder.
- February 1996: Chengde Intermediate Court sentenced the four defendants to death with immediate execution. All four defendants appealed.
- October 6, 1996: Hebei Province Superior Court sent the case for retrial on the grounds that more than twenty items of the prosecution's evidence needed clarification.
- August 12, 1997: Chengde Intermediate Court re-sentenced all four defendants to death with immediate execution. All four defendants appealed.
- February 16, 1998: Hebei Province Superior Court sent the case back for retrial on the same grounds.
- October 13, 1998: Chengde Court again sentenced all four defendants to death with immediate execution. They all appealed.
- December 21, 1998: Hebei Superior Court sent the case back for the third time for retrial.
- October 20, 2000: Defendants Chen and Yang were sentenced to death. Defendant He was sentenced to suspended death and Zhu was sentenced to life imprisonment. They all appealed.
- July 21, 2003: The retrial was commenced by the Hebei Superior Court.
- July 22, 2004: The Hebei Superior Court convicted all four defendants with robbery and sentenced defendants Chen, Yang and He to death with a two year suspension of execution and Zhu with life imprisonment.

Source: See "A Perplex Case of Death Sentence with a Two Year Suspension." Xinhua News Web site at http://news.xinhuanet.com/legal/2005-07/11/content_3202716.htm (accessed 7/11/2005).

on August 26, 2002.[37] Dong was subsequently executed on September 5, 2002.[38]

Case of Chen Guoqing and associates — convicted of murder and robbery

Chen Guoqing and his associates were on death row for almost ten years. They were sentenced to death four times for murder and robbery by a lower court. Their sentences were overturned and sent back for retrial three times by the Superior Court in Hebei Province. The case was extraordinary not only for its lengthy appeals and retrials, but also for its unusual media disclosure of torture and forced confession.

In July and August of 1994, there were two car-jacking incidents that resulted in deaths of the taxi drivers in Chengde City of Hebei province. According to the *Chengde Daily News*, the Chende Public Security Bureau ordered the two branch offices in charge of the region to solve the cases with "whatever it takes." The police first detained Chen Guoqing because he appeared to be gloomy and anxious. Subsequently, with Chen's testimony, the police arrested three additional suspects.

Between 1996 and 2003, the four defendants were charged and convicted of murder and robbery four times by the Chengde City Intermediate Court in Hebei province. The original sentence was returned three times by the Hebei Superior Court for a retrial on the grounds that the facts in the case were insufficient and/or unclear. All four defendants claimed in court that they were physically tortured and their confessions were coerced. According to the judicial judgment of the first trial, all four defendants bared their scares to the courtroom, claiming that the wounds had been inflicted by police officers to extort their confessions. The court stated in the judicial document that "the four defendants' confessions are on the record. The facts are clear and there is sufficient evidence to convict."[39]

After the fourth trial by the low court, the Hebei Superior Court decided to conduct a retrial itself in July 2003. After a year, the high court convicted all four defendants with robbery and sentenced defendants Chen, Yang, and He to death with a two year suspension of execution and Zhu with life imprisonment. The case was not reviewed by the Supreme Court both because of its nature (e.g., ordinary violent crime) and its final sentence (e.g., suspended death sentence does not require the final review of the Supreme Court).[40]

In a most recent report, the four criminals may have been wrongfully convicted for the crime that they did not commit as another criminal, currently serving his prison sentence, revealed to the authority the real criminals in this case. The four offenders' families and lawyers are making efforts to petition for a review of their case.[41]

Criminal process — internal struggle and external influence

All of these complex capital cases activated extraordinary judicial proceedings, assembled unprecedented legal resources and public attention, and in the meanwhile, exposed several major problems associated with the death penalty and its legal process. These problems could be summarized into local protectionism, judicial independence, and the ultimate review and approval authority of the death penalty.

Local protectionism is deeply rooted in China's political, economic and social structure. To put it simply, agencies in performing their duties tend to act in favor of local interests rather than the national, public interests.[42] This is especially apparent when the two are in conflict with each other, due to the enmeshed local relations and concerns for special local interests. The judicial aspects of local protectionism may result in local courts' insistence upon their rulings despite the law and higher courts' dissenting opinions. For example, in the case of Dong Wei, despite the Supreme Court's timely order for a retrial, the superior court of Shaanxi province affirmed twice the lower court's ruling and executed Dong only five months after the Supreme Court's intervention. Similarly, Chengde Intermediate Court affirmed its death sentence on defendant Chen with virtually the same evidence in four different trials, despite the provincial superior court's order for more evidence.

This judicial protectionism that refuses to correct its own rulings is partly due to the internal pressure within the judiciary. One of the recent judicial reforms was the instigation of a judicial responsibility system that makes judges responsible for intentional or major erroneous rulings. Under this system, a change of ruling may eventually affect the presiding judges' career, reputation, and/or their financial interests.[43] Especially when a case grasps the national headline, it becomes even more difficult for the judge to change its original ruling because the entire court's authority and reputation is on the line.[44]

Another aspect of local protectionism may derive from complex local relations. For example, external political pressure may force the court to rule in one way than another to satisfy local interests and demands. The external pressure on the judiciary consequentially affects the judicial independence.

The concern of judicial independence has been a long struggle in the Chinese judiciary's attempts to find its identity and authority. Even though relevant laws clearly state that the Chinese judiciary is fully independent of political and party interference, it is difficult in reality to separate politics and law.[45] For example, in the case of convicted organized criminal leader Liu, the defense attorney solicited fourteen top legal experts to sign an affidavit to influence the judge's opinion on the case. It was also reported that Liu's political and financial influence helped him in his second trial that temporarily spared his life.

These complex capital cases also shed light on the issue of final review and approval of capital cases. With the current waiver of the final review and approval authority of the Supreme Court in many ordinary violent crimes, the Supreme Court had to go through extraordinary steps to prevent miscarriages of justice. Even there, the Supreme Court, as the highest court in the country, may be powerless in preventing an execution that it deemed unnecessary. In the case of Dong Wei, for example, despite the Supreme Court's order to halt the execution and start a new trial, the Shaanxi Superior Court only held a closed hearing with no testimonies from the defendant and witnesses, sustained the original death sentence, and executed Dong without notifying the Supreme Court. In the case of Chen and his associates, despite the repeated returns of the rulings from the high court, the Chengde lower court reaffirmed its death sentence rulings four times. In Liu's case, the Supreme Court had to replace all the judicial officers with its own officers in a retrial in order to prevent judicial corruption.

LENGTHS OF CRIMINAL PROCESS FOR VARIOUS CAPITAL CASES

Due to the grave concerns for individual liberty and freedom, laws in many countries stipulate defendants' due process rights, particularly rights to a speedy trial to prevent criminal suspects and/or defendants from undue detention by the government. There is no exception in China.

The criminal procedure law and other laws specify the time limit for various actions taken by law enforcement and judicial agencies. For example, the police must conduct interrogation of the criminal detainee within twenty-four hours after the detention (1996 CPL Article 65).[46] Upon determining that an arrest is warranted, the police shall submit the arrest warrant application to the procuratorate for review and approval within three days after the detention (Article 69).[47] After arrest, interrogation shall be conducted within twenty-four hours (Article 72).[48] The time limit for detaining a criminal suspect for investigation shall not be more than two months after the arrest. In complicated cases, the time limit may be extended by one month with the approval of the procuratorate at the next higher level (Article 124). In other specified extraordinary circumstances, the detention time could be further extended by two months.[49]

The procuratorate shall render a decision of whether to initiate the prosecution within one month after receiving the case transferred from the police. When involving complicated cases, the time may be extended by another half month (CPL Article 138). Upon accepting the case transferred from the procuratorate, the court shall announce a judgment within one month, or at the latest, not exceeding one and one-half months. However, when involving complicated cases and under unusual circumstances, the announcement of judgment may be postponed for one more month with the approval of a higher court (CPL Article 168). In cases where the jurisdiction of a case is shifted and/or requires supplementary investigation by the procuratorate, the time shall be recomputed (CPL Article 168).

Upon the announcement of judgment by the first trial court, the defense or the prosecution has ten days to appeal or protest the judgment (CPL Article 183). The time limit of the second trial or retrial by the original court is the same as the first trial, except in cases where the Supreme Court receives and agrees to try an appeal or protest case, the time limit of adjudication shall be decided by the Supreme Court (CPL Article 196).

Taken altogether, in a normal criminal proceeding, a defendant shall receive a judgment from the first trial court in four months from the day of the arrest; and receive a judgment from the second trial in one and one-half months if the defendant appeals or the procuratorate protests. In complicated cases, the time from the arrest to the announcement of first judgment may take up to nine months and the time from the announcement of first judgment to the second judgment may take up to three months. In cases involving extraordinary circumstances, the time it takes for the completion of first and second trial may be indefinite.

For various reasons of procedural justice, it is critical for the law to set the maximum time allowed for various criminal proceedings. However, it is equally important to specify a reasonable amount of (minimum) time in law to ensure adequate and sufficient preparation for the case by defense. For example, the CPL stipulates that the criminal suspect may retain a lawyer after the first interrogation (Article 96), presumably after twenty-four hours of the approved arrest. The law also stipulates that special circumstances may warrant a postponement of a trial, even though the time limit for a trial to conclude remains intact.[50] Moreover, the law requires that the defense and the procuratorate have up to ten days to appeal or protest a judgment of first trial.

The length of a criminal proceeding is an important measure of justice in and of itself regardless of the substantive rulings. This is the case because a defendant's due process rights may be deprived if the proceeding does not permit sufficient time for a thorough investigation and preparation of the case by the defense. For example, during strike-hard campaigns, the time limit for appeals was reduced at varying times from the legally stipulated ten days to three days to expedite the process. Similarly, defendants' rights not to be subject to undue governmental coercion and deprival of freedom may be violated if prolonged criminal proceeding is widespread in a legal system.[51] This becomes even more important under the Chinese system because the majority of criminal suspects/defendants were detained while waiting for criminal prosecution and trial.[52]

Using criminal court judgment documents for 1,010 capital and serious, non-capital cases, we conducted analyses of the amount of time it took for cases to move from the three stages of the criminal processing: (1) from arrest to the end of the first trial, (2) from the end of the first trial to the end of the second trial/first review, and (3) from the end of the second trial/first review to the final review in cases involving the death penalty.[53] These results are summarized below.

Arrest — trial of first instance

The criminal case collections included in this analysis included a total of 403 capital cases (with immediate execution only) with information on the time from the defendants' arrest and the completion of their first trial.

As summarized in Table 6.1, the average length of time for these capital cases to conclude from the initial arrest to first trial was 233 days (approximately eight months). This time period exceeds what is considered the normal proceeding of four months but it falls within the range of complicated case of up to nine months that is stipulated in law. Capital cases with the shortest period of time from arrest to first judgment involved three days[54] and the longest time 1,160 days (approximately thirty-nine months).[55]

Table 6.1 Average days between arrest and end of first trial

Sentence	*Violent*	*Property*	*Economic*	*Corruption*	*Public safety*	*Public order*	*All cases*
Death	R:3-1079 $\bar{x}$ = 222 (n = 126)	R: 3-651 $\bar{x}$ = 184 (n = 127)	R: 8-1160 $\bar{x}$ = 331 (n= 27)	R: 12-987 $\bar{x}$ = 337 (n = 60)	R:13-580 $\bar{x}$ = 184 (n = 21)	R:29-916 $\bar{x}$ = 224 (n = 42)	R:3-1160 $\bar{x}$ =233 (n = 403)
Death2 and Life	R:29-627 $\bar{x}$ = 197 (n = 48)	R: 29-998 $\bar{x}$ = 268 (n = 56)	R:114-1549 $\bar{x}$ = 430 (n = 15)	R: 20-861 $\bar{x}$ = 356 (n = 21)	R:30-688 $\bar{x}$ = 216 (n = 10)	R:41-1157 $\bar{x}$ = 415 (n = 29)	R:20-1549 $\bar{x}$ = 293 (n = 179)
> 10 yrs.	R:70-453 $\bar{x}$ = 142 (n = 43)	R:20-1041 $\bar{x}$ = 271 (n = 101)	R:103-1549 $\bar{x}$ = 379 (n = 21)	R:144-1186 $\bar{x}$ = 316 (n = 27)	R:46-316 $\bar{x}$ = 146 (n = 16)	R: 41-937 $\bar{x}$ = 211 (n = 17)	R:20-1549 $\bar{x}$ = 249 (n = 225)

R = Range, $\bar{x}$ = Mean, n = Number of Cases, Death2 = capital sentence with a two year suspension.

Across the six crime categories of capital offenses, corruption and economic cases took the longest time, with an average of about one year for each offense type to complete their first trial. Property crimes and crime against public safety cases took the shortest time, averaging around six months to complete their first trial.

When compared with offenses that received non-capital punishments (e.g., more than ten years, capital sentence with a two-year suspension), the average time it took for capital cases to conclude their first trial was surprisingly shorter. For example, the average time for capital cases to conclude their first trial was about sixty days shorter when compared with cases that received suspended death and life imprisonment. Similarly, the average time from arrest to first trial was sixteen days shorter for capital cases than was true of criminal cases receiving fixed prison sentences of at least ten years.

Comparisons of the average time it took for capital and non-capital cases to be reach for the first trial for each offense category indicated no consistent patterns. Capital offenses took a longer time to complete for

Table 6.2 Average days between first trial and second trial/first review

Sentence	*Violent*	*Property*	*Economic*	*Corruption*	*Public safety*	*Public order*	*All cases*
Death	R: 3-399 $\bar{x}$ = 70 (n = 89)	R: 4-196 $\bar{x}$ = 44 (n = 93)	R: 5-800 $\bar{x}$ = 106 (n = 28)	R: 4-308 $\bar{x}$ = 64 (n = 44)	R: 11-231 $\bar{x}$ = 76 (n = 15)	R: 11-330 $\bar{x}$ = 72 (n = 34	R:3-800 $\bar{x}$ = 65 (n = 303)
Death2 & Life	R: 3-688 $\bar{x}$ = 126 (n = 32)	R:14-706 $\bar{x}$ = 121 (n = 31)	R: 13-800 $\bar{x}$ = 147 (n = 16)	R: 11-560 $\bar{x}$ = 168 (n = 21)	R:35-304 $\bar{x}$ = 130 (n = 3)	R:18-289 $\bar{x}$ = 150 (n = 19)	R:3-800 $\bar{x}$ = 138 (n = 122)
> 10 yrs.	R: 24-399 $\bar{x}$ = 94 (n = 22)	R:27-810 $\bar{x}$ = 177 (n = 30)	R: 70-213 $\bar{x}$ = 109 (n = 12)	R: 15-532 $\bar{x}$ = 166 (n = 8)	R: 35-68 $\bar{x}$ = 45 (n = 5)	R:53-192 $\bar{x}$ = 85 (n = 10)	R:15-810 $\bar{x}$ = 127 (n = 87)

R = Range; $\bar{x}$ = Mean; n = Number of cases.

some offense types (e.g., violent crime) than non-capital offenses, but they took shorter period of time to complete in other offense types (e.g., property and economic offenses).

Second trial/ first review

Table 6.2 presents the range and average time it took for capital and non-capital cases for a judicial decision between the first trial and the second trial or first review. The case with the shortest time until the second trial/ first review was a murder/robbery case. It took the Sichuan Superior Court three days to sustain and finally approve the death sentence with immediate execution in 1998 for the two convicted offenders in this case.[56] The case with the longest time in the second trial/first review involved financial fraud, which took a total of eight hundred days to complete.[57]

Similar to the pattern in the first trial, the second trial for capital cases appeared to be shorter in average (e.g., sixty-five days than for non-capital offenses (e.g., 138 and 127 days). In both the capital and non-capital cases, however, the amount of time it took in second trial all exceeded the regularly required length of no more than one and one-half months that is established by law.

In almost all six offense categories, the average time spent in the second trial was shorter for capital cases than non-capital cases. The exception is the case of public safety where those cases that received a fixed prison sentence of at least ten years took less time to complete ($\bar{x}$ = 45 days) than their capital case counterparts ($\bar{x}$ = 76 days).

Table 6.3 Average days between first review and final review/approval of the death sentence by the Supreme Court

Sentence	*Violent*	*Property*	*Economic*	*Corruption*	*Public order*	*All cases*
Death*	(n = 0)	R:108-389 $\bar{x}$ = 248 (n = 2)	R: 5-297 $\bar{x}$ = 53 (n = 23)	R: 2-388 $\bar{x}$ = 82 (n = 41)	R: 148-210 $\bar{x}$ = 67 (n = 14)	R:2-389 $\bar{x}$ = 74 (n = 82)
Death2 & Life**	R:516-554 $\bar{x}$ = 535 (n = 2)	R: 1223 $\bar{x}$ = 1233 (n = 1)	R: 5-14 $\bar{x}$ = 10 (n = 6)	R:94-355 $\bar{x}$ = 213 (n = 5)	R: 14-607 $\bar{x}$ = 247 (n = 3)	R:5-1223 $\bar{x}$ = 249 (n = 17)

R = Range; $\bar{x}$ = Mean).

* Fewer cases went through the final review and approval proceeding by the Supreme Court because of the earlier practice that waived the Supreme Court's final review and approval authority over the death penalty case and granted it to superior courts. The cases involved in the waiver were mainly violent crimes (murder, rape), property crimes (e.g., robbery), and crimes against public safety (e.g., explosion, arson).

** This category of suspended death sentence and life imprisonment may contain cases that originally received a death sentence with immediate execution and had the original sentence modified to the death sentence with a two year reprieve or life imprisonment by the Supreme Court. In addition, cases in this category may also have cooffenders who were sentenced to death with immediate execution. When a codefendant's case is forwarded to the higher court for trial and review, all other defendants in the same case were reviewed as well.

Final review

The Supreme Court has the final review and approval authority over the death penalty cases, except in some cases (e.g., murder, rape, robbery, explosion, arson) where the authority was granted to the superior court of each province, autonomous municipality, and autonomous region. Table 6.3 presents the range and average length of time between the first review and the final review for capital cases by the Supreme Court.

The average capital case took seventy-four days for the Supreme Court to conduct the final review and approval of capital cases. The fastest review involved a corruption case where two codefendants were convicted of graft in 1989 and had their death sentence approved by the Supreme Court in only two days. In contrast, a case involving a forty-year-old female offender convicted of fraud in 1997 took 389 days to complete the final review and approval process. This case was the lengthiest review conducted by the Supreme Court among all the cases in our analysis.

Four offense categories of property (mainly fraud and theft cases), economic, corruption and public order offenses (e.g., drug trafficking, forcing into prostitution) went through the final review and approval by the Supreme Court. The shortest time it took for the final review and approval to complete among these offenses involved economic crimes ($\bar{x}$ = 53 days). Robbery and other property crimes had the longest time of final review ($\bar{x}$ = 248 days).

Similar to the patterns in the first and second trial where capital cases appeared to take less time than non-capital cases, the final review and approval process conducted by the Supreme Court was also much shorter for cases resulting in the death sentence with immediate execution than cases with a suspended death sentence or life imprisonment. The average final appeal was completed with seventy days for capital cases compare to 249 days for non-capital sentences.

Length of criminal proceeding for capital cases

The Chinese criminal procedure law requires the Supreme Court's mandatory final review and approval for some capital offenses but not for others. Because of these differences, it is interesting to compare the average length of the entire criminal proceeding for capital cases with and without the final review and approval of the Supreme Court.[58] Table 6.4 summaries the average time of the entire criminal processing from initial arrest to final disposition of cases with and without Supreme Court review.

As shown in Table 6.4, the length of criminal processing was far longer for capital cases with Supreme Court review than those without ($\bar{x}$ = 449 days and 273 days, respectively). Similar patterns were found when each type of crime categories was considered separately. The exception was public order offenses, where capital cases with Supreme Court review ($\bar{x}$ = 249

Table 6.4 Average days for capital cases to conclude with or without the final review and approval by the Supreme Court

Review type	*Violent*	*Property*	*Economic*	*Corruption*	*Public safety*	*Public order*	*All cases*
Death without Supreme Court's review	R:7-852 $\bar{x}$ = 244 (n = 79)	R: 7-1274 $\bar{x}$ = 229 (n = 93)	R: 13-1960 $\bar{x}$ = 441 (n = 25)	R: 113-998 $\bar{x}$ = 308 (n = 42)	R:41-491 $\bar{x}$ = 211 (n = 15)	R: 44-1137 $\bar{x}$ = 249 (n = 32)	R:7-1960 $\bar{x}$ = 273 (n = 286)
Death with Supreme Court's review	n/a	R:879-1382 $\bar{x}$ = 1130 (n = 2)	R:147-1965 $\bar{x}$ = 519 (n = 22)	R:119-1001 $\bar{x}$ = 458 (n = 37)	n/a	R: 62-707 $\bar{x}$ = 215 (n = 14)	R:62-1965 $\bar{x}$ = 449 (n = 75)
Death2 & Life without SC's review	R:88-825 $\bar{x}$ = 289 (n = 28)	R:65-1525 $\bar{x}$ = 412 (n = 30)	R:139-1960 $\bar{x}$ = 638 (n = 11)	R:40-1018 $\bar{x}$ = 526 (n = 16)	R:119-992 $\bar{x}$ = 415 (n = 3)	R:149-1437 $\bar{x}$ = 643 (n = 18)	R:40-1960 $\bar{x}$ = 456 (n = 108)
Death2 & Life with SC's review	R:673-900 $\bar{x}$ = 786 (n = 2)	n/a	R:147-1965 $\bar{x}$ = 602 (n = 6)	R:217-1149 $\bar{x}$ = 552 (n = 5)	n/a	R:163-2044 $\bar{x}$ = 971 (n = 3)	R:147-2044 $\bar{x}$ = 689 (n = 14)
> *10 yrs. without* SC's review	R:104-852 $\bar{x}$ = 230 (n = 21)	R:127-1274 $\bar{x}$ = 628 (n = 30)	R:302-1672 $\bar{x}$ = 5 71 (n = 12)	R:88-980 $\bar{x}$ = 402 (n = 8)	R:128-159 $\bar{x}$ = 141 (n = 5)	R:114-1129 $\bar{x}$ = 29 (n = 10)	R:88-1672 $\bar{x}$ = 434 0 (n = 86)

days) took over a month longer for final legal resolution than capital cases without this review ($\bar{x}$ = 215 days).

When cases with capital and non-capital sentences are compared on their overall length of processing, the average criminal proceedings for capital cases tended to take far less time than serious, non-capital cases. This pattern was consistent for cases with and without final review and approval by the Supreme Court.

There are several plausible explanations for the less time it often took for capital cases to move from one criminal proceeding to another when compared with other serious, non-capital offenses. First, these criminal cases were primarily tried in the past ten years when strike-hard campaigns were at their peak of enforcement. Strike-hard campaigns tended to target the most serious violent and property offenses and were designed to quickly dispose those cases to enhance the impact of punishment. In this unusual sociopolitical context, the more rapid imposition of the death sentence and execution may have become a top priority for law enforcement and judicial agencies.[59] Second, capital cases typically receive more manpower and resources from the law enforcement and the judiciary due to political and public pressure to solve the case in the timely fashion. As a result, these cases may be disposed faster than other serious, non-capital cases.[60] Third, compared to average cases with suspended death sentence and life imprisonment, capital cases with immediate execution may involve more clear-cut facts and circumstances (e.g., multiple deaths involved, extremely large amount of monetary damage involved, repeat offenders), thus required less time to reach the legal ruling.[61]

PROCESS OF EXECUTION

The 1997 Criminal Procedure Law (Article 211) states: "After receiving an Order to execute the death sentence from the Supreme People's Court, the people's courts at lower levels shall, within seven days, deliver the criminal for execution of the sentence." The temporary waiver of the final review and approval authority of the Supreme Court allows the superior courts to send the order of execution to the intermediate courts to carry out the execution. After 1996, the methods of legal execution in China have been shooting and lethal injection.

Various myths and misconceptions often surround legal executions in China and elsewhere. After China's economic reforms in the late 1970s, there is greater uncertainty about how these lethal punishments are actually imposed because public executions are not permitted under the new laws. Media outlets in last two decades are rarely allowed access to actual executions. However, some media coverage of eyewitness accounts of actual executions, particularly execution by lethal injection, has occurred in the past few years. The following depictions of execution process were derived from various media outlets, particularly Web sites as very little scholarly research has documented the process.

Death row

Death row is often considered the physical space that is reserved in prisons for capital offenders awaiting their execution. When compared to their Western counterparts, most Chinese offenders spent little time on death row. In fact, many offenders spent just a few minutes or hours on death row prior to their execution. In the case of Liu Yong, for example, immediately after the Supreme Court's final ruling was announced, Liu was taken from the court to a nearby funeral home to be executed by lethal injection and cremated.[62] Others had their execution date set with the announcement of their final death sentence rulings, typically within days after their death sentence ruling went into effect. For example, Dong Wei was executed ten days after his retrial (also the final review) ended. In contrast, others may wait until after a sentencing rally is held and then be executed in a group.[63]

Even for capital offenders who only had a few days to live, it has been reported that prison officials have tried to conduct political and moral education, psychological counseling, and to encourage the offender to repent and contribute to society. For example, condemned offenders have often been encouraged by the officers to write to their family and the victim's family to express their regret and repentance. Some offenders have also been encouraged to leave a will to donate their organs after execution to repay the society.[64]

Humanitarian measures were also taken in recent years to alleviate death row inmates' suffering while awaiting execution. Death row inmates are now allowed to have a final meeting with their family and some were allowed to take a picture with the family.[65] To reduce their family's psychological pressure, a recent Beijing notice on the meeting between the condemned and the family stipulated that upon been escorted into the meeting room, offender's handcuffs and ankle-fetters shall be removed, and the prison guards shall sit down rather than standing during the meeting.[66]

A report of a twenty-six-minute meeting between offender Wang (convicted and sentenced to death for kidnapping and murder) and his family provided an example of such a final meeting between the condemned and the family. In September 2005 prior to his execution, Wang's mother and sister arranged to meet with Wang at Beijing No. 2 Intermediate Court. Wang, in a t-shirt with a yellow prison vest, was escorted by prison guards to a meeting room and ordered to sit in a chair.[67]

He was able to see and talk to his sister and mother through a sheet of reinforced glass and a telephone linking either side of a partition wall. When he saw his mother being escorted by his sister into the other room, he asked the guard to get a chair for his mother. He tried to stay calm during the meeting, comforting his mother to take care of herself. When asked by his sister whether to further petition for the case, Wang said that "I killed the man. I deserve the death. As long as I meet with you, I have no regret." His sister said "do not live like this in the afterlife." Wang replied with his legs shaking: "I will repay you in the next life." Seeing pictures of family and friends brought by the sister, Wang said "I only treated myself well in this life. I did not treat others right. With the money I got (from the crime), I spent them all on myself." He wiped tears three times when talking to his mother. He turned toward his sister asking her to take care of the mother. "Do not forget to take mother to the hospital for regular check ups." His sister brought him new clothes in a black color. He wore them on the day of the execution.[68]

Final moments prior to the execution

Various descriptive accounts indicate that condemned offenders exhibited different emotions and behaviors in their final moments before execution. Some ask for papers and a pen to write letters to their family. Illiterate offenders typically ask others to write on their behalf. Many spoke little the entire night while others cried. The detention officials, for the most part, tried to satisfy the condemned offenders' request for food, cigarettes, and new clothes if their family had not sent them one, or shaving.[69] It is also reported that some officers stay in the jail cell the entire night to chat with the condemned about their wishes, regrets, and last words.[70]

On the morning of an execution, court and police officials came to the condemned's cell and read the sentencing documents to the condemned offender one last time. The offender was asked about their final words and once again granted the last breakfast (e.g., one report showed that the condemned offender's last breakfast was noodles with minced pork and pickled cucumber).[71] Some offenders were allowed a final meeting with the family.[72]

Execution by shooting

The current Chinese criminal law stipulated two methods of execution: by shooting and by lethal injection. Execution by shooting has been the standard method of execution for the last half a century in the PRC history. In the past, execution by shooting was carried out by the special armed police. In recent years, with the legal reforms of judicial independence, shootings have been carried out by judicial officers who undergo special training for the task.

There is wide regional variability in the physical location of executions by shooting. Some jurisdictions have their own executing grounds, but many other jurisdictions, especially in the countryside, must find an appropriate execution ground every time when executing an offender. Narrative reports also indicate that officers are often sent out to the nearby suburban or rural areas days before the execution to find a place that is both accessible and secure. Upon identifying the spot, the place would be secured by armed police.[73]

On the morning of an execution, the court officials come to the detention center to read the sentencing documents to the condemned offender. After recording the offender's last words and satisfy his/her last wishes (e.g., meeting with family, last breakfast), the offender is placed in handcuffs and ankle-fetters and escorted to the execution ground by the armed court officials in an unmarked court vehicle.[74]

Condemned offenders usually are forced to kneel on the ground with their hands tied behind their back. Upon further verifying the offender's identity, an armed court officer fires a single high-calibre bullet usually into the back of the offender's head from point-blank range.[75]

Execution by lethal injection

Lethal injection only became a valid legal method for execution in China in 1997. Execution by lethal injection quickly gained favor among legal authorities for obvious reasons of humanity and practicality (e.g., less disturbance of nearby residents, implemented in a private place). It was hailed as "scientific" and "civilized development" by public officials, legal scholars and journalists alike, and some even viewed it as paving the way for the ultimate abolition of the death penalty in China.[76]

Regardless of its relative attractiveness as a lethal method, lethal injection is nonetheless far less commonly used than shooting as the execution method in contemporary China. Several factors related to retribution, deterrence, and economic costs account for its lower usage. In particular, citizens openly questioned lethal injection's impact on retribution. "To let offenders die with little pain (with lethal injection)," one Kunming resident wrote to the Yunnan Superior Court, "does not serve the fundamental purposes of punishment." Many residents have also expressed dissatisfaction with the deterrent and retributive effect of lethal injection, and were particularly concerned about favoritism given to corrupt officials.[77] The economic costs (e.g., a typical execution van for lethal injection could cost an average of 400,000 Chinese yuan) is another basic obstacle in the widespread use of this method.

It appears, however, lethal injection will become the dominant method of execution in the near future in China. Since its inaugural use in 1997 by Kunming Intermediate Court of Yunnan Province,[78] other jurisdictions such as Chengdu, Changsha, Beijing, Huangzhou, Qingdao, Shenyang, Xian, and Lanzhou have all experimented with the use of this method of execution.[79] As early as 2001, the Supreme Court urged courts with economic resources to adopt lethal injection.[80] In 2002, the Court issued the *Notice on Using Lethal Injection in Executions* to ensure the standardization of execution procedures through lethal injection.[81]

A recent report disclosing an execution chamber customized for Chengdu Intermediate Court may be illustrative of a typical execution chamber in China.[82] According to the report, the execution chamber was converted from a regular passenger van, cost 400,000 Chinese yuan to build, and has the following characteristics:

> The exterior of the execution van looked no different from an ordinary van, except the red siren on the top of its roof. The van was about 7-meter long with dark tinted windows. The main front door was 1.3 meter in height and 0.6 meter in width. The back of the van was enclosed in the original design and was redesigned to have a double-door to allow the execution bed to be pushed in and out of the van. On the back of the van, there was also a video camera installed to monitor the surrounding premises.
>
> The interior of the van looked completely different from an ordinary van. All seats (more than 20 of them) originally installed in the van were removed. The inside of the van was now divided into two areas, a front area and a back area, with a clear glass window separating the two areas.
>
> The front area contained an area for the driver and an area for directing and monitoring the execution. There was a desk with a telecom and a microphone. From there, the entire execution area in the back could be observed from the clear window.
>
> The back area was where the actual execution would take place. This entire back area was less than 5 square meters. Walking into the van via the front door, on the left hand side of the back area, there was a sink with four foldable seats placed nearby. In the middle of this area, there was an execution bed of 0.8 meter high and 1.8 meter long. The bed was made of aluminum metal, covered with mattress and a sponge pillow. The bed could withhold at least 400 pounds in weight. An anti-bacterial light was installed on the interior ceiling, along with two video cameras.

This report also demonstrates how to prepare for the execution.[83] Specifically, the condemned's left hand is placed on one of the holders of the bed. The condemned is securely fastened with three belts, on the leg, stomach, and chest. When necessary, the offender's hand is handcuffed onto the iron ring installed on the right hand side of the execution bed to ensure the entire process runs smoothly. The executioner sitting in the second foldable seat has easy access to medical equipments and medicines in the small refrigerator. Two stereos play music to ease the condemned's tension. Once the door of the van is closed, the conducting officer issues the order to the executioners through the microphone. From then on, the entire process takes less than two minutes, with the executioner inserting the needle into the condemned's left arm. The computers connected with the video cameras record the entire execution process, including the executed offender's last words. The electrical heart monitor shows whether the condemned's heart stopped beating. Once the heart stops beating, it is recorded and the execution is completed.[84]

A journalist's account of an actual execution in the Gansu province further reveals elements of the process of lethal injection. As reported by Amnesty International, this journalist watched the execution of Dong Jun, who was convicted and sentenced to death for robbery. The following description was provided in this report:

> Dong Jun's ankle chains had already been taken off when he was taken into the execution chamber. He seemed calm and his face was expressionless. On the direction of the person carrying out the execution, Dong Jun climbed onto the execution bed on his own volition, and then put his arm through a hole in a one-way mirror to the other side. Specialist personnel quickly inserted a needle into Dong Jun's arm, connecting a hypodermic pump to a vein. The executing personnel then started the pump and the injecting work was underway. Dong Jun closed his eyes, and there was no sign of pain in his expression. Around a minute later, the computer showed that Dong Jun was brain dead with the monitor displaying a flat line. His heart gradually slowed until it eventually stopped beating.[85]

Several witness reports of lethal injection confirm that these executions took a very brief period of time to complete (as few as seconds and as long as a couple of minutes) and the condemned showed no apparent expression of pain in the process. For example, the first lethal injection execution in Xi'an involved a sixty-eight-year-old convict of murder and took only about ninety seconds to complete.[86] Nanchang Intermediate Court reported an execution with lethal injection in less than a minute.[87]

Liu Yong's final days

The legal drama surrounding the sentence and execution of the convicted organized criminal gang leader, Liu Yong, was saturated and sensationalized in various media accounts (e.g., Internet, newspaper, and television). Given that inside stories about last-minute legal maneuvers in capital cases are rarely reported by the news media, the detailed account of the last 84 hours of Liu Yong's life by a local newspaper is an exceptional and invaluable descriptive narrative of this often low visible process.[88]

Liu's life was temporarily spared on August 15, 2003, by Liaoning Superior Court's modified ruling of a death sentence with a two year suspension of execution. However, Liu received a notice from the Supreme Court for retrial on October 8, 2003. According to the report, he sighed on the way back from the Jinzhou prison to the detention center: "all the efforts we spent on saving my life seemed to be in vain."[89] He seemed to have anticipated the outcome of the Supreme Court's unprecedented retrial. The last four days Liu spent between the recess of the Supreme Court at 6:00 p.m. on December 18 and the last day of his life on December 22, 2003, are chronicled below.

According to the reports, Liu felt depressed when returning to his cell at Jinzhou No. 2 Detention Center after the Supreme Court's recess on December 18, 2003. He refused to eat and to be treated for his wound on his ankle.[90] Liu's emotional state became unstable. He would shed tears at one time when talking about his family, and felt comfort about his accomplishments in life at another time.[91] He only slept for three hours that night.

Officers at the detention center tried to keep Liu physically strong enough to stand the trial by providing him with a variety of foods.[92] They also started political education with Liu.[93] It was reported that with constant counseling and education, Liu's mood changed. He started to eat meals regularly, watch movies, and listen to CDs. He even wrote a letter of thanks for the humanitarian treatment the detention center granted him during his two year stay.

At 7:30 a.m. on December 22, Liu was escorted by eleven police cars to Jinzhou Intermediate Court to hear the verdict.[94] At 8:30 a.m., the trial resumed. Liu's family along with journalists and spectators gathered outside the courtroom. The mood was mixed. While Liu's family members were more reserved and showed sobering expressions, most people were chatting and laughing, and some were optimistic about the outcome.[95] At 9:30 a.m., a few armed police officers left the premise, which was seen as a good sign by Liu's family. Around 10:00 a.m., the two defense attorneys came out the courtroom with one telling the reporters "not good, not good...." Both of them quickly got into Liu's family car and drove away.[96]

At 10:04 a.m., the reporter received a phone message indicating that Liu was sentenced to death with immediate execution. Upon hearing the news, Liu's family quickly gathered and some left the scene immediately. The crowd did not erupt, showing no apparent signs of cheerfulness or somberness.

After the announcement of the final verdict, Liu was allowed to meet with the family members briefly, smoked two cigarettes, drank water, and asked the family member to stick one yuan into his sock. At 11:00 a.m., more than ten police vehicles escorted Liu to the Jinzhou Funeral Home. Along the way, there were police cars every 50 meters to provide security. All nonauthorized vehicles were stopped at 100 meters outside the funeral home. All cars with local license plates were cleared out at the premises to prevent a possible bombing.[97]

At 11:35 a.m., Liu was escorted out from a white van and into an execution van. The van was equipped with technology that allowed the transmission of the execution process live to a projection screen in a room at the funeral home, where officials of the Supreme Court, Liaoning Superior

Court, and Jingzhou Intermediate Court were watching the live coverage of the execution. Liu was executed through lethal injection. Ten minutes later, Liu's body was placed into a yellow box used by the funeral home and it was sent in another van to be cremated.[98]

Around 12:00 p.m., all police cars left the scene. Ten minutes later, Liu's brother called the family waiting outside the funeral home asking them to prepare 5,000 yuan (approximately $600), presumably to pay for the lethal injection and cremation. At 1:30 p.m., all major television channels reported Liu's execution.[99]

CONCLUSION

This chapter described the actual process in death penalty cases in China. It first described the regular three-tiered trial/review process of capital cases, and then discussed extraordinary proceedings involving major, complex capital cases in recent years. As timing in capital cases is critical both for ensuring the defendants' due process rights and the maximum impact of punishment, this chapter also examined the length of time that average capital cases took from arrest to first trial, second trial/first review, and the final review and approval of the death sentence. The execution process involving methods of shooting and lethal injection was also described.

7 Reforms and the future prospects of the death penalty

The death penalty is at a major crossroad in contemporary Chinese society. From a historical perspective, its imposition in the current context has become more rational and civilized. However, from a modern global perspective, the Chinese government's desire to become a major player and leader of the international community will inevitably lead to its reassessment of the death penalty practice. Under the current sociopolitical conditions in China, the death penalty seems to have sufficient official and grass-roots support to play a continued role in crime control and order maintenance even in the face of a global movement toward its abolition.

This concluding chapter discusses the future prospects of the death penalty in China. We review the death penalty debate from different perspectives, including the general public, scholars and practitioners, the ongoing legal reforms pertinent to the death penalty, and its theoretical and practical dilemmas in the context of law and society. The chapter concludes with speculations on the future of the death penalty in China.

DEATH PENALTY DEBATE

The public's view

The use of the death penalty has frequently been portrayed and justified by the strong public support in China's official records and statements.[1] It was quite common for official documents to indicate the reliance on the death penalty by emperors to suppress revolts, executing bandits, maintain social stability and appease the public's indignation.[2] In the PRC, the death penalty has been relied upon as one of the most potent measures to eliminate political opponents and the criminal elements. Major political leaders of the past (e.g., Mao, Deng, Jiang) and the present (e.g., Hu) have all mentioned the public's indignation and outrage about crime when commenting on the imposition of the death penalty for particular criminals involved in corruption and robbery.[3]

Public sentiments about the death penalty are most intensely highlighted in sentencing rallies. Visual images of audiences with facial expressions of anger, rage, disgust, despair and sorrow are common in these public events. Other expressions of condemnation through shouting and holding signs that vilify the offender are transmitted to the living rooms of millions of Chinese people with the aid of television coverage.

As a result of official reports of the public's outrage over the criminal elements of the society and the strong images of pro-death penalty sentencing rallies portrayed by the media, it is commonly assumed that the support for the death penalty is extremely high in China.[4] This perception is further reinforced by scholarly works on the general punitive culture in China, and its lack of humanitarian tradition and rights consciousness.[5]

The degree of support for capital punishment in China, however, has never been scientifically documented and/or empirically verified by research.[6] No national surveys on the death penalty opinions have ever been conducted in China. No studies of random samples of subgroups of the Chinese population have been performed either.[7] The only existing survey data on public attitudes about capital punishment involve small, nonrandom samples (e.g., student populations) and Internet surveys.[8]

Western studies of death penalty opinions indicate that survey results may dramatically change depending on (1) the specificity of the questions posed, (2) the questioning sequence, (3) the alternative measures used, and (4) the participants' demographic composition.[9] Due to the lack of opinion surveys in China, few measurements and indicators have been developed to address these conceptual and methodological issues. While some Chinese surveys asked questions about respondents' general attitude towards the death penalty (e.g., "Are you in favor of the death penalty for a person convicted of a crime?"),[10] other surveys are more case specific. For example, an Internet survey (see http://www.sina.com.cn) has posted the following question for a period of time since December 22, 2003:

> The Supreme Court ruled in its retrial to sentence Liu Yong to death with immediate execution. Some legal experts believed that this ruling reflected the law's fairness and justice. Do you agree with this statement?[11]

An examination of the available survey results from Internet surveys and student samples reveals a general supportive attitude towards the death penalty. For example, Cao and Cullen's study found 78 percent of respondents supported the death penalty.[12] The study by Liang and colleagues in 2005 found that 72 percent of Chinese students (domestic and abroad combined) favored the death penalty as a criminal punishment in China. When alternative punishments (e.g., life imprisonment without the possibility of parole) were listed for particular offenses, the magnitude of support for the death penalty was reduced to 62 percent. In addition, specific deterrence was the most robust predictor for the support of the death penalty found by this study.[13]

The results of various Internet polls also provide some evidence of strong pro-death penalty attitudes in China. These online surveys include the following findings:

- About 70 percent of the 137,127 Internet poll responses were in support of the Supreme Court's death sentence in the retrial of Liu Yong (a convicted organized criminal gang leader). The remaining Internet respondents from December 2003 to November 2005 were either nonsupportive (14 percent) or not sure about the ruling (15 percent).[14]
- A survey of death penalty opinions posted in January 2003 indicates that over three-fourths of the respondents were in support of retaining the death penalty.[15]
- A survey by the Chinese Social Science Academy suggested that less than 1 percent of the respondents supported the complete abolition of the death penalty in China.[16]
- Another online survey conducted by the Web site of the *Legal Morning Newspaper* suggested that by April 11, 2005, 59 percent of votes were against abolishing the death penalty and 10 percent of votes were in favor of completely abolishing the death penalty.[17]
- A popular Chinese Web site Wangyi (http://www.163.com) posted a question on its homepage: "Death Penalty, For or Against," sparked by a controversial hanging of a drug trafficker (a Viet Nam born, Australian citizen) in Singapore on December 2, 2005.[18] All nineteen messages, which were posted within three days of the question posted online, expressed strong support for the retention of the death penalty in China. Most citizens called for stiffer punishment and wider application of the death penalty for corrupt officials, and some insisted that the death penalty was absolutely needed to get rid of the most heinous criminals in society.[19]

Taken together, these public opinion surveys suggest a rather strong level of support for the death penalty among the Chinese general public who participate in these online and student surveys. If these results are representative of Chinese citizens in general, they further suggest that the Chinese support for the death penalty is quite comparable with their Western counterparts in the United States, the United Kingdom, France, and Germany. For example, studies showed that public support for the death penalty in the United States has been relatively high and stable since 1982, ranging from 70 percent to 75 percent in support of capital punishment.[20] In the United Kingdom, only about 20 percent of the public were supportive of abolishing the death penalty for murder in 1965. Since the abolition of the death penalty for ordinary crimes in the U.K in 1966, an estimated 85 percent of these citizens still support the death penalty. In addition, a clear majority (60 percent) of British citizens were in favor of reintroducing the death penalty for all murders in the mid-1990s.[21]

As in China, the public support for the death penalty in Western countries is also primarily justified on the basis of deterrence, retribution and incapacitation.[22] Even when informed of the lack of empirical proof of the deterrence effect of capital punishment, it has been found that proponents of capital punishment remain supportive of the death penalty.[23]

Scholars' views

Scholars' views, particularly of social scientists, are generally not transformed directly and immediately into public policies. They nevertheless provide an important source of knowledge for the general public and may serve as a catalyst for social and policy changes in the long run. There is no exception in the area of the death penalty. For example, in eighteenth-century Europe, when public opinion was overwhelmingly in favor of the death penalty, Italian scholar Beccaria in his 1764 publication "*On Crimes and Punishment*" proposed to abolish the death penalty. While ignored by his contemporaries, Beccaria's view gradually gained support in the following millennium as nations reconsidered their position on the death penalty. Today, almost all nations in Europe have abolished the death penalty either in law or in practice.

In the scholarly community of China, both the abolitionist and retentionist views are present.[24] Qiu Xinglong, Dean of the Law School at Hunan Xiangtan University, represents one of the most prominent scholars who proposed the complete abolition of the death penalty in China.[25]

Qiu was very critical of many Chinese scholars' position on the death penalty, pointing out that "thus far, there has not been one scholar who was a steadfast believer in the complete abolition of the death penalty (in China)."[26] He criticized the current Chinese academic circle for the lack of academic independence and professional integrity. He said that Chinese scholars tended to submit their views to the public policy (in this case, the death penalty) instead of the other way around. If, he said, the scholarly community continues to assert that the death penalty should be abolished in the long run but is needed for the current politico-social conditions, the death penalty will never be abolished.[27] Hao Shoucai, professor of law at Henan University, was also a strong supporter for the abolitionist movement, citing moral and humanitarian reasons in his recent talk at the 2004 Annual Chinese Society of Criminology.[28]

The most popular scholarly view on the death penalty, however, is articulated by Xingliang Chen, professor of law at Beijing University. Chen supported the eventual abolition of the death penalty in China, but regarded the abolition of the death penalty premature under the current conditions in China.[29] His arguments were primarily based on two levels: the current level of economic development and moral development in China.

According to Chen, current Chinese society is at a relatively low level of economic development, providing a context for supporting capital punishment because the relative value of human life is not very high. In particular, he argued that in a less economically developed society, the societal damage caused by a crime is relatively higher than in a more economically advanced society. When compounded with a low level of tolerance on crime, and the lack of means and resources to prevent crime, the death penalty becomes an attractive alternative (e.g., cheaper and easier) to punish wrongdoers under the current economic conditions.

Chen further argued that the level of moral or spiritual development was also crucial for the abolition of the death penalty. He reasoned that in a society with relatively low moral values (e.g., the value of retribution is upheld as much more important than the value of humanness), the support for the death penalty is likely to be strong. He stressed the Chinese cultural tradition of retribution and lowly regarded individual rights, and concluded that the current economic and social conditions make it premature to abolish the death penalty in China.

Chen's views on the death penalty have been widely accepted among the scholarly community and the general public in China. This acceptance, however, is not necessarily because of his retentionist position, but because of his progressive ideas on the death penalty. In particular, Chen was a strong advocate for limiting the scope of the death penalty. He proposed to reduce the current sixty-eight capital offenses to approximately twenty, eliminating one-third of the offenses never used, and the other one-third of nonviolent, economic, and property offenses to be more in line with the international practice.[30] He also proposed to set up more long-term prison sentences (e.g., twenty- or thirty-year sentences) to reduce the use of the death penalty.[31] Other legal scholars have also suggested that the abolition movement in China may be of a gradual process, encompassing the abolition of death penalty for nonviolent crimes first, then for nonlethal crimes, and finally the complete abolition of the death penalty for all crimes.[32]

Influenced by progressive views, recent scholarly discussions on China's death penalty have revolved around how to improve the current system. These current issues include how to prevent torture and coerced confessions, improve the system of legal representation, strengthen the process of final review and approval, abate judicial corruption, and enhance the overall judicial effectiveness and efficiency so that arbitrary and erroneous death sentences and executions could be minimized and the rights of the defendants could be enhanced.[33] As a sign of gradual abolition of the death penalty, representatives of the Fourth Meeting of the Tenth Session of the National People's Congress held in 2006 proposed to abolish the death penalty for corruption-related crimes.[34]

Views by public officials and legal practitioners

Several public official and legal practitioners recently expressed their opinions on the death penalty. The most authoritative official position was expressed by Premiere Wen Jiabao on March 14, 2005, in response to journalists' questions on the current status of the death penalty in China in lieu of the recent cases of wrongful convictions and executions of Li Jiuming, Du Peiwu, Nie Shubin, Huang Yaquan, Huang Shengyu, Sun Wanggang, and Yu Xianglin. Within this context, Premiere Wen asserted that China can not abolish the death penalty given its particular social conditions in the current time, but that is also imperative to mete out the death sentence more carefully and with fairness through the improvement of the legal system.[35]

President of the PRC, Hu Jintao, has also recently pointed out that the death penalty cannot be abolished. Consistent with Premiere Wen's views, President Hu has also stated that the death penalty remains an effective way to deal with the most serious offenders, even though its application must be careful.[36]

President of the Supreme Court, Xiao Yang, in the recent Fourth Meeting of the Tenth Session of the National People's Congress pointed out that abolition of the death penalty does not fit the current social conditions. He further commented on the representatives' proposal of gradual abolition of the death penalty for corruption related offenses by indicating that the current social conditions do not permit the abolition of the death penalty for those nonlethal offenses either.[37]

Vice president of the Supreme Court, Cao Jianmin, stressed the importance of "kill fewer, kill carefully" policy on the death penalty. He has also urged judicial officers to "rigidly execute" every procedure of the legal process to ensure no innocent individual been wrongfully sentenced to death.[38]

Vice-Minister of Justice Zhang Jun has been supportive of gradually replacing the death penalty with the set up of the long-term imprisonment system. He has said that there is currently a lack of alternatives to the death penalty. Based on a survey by the ministry in 2004, most serious criminals who were sentenced to life imprisonment actually stayed in prison for about fifteen years before being released.[39] If longer prison sentences (e.g., thirty to forty years) were available, judges might be more willing to sentence defendants to long-term imprisonment, not the death penalty.

Zhu Zhanping, the defense attorney representing Dong Wei in his appeals, has taken a more practical perspective on the death penalty. In particular, he has said that if the current conditions do not permit the complete abolition of the death penalty, the system should at least maintain respect for human lives and implement this punishment with great care and caution. Zhu has been most critical of the review process, especially based on his personal experiences in the Dong Wei's case. He echoed many scholars' concerns about the need for the Supreme Court to take back the final review and approval authority for all death penalty cases. If the main obstacle for the Supreme Court taking back its final review and approval authority is the lack of financial resources and manpower, Zhu contends that measures such as collecting fees from the defendant's family who wish to appeal the case should be contemplated so that defendants have more legal protections in cases in which they were wrongfully convicted.[40]

A judicial officer from Xuzhou Intermediate Court, Jiangsu province, also has voiced some opposition to the death penalty. In particular, she stated that the current death penalty reform should most urgently focus on improving the legislation on the death penalty, restricting the qualifications of the death penalty, reducing capital offenses, and limiting the imposition of the death penalty.[41] Similar to other officials, this judicial official also contends that to discuss the abolition of the death penalty in the current context is premature.

ONGOING REFORMS

A series of legal developments have been underway to reform many aspects of the legal system in China since the 1990s. These reforms have been directed at the police, the procuratorate, and the judiciary. Of relevance to the death penalty are reforms of the substantive law (e.g., limiting the scope of capital offenses), and procedural law (e.g., the use of torture, confessions, legal representation, the Supreme Court's final review and approval authority).

Limited capital offenses

While divergent opinions exist on the future direction of the death penalty in China, scholars and practitioners seemed to converge on the need to restrict the scope of capital offenses. As discussed previously, the current 1997 criminal law stipulated a total of 68 capital offenses, encompassing a broad categories of violent, property, public safety, public order, economic, and corruption offenses. This dramatic expansion of the scope of capital offenses in the 1990s contradicted the global trend of the restrictive use of capital punishment, and was inconsistent with the Chinese legal reforms of professionalism, formalism, and humanism.

Chen laid out convincing arguments on the feasibility of limiting the scope of capital offenses in contemporary China. He pointed out that among the total of sixty-eight current capital offenses, about one-third of the capital offenses have never been used in practice; and another one third of these capital crimes consisted of nonviolent, nonlethal offenses (e.g., corruption, economic offenses, and public order offenses). Following international practices, if these nonviolent and nonlethal offenses could be sanctioned with non-capital punishment (e.g., long-term incarceration and severe economic penalties), the number of capital offenses could be substantially reduced to around twenty.[42]

The major obstacle to the abolition of capital punishment for economic and corruption offenses is the law's apparent deterrence effect. In particular, given the current sociopolitical context, many fear that offenders convicted of economic and corruption crimes (e.g., smuggling and graft) will easily get away with the crime if a non-capital punishment is imposed because of the rampant political and judicial corruption.[43]

Other scholars have argued that restricting the scope of the death penalty also required that ad hoc interpretations and amendments issued by the National People's Congress and other governmental agencies should be eliminated. By abolishing these practices, a primary means of expanding the scope of the death penalty and implementing mandatory punishments in some cases (e.g., corruption) is severely restricted.[44]

Defendants' rights to silence and legal representation

One of the major challenges in curbing erroneous death sentences and executions involves the role of torture and coerced confessions. Even though the 1996 revised criminal procedure law stipulated the principle of presumption of innocence and entitled more rights to attorneys to curb police abuse, almost all cases of wrongful convictions and/or executions exposed by the media in recent years involved some forms of physical torture and forced confessions. For example, She Xianglin, a former security guard in Hubei province, spent eleven years in jail for murdering his wife. He was released in April 2005 after his wife reappeared in the village. She told reporters that he was tortured by the police interrogators, deprived of sleep for ten days and forced to leave his finger mark on the documents that stated that (1) he admitted to the killing of his wife and (2) the body discovered, which was unidentifiable, was his wife's.[45] In another case involving rape and murder in Hebei, a twenty-one-year-old man was recently found to have been wrongfully executed in 1994 for a crime he did not commit. His attorney recalled that the defendant said that he was beaten prior to confessing the crime.[46]

Holding suspects for prolonged custody and collecting evidence by torture is especially prevalent in rural areas where legal training is lacking among the legal professionals and traditional views and methods of brutality and abuse are more tolerated.[47] According to Chief Justice Xiao Yang's work report to NPC sessions, 80 percent of lawsuits on police torture nationwide were filed at courts of the grassroots level (e.g., rural areas and urban districts).

The widespread police interrogation practices of torture and coercion to extract confession, while having its deep historical roots, reflects more of the weaknesses in the current legal system. For example, the current law does afford a defendant's rights to remain silent and adequate legal representation. Though the law prohibits police torture and brutality, it does not provide mechanisms to ensure its enforcement (e.g., no exclusionary rules; rare and lenient disposition on violators, overemphasis on confession evidence).[48] Any legal safeguards are further restricted because defense attorneys are not allowed to be present in critical stages of the initial criminal investigation before suspects/defendants make their confessions.[49]

Reforms to curb torture and forced confessions have been placed on the top agenda of several agencies. For example, the procuratorate in China is in charge of supervising the police and judicial activities. It bears the direct responsibility and authority to regulate, monitor, and investigate police misconduct in torture and forced confessions. A report showed that the procuratorate in 2004 had probed and dealt with more than seven hundred cases involving illegal police detention and torture nationwide[50] and an approximately 1,600 police officers were charged with abuse power. [51]

Internally, the procuratorate attempts to strictly follow the agency protocol to detect and investigate any allegations by criminal defendants of the possible claims of confessions extracted by torture. The top official of the Supreme People's Procuratorate (SPP) told a reporter that in the future, before prosecuting a case, criminal suspects will be asked whether they were forced to make a false confession, and the lead prosecutor must carefully examine reports prepared by the police to detect any signs of forced confessions. Once determined, prosecutors must immediately report the police abuse to the higher level of the procuratorate and ask the police to rectify the problem. For serious abuse, the police will be investigated and held legally responsible.[52]

Recognizing that forced confession is a "salient problem" in the criminal justice system, the legislative body is likely to amend a bill on Offenses against Public Order, aiming at increasing criminal penalty for the violation of public order and limiting police power.[53] This bill is expected to stipulate in more stern language that forced confessions are "strictly forbidden and legally invalid." Police officers who are involved in extorting confessions through torture will be held either criminally or administratively responsibilities based on the severity of their conduct.[54]

While it is important for the oversight judicial and procuratorate agencies to be more alert of police misconduct, it seems more effective to simply reform the process of police interrogations. A recent report from the Ministry of Public Security suggests that China will gradually adopt live voice recording of the entire police interrogation involving lethal cases and organized crime cases.[55] Another pilot project led by the top prosecution offices and the Chinese University of Political Science and Law was recently launched to allow suspects to be interrogated in the presence of lawyers, or by recording and videotaping the entire process.[56] Other reform attempts included allowing defense attorneys' greater access to police and prosecution files, increasing their presence during police interrogation at all times, and improving and enforcing the State Compensation Law that was passed in 1995.[57] The State Compensation Law mainly affords plaintiffs' rights to seek financial compensation from the government when affected by wrongful and illegal administrative decisions and measures (e.g., policing coercion and torture).[58]

The Supreme Court's final review and approval authority

According to several speeches in 2004 and 2005 by Xiao Yang (President of the Supreme Court), China's Supreme Court is contemplating whether to take back the final review and approval authority for the death penalty in all cases.[59] Premiere Wen in 2005 also stated that one of the judicial reforms will include the recall of the final review and approval authority by the Supreme Court.[60] Recently, legal scholars and lawmakers have urged the Supreme Court to take back the final review and approval authority on all death penalty cases.[61] All of these official, scholar and practitioners' comments and activities indicate that the use of the Supreme Court as the only final authority over capital cases will become inevitable in the near future in China.

The current debate on the final review and approval of the death penalty cases has converged on the need for a central, national authority for this function. However, different groups diverge on their views about how the system will be set up. More specifically, the debate focuses on the goals, the nature of the review and approval process, and the organizational structure.[62]

Competing theories and justifications have been advanced to support the Supreme Court's reestablishment as the final review and approval authority on the death penalty cases. Some of these supporting arguments include (1) preventing erroneous killings, (2) reducing the use of death sentences, (3) providing uniform standards for death sentences, and (4) serving the symbolic function that the Chinese government is cautious when meting out the death sentence.

Different goals of capital punishment may place different demands on financial resources and professional expertise on the Supreme Court. For example, if the goal is serving as a symbolic function to show the world that all death sentences are finally reviewed and approved by the Supreme Court in China, it may only mean an additional administrative layer that capital cases must go through, rather than involving any substantive review of either the facts or evidence in the process. In this regard, other goals such as preventing erroneous killing and limiting the use of death sentences may not be fulfilled. In contrast, if the main goal is to unify the standards and limiting the scope of capital punishment, the Supreme Court must more carefully review the facts and the laws in the case, which requires more resources and experienced judicial officers in this area.

Two different processes have been proposed for the final review and approval authority on the death penalty. One involves administrative review. This administrative review refers to the process of review that focuses primarily on procedural justice. Under this perspective, if the application of the law was correct and no obvious illegal conduct was involved (e.g., coerced confessions, erroneous judgments), the lower court's ruling should be sustained. This type of review is driven by formality and process, involves little witness testimony in court, no public hearings, and focuses primarily on documents prepared by procuratorate, the defense, and the lower courts. Under this model of administrative review, the scope of the review is quite limited and the symbolic function is greater than its actual value of preventing possible errors in judgment.

The other process for the final review and approval authority involves an adjudicative component. This adjudicative process is similar to a normal trial. Facts, evidence, and the application of law must be reviewed more closely and carefully. It involves necessary hearings and testimonies from both sides, particularly from the condemned offender and the defense attorney. The advantage of this adjudicative process certainly is the reexamination of facts and evidence and possible prevention of any erroneous facts and evidence admitted to the court. Its drawback is that it demands more resources.[63]

Scholars and legal practitioners have also debated about how to set up the organizational structure for the final review and approval of capital cases. Three views emerged: (1) to set up regional district courts (e.g., similar to the U.S. federal district courts); (2) to set up circuit courts; and (3) to entrust the Supreme Court, headquartered in Beijing, to review and approve all cases. Generally speaking, legal practitioners preferred the Supreme Court to be the only and final authority over the review and approval of all capital cases because it requires little organizational restructure and prevents local protectionism and corruption. In contrast, scholars seemed to be more in favor of setting up circuit courts in each province for the following reasons. Circuit courts can significantly reduce financial costs associated with the increasing number of capital cases reviewed by the Supreme Court by cutting down the costs for transporting and providing accommodations for defendants, witnesses and legal professionals from one province to the capital city of Beijing for live hearings. Circuit courts could also prevent local protectionism and corruption from judicial officers and legal personnel appointed by the Supreme Court and through a rotating work schedule (e.g., judicial officers change their post every few years to prevent from establishing local ties).

Currently, the more pragmatic approach proposed by the legal practitioners seemed to win over other arguments. In fact, the Standing Committee of the National Peoples' Congress announced the creation of the No. 3, No. 4, and No. 5 Criminal Courts within the Supreme Court. Many predict that the creation of these new courts within the Supreme Court will help pave the way for the Court to take back its final review and approval authority over the death penalty cases.[64]

DEATH PENALTY IN THE CONTEXT OF LAW AND SOCIETY

Scholars of sociological jurisprudence and legal realism invariably believed that law is a product of particular political, economic and social conditions in a society. Different from social morality and community norms, law nevertheless must be rational, formal, and consistent in reflecting social justice. When the rule of law is challenged, the legitimacy of the political, economic, and social systems is also likely to be questioned.

The death penalty in law and practice is often at the center of the public attention as the testing ground for law and justice. On the one hand, it is expected that law be applied equally, uniformly and objectively. In contrast, law is also expected to be pliable and flexible to accommodate particular circumstances. This contradiction can be best illustrated in the case of Wang Binyu, currently on trial for murder. This fairly routine murder case has raised several complicated social and legal issues.

Case of Wang Binyu

The facts and evidence against convicted defendant Wang Binyu for the murder of four people is not very complicated. Wang is a twenty-seven-year-old, rural migrant worker from a poor, western region of Gansu province. He experienced many of the same life challenges as other migrants working in urban China: low pay, poor living conditions, little social security protections, and prejudice from urbanites. Like millions of migrant rural works in China, Wang's low wages were withheld in back pay by his employer, Wu Xingguo, in the amount of more than 5,000 yuan (equivalent to $620). Needing to pay for his father's leg surgery, Wang asked Wu Xingguo for the back pay in May, 2005. Initially refusing to pay and then forced by the local labor bureau, Wu Xingguo, agreed to pay Wang within five days. Returning from the labor bureau on May 11, Wang was locked out from his factory dorm.

Without money and a place to sleep, Wang went with his brother (Wang Binyin) to Wu Xingguo's residence to ask for the back pay that evening, carrying a knife with him. Wu refused to open the door, and said that he just gave Wang 50 yuan that afternoon, and he did not have any money. They argued by the window. As Wang continued to knock on the door, Wu Xinguo called Wu Hua (a supervisor of Wang's work team) to help make Wang leave. Wu Hua then called Su Wencai (his father-in-law), Su Zhigang (brother-in-law), and Xu Xianglan (his wife) for help.

The court document stated that over the heated arguments, Su Wencai slapped Wang Biyu on his face, and the argument quickly escalated. Wang pulled out the knife and stabbed all four people on the scene. Wu Xinguo became scared and went to call the police. Meanwhile, Wang saw Wu Xinguo's wife Tang Xiaoqin helping wounded Su Zhigang. He stabbed Tang five times on the stomach, arms, and legs, causing Tang severe injury. When Wang saw Wu Xinguo come back, Wang gave him a chase with a bloody knife in his hand and yelling "I have nothing to live for now!" Losing Wu Xinguo in the chase, Wang returned to the scene and again stabbed the four victims. He then left the scene and threw the knife in the nearby Yellow River. At 11:55 p.m., Wang surrendered to the local police and confessed to the crime.

According to the police report cited in the court document, Wang stabbed a total of forty-seven times, causing four deaths and one severe injury. There were numerous witnesses at the scene, but none tried to stop the crime.[65]

On June 29, 2005, Wang was convicted and sentenced to death with immediate execution by the Intermediate Court of Shizuishan in Ningxia province. Currently, the case is been reviewed by the Ningxia Superior Court.[66]

Although Wang's fate is unknown as the final ruling is pending, widespread public debate over the incident has emerged involving both legal scholars and the general public. The debate sheds light on issues of law and social justice, but ultimately questioned the legitimacy of the death penalty by asking "does Wang deserve the death penalty?"

Social background of the case of Wang Binyu

Wang Binyu's case sparked huge public debate and outcry for sympathy and justice because Wang was a rural migrant worker and the situational events precipitating the tragedy (Wang's wages were withheld by the employer) was a common experience shared by millions of rural migrant workers in China.

Since the economic reforms, major social conflicts in China involve disputes between migrants and urbanites and, more specifically, rural migrant workers and local employers. On the one hand, rural migrant workers contributed significantly (e.g., more than 530 billion yuan a year, the equivalent of $66 billion) to local economies outside their homes, helping improve both the urban and rural living standards. Nonetheless, the gap between urban and rural earnings continued to widen because rural migrant workers have to endure long hours of physical labor with minimal security protection, poor living conditions, humiliation and abuse by their employer, and prejudice by urbanites.[67] Worse yet, their economic rights are not protected with their payments frequently defaulted by the employer.[68]

Wang Binyu's experience was typical of other rural migrant workers. Wang's tragedy reflected a deeply imbedded social system prejudicial to rural migrant workers — the urban household registration system (e.g., rural migrant workers are a marginalized population in the city without the permanent urban registration), low social status as a migrant worker, and the lack of social security protection.[69]

Like millions of peasants, Wang quit school after the fourth grade to help his parents support the family by working on a farm. Upon turning seventeen, he went to work at the Gansu Tianshui construction site for more money, earning 7.5 yuan ($1) per day. One time, he fell into a seven-meter deep well and nearly drowned while working on the construction frame. When he was pulled up, he was only given cold pills for his illness.

In 2003, Wang found work at a heat-preservation factory in Ningxia province. His job was to apply rockwool and iron sheeting around steel pipes. Supplied with only a hat and gloves but no special protective clothing, the workers suffered allergic reactions to rockwool (i.e., red and itchy skin). Later Wang became the team leader, earning 35 yuan ($4.5) per day, payable at the end of the year subject to a deduction of 300 yuan ($40) as personal bond and more than 1,000 yuan ($120) for board and meals. During work, Wang often had arguments with the technician/foreman Wu Hua (one of the victims in the case), and had been verbally abused and physically beaten by him. Even though Wang's contract stated free room and board, and paid medical insurance by the employer, Wang did not receive any of these benefits.[70] Wang Binyu, in an interview, told the reporter that "life in jail is much better than on the construction site, here at least he was not beaten, and has his rights."[71]

Objectivity of law and relativity of social context

Wang's murder case had both obvious aggravating circumstance and several mitigating factors. The first trial court appeared to place a greater emphasis on the aggravating circumstances when issuing the ruling. These aggravating circumstances cited by the court included the extremely severe consequence of the crime (e.g., four deaths and one serious bodily injury), the repeated and brutal stabbing of a total of forty-seven times (particularly involving the innocent wife of Wu Xingguo, who was there to help another victim and begged the defendant not to hurt her), and the offender's murderous intent derived from the knife he carried that night.[72]

The defense attorneys in this case argued for a lesser sentence based on various mitigating factors. In particular, the defendant Wang voluntarily surrendered himself to the police authority and confessed to the crime, which in accordance to the Chinese law warrants a sentencing reduction. The defense attorney claimed "self-defense" with a series of events preceding the incident, that the incident was precipitated by the victim (e.g., the slap on Wang's face by one of the victims and verbal abuse, being called a "dog" by one of the victims, and a long history of physical and verbal abuse at the hands of supervisors and contractors), the cause of the crime was the back pay owed by the employer of the victim to the offender, and Wang's frustration resulting from the lack of support from social and legal aid agencies to resolve the issue of withheld wages. To appeal to the victims' family, Wang also openly apologized to the victims' family and begged for forgiveness and judicial leniency.

From the standpoint of law's objectivity, the lower court insisted upon the death sentence with immediate execution, arguing that even though Wang was owed wages and was humiliated when asking for the payment, these facts did not justify his murderous act of killing four people and severely wounding one. The method of killing was cruel, circumstances involved were severe and the consequences were extremely grave. Even though he voluntarily surrendered and confessed to the crime, he should not be granted judicial leniency.[73]

In the appeal that is currently pending, the defense attorney further raised the appeal issues that were not only related to the legal aspect of this case, but also its human and social aspect. The defense attorney reasoned that according to the Chinese law, only the most heinous crimes (*zuida erji*) deserve the death penalty. In this case, the attorney argued, even though Wang's crime was severe (*zuida*), it was not heinous (*erji*). Wang did not have an evil intent. All he wanted was to get back his wages withheld by his employer to support the family and pay for his father's leg surgery.

Citing the recent outpouring of sympathy and support by the public, the attorney further argued that for the death penalty to be imposed, a crime must have incited public's indignation and outrage. In this case, contrary to the public's indignation, there was overwhelming public sympathy for Wang and for what he represents — millions of rural migrant workers who experience prejudice and abuse in their everyday lives. The defense attorney asked for the court to modify the sentence to the suspended death sentence.[74]

While the final sentence ruling remains pending (if Wang were to be sentenced to death with immediate execution by the superior court, the sentence would be final and Wang would be executed immediately), we can preview the possible arguments to be used by the high court to sustain the low court's ruling. One such argument was provided by Professor Zhou of Qing Hua University. Arguing from both aspects of law's absoluteness and possible societal impact of a legal decision, Zhou stated that executing Wang was justified because (1) the right to life is absolutely guaranteed for everyone, not just for the defendant; (2) Wang did not act in the legal sense of self-defense even given the special circumstances of the owed wages, and verbal and physical abuse; (3) the extremely grave nature of Wang's act canceled the effect of Wang's voluntary surrender; and (4) to spare Wang's life will send a dangerous signal to other migrant workers that taking laws into one's own hand is acceptable, and will likely to cause further instability and social unrest.[75]

It is not rare for Chinese courts to consider circumstances involved in a particular case when rendering criminal sentences (e.g., offender's good attitude and meritorious service, compensation to the victim). In fact, it is almost a requirement for judges to consider particular circumstances, criminal motivations, and possible social and legal impact, when meting out sentences. Xiao Yang, President of the Supreme Court, once said that :

> The Chinese society has had a long historical tradition of ritual propriety. Law cannot be a panacea for all social problems. Extra-legal factors, such as morality and community norm cannot be ignored in the judicial process. Judicial decisions must be based on whether they can help advance social stability and economic development, rather than purely pursue the objectivity of the law.[76]

The case of Wang Binyu is unusual because it magnified the influence of social context on legal decisions to the point where it almost overwhelmed the objectivity of the law. Take public opinions in this case for example. A sample of posted messages on the Internet cited below illustrates the public's sentiment on the case.[77]

- Wang's action fits the broad interpretation of self-defense. He does not deserve the death penalty.
- If Wang was sentenced to death, contractors who owed Wang's wages should be held to legal responsibilities too.
- In Liu Yong's case (organized criminal gang leader reviewed in chapter 6 of this book), many legal experts came out to support Liu. How come no experts expressed their sympathy toward a poor peasant?
- We should establish a jury system. We cannot let the crooked judges, who only work for special interests, to rule whatever they want.
- The only way to appease the public's indignation over the employers' exploitation of rural migrant workers is to spare Wang's life.
- The employers after the Liberation (referring to the establishment of the PRC) are even worse than the landlords prior to the Liberation. My dad told me that even though peasants were exploited by the landlords in the old society, they were paid daily for their work.
- Wang Binyu's case is a wake-up call for the privileged and the government in our society. If millions of rural migrant workers continued to receive the second-class citizen treatment by urban residents, they would erupt and rebel as they had nothing to live for. It would be a slap on the face of millions of rural migrant workers if Wang were sentenced to death.

Consequentially, scholars worry that the strong public opinion and sentiment in Wang's case may affect judicial independence and impartiality. They argued that judges must try cases based on judicial documents, not public opinion. The public only observed parts of the case, not the complete picture. The brutality in this case was not sufficiently portrayed by the media, but only the selected stories of Wang. They said that if you look at the victims in this case, all four of them were innocent victims, who did not owe Wang money, and were all poor rural migrant workers. Judges must consider all facts and evidence in this case in order to uphold the integrity of the law.[78]

Some cautioned that media overexposure in this case, just as in Dong Wei's case, may cause backlash, eliminating the slim chance, if any, to revive the case because of the possible media speculation and finger-pointing if the verdict was modified.[79] Other legal scholars believe that law exists in society, and must be subject to social influence. However, such influence should be formalized and institutionalized, not driven by sporadic public sentiment and particular criminal events.[80] Absence of the common law jury system where public opinion and societal norm may be introduced by the average citizens serving on the jury and through a standard court proceeding, the Chinese courts are experimenting with a sentencing revaluation report that will integrate offenders' past experiences and behaviors into sentencing considerations.[81]

FUTURE PROSPECTS AND IMPLICATIONS

While China certainly has had a long history of the use of the death penalty for order maintenance and crime control, the recent series of economic and legal reforms indicate that the scope of the death penalty is likely to be restricted and the standards for its application will be made more uniform. Within this context of legal reforms, several social forces have been playing an indispensable role in helping shape laws and public policies on the death penalty.

One such social force is the media and public opinion, primarily driven by the information age of the Internet. As China is a vast country with great disparities in political, economic, and cultural development, public opinions and sociocultural values may dramatically diverge by region and population. In several high-profile capital cases in recent years, it was not the legal agencies (e.g., the police, the procuratorate, the court) that first exposed the case, but rather the media. Interestingly, several high-profile cases in recent years were first reported not by the local media, but by a media from another region of the country. For whatever the reasons that the local media in China tended to remain silent on major issues (e.g., local protectionism, desensitized with local practices and norms), media, aided by the Internet, is able to quickly rally the public's sentiment and opinion on certain issues and exert its impact on the legal practice in some high-profile cases.[82]

The second social force is the external environment, driven by the international abolitionist movement. The past century witnessed dramatic development in the death penalty law and practice in the global context, with the current number of abolitionist countries exceeding the retentionist countries. Even among the retentionist countries, laws and practices are changing to reduce unnecessary suffering of the condemned and increase the exempt populations from the death penalty.[83] China, determined to become the major player and leader of the world in the twenty-first century, is greatly aware of these developments, as indicated by many public officials' speeches and legal scholars' work, and has tried to adapt to the international trend with recent reforms of its legal system.[84]

The third major force is the desire of the Chinese government to improve its citizens' living standards, including the rights of the individual. In numerous occasions when questioned about its human rights records. Chinese political leaders invariably comment that they respect the rights of individuals in a broader sense, including not just political rights, but more importantly economic, social and cultural rights. If, they reasoned, the very survival of the Chinese citizens was at the stake (e.g., shortage in basic living necessities such as food, medicine), mere discussions of political freedom and rights would become ludicrous. The leaders believed that the most urgent need for China was to feed its 1.3 billion people and provide them with adequate shelter and education. From the perspective of the Chinese leadership, only after achieving these basic requirements is it meaningful to discuss the protection of individual rights within the Western interpretation of that concept.

After more than twenty years of economic reforms, China's economy has experienced unprecedented growth, living standards have improved dramatically, and citizens have enjoyed growing freedom of employment, housing, school, and travel. Under these conditions, more and more attention is now focused on improving citizens' rights through the reforms of the legal system (e.g., the passage and revision of the state compensation law, administrative litigation law, and various procedure laws, and the elimination the practice of "Shelter and Investigation" that subjected many citizens, particularly migrants, to random police search, detention and investigation). Among them, the reforms of the death penalty law and practice have taken the center stage.[85] According to public officials and legal scholars, the next few decades may be characterized by major changes in the Chinese death penalty laws and practices, primarily in areas of restricting its scope, improving fairness of the proceeding, and gradually replacing the death sentence with a long-term imprisonment sentence.[86]

CONCLUSIONS AND A COMPARATIVE PERSPECTIVE

This review and analysis of the death penalty law, theory, and practice in China has revealed that the death penalty is a product of a particular political, economic, and social condition. Even though international patterns of the abolitionist and retentionist countries suggest that the death penalty is becoming more independent of particular political structure (e.g., democracy or totalitarian regime), economic development, and social conditions (e.g., high or low crime rates), the death penalty in China remains strongly related to its political, economic, and social development. For example, the justification for corruption being a capital offense lies primarily in the need to protect the integrity and legitimacy of the government. Economic crimes such as smuggling and financial fraud are subject to the death penalty because the current socialist market economic system remains fragile, and a sound and orderly economic order is vital to the entire nation's vitality. In addition, many illicit crimes such as prostitution and drugs, if uncontrolled, are often thought to erode social morality and pollute the spiritual health of the nation.

These justifications are widely accepted in China because of the value differences between the East and the West. In Western countries, individual freedom and rights are upheld as the most important fundamental value of the society. The death penalty is questioned within the context of undue governmental coercion and deprival of individual's rights to life. In the Chinese context, however, rights of the collectives and political, economic and social stability are the most important value. The Chinese are willing to sacrifice individual freedom and rights to achieve stability and social good. One example of this approach is the current effort in building a "harmonious society" (*hexie shehui*) in China to strengthen the weakening collectivism in the process of moving toward the market economy. Even though some scholars have already voiced concerns about the danger of using oppressive and punitive means to suppress elements of the society that cause social disharmony,[87] the legitimacy of the death penalty is less questioned as it is seen as one of the most potent weapons to protect the social interest against a few bad elements of the society.

In contrast to the theoretical and structural justification for the death penalty, the majority of studies on the death penalty in China have been law-oriented. That is, the studies have primarily focused on law's rationality, consistency, fairness, and implementation, but they tend to ignore its implications on the larger society (e.g., whether the death penalty reduces crime). This is partly due to the slow development of social science research in China. However, recent public debates on the Internet over several high-profile death penalty cases may help shift scholars' attention from law to society.

It seems that any movement toward abolition of capital punishment in China must involve both legal infrastructure (e.g., setting up a long-term incarceration as a viable alternative) and public education. The primary elements of public education would involve greater discussions of the social science evidence on the deterrent value of capital punishments, humanitarian issues, and increased public awareness of the sociopolitical disparities that often arise in the imposition of these legal sanctions.

As China moves through the twenty-first century, there has been a growing debate among people in all segments of this society about the value of the death penalty. However, current policies and practices focus primarily on its fair and impartial implementation of capital punishment rather than abolishing the death penalty. It remains a primary mechanism of social control in modern China.

Appendix: Judicial judgment documents for a sample of capital cases

Appendix contains selected judicial judgment documents issued by courts of various levels. These documents were translated by the first author of this book, Hong Lu.

Each judicial judgment document involves at least one offender sentenced with the death penalty or the suspended death penalty. Ten cases from six offense categories were selected, including violent crime: murder (cases 1 & 2), rape (case 3), intentional assault (case 4), property crime (theft, case 5), economic crime (manufacturing counterfeited currency, case 6), corruption (bribery taking, case 7), public safety (bombing, case 8), and public order crime (selling narcotics, case 9; and forcing others into prostitution, case 10).

CASE 1

Wang Hua et al.: murder, firearm theft, and dereliction of duty case

Judicial Judgment Document of First Trial:
 Yichang Intermediate People's Court of Hubei Province (1998).
 Yi Intermediate Criminal First #1.
Judicial Judgment Document of Second Trial:
 Superior People's Court of Hubei Province (2001).
 Er Criminal Final #17.
Judicial Judgment Document of Retrial:
 Yichang Intermediate People's Court of Hubei Province (1998).
 Yi Intermediate Criminal First #3.
Judicial Judgment Document of Retrial Review:
 Superior People's Court of Hubei Province (2001).
 Er Criminal Final #112.
Original Prosecutorial Agency:
 The People's Procuratorate of Yichang, Hubei Province.
Appellant (Defendant in the first trial):

Wang Hua

Male, twenty-five years old, Tujia ethnicity, originally from Changyang Tujia (Autonomous County, Hubei Province, middle school education, self-employed, arrested on December 19, 1997.)

Defense Attorney:

Jiang Hua

Zhongtian Law Firm, Yichang.

Appellant (Defendant in the first trial):

Deng Xinping

Male, twenty-seven years old, Tujia ethnicity, originally from Changyang Tujia (Autonomous County, Hubei Province, two-year college education, formerly employed as coach and security guard of the People's Military Cadre Training Center of Yichang City, arrested on December 19, 1997.)

Defense Attorney (first trial):

Li Chunlin

Yichang #2 Law Firm.

Defense Attorney (retrial):

Chen Aihua

Zhenyuan Law Firm of Yichang.

First Trial Completed

January 4, 1998

Second Trial Completed:

January 13, 1998

Retrial Completed:

March 24, 1998

Review of Retrial Completed:

April 22, 1998

Prosecuting and defense arguments in the first trial

The People's Procuratorate of Yichang, Hubei Province accused the defendants Wang Hua and Deng Xinping of conspiring to steal firearms for murder. Defendant Deng went to Yichang People's Military Cadre Training Center and stole a handgun on November 13, 1997. That afternoon, Wang and Deng went to Yichang Haitong Building and attempted to kill Deng Dong, who had conflicts with Deng Xinping, They were not successful. The two defendants then went to Hubei Sanxia Technology College. Wang Hua fired shot that killed Li Xiaorong and Zhang Kailai, both students of the College.

While on the run, the defendants also killed Tong Xiaoli in Luo Yang City of Henan Province on November 19, 1997, and Mu Yong in Dangyang City of Hubei Province on November 20. Defendant Li Qiang allowed

Deng Xinping to stay at the Office of the Training Center in violation of the Center's policy, and was considered responsible for a handgun that was stolen because of the failure to carry a key with him at all time that locked up the weapon. Defendant Wang Hua had committed murder; defendant Deng Xinping had committed murder and firearm theft; and defendant Li Qiang had committed dereliction of duty.

Defendant Wang, Deng and Li provided testimonies about the crime. Defendant Wang's defense attorney claimed that the victim shared some blame for the crime. Defendant Deng's defense attorney claimed that Deng's theft of firearm was for the purpose of committing murder, thus should not be counted as separated offenses. Defendant Li's defendant attorney argued that Li's supervisor should share some responsibilities, not just him.

Facts and evidence in the first trial

Yichang Intermediate People's Court of Hubei Province conducted a public trial. The court presented the following facts and evidence:

Defendant Wang Hua resigned from his job and started a small business in July 1996. He opened a photo shop with a rented office from the landlord Li and started to date Li's daughter, Li Xiaorong, then an eighteen-year-old college student. In October 1997, Li Xiaorong started to date classmate Zhang Kailai (then twenty years old). Defendant Wang was resentful of both Li and Zhang and wanted to seek revenge. In November 1997, Wang and Deng conspired to murder. Deng suggested to kill Deng Dong, with whom he had previous conflicts. To achieve the goal, the two defendants sought to steal firearms from the Training Center where Deng's friend, Li Qiang, worked.

On November 7, the two defendants went to the Training Center and found Li. Deng suggested that they go target shooting. Li did not seek the approval from the supervisor, and took the two defendants to the target shooting location. Li took out firearms and ammunitions from the storage garage in front of the two defendants.

On November 12, Deng went to the Training Center and invited Li to play cards until 3:00 a.m. the next day. While Li needed to go out, Li took Deng to sleep in his office. Deng took the key, opened four security doors, and stole one handgun.

At noon of November 13, Deng gave Wang the stolen handgun. They went to the workplace of Deng Dong and attempted to kill him. They then went to the Sanxia Technology College and killed Li and Zhang with five shots fired by Wang. The two victims were dead at the scene. At 7:00 p.m., they went back to Deng Dong's place to try to kill him, and again were unsuccessful. They fled to Luoyang, Hunan province the same night. On November 16, defendant Deng left Luoyang alone and was arrested in Huainan City, Anhui province.

At 9:00 a.m. of November 18, defendant Wang had an altercation with saloon worker Tong Xiaoli for unpaid service. Wang shot Tong to death at the scene. At 3:00 p.m. of November 20, 1997, defendant Wang tried to escape from the Yanwu training station of Dangyang City, Hubei Province, and was stopped and interrogated by security guard Mu Yong. He fired a shot at Mu and killed him instantly. Defendant Wang was finally caught in Huihua City, Hunan province on December 9, 1997, with a handgun and 20 rounds of ammunition.

The above facts were supported by the following evidence:

1. Crime report;
2. Crime scene investigation report and recovered handgun and ammunitions;
3. Coroners' reports on victim's Li, Zhang, Tong, and Mu;
4. Forensic report;
5. List of confiscated handgun and ammunitions;
6. Witnesses Chen, Q., Chen, Y., He, Wang, SQ., Wang, SZ., Guan, Wang, RL., Li, J., Li, Y., Zhu, and Deng's testimonies;
7. Training Center's certification of a lost handgun;
8. Police report;
9. Defendant Wang Hua and Deng Xinping's testimonies.

Legal reasoning by the first trial court

Yichang Intermediate People's Court of Hubei Province ruled that defendants Wang Hua and Deng Xinping conspired to steal firearms for the purpose of committing murder for revenge. Their act constituted murder. Their criminal circumstances were extremely severe, consequences were extremely grave, and should be punished accordingly. Defendant Li Qiang did not perform his job function with due diligence and this action resulted in the theft of a handgun. His act constituted the dereliction of duty. His criminal circumstances were extremely severe and thus should be punished with severity.

Defendant Deng's defense attorney claimed that Deng's crime should not be counted separately. The procuratorate's charge for defendant Wang and Deng was murder. Defendant Li's charge for dereliction of duty was based on clear facts and accurate and sufficient evidence. The procuratorate's charge of defendant Deng for theft of firearms was not supported by the court.

Sentences by the first trial court

Yichang Intermediate People's Court of Hubei Province issued the following rulings based on Article 232, the first clause of Article 397, and the first clause of Article 57, the first clause of Article 25, and Article 36 of the PRC Criminal Law:

1. Defendant Wang Hua was convicted of murder and sentenced to death and deprival of political rights for life;
2. Defendant Deng Xinping was convicted of murder and sentenced to death and deprival of political rights for life;
3. Defendant Li Qiang was convicted of dereliction of duty and sentenced to five years of imprisonment;
4. Defendant Wang Hua was ordered to pay for the funeral costs of 2,000 yuan each for victims Li and Zhang.

Summary of the second trial court

After the announcement of the sentence by the first trial court, all three defendants appealed. Defendant Wang claimed that Deng's theft of firearms was the cause of crime. He suffered from mental illness. He showed good attitude and confessed to the crime. Defendant Deng claimed that he did not encourage Wang to murder. He did not have the intent to kill Li and was not at the scene when Wang killed Li. He showed remorse. Defendant Li claimed that the management of the training center had major problems. He did not receive any necessary training for the job. The night that he left from the job post was requested by the supervisor.

The high court ruled that the facts presented by the procuratorate on defendant Li's dereliction of duty were clear and the evidence was sufficient. However, facts used to charge defendant Wang and Deng were unclear. The High Court also ruled that defendant Deng not only committed murder, but also theft of firearms, thus should be sentenced and punished for both offenses.

Based on the third clause of Article 189 of the PRC Criminal Procedure Law, the Superior People's Court of Hubei ruled:

1. Dismiss the original ruling of Yichang Intermediate People's Court;
2. Return the case to Yichang Intermediate People's Court for a retrial.

Summary of the retrial

Yichang Intermediate People's Court of Hubei Province adopted the facts and evidence used in the original trial and concluded:

Defendant Wang Hua intentionally deprived other persons' lives. His acts constituted murder, and circumstances involved were extremely severe, consequences were grave, thus deserved severe punishment. Defendant Deng Xinping secretly stole firearms for the purpose of revenge and murder. Defendant Deng gave Wang the handgun, which caused serious consequences. His theft of firearms involved serious circumstances. In addition, he was involved in Wang's killing of two persons, thus constituting murder. Defendant Li Qiang, as a security guard for safeguarding firearms, acted irresponsibly, leading to the loss of handguns, and causing severe consequences. His act involved extremely serious circumstances, thus constituted dereliction of duty.

Based on Article 232, Clause 2 of Article 127, Clause 1 of Article 397, Clause 1 of Article 57, Article 69, Clause 1 of Article 25, and Article 36 of the PRC Criminal Law, Yichang Intermediate People's Court of Hubei Province ruled:

1. Defendant Wang Hua was convicted of murder, and sentenced with the death penalty and deprival of political rights for life.
2. Defendant Deng Xinping was convicted of theft of firearms and sentenced with the death penalty and deprival of political rights for life; convicted of murder and sentenced with life imprisonment and deprival of political rights for life. The death sentence and deprival of political rights for life shall be carried out.
3. Defendant Li Qiang was convicted of dereliction of duty and sentenced to five years of imprisonment.

Appeal of the retrial

After the ruling of the retrial, defendant Deng and Li appealed the rulings to Hubei Superior People's Court. Upon investigation, the high court adopted all facts and evidence presented by the original court and regarded the facts and the evidence as clear and sufficient.

The Hubei Superior Court sustained the ruling of the retrial court.

Source: Mingshan Zhu. *Selected Chinese Criminal Court Cases — 1999*. Beijing: Chinese People's University Publishing House, 2002, 146–52.

CASE 2

Luo Jianxin: Murder case

Judicial Judgment Document of First Trial:
Production and Construction Group No.10 Intermediate People's Court of Xinjiang Province (2001) Nong 10 Intermediate Criminal First #3.
Judicial Judgment Document of Second Trial:
Superior People's Court of Xinjiang Autonomous Region (2001). Xin Criminal Final #54.

Original Prosecutorial Agency:
The People's Procuratorate of Production and Construction Group No. 10, Xinjiang Autonomous Region.
Appellant (Defendant in the first trial):
Luo Jianxin
Male, born on July 24, 1974, at Production and Construction Group No.10-181, Xinjiang Autonomous Region, Han ethnicity, middle school education, unemployed, detained on January 23, 2001, and arrested on February 14, 2001.
Defense Attorney (first trial):
Chen Jingwei (Law firm unavailable)
First Trial Completed:
August 20, 2001
Second Trial Completed:
December 23, 2001

Prosecuting and defense arguments in the first tial

The People's Procuratorate of Production and Construction Group No. 10, Xinjiang Autonomous Region accused that due to family conflicts, defendant Luo Jianxin became suspicious of whether his mother, victim Xu, was his biological mother. At around 6:00 a.m. of January 23, 2001, while burning household items in the house, defendant Luo questioned his mother whether she was his biological mother. His mother screamed for help and tried to escape from the window. Luo hit his mother on the head with an iron hook. While Xu went outside for help, Luo hit her again with a pole and repeatedly hit her until she passed out. Luo then cut Xu's stomach open and burned her body. Defendant Luo had committed murder, and in accordance to Article 232 of the PRC Criminal Law, Luo shall be given the death sentence.

Defendant Luo Jianxin did not contest the facts of the case, but denied that his motive for killing his mother was for financial reasons. The defense attorney pointed out that defendant Luo suffered from mental disability. According to stipulations of the criminal procedure law, an evaluation of mental illness must be done by a provincial government-designated hospital. The evaluation of Luo's mental health in this case was done by Beijing Anding Hospital, which was not designated by the provincial government to evaluate individuals' mental heath for criminal trial purposes. Based on the evaluation results of Luo's mental health derived by the Beijing Anding Hospital, Luo's mental conditions qualified him as a person with "limited criminal liability." Luo had confessed and showed remorse, which in accordance to clause 3 of Article 18 of the PRC Criminal Law, a lighter sentence could be granted.

Facts and evidence in the first trial

Production and Construction Group No.10 Intermediate People's Court of Xinjiang Province's own investigation concluded that defendant Luo had been spoiled since he was little as the youngest child in the family with a single mother. Because his older half-brother and sister borrowed money from his mother without returning it, Luo was resentful and asked his mother to deposit 30,000 yuan into his account. His mother refused. In October, 2000, Luo went to Qinghai province to try to find a mate, but was unsuccessful. When he came back home, he felt that his mother treated him differently and became suspicious of whether his mother was his biological mother.

At 6:00 a.m. of January 23, 2001, Luo told his mother that he could not sleep, and started to burn household items while questioning whether Xu was his biological mother. Xu was scared and tried to escape, but was hit on the head by an iron hook. Xu ran outside for help, and was hit again by Luo on the head with a wood stick. Luo repeatedly hit Xu until she fell on the ground. Luo thought that his mother was dead, and started to cut her stomach open with a knife, and burned her body. At 9:40 a.m., Luo was detained by residents and police were summoned to the scene.

The court also recognized that the People's Procuratorate of Production and Construction Group No. 10, Xinjiang Autonomous Region requested Beijing Judicial Evaluation Committee contact Beijing Anding Hospital to conduct an evaluation of Luo's mental health. It was concluded that Luo's motivation was mixed with both reality and pathology. His mental illness was precipitated by conflicts with his mother. While in the heat of passion, he could not control his behavior and committed the crime. The evaluation report suggested that Luo must undergo treatment and be placed under supervision to prevent another incidence.

The above facts were supported by the following evidence.

1. The police recovered iron hook, knife, and corner's report.
2. The police report showed the blood stains on Luo's hands and clothes were victim Xu's.
3. Witnesses Zhang's statement that Luo, after killing his mother, went to Zhang's house, and exhibited unusual demeanor.
4. Beijing Neurological Judicial Evaluation Committee Beijing Anding Hospital's evaluation report indicated Luo suffered from mental illness, could not fully control his behavior, and shall be deemed as a person with limited liability.
5. Court's records that corroborated the above evidence.

Legal reasoning by the frst trial court

Production and Construction Group No.10 Intermediate People's Court of Xinjiang Province ruled that the procuratorate's charge of Luo's murder of his mother Xu was based on clear facts and accurate and sufficient evidence. Luo's act had constituted murder and shall be punished according to law. In this country, stamps obtained by governmental agencies and institutions must go through a series of evaluation and approval. Beijing Anding Hospital had a stamp engraved as "Beijing Neurological Judicial Evaluation Committee Beijing Anding Hospital." This stamp is sufficient in proving that Beijing Anding Hospital had the expertise and authority to conduct mental health evaluation for judicial purposes. In addition, its evaluation results were corroborated with other evidence in this case, thus should be reliable, and admitted into evidence. The court therefore denied the defense's request to seek another mental health evaluation. According to clause 3 of Article 18 of the PRC Criminal Law, "for those individuals who suffer mental illness but have not completely lost control of their behaviors or know the consequences of their behaviors, shall be held with criminal liability, but may be given a lighter or reduced sentence."

Based on this legal stipulation, the court may exercise discretion not to grant judicial leniency in cases where individuals suffered minor mental illness and their criminal act was particularly severe. In this case, defendant Luo knew that he was attacking his mother, and he had some control over his judgment and behavior. But because of his resentment and suspicion, he murdered his mother with extremely cruel methods. The court cannot give a lighter sentence in this case. Otherwise, it would be difficult to appease the public's indignation. The court thus denied the defense's request for a lighter sentence and supported the procuratorate's request for the death penalty.

Sentences by the first trial court

Production and Construction Group No.10 Intermediate People's Court of Xinjiang Province issued the following rulings based on Article 232, the third clause of Article 18, and the first clause of Article 48, 57, and 64 of the PRC Criminal Law:

1. Defendant Luo Jianxin was convicted of murder and sentenced to death and deprival of political rights for life;
2. Defendant Luo's knife used in committing the crime was confiscated.

Summary of the second trial court

After the announcement of the sentence by the first trial court, defendant Luo did not appeal. The procuratorate did not protest. The first trial court, in accordance to the legal procedure, forwarded the case to the Superior People's Court of Xinjiang Autonomous Region for final approval of the death penalty.

The high court ruled that the facts presented by the procuratorate were clear, and evidence was accurate and sufficient, and the legal process was strictly followed by the first trial court. However, the court did not appropriately assess the sentence. According to the available evaluation report of Luo's mental health, Luo suffered mental illness at the time of murdering his mother. He could not completely control his behavior, and was a person with limited liability. Even though the Chinese criminal law Article 18 clause 3 did not require that individuals with limited liability must be given a lighter or reduced sentence, its original intent was to grant leniency to those types of individuals. The high court thus regarded the original sentence as not appropriate and thus shall be modified. Based on the second clause of Article 276 of the Supreme Court's Interpretation on Several Issues Regarding the Implementation of the PRC Criminal Procedure Law and Article 232, the first clause of Article 57 and the second clause of Article 18 of the PRC Criminal Law, the Superior People's Court of Xinjiang Autonomous Region ruled:

1. Sustain the original sentence of confiscating the defendant's knife used in the murder;
2. Remove the original sentence of the death penalty;
3. Sentence defendant Luo Jianxin with life imprisonment and deprival of political rights for life.

Source: Mingshan Zhu. *Selected Chinese Criminal Court Cases — 2002*. Beijing: Chinese People's University Publishing House, 2003, 12-5.

CASE 3

Sun Aijun: intentional assault and rape case

Judicial Judgment Document of First Trial:
Huaian Intermediate People's Court of Jiangsu Province (2001).
Huai Criminal First #27.
Judicial Judgment Document of Second Trial:
Superior People's Court of Jiangsu Province (2001).
Su Superior Criminal Final #318.
Original Prosecutorial Agency:
The People's Procuratorate of Huaian City, Jiangsu Province.
Appellant (Defendant in the first trial):
Sun Aijun
Male, born on December 26, 1973, Han ethnicity, unemployed, originally from Jiangsu Huaian. In March of 1992, he was convicted of rape and sentenced to nine years of incarceration. His sentenced was reduced by two years and ten months. He

was released on May 1, 1998. He was detained for suspected involvement in intentional assault on November 24, 2000, and was formally arrested on December 1 of the same year.

Defense Attorney (appointed by court):
Wu Zhenglin
Legal Aid Center of Huaian City.

First Trial Completed:
August 14, 2001

Second Trial Completed:
September 6, 2001

Prosecuting and defense arguments in the first trial:

Huaian People's Procuratorate of Jiangsu Province accused that on a day of July, 2000, defendant Sun Aijun attempted to rape a female named Shao. On the night of September 7, Sun accidentally met Shao and her friends, and was assaulted by Shao's boyfriend and others. Sun called several of his friends for help. The two groups had a fight that resulted in one of Shao's friend's death. In addition, between October 1999 and May 2000, Sun was accused of fondling four other females. The procuratorate charged Sun with multiple counts of intentional assault and rape. The procuratorate recommended to the court a more severe sentence given that Sun was a recidivist (he reoffended within five years of his release from the prison) and despite the fact that Sun performed meritorious deeds for the authorities by disclosing others' crimes upon his arrest.

Defendant Sun Aijun claimed that he performed meritorious services to the authorities and deserved lenient sentences. The court-appointed defense attorney argued for the mitigating circumstances of Sun's important services for the authorities and called for a lenient sentencing disposition.

Facts and evidence in the first trial:

The Intermediate People's Court of Huaian City conducted a public trial and concluded the following:

In July 2000, defendant Sun attempted to rape Shao under a bridge by hitting her in the face. He was unsuccessful because of Shao's resistance and screaming for help. Around 9:00 p.m. on September 7, defendant Sun met Shao at the Xinmin Square when he and his friends went for Karaoka. Shao's boyfriend and other friends went to pick a fight with Sun. Sun's friends joined the fight. During the fight, Sun along with his friends Wang, Li, and Zhu repeatedly beat Shao's friend Bi, severely injuring Bi at the scene. Bi died from these injuries three days later.

The court also found that between October 1999 and May 2000, defendant Sun resorted to violence by fondling four other female victims both near where he lived and other locations.

After being arrested, Sun provided leads for the police to catch other cooffenders in the intentional assault case of Bi.

The above findings were supported by the following evidence:

1. Victim Shao's testimony about the attempted rape on a July night, 2000, which was corroborated with Sun's testimony.
2. Two eyewitnesses who testified that they saw Sun trying to catch Bi. Sun also admitted to hitting Bi.
3. The police report showed that two bricks with blood stains were recovered from the crime scene. Sun admitted that the smaller brick was used by him to hit the victim Bi. Forensic examination revealed that Bi died of a brain damage.
4. The police recorded Sun's meritorious services to the authority with the disclosure of another murder case by Wang, Li and Zhu. After police investigation, Sun's disclosure was consistent with the evidence discovered for the crime.
5. Sun confessed to all the charges by the procuratorate and his confessions were corroborated by other witnesses' testimonies.

Legal reasoning by the first trial court

Based on evidence and arguments presented by both the procuratorate and the defense, Huaian Intermediate People's Court made the following rulings:

Defendant Sun along with his cooffenders violently beat the victim to death in an incident caused by his attempted rape of Shao and altercations with Shao's friends. His actions involved an intentional assault. Sun also committed multiple counts of rape with violent and coercive means. Even though he disclosed important information for the police to solve other major crimes and may be given a lenient sentence, his recidivist status is a mandatory aggravating factor required by law. In addition, Sun committed multiple counts of crime, and did not show remorse. Thus, the court does not grant leniency to Sun.

Sentences by the first trial court

Based on the second item of Article 234, the first clause of Article 236, the first, third (second and forth items) of Article 236, the first clause of Articles 65, 68, 69, 48, and 57, Huaian Intermediate People's Court of Jiangsu Province issued the following sentences:

Defendant Sun Aijun was convicted of intentional assault and sentenced to death and deprival of political rights for life. He was also convicted of rape and sentenced to death and deprival of political rights for life. When combined, the death sentence shall be carried out and the political rights shall be deprived for life.

Summary of the second trial court

After the announcement of the sentence by the first trial court, the defendant appealed to Jiangsu Superior People's Court on the ground that the sentence was too severe.

Upon reviewing documents and conducting investigation, Jiangsu Superior People's Court concluded that the facts for convicting Sun for intentional assault and rape were clear, and the evidence was truthful and sufficient. It reasoned that defendant Sun along with other cooffenders were collectively involved in a fight, in which they used violent means that caused bodily injuries and resulted in a death. Their actions constituted intentional assault. Sun also resorted to violent and coercive means in the rape of five female victims a total of nine times. His acts constituted rape. Given that Sun committed a series of multiple offenses that involved multiple victims, had extremely severe circumstances and that his crime had aroused the public's indignation, he should be punished severely by law. Even though he performed meritorious services to the authority by providing valuable leads for other crimes, due to the severity of his offense, the service did not necessarily warrant sentencing reduction in this case.

Based on the above reasons, facts and evidence in this case, and in accordance to the first clause of Article 189 of the PRC Criminal Procedure Law, the court issued the following ruling:

> The appeal was denied and the original sentence was sustained.
> The court also approved Huaian Intermediate People's Court's death sentence ruling for defendant Xing Yanrong.

Source: Mingshan Zhu. *Selected Chinese Criminal Court Cases —2002*. Beijing: Chinese People's University Publishing House, 2003, 242–5.

CASE 4

Lu Xiaoer: Intentional Assault Case

Judicial Judgment Document of First Trial:
  Nantong Intermediate People's Court of Jiangsu Province (2001).
  Tong Intermediate Criminal First #16.
Judicial Judgment Document of Second Trial:
  Superior People's Court of Jiangsu Province (2001).
  Su Criminal Final #193.
Original Prosecutorial Agency:
  The People's Procuratorate of Nantong City, Jiangsu Province.
Appellant (Defendant in the first trial):
  Lu Xiaoer
  Female, born on September 25, 1974, Han ethnicity, unemployed, originally from Weisheng Street #33, Yangzhou Zhen, Yang

Zhou, Shaanxi Province, detained on September 24, 2000, and arrested on October 24, 2000.

Defense Attorney (First trial—court appointed):
Yuan Zhongping and Zhu Yu
Pingfan Law Firm, Nantong City.

Defense Attorney (Second trial):
Li Zong and Zhou Yue
Lizheng Law Firm, Nantong City

First Trial Completed:
May 18, 2001

Second Trial Completed:
August 1, 2001

Prosecuting and defense arguments in the first trial

Nantong People's Procuratorate of Jiangsu Province accused that at around 2:00 p.m. of September 24, 2000, defendant Lu Xiaoer used high-density acid to pour on her ex-husband's face and back at the location of his temporary residence. She then escaped the scene. According to forensic tests, the victim suffered severe injury with third-degree burns. The procuratorate argued that defendant Lu committed intentional assault with employment of extremely cruel methods. Even though defendant Lu voluntarily surrendered to the police authority, because of the criminal circumstances and social harm in this case, the procuratorate argued that leniency shall not be granted in this case.

Defendant Lu confessed completely to the crime, and was willing to compensate the victim's financial losses. She begged for the court's leniency. Her defense attorney argued that in this case, both the cause of the crime and the voluntary surrender after the crime warranted leniency and suggested to the court to give a lighter sentence.

Facts and evidence in the first trial

The Intermediate People's Court of Nantong City conducted a public trial and concluded the following:

Defendant Lu and her ex-husband began their relationship in 1996 and got married in the beginning of 1999. Due to personality conflicts and conflicts between Lu and her ex-husband's mother, they frequently quarreled and started to separate. On August 9, 2000, the ex-husband filed for divorce. On September 5, 2000, through the mediation of Congchuan District People's Court of Nantong City, the two got divorced. Lu suspected that her ex-husband had an affair.

To make his life miserable, Lu purchased acid of 95–98 percent purity with a fake introduction letter. She was imitating a recent high-profile case in which the offender burned a sister's face with acid (the offender in the case was sentenced to death in the first trial). Upon obtaining the acid, Lu hid it in two plastic drinking bottles as a disguise. At 2:00 p.m. of September 24, Lu went to the ex-husband's place. While the husband was reading Lu's diary, Lu took out the bottles with acid and poured them toward Li's face. Yu went outside for help. Lu followed and poured the other bottle on Yu's back. Afterwards, Lu escaped the scene. Eyewitnesses at the scene called 110 to report it to the police. The police took Yu to the hospital. Lu also called 110 to report the crime. Based on the hospital record, Yu suffered severe disfigurement on his face and body, losing his right eye. The total cost for medical, nursing, missed work, and nutrition, disability compensation and other expenses was estimated at 151,337 yuan.

The above facts were supported by the following evidence.

1. Nantong Congchuan District Court's (2000) Cong Civil First #1115 civil mediation judgment document indicating that Lu Xiaoer and Yu Xiaohua voluntarily dissolved their marriage.
2. Nantong Mingquan Trading Company's certificate, Nantong Medical Company's receipt and witnesses Ding and Ma showed that Lu purchased a bottle of high-density acid with a forged certificate.
3. Eyewitnesses outside of Yu's house testified that they saw Lu pour a bottle of acid on Yu's back.
4. Lu's friend testified that she heard Lu say that Lu poured acid onto her ex-husband and her friend reported it to the police.
5. Victim Yu's statement of the entire incident to the police.
6. Nantong Police Department's crime scene investigation reports, Lu's confessions, retrieved bottled with left over acid, Yu's bed sheets burned by acid.
7. Nantong Police Department's certificate that Yu suffered the third-degree injury.
8. Lu's complete confessions.

Legal reasoning by the first trial court

Nantong Intermediate People's Court ruled that defendant Lu Xiaoer intentional injured the victim with acid. Her act constituted intentional assault. Due to the extremely cruel methods involved and severe consequences, Lu should be punished severely. In addition, Lu must compensate the victim's financial losses as a result of the crime. The facts presented by the procuratorate were clear, evidence was sufficient, and the charge was appropriate. As to the defense attorney's claim that Lu voluntarily surrendered and fully confessed to the crime, the court ruled that due to the extremely cruel methods and severe consequences of this crime, leniency cannot be granted.

Sentences by the first trial Ccourt

Based on the second item of Article 234, the first clause of Article 57, and the first clause of Article 36 of the PRC Criminal Law, Nantong Intermediate People's Court of Jiangsu Province issued the following sentences:

1. Defendant Lu Xiaoer was convicted of intentional assault and sentenced to death and deprival of political rights for life;
2. Defendant Lu Xiaoer must pay the total amount of 151,337.52 yuan for the victim's medical expenses, missed working days, and other direct costs. The payment is due one month from the judgment date.

Summary of the second trial court

After the announcement of the sentence by the first trial court, defendant Lu appealed by claiming that the victim shared some responsibilities in the crime. She voluntarily surrendered to the police authority, thus deserved leniency. Her attorney also made similar claims and asked the court for leniency.

Upon reviewing documents and conducting investigation, Jiangsu Superior People's Court adopted the facts and evidence admitted by Nantong Intermediate People's Court.

The high court reasoned that defendant Lu sought revenge after divorcing Yu, intentionally assaulted Yu with acid, and caused Yu severe bodily injury and disability. Her act constituted intentional assault. In addition, her method of crime was extremely cruel, consequences were extremely grave, and thus she must be severely punished. Even though the court recognized that Lu voluntarily surrendered to the police after the crime, it ruled that leniency should not be granted because of the severity of the crime. The first trial court's ruling that required Lu to compensate Yu's direct costs associated with the crime was considered correct and appropriate. As to defendant Lu and her attorney's claim that Yu shared some criminal responsibility, the court's investigation suggested that it could not determine whether Yu had extra-marital affairs, but it was sure that the divorce was caused by irreconcilable differences between the couples and Lu's relationship with her in-laws. The defense was thus denied.

According to the first clause of Article 189 of the PRC Criminal Procedure Law, Jiangsu Superior People's Court ruled that the appeal was denied and the original sentence was sustained.

According to the Supreme Court's Notice on Granting Superior People's Courts and Military Courts Final Approval and Review Authority over Some Types of Death Penalty Cases, the high court finally approved Lu's death sentence and deprival of political rights for life sentence.

Source: Mingshan Zhu. *Selected Chinese Criminal Court Cases — 2002*. Beijing: Chinese People's University Publishing House, 2003, 114–7.

CASE 5

Wang Ming et al.: theft appeal and retrial case

Judicial Judgment Document of First Trial:
Jiaxing Intermediate People's Court of Zhejiang Province (1996). Criminal First #65.
Judicial Judgment Document of Second Trial:
Superior People's Court of Zhejiang Province (1996).
Zhe Superior Criminal Final #579.
Judicial Judgment Document of Retrial:
Superior People's Court of Zhejiang Province (2000).
Zhe Superior Criminal Retrial Final #18.
Original Prosecutorial Agency:
The People's Procuratorate of Jiaxing City, Zhejiang Province.
Appellant (Defendant in the first trial):
Yu Jianmin
Male, born on January 23, 1971, Han ethnicity, originally from Tongxiang City, Zhejiang province, peasant, lived at Nanri Yuefeng Village of Tongxiang City, currently serving at #4 Prison of Zhejiang Province.
Appellant (Defendant in the first trial):
Lu Fengqiang
Male, born on June 20, 1971, Han ethnicity, originally from Tongxiang City, Zhejiang province, employed, worker, lived at Qitang Caojing Village of Tongxiang City, currently serving at #4 Prison of Zhejiang Province.
Appellant (Defendant in the first trial):
Yu Jianguo
Male, born on June 27, 1966, Han ethnicity, originally from Tongxiang City, Zhejiang province, employed, worker, lived at Qitang Caojing Village of Tongxiang City, previously sentenced with three years of incarceration for theft on September 20,1986 and released from prison in May 1989, currently serving at #4 Prison of Zhejiang Province.
Appellant (Defendant in the first trial):
Chen Yuekang
Male, born on September 17, 1973, Han ethnicity, originally from Tongxiang city, Zhejiang Province, employed, worker, lived at Qitang Caojing Village of Tongxiang City, currently serving at Juvenile Reform Facility of Zhejiang Province.
Appellant (Defendant in the first trial):
Wang Ming
Male, born on October 28, 1970, Han ethnicity, originally from Tongxiang City, Zhejiang Province, employed, worker, lived at

Qitang Caojing Village of Tongxiang City, currently serving at #6 Prison of Zhejiang Province.

Appellant (Defendant in the first trial):

Zhang Ping

Male, born on March 18, 1966, Han ethnicity, originally from Tongxiang City, Zhejiang Province, employed, worker, lived at Qitang Caojing Village of Tongxiang City, currently serving at #6 Prison of Zhejiang Province.

Appellant (Defendant in the first trial):

Yu Guoqiang

Male, born on October 13, 1972, Han ethnicity, originally from Tongxiang City, Zhejiang Province, employed, worker, lived at Qitang Caojing Village of Tongxiang City, currently serving at Qiaosi Prison of Zhejiang Province.

Appellant (Defendant in the first trial):

Zhu Lichu

Male, born on December 18, 1972, Han ethnicity, originally from Tongxiang city, Zhejiang Province, employed, worker, lived at Qitang Caojing Village of Tongxiang City, currently serving at Qiaosi Prison of Zhejiang Province.

Appellant (Defendant in the first trial):

Zhang Boxing

Male, born on January 7, 1938, Han ethnicity, originally from Tongxiang City, Zhejiang Province, employed, worker, lived at Qitang Caojing Village of Tongxiang City, currently serving at Qiaosi Prison of Zhejiang Province.

Appellant (Defendant in the first trial):

Yu Xiaochun

Male, born on January 13, 1969, Han ethnicity, originally from Tongxiang City, Zhejiang Province, peasant, lived at Qitang Caojing Village of Tongxiang City.

First Trial Completed:

August 13, 1996

Second Trial Completed:

November 26, 1996

Jiaxing People's Procuratorate of Zhejiang Province accused defendants Wang Ming, Yu Jianmin, Zhang Ping, Yu Guoqiang, Zhu Lichu, Zhang Boxing, Lu Fengqiang, Yu Jianguo, Chen Yuekang, Yu Xiaochun of theft. Jiaxing Intermediate People's Court of Zhejiang Province issued the judicial decision on August 13, 1996. The Superior People's Court of Zhejiang issued its final judicial decision on November 26, 1996. After the above decision took effect, Wang Ming's father, Yu Jianming's father, Zhang Ping's wife, Yu Guoqiang's father, Zhu Lichu's father, Zhang Boxing's father, Yu Jianguo's wife, Chen Yuekang's father filed a petition to the Superior Court for reconsideration of the case. The Court decided to retry the case on April 4, 2000. Accordingly, the Court set up a collegiate bench. Upon review of the related materials, the Court found that the facts of the cases were clear and thus it was not to hold a public hearing. The case has now concluded.

The first trial court determined, between June 1994 and September 1995, defendants Wang Ming, Yu Jianmin, Zhang Ping, Yu Guoqiang, Zhu Lichu, Lu Fengqiang, Yu Jianguo, Chen Yuekang committed a series of thefts alone or collectively in several factories, obtaining sheep skins and pig skins of various colors. More specifically, defendant Wang Ming was involved in eight thefts, stealing goods valued at 156,050 yuan; Defendant Yu Jianmin was involved in five thefts, stealing goods valued at 99,700 yuan; defendant Zhang Ping was involved in three thefts, valued at 74,600 yuan; defendant Yu Guoqiang was involved in three thefts, valued at 54,100; defendant Zhu Lichu was involved in three thefts, valued at 50,350; defendant Zhang Boxing was involved in one theft, valued at 40,250; defendant Lu Fengqiang was involved in four thefts, valued at 37,915; defendant Yu Jianguo was involved in one theft, valued at 28,600; defendant Chen Yuekang was involved in two thefts, valued at 28,200 yuan. In addition, defendants Yu Jianguo, Lu Fengqiang and Yu Xiaochun knowingly sold stolen goods (defendants Yu Jianguo and Lu Fengqiang sold stolen goods totaled at 108,150 yuan and defendant Yu Xiaochun sold stolen goods of 6,900 yuan).

The first trial court also determined that defendants Wang Ming, Zhang Ping, Zhu Lichu, Chen Yuekang voluntarily turned themselves in and confessed to the crime on November 14, 1995. The next day, defendants Yu Jianming, Yu Jianguo also turned themselves in voluntarily. The Public Security agency was able to retrieve stolen property and money valued at 109,880 yuan. The defendants' families provided a total of 91,800. A total of 194,140 yuan was returned to the victimized factories.

Accordingly, the first trial court decided to give defendant Wang Ming a death penalty with a two year suspension and deprival of political rights for life; give defendant Yu Jianmin a life imprisonment and deprival of political rights for life; give defendant Zhang Ping and Yu Guoqiang each a prison sentence of fifteen years and deprival of rights for three years; give defendant Zhu Lichu a prison sentence of thirteen years and deprival of political life for one year; give defendant Zhang Boxing a prison sentence of five years. Defendant Lu Fengqiang was given twelve years of imprisonment for theft and two years of imprisonment for knowingly purchasing stolen goods, fines of 5,000 yuan. Defendant Lu was thus sentenced to serve a total of thirteen and one-half years in prison and pay fines of 5,000 yuan. Defendant Yu Jianguo was given ten years of imprisonment for theft and two years of imprisonment for knowingly purchasing stolen goods, fines of 5,000 yuan. Combined together, defendant Yu was thus sentenced to serve a total of eleven and one-half years in prison and pay fines of 4,000 yuan. Defendant Chen Yuekang was sentenced with ten years of imprisonment for theft and one year of surveillance and fines of 1,000 yuan.

The Appeals Court determined that the facts were clear, evidence was sufficient, and the first trial court's application of law and procedure were lawful, thus decided to turn down the appeal and sustain the original sentence. The Appeals Court also review and approved defendant Wang Ming's death sentence with a two year suspension and deprival of political rights for life.

The petition states that the previous courts' decisions wrongfully determined the nature of the crime. Instead of theft, those defendants should have been convicted for criminal possession, a lesser serious crime, because they committed theft by taking advantage of their work.

The Court investigated the case and determined:

> The first trial court determined that between November 1994 and July 1995 defendants Wang Ming, Yu Jianmin, Yu Guoqiang, Zhu Lichu, and Chen Yuekang committed five thefts alone or collectively, stealing a variety of sheep skins and products, valued at 82,300 yuan. Defendants Yu Jianguo and Lu Fengqiang knowingly purchased stolen goods totaled at 50,650 yuan. Defendant Yu Xiaochun knowingly purchased stolen goods totaled at 6,900 yuan. The above facts were clear. The court had several witnesses' testimonies, confiscated property by the public security agency, and also had the offenders' own confessions.

It was also confirmed that between June 1994 and September 1995, defendants Wang Ming, Yu Jianmin, Zhang Ping, Zhang Boxing, Zhu Lichu, Lu Fengqiang, and Yu Jianguo committed ten thefts alone or collectively, stealing goods from their own workplace by taking advantage of their work. The crimes were documented below:

1. In an evening of June 1994, defendant Lu Fengqiang, while at work, stole 21 pieces of sheep skins valued at 2,415 yuan. He sold them for 1,200 yuan.
2. In September 1994, defendant Wang Ming conspired with Xu Jinkun and Zhu Hanhua (tried in a separate case) stole 180 pieces of sheep skins during lunch recess, valued at 21,600 yuan. They sold the goods for 12,000 yuan.
3. On October 14, 1994, defendant Lu Fengqiang conspired with She Dejiang (already been sentenced) and stole eighteen pieces of sheep skins at work, valued at 2,070 yuan. They sold the goods for 1,050 yuan.
4. On November 4, 1994, defendants Lu Fengqiang, Lu Weida (tried separately), and She Dejiang stole forty-two pieces of sheep skins, valued at 4,830 yuan. They sold the goods for 3,750 yuan.
5. In April 1995, defendant Wang Ming conspired with Xu Jinkun stealing one hundred pieces of sheep skins valued at 11,500 yuan. They sold the skins for 5,000 yuan.

6. In June 1995, defendants Zhang Ping and Zhu Lichu conspired to steal fifty pieces of sheep skins, valued at 5,757 yuan. They sold the goods for 2,400 yuan.
7. In July 1995, defendants Wang Ming and Zhang Ping conspired to steal 350 pieces of sheep skin, valued at 40,250 yuan. They sold the goods for 10,000 yuan. Defendants Yu Jianguo and Lu Fengqiang knowingly purchased the stolen goods and resold the goods for 20,000 yuan.
8. In July 1995, defendants Wang Ming, Zhang Ping, Yu Jianguo, Lu Fengqiang conspired to steal 240 pieces of sheep skin and 40 pieces of pig skin, valued at 28,600 yuan. They sold the goods to Yu Jianguo and Lu Fengqiang for 10,000 yuan.
9. In September 1995, defendants Zhu Lichu and YU Jianmin stole 150 pieces of sheep skin valued at 17,000 yuan. They sold the goods to Yu Jianmin and Lu Fengqiang. Most of these goods were confiscated after the case broke.

The above facts were supported by witnesses' testimonies and defendants' confessions. Values of the goods were appraised by related governmental agencies.

This court determined that defendants Wang Ming, Yu Jianming, Yu Guoqiang, Zhu Lichu, and Chen Yuekang, motivated by illegally possessing others' goods, conspired or worked alone to steal property valued at 82,300 yuan. The amount was extremely large, and the act has constituted theft. Among them, defendants Wang Ming, Yu Jianmin, and Yu Guoqiang conspired to commit thefts three times, having stolen goods valued at 54,100 yuan; defendant Zhu Lichu was involved in one crime, stealing goods valued at 27,600 yuan; defendant Chen Yuekang was involved in two crimes, stealing goods valued at 28,200 yuan.

Defendants Wang Ming, Yu Jianming, Zhang Ping, Zhang Boxing, Zhu Lichu, Lu Fengqiang, and Yu Jianguo, taking advantage of their work, secretly stole products at the workplace. The amount involved was either large or extremely large, thus constituted the crime of illegal possession. Among them, Wang Ming was involved in five illegal possession crimes, stealing goods valued at 101,950 yuan; Yu Jianming was involved in two crimes, stealing goods valued at 45,600 yuan; Zhang Ping was involved in three crimes, stealing goods valued at 74,600 yuan; Zhang Boxing was involved in one crime, stealing goods valued at 40,250 yuan; Zhu Lichu was involved in two crimes, stealing goods valued at 22,750 yuan; Lu Fengqiang was involved in four crimes, stealing goods valued at 37,915 yuan; Yu Jianguo was involved in one crime, stealing goods valued at 28,600 yuan. The first court determined the above crime as theft, which was inappropriate and should be reversed.

Defendants Yu Jianguo, Lu Fengqiang, and Yu Xiaochun knowingly purchased stolen goods, which constituted a crime. Among them, defendant

Yu Jianguo and Lu Fengqiang purchased stolen goods at 107,900 yuan; defendant Yu Xiaochun purchased stolen goods at 6,900 yuan.

Defendants Yu Jianming, Zhang Ping, Zhu Lichu, and Chen Yuekang voluntarily turned themselves in after the crime. Defendant Yu Jianming also performed meritorious services after confessing to the crime and shall be given a lighter sentence. Defendant Zhang Ping may receive a lighter sentence. Defendants Wang Ming, Zhu Lichu, and Chen Yuekang may be given a lighter sentence. Defendant Yu Jianguo committed a crime after being released from prison, and shall be given a heavier sentence.

Petitioners' claims that the first trial court wrongfully determined the crimes as theft, not illegal possession, were supported by this court. Other claims such as defendants Yu Jianguo and Lu Fengqiang did not conspire were not supported by this court.

Based on Article 206, the second item of Article 189 of Criminal Procedure Law and Article 152, 172, the first item of Article 22, Article 63, Article 59, the first item of Article 51, Article 52, 60 and 64 of Criminal Law (1979) and Article 10 of The Resolution of Punishing Those Who Violated the Company Law, and the second item of Article 2 of the Resolution on Punishing Those who Escaped from Prison or Recidivate, issued by the National People's Congress, the court issued the following sentences:

1. Overturn Jiaxing Intermediate People's Court's decision and the previous Superior Court's decision.
2. Sentence defendant Wang Ming with fifteen years of imprisonment for theft and deprival of political rights for five years; with six years of imprisonment for criminal possession. A total of twenty years of imprisonment and deprival of political rights for five years shall be carried out.
3. Sentence defendant Yu Guoqiang with fifteen years of imprisonment and deprival of political rights for three years for theft.
4. Sentence defendant Yu Jianmin with twelve years of imprisonment and deprival of political rights for three years; with two years of imprisonment for criminal possession. A total of thirteen years of imprisonment and deprival of political rights for three years shall be carried out.
5. Sentence defendant Zhu Lichu with six years of imprisonment; with one year of imprisonment for criminal possession. A total of six years of imprisonment shall be carried out.
6. Sentence defendant Chen Yuekang with six years of imprisonment for theft.
7. Sentence defendant Zhang Ping with four years of imprisonment for possession.
8. Sentence defendant Zhang Boxing with two years of imprisonment for possession.
9. Sentence defendant Lu Fengqiang with two years of imprisonment

for possession; two and half years of imprisonment for knowingly purchasing stolen goods, fines of 5,000 yuan. A total of four years of imprisonment and fines of 5,000 yuan shall be carried out.

10. Sentence defendant Yu Jianguo with one and half years of imprisonment for possession; two and one-half years of imprisonment for knowingly purchasing stolen goods, fines of 4,000 yuan. A total of three years of imprisonment and fines of 4,000 yuan shall be carried out.
11. Sentence defendant Yu Xiaochun with surveillance of one year and fines of 1,000 yuan for knowingly purchasing stolen goods.

This decision is final.

Source: Qimei Zhang. Judicial Document Selections of the People's Court — Zhejiang 2000. Beijing: Law Press, 2001, 107–11.

CASE 6

Wan Guohai et al.: manufacturing and possession of counterfeited currency case

Judicial Judgment Document of First Trial:
  Zhumadian Intermediate People's Court of Henan Province (2001).
  Criminal First #56.
Judicial Judgment Document of Second Trial:
  Superior People's Court of Henan Province (2001).
  Criminal Final #416.
Original Prosecutorial Agency:
  The People's Procuratorate of Zhumadian City, Henan Province.
Appellant (Defendant in the first trial):
  Wan Guohai
  Male, thirty-six years old, Han ethnicity, originally from Henan Guangxian, peasant, arrested on April 16, 2001.
Defense Attorney (first trial):
  Lou Shijun
  Jishiyu Law Firm.
Defense Attorney (second trial):
  Deng Hande & Hua Xiaopeng
  Jinxueyuan Law Firm.
Appellant (Defendant in the first trial):
  Zhao Jianguo
  Male, twenty-seven years old, Han ethnicity, originally from Henan Fanxian, peasant, arrested on April 16, 2001.

Defense Attorney:
Yan Chao
Hexiang Law Firm.
Appellant (Defendant in the first trial):
Li Guoxi
Male, thirty-one years old, Han ethnicity, originally from Henan Queshan, peasant, arrested on April 16, 2001.
Defense Attorney:
Gao Cheng
Shangcheng Law Firm.
First Trial Completed:
September 13, 2001
Second Trial Completed:
December 30, 2001

Prosecuting and defense arguments in the first trial

Zhumadian People's Procuratorate of Henan Province accused that in July 2000, defendant Wan Guohai started to plan manufacturing counterfeited U.S. dollars, and contacted defendant Zhao Jianguo. The two defendants purchased printing equipment, and started manufacturing counterfeited U.S. dollars along with defendant Li Guoxi in a rented house since January 2001. On March 19, 2001, the three defendants were arrested by the police while manufacturing the counterfeited currency. The police also confiscated 3,286 pieces of $100 (one-side printed), equivalent of 2,651,868 yuan. In addition, in June 2000, defendant Li Guoxi purchased 450 counterfeited $100 bills, and three counterfeited $50 bills, equivalent of 364,370 yuan. He stored these counterfeited currencies in the rented house. This currency was confiscated by the police. The above facts and evidence were supported by the police search report, list of confiscated properties, pictures taken at the scene, witness Li Min and Chen Guofan's testimonies, and three defendants' testimonies.

Defendants Wan, Zhao, and Li manufactured counterfeited currencies, and have committed the crime of manufacturing of counterfeited currency in accordance to the second clause of Article 170 of the PRC Criminal Law. The amount involved was extremely large. Defendant Li also committed crime of purchasing and transporting counterfeited currency according to the first item of Article 171 of the PRC Criminal Law and the amount involved was extremely large. The procuratorate requested for severe criminal punishment for all three defendants.

Defendant Wan claimed that Zhao rented his house for printing business cards. All the money Zhao used to purchase the equipment was borrowed from Wan. Later, Wan learned that Zhao used the equipment to manufacturing counterfeited currency but was not involved. Wan's defense attorney argued that facts presented by the procuratorate were unclear and evidence was insufficient because Wan denied his involvement in manufacturing counterfeited currency and his statement was corroborated by Zhao's testimony. The attorney asked the court to exonerate Wan.

Defendant Zhao claimed that he borrowed money from Wan to purchase equipment to manufacture counterfeited U.S. dollars. Wan asked him to set up the factory at Wan's house in case that Zhao was unable to pay back the debt. But Wan was not involved in the process. Zhao claimed the counterfeited money was meant to be used for funeral services. Zhao's defense attorney claimed that Zhao was employed by Wan to manufacture counterfeited currency and was an accomplice, thus shall be grant leniency.

Defendant Li Guoxi claimed that he was not involved in manufacturing counterfeited currency. His defense attorney argued that the facts were unclear and evidence was insufficient in charging Li with the crime because according to Zhao's statement that Zhao manufactured counterfeited currency alone.

Facts and evidence in the first trial

The Intermediate People's Court of Zhumadian City conducted a public trial and concluded the following.

In July 2000, defendant Wan Guohai suggested to defendant Zhao Jianguo to manufacture counterfeited U.S. dollars. Conspiring together, the two defendants purchased the necessary printing equipments and materials with Wan's money. Zhao provided a laser scanner, a computer, and a printer. After the spring festival of 2000, the two defendants started to manufacture counterfeited U.S. dollars in the house rented by Wan. Zhao was responsible for printing, Wan supervising overall quality, and Li, employed by Wan, was to take care of miscellaneous businesses. On March 29, 2001, the police arrested Wan and Zhao on the scene and confiscated 3,286 $100 bills. Later that day, the police caught Li as well.

In October, 2000, Li hid 453 $100 bills and three $50 bills in Wan's bathroom. The money was confiscated on March 19, 2001.

The above facts were supported with the following evidence:

1. Witness Li Min's testimony that the three defendants jointly manufactured counterfeited currency.
2. The police confiscated a total of 3,286 U.S. dollar bills (with one side printed) and printing equipment and materials in Wan's rented house and Li's residence.
3. The police confiscated 453 U.S. dollar bills (completed) from Wan's bathroom, and concluded that these bills were not manufactured with this equipment.
4. The three defendants's testimonies were consistent.

5. Defendant Li stated that he purchased 453 U.S. dollar bills from Guangdong, brought the counterfeited money from Guangdong to Zhumadia, and hid it in Wan's bathroom.
6. The published currency exchange rate for date of March 19, 2001, was $100 = 807.02 yuan.
7. The Zhumadian Branch of China People's Bank issued a receipt for confiscating the counterfeited U.S. dollars.

Legal reasoning by the first trial court

Based on evidence and arguments presented by both the procuratorate and the defense, Zhumadian Intermediate People's Court made the following rulings:

Defendant Wan Guohai conspired with defendant Zhao Jianguo and Li Guoxi to manufacture counterfeited U.S. currencies. The facts were clear, and evidence was sufficient. In accordance to Article 170 of the PRC Criminal Law and the second clause of Article 1 and Article 7 of the Supreme Court's Interpretation of Several Legal Issues regarding Adjudicating Counterfeited Currency Cases, the court ruled that the three defendants committed the crime of counterfeiting currency. The amount involved was extremely large. All three defendants shall be held criminally liable. As for the 453 U.S. dollar bills confiscated from Wan's bathroom that Li claimed that he purchased and transported from Guangdong to Zhumadia, because no other evidence could corroborate Li's account, the charge against Li for purchasing and transporting counterfeited currency is insufficient. However, the court recognized that Li has committed the crime of possessing counterfeited currency. Because the amount involved was extremely large, according to the Supreme Court's Interpretation of Several Legal Issues regarding Adjudicating Counterfeited Currency Cases, Li must be held with criminal liability.

Defendant Wan first suggested to manufacture counterfeited U.S. dollars, and conspired with Zhao to purchase equipments and materials. Wan provided the manufacturing place and Zhao provided skills. Both were major and cooffenders in this case. Defendant Li was employed by Wan, helping them clean the house, serve water, and shall be regarded as an accomplice. The confiscated currency was not completed because of police intervention, thus no social damage was made. The crime is thus attempted, not completed.

Based on the above facts and evidence, the court ruled to sustain the procuratorate's charge that defendant Wang, Zhao, and Li committed the crime of manufacturing counterfeited currency. The court did not affirm the procuratorate's charge that Li committed the crime of purchasing and transporting counterfeited currency. The court further denied defendant Wan, defendant Li and their defense attorneys' claims that these two defendants were not involved in the process. Defendant Zhao's assertions that the purpose of making the counterfeited currencies was for the use in funeral services were inconsistent with the equipment, sample products, thus were denied. Zhao's defense attorney's argument that Zhao was an accomplice was based on insufficient evidence, and was thus denied.

Sentences by the first trial court

Based on the second item of Articles 170, 172, 23, the first clause of Articles 26, 27, 48, the first clause of Articles 57, 55, 59, 64, and 69 of the PRC Criminal Law, and the second clause of Articles 1, 5, and 7 of the Supreme Court's Interpretation of Several Legal Issues regarding Adjudicating Counterfeited Currency Cases, Zhumadian Intermediate People's Court of Henan Province issued the following sentences:

1. Defendant Wan Guohai was convicted of manufacturing counterfeited currency, and sentenced to death with a two year reprieve, deprival of political rights for life, and confiscation of all personal property;
2. Defendant Zhao Jianguo was convicted of manufacturing counterfeited currency, and sentenced to death with a two year reprieve, deprival of political rights for life, and confiscation of all personal property;
3. Defendant Li Guoxi was convicted of manufacturing counterfeited currency, and sentenced to ten years of prison sentence, deprival of political rights for three years, fines in the amount of 50,000 yuan; convicted of passing counterfeited currency, convicted for ten years of incarceration, deprival of political rights for three years, and fines in the amount of 50,000 yuan. Combined, Li shall serve eighteen years of incarceration, deprival of political rights for five years, and fines in the amount of ten years (the fines are due three months from the sentence taking effect).

Summary of the second trial court

After the announcement of the sentence by the first trial court, all three defendants appealed.

Appellant Wan claimed that he was not involved in manufacturing counterfeited currency. His defense attorney claimed that the sentence was too severe because the defendant manufactured the U.S. dollars, not the Chinese yuan. Its societal damage was much smaller, and therefore he should not be given the death sentence.

Appellant Zhao claimed that the purpose for manufacturing the counterfeited currency was not to make illegal profits, but for the use in funeral services. There is no social harm, thus should not be considered a crime.

Appellant Li claimed that he was not involved in manufacturing the counterfeited currency. He was there to assist in house work. His sentence was too heavy.

Upon reviewing documents and conducting investigation, Henan Superior People's Court adopted the facts and evidence admitted by Zhumadian Intermediate People's Court.

The high court reasoned that appellant Wang repeatedly confessed to the crime during the police investigations, and his testimonies were largely consistent and corroborated by Zhao's testimonies given to the police during the initial police investigations in terms of the process of purchasing the equipment and materials and the production process. This was also supported by the confiscated properties by the police. This evidence thus did not support the two defendants' claims that they did commit the crime. Appellant Li claimed that there were mitigating circumstances in his case. The high court commented that the first trial court had already taken that into account when meting out the sentence for Li, thus Li's argument that the sentence was too severe was deficient.

The high court ruled that appellants Wan, Zhao, and Li were involved in manufacturing counterfeited U.S. currency, the amount was extremely large, thus constituting a serious crime. During the crime, Wan and Zhao were major cooffenders, and should be punished with severity. Li should be punished severely for his crime of possessing large amount of counterfeited currency. The first trial court's rulings were based on clear facts, sufficient evidence, and appropriate application of substantive and procedural laws.

According to the first clause of Article 89 of the PRC Criminal Procedure Law, Henan Superior People's Court ruled:

> The appeal was denied and the original sentence was sustained.

According to Article 201 of the PRC Criminal Procedure Law, this ruling serves as the final approval of Wang and Zhao's death sentence with a two year reprieve, and deprival of political rights for life.

Source: Mingshan Zhu. *Selected Chinese Criminal Court Cases — 2002*. Beijing: Chinese People's University Publishing House, 2003, 154–8.

CASE 7

Judicial Judgment Document of the Superior People's Court of the Beijing Municipality (2000) Superior Criminal Final Ruling #434 Appeal of Cheng Kejie's Bribery Case

Original Prosecutorial Agency:
The No.1 People's Procuratorate of Beijing Municipality.
Appellant (Defendant in the first trial):
Cheng Kejie

Male, sixty-six years old, born on November 13, 1933, Zhuang ethnicity, born in Guangxi Zhuangzu Municipality, Shanglin County of Guangxi Zhuangzu Autonomous Region, college educated, formerly employed as Vice-Chairman of the Standing Committee of the 9th National People's Congress, Vice-Secretary of the Committee of Guangxi Zhuangzu Autonomous Region, and Chairman of the People's Government of Guangxi Zhuangzu Autonomous Region, resided at the Communist Party Committee Courtyard seven star-road No.128, Xincheng District, Nanning City, Guangxi Zhuangzu Autonomous Region, arrested on April 25, 2000 for suspected bribery, and currently in police custody.

Defense Attorney:

Zhang Jianzhong
Beijing Gonghe Law firm.
Guo Jinhai
Guangxi Dahai Law firm.

The No.1 Intermediate People's Court of Beijing tried the case brought by the No.1 People's Procuratorate of Beijing Municipality on Cheng Kejie's bribery case and issued a judgment on July 31, 2000 (No.1 Intermediate Criminal First Trail #1484). The defendant Cheng Kejie appealed. This court formed a collegiate bench according to law, reviewed documents, and heard from the defense attorneys. Due to clear facts in this case, the court decided not to conduct a public hearing. The review is now completed.

The No.1 Intermediate People's Court of Beijing ruled:

At the end of 1993, defendant Cheng Kejie and Li Ping (tried in another case) discussed to get a divorce from their spouses and get married with each other. Toward this end, Cheng's then secretary Zhou Ningbang suggested to Li Ping to profit from Cheng's political power to make the future married life better. Li told Zhou's suggestions to Cheng and Cheng agreed. Between 1994 and 1997, Cheng and Li took in an excessively large amount of bribery by offering favors to numerous units and individuals. The detailed facts are as follows:

- Between 1994 and June 1995, Cheng learned from Li that they could take a large sum of kickbacks if Yinxing Company could get a contract for the construction project of the Jiangnan Parking and Shopping Mall of Nanning City, and have their construction capitals provided. Cheng agreed to let Li accept funds from Zhou Kun, Chief Manager of the Yinxing Company. He ordered to place Yinxing Co. under the management of the Autonomous Region government office. He then gave Yinxing Company the contract to build the Jiangnan Parking & Shopping Mall, and pushed the Auditing Department of the Autonomous Region to establish the construction project. In addition, Cheng instructed the government of Nanning City to lend the eighty-eight acres of land for a much reduced price of 550,000 yuan (an assessed value was 960,000 yuan) to Yinxing Company and repeatedly requested loans from the Guangxi Branch of China Construction Bank in the total amount of 70,000,000 yuan on behalf of Yinxing Company. Afterwards, based on Zhou Kun and Li Ping's agreements, Yinxing Company deposited a total of 20,211,597 yuan into Li's designated bank account. Li later gave 9,000,000 yuan to Zhang Jinghai, who helped transfer the funds. She then converted the rest funds into Hong Kong dollars and deposited them into her account at Hongkong Zhejiang Xingye Bank. Li told about the kickbacks to Cheng.

- From 1996 to the end of 1997, defendant Cheng learned from Li that if Yinxing Company could get the contract for the construction project of Guangxi Ethnic Palace and have their construction capital provided, a huge amount of kickbacks would be offered. Li again accepted funds from Zhou, and arranged to have the project jointly developed by Yixing Company and Civic Committee of the Autonomous Region. Cheng managed to change the original legal entity for the project from the Civic Committee to Yixing Company and applied loans in the amount of 30,000,000 yuan from the Guangxi Branch of China Industrial and Commercial Bank. Cheng also instructed the Autonomous Region's Housing Reform Office to lend the housing reform funds in the amount of 25,000,000 to Yinxing Company in violation of the law. He twice instructed the Financial Department of the Autonomous Region to lend Yixing Company a total of 50,000,000 yuan from the circulating funds. He also helped Yinxing Company to apply the subsidiary funds from the State Planning Committee in the amount of 13,000,000 yuan. Afterwards, Yinxing Company wired 9,000,000 yuan, and 8,040,000 Hong Kong yuan to Li. Li paid 2,500,000 yuan to Zhang, who helped transfer money for Li. She converted the remaining Chinese yuan into Hong Kong dollars, deposited all funds into her Hong Kong bank account, and told Cheng about it.
- From July 1994 to the end of 1997 during the construction projects of the Shopping Mall and Ethnic Palace, defendant Cheng and Li accepted additional bribery from Zhou Kun in the total amount of 559,428 yuan (e.g., 20,000 yuan, 20,000 Hong Kong dollars, $20,000, a pair of diamond rings, a loaf of gold, a pair of decorative golden lions, a pair of Rolex watches, one man's Rolex watch). Among them, Cheng received the loaf of gold, the pair of decorative golden lions, the man's Rolex watch, $20,000, and 20,000 Chinese yuan (a total of 455,000 yuan). The rest was deposited by Li in her Hong Kong bank account after notifying Cheng.

- Between July and October of 1994, defendant Cheng learned from Li that they would get kickbacks if they could help get loans for Guangxi Trust and Investment Company and its subsidiary company — Guangxi Guixin Industrial Development Company. Cheng arranged Li to help apply loans from the Guangxi Brach of China Construction Bank and Bank of China and received loans in the amount of 6,000,000 yuan and 10,000,000 from these banks respectively. Li received kickbacks for the favor in the amount of 600,000 yuan. She notified Cheng, converted the money into Hong Kong dollars, and deposited the money into her Hong Kong bank account.
- In July of 1997, defendant Cheng learned from Li that they would get kickbacks if they could arrange the Tunnel Bureau of the Railway Ministry to get the construction project of Yantan Hydropower Station reservoir. Li was sent to accept funds from Liu Xingmin, CEO of Guangxi Guilong Finance and Trade Limited Corporation, and instructed the Migration Office of the Autonomous Region to give the project to the Tunnel Bureau. Meanwhile, Cheng interfered in the bidding process by allowing the Tunnel Bureau to get the more profitable portion of the project. As a result, Li received kickbacks from Liu in the amount of 1,800,000 yuan, converted the amount into Hong Kong dollars, and deposited the money into her Hong Kong bank account. Li told Cheng about the kickbacks.
- From the beginning of 1994 to April of 1997, defendant Cheng accepted Gan Weiren's funds through Li, helped promote Gan from Vice-Chairman of the Hepu County to Chairman of Tieshangang District of Beihai City, then to be Vice-Secretary of Guangxi Autonomous Region Government. Gan gave Li four bribery funds in the total amount of 270,000 yuan. Li told Cheng about taking the bribes from Gan.
- During 1996 and 1997, defendant Cheng accepted the request from Zhou Yisheng, Chief of Haicheng Division of Beihai City Police Bureau, to promote him to be the chief of Beihai City Police Bureau. Cheng received $3,000 for the favor, and gave the money to Li.
- From the beginning of 1996 to Feburary of 1997, defendant Cheng accepted the request of Li Yihong, Chief of the Service Centre of the Planning Bureau, Autonomous Region, to help promote and endorse Li to serve as Vice-Director of the Beijing Office of the Autonomous Region. Cheng accepted 18,000 yuan for the favor.

In sum, defendant Cheng took advantage of his official position, individually and collectively with Li, collected a total amount of 41,090,373 yuan in bribery. After the case broke, all of the above cash and property were confiscated.

The No.1 Intermediate People's Court of Beijing ruled that defendant Cheng, taking advantage of his high ranking governmental positions as Vice-Secretary of Guangxi Autonomous Region Committee and Chairman of the Autonomous Region Government, offered favor to individuals and units to illegally collect kickbacks and bribery both individually and jointly with Li. His activities constitute the crime of bribery. The facts of the case presented by the No.1 People's Procuratorate of Beijing were clear, evidence was credible and sufficient, and the accusation was found to be truthful. Defendant Cheng accepted extremely large amounts of money for bribery. As a high ranking governmental official, his act obstructed the normal operational order of the governmental agencies, tainted governmental officials' integrity and credibility. His criminal circumstances were extremely severe, and shall be punished severely in accordance with the law. Though his illicit money had been fully retrieved, it shall not serve as ground for leniency.

According to the first clause of Article 385, Article 386, item one of the first clause and the second clause of Article 383, and the first clause of Article 57 stipulated in the PRC Criminal Law, defendant Cheng was convicted of bribery and sentenced with the death penalty, deprival of political rights for life, and confiscation of all personal property.

The main reasons of defendant Cheng's appeals included: (1) the first trial court did not sufficiently establish that Cheng and Li collectively accepted bribery for the preparation of marriage; (2) Cheng should not be held responsible for bribery taken by Li; (3) Cheng did not take advantage of his governmental position to help those companies obtain bank loans; (4) the money Cheng collected from Zhou and gave to Li was meant for Li to return to Zhou, not for a bribe; (5) the sentence rendered by the first trial court was too heavy-handed without considering mitigating factors. Cheng claimed that he voluntarily confessed to the crime, wrote letters to Li to ask her to return 50,000,000 yuan in money and property, and was able to retrieve all the state funds. Based on these mitigating factors, Cheng pled to the appellant court for leniency.

The appeals defense attorney, Zhang Jianzhong, offered several defense opinions: (1) Defendant Cheng had extra-marital affairs with Li. The first trial court's ruling that Cheng and Li planned to get married and collect money for their future life together lacked factual basis. (2) The first trial court's ruling that Cheng shall be responsible for bribes taken by Li lacked factual basis. (3) Cheng's voluntary confession shall deserve lenient punishment.

The No.1 Intermediate People's Court of Beijing listed evidence recognized by the court in its judicial judgment document and read out loud in the open court these cited pieces of evidence and related documentations. During the review of this case by this court, defendant Cheng and his defense attorney did not offer new evidence. This court thus recognized all evidence admitted by the first trial court. Upon completing the review of the case, this court ruled that the facts presented by the first trial court were clear and evidence was credible and sufficient.

To refute the arguments presented by defendant Cheng and his defense attorney that Cheng and Li were merely involved in extra-marital affairs, and were not planning to get married soon, thus could not possibly have conspired to collect bribes, this court's investigation found evidence contrary to their claims. This evidence included Li's testimonies (e.g., in numerous occasions, Cheng and Li discussed divorcing their spouses and getting married); Zhou Ningbang's testimonies (upon learning their divorce and marriage plans, he suggested that they get money first by taking advantage of Cheng's high ranking governmental post); and Cheng's own testimonies in the initial investigation stage. Based on these corroborating testimonies, the court did not recognize Cheng and his defense attorney's claims.

To refute the defendant and his defense attorney's claim that Cheng should not be held criminally liable for bribes taken by Li, the court's investigation suggests that Cheng helped Li make arrangements for units and individuals and knew every transaction and bribe taken by Li. Even though Li accepted and deposited most of the bribe money into her bank account, Cheng and Li were both the beneficiaries, thus their actions constituted conspiracy.

Defendant and his attorney also claimed that local governments had not direct supervisory relations with the professional banks. Thus, even though Cheng asked the banks to loan money to those companies, his act should not be deemed as taking advantage of his official position. The court's investigation showed that at the time of the crimes, the appointment of major posts of the financial institutions must be approved by the local government. As a major public official in the local government, Cheng held some supervisory role to the financial institutions. This court thus ruled that Cheng did take advantage of his official post to do favor for units and individuals in an effort to personally profit from it.

As to Cheng's claim that by giving Li Zhou Kun's bribes, he meant for Li to return the money and property to Zhou, not to accept the bribes, the court found that according to Zhou, Cheng did not refuse to accept the bribes when he gave the money and property to Cheng. According to Li, Cheng gave the money and property to her for safe keeping purposes. Cheng also testified during the initial investigation stage that he gave the bribery goods taken from Zhou to Li for safe keeping. Despite Cheng's denials in the first and second trial, given that Cheng could not offer additional evidence to support his claims, the court denied his claims.

As for the claims of voluntary surrender and cooperation with the investigative agencies to retrieve the lost state property, the court found that Cheng did not voluntarily surrender to the authorities. Only when his act was discovered by the authority, did Cheng confess to the crime. Even there, Cheng was not honest and truthful about his criminal activities, often denying what he confessed of later. He did not show remorse.

Even though Cheng wrote letters to Li to retrieve the money, the money was primarily retrieved with the help of Li, not Cheng. The rulings of the first trial court were correct and appropriate. Cheng and his defense attorney's defense were not supported by evidence and thus denied by the court.

This Court ruled, the appellant Cheng Kejie, taking advantage of his high ranking governmental positions, conspired with Li Ping and acted on his own to offer favors for units and individuals in exchange for bribes. His act constituted bribery. The first trial court's rulings were supported by clear facts, appropriate application of law, proper sentence, and legal process. Cheng Kejie took in an excessively huge amount of bribery by taking advantage of his official position, severely threatened the integrity and credibility of the governmental officials, and infringed upon the normal working order of the governmental agencies. His crime was serious and deserved to be punished severely. Based on Cheng's criminal activities, the nature, circumstances and social harm of his crime, and according to the first clause of Article 189 of the PRC Criminal Law, the court ruled:

> Reject Cheng Kejie's appeal and uphold original ruling.

This judgment will be forwarded to the People's Supreme Court for final review and approval.

Chief justice: Wang Ming
Judge: Tan Jingsheng
Judge: Li Yan
August 22, 2000
Clerk: Yan Ying
Clerk: Zhou Chuan

Source: Zhengan Qin. 2001. *Judicial Document Selections of the People's Court — Beijing 2000* (Beijing: Law Press, 2001), 197–202.

CASE 8

Chen Guoguang: bombing case

Judicial Judgment Document of First Trial:
Wenzhou Intermediate People's Court of Zhejiang Province (1999).
Criminal First #293.
Judicial Judgment Document of Second Trial:
Superior People's Court of Zhejiang Province (2000) Zhe Superior Criminal Final #197.
Original Prosecutorial Agency:
The People's Procuratorate of Wenzhou City, Zhejiang Province.

Defendant:
Chen Guoguang
Male, born on August 29, 1972, Han ethnicity, driver, originally from Yongjia County, Zhejiang Province, lived at Oubei Zhen, Najiangdong Road #248, Yongjia County, detained on October 23, 1999, and arrested on November 5, 1999.
Defense Attorney:
Xin Benfeng
Wuxing Guotai Law Firm, Zhejiang Province.
Defendant:
Chen Guohe
Male, born on September 8, 1974, Han ethnicity, driver, originally from Yongjia County, lived at Oubei Zhen, Najiangdong Road #248, Yongjia County, detained on October 6, 1999, and arrested on November 5, 1999.
Defense Attorney:
Jin Keming
Jin Keming Law Firm, Zhejiang Province.
First Trial Completed:
January 10, 2000
Second Trial Completed:
September 31, 2000

Prosecuting and defense arguments in the first trial

Wenzhou Intermediate People's Court of Zhejiang Province investigated the case and concluded that on September 30, 1999, defendant Chen Guoguang had a fight with a couple, Gu Linyun and Zhou Xiaohong at Chen's house due to disputes over debts. The couple was later persuaded to leave the premise. Defendant Chen Guohe learned the news and drove to the scene. When he saw the couple in Ye Changqui's van, Chen went up and started beating Gu. The couple stepped out the van and started fighting with Chen. While several people tried to intervene and stop the fight, many more watched. Upon learning the news, Chen Guoguang took a grenade from his house and went to the scene. He first knocked Gu's head with the grenade, and then threw the grenade into the crowd. The grenade exploded causing two deaths, and more than twenty injuries. After the case broke, seventeen victims brought the lawsuit to Wenzhou Intermediate People's Court for civil compensation. Through mediation, eleven victims voluntarily withdrew their case after receiving a total of 31,200 yuan.

The first trial court convicted defendant Chen Guoguang with bombing and sentenced him with the death penalty and deprival of political rights for life. The court convicted defendant Chen Guohe with disturbing the peace and sentenced him to three years of imprisonment. The court also ordered defendants Chen Guoguang, Chen Guohe, and another defendant to provide financial compensation to Zhou Lixian in the amount of 65,768 yuan, Zhou Xiaohong in the amount of 121,300 yuan, Ji Guohua in the amount of 77,098 yuan, Zhang Cunmei in the amount of 63,830 yuan, Wang Guojin in the amount of 57,324 yuan, and Mao Xiufen in the amount of 54,967 yuan.

After the announcement of the sentence, the defendants appealed. Defendant Chen Guoguang and his defense attorney argued that victim Gu Linyun shared some responsibility for his own death. The first trial court did not have sufficient evidence to prove that Chen Guoguang ignited the grenade, and that Chen Guoguang revealed information about other crimes, thus provided meritorious services to law enforcement, and should be given leniency. Chen Guohe and his attorney argued that Chen voluntarily turned himself in, thus should deserve judicial leniency.

The Superior Court of Zhejiang Province investigated the case and determined that the facts presented by the first trial court regarding Chen Guoguang's bombing and Chen Guohe's disturbing peace convictions were truthful and supported with sufficient evidence. Defendant Chen Guoguang's arguments that victim Gu shared some fault, Chen did not ignite the grenade, and that Chen performed meritorious deeds were not credible, thus were not accepted by the court. Chen Guohe did voluntarily turn himself in, but it had already been taken into consideration in the sentencing by the first trial court, thus will not be considered by this court.

The Superior Court of Zhejiang Province ruled that defendant Chen Guoguang's bombing threatened the public safety, causing two deaths, and more than twenty injuries. The crime was extremely severe and the consequences were extremely grave. This is especially the case given that it was only due to a trivial altercation. Chen Guoguang's behavior constituted bombing and should be given a heavier penalty. Defendant Chen Guohe was involved in the fight that caused severe consequences, thus it constituted disturbing the peace, and should be severely punished. Chen Guohe voluntarily turned himself in. His sentence thus may be reduced. Both Chens' crimes have caused severe financial losses for the victims and thus they should provide adequate compensation to the victim. Chens' arguments for reduced sentence are not valid and thus are not supported by the court.

In accordance to the first item of Article 115, the first item of Article 293, the first item of Article 57, the first item of Article 67, the first item of Article 36 of the Criminal Law, Articles 119 and 130 of the Civil Law, the first item of Article 189 of the Criminal Procedure Law, and Articles 1 and 3 of the Civil Procedure Law, the court issued the following ruling:

1. Dismiss the appeals;
2. Remove the original rulings regarding Zhou Xiaohong's civil compensation, and sustain other parts of the original rulings;

3. Defendant Chen Guoguang and Chen Guohe are ordered to pay Zhou Xiaohong a total of 180,130 yuan.

This decision is final.

Based on the Supreme People's Court's Notice of Authorizing Superior Courts and Military Courts Approval of Some Death Penalty Cases, this court decision also served as an approval of Chen Guoguang's death sentence and deprival of political rights for life for the crime of bombing.

Source: Qimei Zhang. *Judicial Document Selections of the People's Court — Zhejiang 2000*. Beijing: Law Press, 2001, 4–7.

CASE 9

Xiang Yanrong: selling narcotics

Judicial Judgment Document of First Trial:
Kunmin Intermediate People's Court of Yunnan Province (2001).
Criminal First #70.
Judicial Judgment Document of Second Trial:
Superior People's Court of Yunnan Province (2001).
Yun Superior Criminal Final #770.
Original Prosecutorial Agency:
The People's Procuratorate of Kunming City, Yunnan Province.
Appellant (Defendant in the first trial):
Xiang Yanrong
Female, born on March 24, 1960, Han ethnicity, high school educated, unemployed, originally from Sichuan Yunyang County, lived at Zhangfeng Trading Station of Long Chuan County, Yunnan Province, detained on April 23, 2000, and arrested on May 31 the same year.
Defense Attorney:
Hu Tuanxiang
Beichuan Law Firm.
Appellant (Defendant in the first trial):
Xiang Mingyan
Female, born on August 27, 1970, Han ethnicity, high school educated, unemployed, originally from Sichuan Yunyang County, lived at Tuanje Road #27, Longyang County Chengzi Zhen, Yunnan Province, detained on April 23, 2000, and arrested on May 31 the same year.
Defense Attorney:
Sun Xiang
Beichuan Law Firm.

First Trial Completed:
April 4, 2001
Second Trial Completed:
July 25, 2001

Prosecuting and defense arguments in the first trial

Kunmin People's Procuratorate of Yunnan Province accused that on April 22, 2000, defendants Xiang Yanrong and Xiang Mingyan were arrested by the police officers on the scene when selling illicit drugs in room 305 of the Beilong Hotel. The procuratorate charged both defendants with the crime of selling narcotics and brought them to prosecution based on the first item of the second clause of Article 347 of the PRC Criminal Law.

Both defendants Xinag Yanrong and Xiang Minyan denied the charges by the procuratorate. Defendant Xiang Yanrong argued that she was induced by the police and police informants to help sell illicit drugs. She was merely to introduce the buyer and the seller. Her sister (Xiang Mingyan) was not involved in the deal at all. She said that she voluntarily surrendered and performed meritorious services and pled for leniency. Her defense attorney argued that the police informant who posed as a buyer offered written testimony only after the procuratorate office returned the police's initial case for additional investigation in September, 2000. But the written testimony was signed and dated as April 22, 2000. Apparently it was a forged document. In addition, the police informant's testimonies were inconsistent and could not be trusted. Defendant Xiang Yanrong was induced by the police informant, and merely served to introduce the buyer and seller, and was not a major offender. The defense urged the court to consider Xinag's voluntary surrender to the authority and give a lenient sentence.

Defendant Xiang Mingyan argued that she had no knowledge of the drug transactions in the hotel room. Her defense attorney argued that his client did not have a criminal motive and was not involved in the transaction. In addition, the interrogation and recoding of Xiang Minyan's guilty confessions was conducted by one police officer, in violation of Article 91 of the PRC Criminal Procedure Law, and thus should not be admitted into evidence.

Facts and evidence in the first trial

The Intermediate People's Court of Kunming City conducted a public trial and concluded that defendant Xiang Yanrong invited Xiang Mingyan to sell illicit narcotics in room 305 of the Beilong Hotel and was arrested on the scene by the police authority. A total of 245 grams of heroin was confiscated.

This was supported by the following evidence:

1. The Vice Unit of the Public Security Bureau of Kunming City issued a report on the sting operation, in which it reported that on April 18, 2000, Xiang Yanrong and Xiang Mingyan claimed to have 2,000–3,000 grams of heroin for sale, and intended to find buyers in Kunming. The police bureau arranged an informant to contact the two defendants. When the transaction took place in the hotel, the two defendants were arrested and 245 grams of heroin was confiscated at around 2:00pm of April 22, 2000.
2. Physical evidence included confiscated drugs, pictures of the confiscated drugs, scientific examination records that identified the confiscated drugs as heroin and its weight of 245 grams.
3. The police informant testified that upon learning from the two defendants that they had drugs to sell, he immediately informed the police. The police instructed the informant to tell the defendants that a client from Beijing was interested in buying drugs. On April 21, the informant told the defendants that the Beijing buyer had already arrived at Kunming. The next day, the informant scheduled an appointment with the defendants to have the deal in a room at the Beilong Hotel. The defendants requested to examine the money first. At around 5:00 p.m., the two defendants came to the hotel and examined the money. They told the buyer that this time they only had one piece of drugs. They weighed it at 260 grams. The Beijing buyer gave them 20,000 yuan and was told that it was short 5,000 yuan. The Beijing buyer took out more money and paid in full for the drugs. The defendants saw that the buyer had lots of money and suggested that they would deal again in the future. The Beijing buyer said ok. When walking out of the hotel room, they were arrested. (The police informant's written testimony was dated September 29, 2000).
4. Another witness testified that after the spring festival of 2000, Xiang Yangrong and Xiang Mingyan showed him samples of drugs three times. Each time the sample was different. They asked him to get buyers for them. The witness told the police that the defendants had told him that they sold "mahuangsu" in Reili.
5. Another witness, Luo Shaojia, testified that on April 22, 2000, he was appointed by the Police Vice Unit, disguised as the Beijing buyer, and went to room 305 of the hotel to buy drugs from the defendants. He testified that he gave the defendants a total of 25,000 yuan for the drug, and when stepping out the hotel room, the two defendants were arrested by the police.
6. Defendant Xiang Yanrong stated that on April 22, 2000, she was told by another drug dealer (in the name of Xiang Jing) that there were 3,000–4,000 grams of heroin available for sale. Xiang asked for an old contact to find a buyer. On April 22, she was told by the old contact to go to the Beilong Hotel. She waited in room 305 for

three hours before the Beijing buyer showed up. The Beijing buyer paid 25,000 yuan for the drug. After counting the money and ready to leave the hotel, they were arrested. She said that when she called to contact the buyer, her sister overheard the conversation, but her sister was not involved in drug dealings. Her sister only knew that she was dealing drugs when she took out the drug to give it to the buyer. She said that she never talked to her sister about drug dealings because she did not want her sister to be involved.

7. Defendant Xiang Mingyan (Xiang Yanrong's sister) provided testimony twice on April 22, 2000. She stated that Xiang Yanrong asked her to go to the Beilong Hotel to help another drug dealer to sell heroin. After they were done with the deal in the hotel room, they were arrested by the police.

Legal reasoning by the first trial court

Based on evidence and arguments presented by both the procuratorate and the defense, Kunming Intermediate People's Court made the following rulings:

The court adopted defendant Xiang Mingyan's defense attorney's arguments that Xing Mingyan's testimonies were taken by the same and only one police investigator, which was in violation of Article 91 of the PRC Criminal Procedural Law, and shall not be admitted into evidence. The court recognized the testimonies by the disguised Beijing buyer as evidence as his testimonies were consistent with other witnesses and defendants' testimonies. The court further recognized the amount of heroin involved in this case based on testimonies of the defendants, other witnesses, and the police report. The court denied the defense attorney's argument that Xiang Yanrong was an accomplice as she was selling drugs for a major drug dealer. However, the court noted that defendant Xinag Yanrong did perform meritorious services to the authorities. The court denied Xing Mingyan's attorney's claim that she did not have criminal motive.

Based on the above reasoning, the court ruled that to make a profit, defendant Xiang Yanrong invited Xiang Mingyan to sell heroin. Her act had constituted drug trafficking. In addition, the amount of quantity involved was extremely large and the circumstances were severe. Defendant Xing Yanrong contacted the buyer and arranged the drug deal, thus should be deemed as a major offender. Due to her remorseful attitude, immediate execution is not necessary. Defendant Xiang Mingyan was invited to deal drugs, served as an accomplice, and shall be sentenced with leniency.

Sentences by the first trial court

Based on the first item of the second clause of Article 347, Articles 25, 26, and 27, the first item of Article 48, the first item of Article 57, and

Article 64, Kunming Intermediate People's Court issued the following sentences:

1. Defendant Xiang Yanrong was convicted of drug trafficking, and sentenced to death with two-year reprieve, deprival of political rights for life, and confiscation of personal property in the amount of 50,000 yuan (the death sentence with two-year reprieve shall start after the final review and approval date by the Supreme People's Court).
2. Defendant Xiang Mingyan was convicted of drug trafficking, and sentenced to seven years of incarceration, and confiscation of personal property in the amount of 10,000 yuan (the sentence should start from the day of the announcement of the sentence). The days spent in detention prior to the sentence shall be counted toward the total incarceration time. Her actual prison sentence thus should be between April 23, 2000 and April 22, 2007.
3. The 245 grams of heroin shall be confiscated.

Summary of the second trial court

After the announcement of the sentence by the first trial court, both defendants appealed to Yunnan Superior People's Court on the ground of insufficient evidence.

Upon reviewing documents and conducting investigations, Yunnan Superior People's Court concluded that the facts were clear, evidence was truthful and sufficient, sentence was proportional to the crime, and the legal procedure was followed in this case. In accordance to the first item of Article 89 and the first item of Article 201 of the PRC Criminal Procedure Law, the court issued the following ruling:

> The appeal was denied and the original sentence was sustained.

The court also approved Kunming Intermediate People's Court's death sentence with a two-year reprieve ruling for defendant Xing Yanrong.

Source: Mingshan Zhu. *Selected Chinese Criminal Court Cases — 2002*. Beijing: Chinese People's University Publishing House, 2003, 480–4.

CASE 10

Gong Liangchao et al.: organizing others in prostitution

Judicial Judgment Document of First Trial:
Enshi Tujiazu Miaozu Autonomous Region Intermediate People's Court of Hubei Province (2001). Criminal First #51.

Judicial Judgment Document of Second Trial:
Superior People's Court of Hubei Province (2001).
Er Superior Criminal Final #441.
Original Prosecutorial Agency:
The People's Procuratorate of Enshi Tujiazu Miaozu Autonomous Region, Hubei Province.
Appellant (Defendant in the first trial):
Gong Liangchao
Male, thirty years old, Tujia ethnicity, self-employed, originally from Xianfeng County, Hubei Province, arrested on January 26, 1996.
Defense Attorney:
Lan Kunshan
Xianfeng County Law Firm, Hubei Province.
Appellant (Defendant in the first trial):
Xu Xiaomei
Male, twenty-nine years old, Tujia ethnicity, worker, originally from Xianfeng County, Hubei Province, arrested on January 26, 1996.
Appellant (Defendant in the first trial):
Liao Kangying
Female, twenty-one years old, Tujia ethnicity, peasant, originally from Enshi County, Hubei Province, arrested on January 26, 1996.
Defense Attorney:
Lu Ming
Wuling Law Firm, Enshi Autonomous Region, Hubei Province.
First Trial Completed:
August 28, 1996
Second Trial Completed:
September 24, 1996

Prosecuting and defense arguments in the first rrial

Enshi Tujiazu Miaozhu Autonomous Region People's Procuratorate of Hubei Province accused that between fall 1994 and December 9, 1995, defendant Gong Liangchao, along with defendants Xiao Xiaomei and Liao Kangying, recruited, induced, and provided shelter for eighteen young women to engage in prostitution using his restaurant business as a disguise. They engaged in prostitution with more than one hundered customers. During that time, defendants Gong Liangchao and Xu Xiaomei also engaged in illicit sexual activities with the prostitutes for numerous times. The Prosecutorate argued that defendants Gong and Xu's behavior has constituted organizing others into prostitution and hooliganism, and defendant Liao Kangying's behavior has constituted assisting in organizing others into prostitution.

Defendants' and the defense attorneys' defense

Gong and his defense attorney claimed that Gong recruited some waitresses for the purpose of running his restaurant business, not for engaging in illegal activities. The waitresses did not follow his order and secretly engaged in prostitution. Upon learning that his employees were engaging in prostitution, Gong did not stop them immediately, but never did he force and order them to engage in prostitution. Therefore the procuratorate's accusation was inappropriate. Xu Xiaomei claimed that he was employed by Gong to assist him to operate the restaurant business. He was not involved in recruiting the waitresses, let alone inducing, forcing, and organizing them into prostitution, thus he should not be charged with the crime. Liao Kangying and her defense attorney claimed that she was induced by others to commit the crime. She confessed to the crime and had no criminal motivation, thus pleading for leniency.

Facts and evidence in the first trial

The Enshi Tujiazu Miaozu Autonomous Region Intermediate People's Court of Hubei Province investigated with a closed hearing and concluded below:

In February 1994, defendant Gong Liangchao rented a house and started Heyi Restaurant. In August 1994, he added a bar and changed the name of the restaurant to Heyi Teahouse. To attract customers, Gong started to organize young women Zhang, Chen, and Wu to engage in prostitution. In December, Dong hired defendant Xu Xiaomei. While Gong was in charge of hiring, managing, and arranging prostituting services, when Gong was not available, Xu was authorized to make decisions for him. In May 1995, Gong hired defendant Liao Kangying with 300 yuan per month to be in charge of the waitresses. She has some managing responsibilities, including managing the keys to rooms for prostitution, and collecting fees. Liao was also asked by Gong to recruit prostitutes. In July, the name of the restaurant was once again changed to Sili Bamboo Village.

Gong and Xu openly recruited young women for prostitution. They clearly stated that the women are not allowed to go out with customers on their own; they must get permission from Gong and be arranged by Xu when going out with customers. Liao was in charge of all businesses in the restaurant. If the women did not provide satisfactory services to the customer, their salary may be deducted. At one time, Liu and He went out with customers without notifying the boss. Upon learning the news, Xu beat the two women. Meanwhile, Gong and Xu engaged in illicit sexual activities with five and six employees, respectively.

Between August 1994 and November 1995, Gong and Xu, along with Liao recruited, induced, and provided shelter for twenty-one young women to engage in prostitution in the restaurant. Each woman was paid 200 yuan per month with room and board accommodations. In addition, pimps, after getting consent from Gong and Xu, rented nine prostitutes from the restaurant and engaged in thirty-nine sexual activities in thirteen different locations. After the case broke, more than one hundred pimps were investigated, among them, sixty-two were public officials (sixty were given fines, and forty-one were given administrative and Party warnings and administrative sanctions). To cover up the illegal operation, Xu destroyed most of the account books. From the confiscated accounting books of three months, Gong, Xu, and Liao profited a total of 39,535 yuan by providing prostituting services.

The above facts were supported by the following evidence:

1. Prostitutes' testimony;
2. Pimps' testimony;
3. Documents confiscated by the public security agency.

Legal reasoning by the first trial court

Enshi Tujiazu Miaozu Autonomous Region Intermediate People's Court of Hubei Province ruled that defendant Gong and Xu recruited, induced and provided shelter for twenty-one young women to engage in prostitution, profited an extremely large amount of money, and caused grave social harm. Their acts have constituted organizing others into prostitution. After being arrested, they tried to cover up their crimes and their attitude was bad. Defendant Liao assisted Gong and Xu to organize young women to engage in prostitution. Her behavior has constituted assisting in organizing others into prostitution. After being arrested, she confessed to the crime, and showed good attitude. Gong and Xu engaged in illicit sexual activities, though immoral, did not constitute criminal activities.

According to Criminal Law and the NPC Resolution on Prohibiting Prostitution and Pimping, the court decided to severely punish these criminals.

Sentences by the first trial court

Based on the facts and evidence presented in this case, the overall circumstances (e.g., nature, circumstances, social harm, and defendants' role) surrounding the case, the first item of Article 53, Articles 22 and 23 of the Criminal Law and the first Item of Article one and Article two of the Resolution on Prohibiting Prostitution and Pimping issued by the National People's Congress, Enshi Tujiazu Miaozu Autonomous Region Intermediate People's Court of Hubei Province issued the following ruling:

1. Defendant Gong Liangchao was convicted of organizing others into prostitution, and sentenced to death, deprival of political rights for life, and confiscation of personal property.
2. Defendant Xu Xiaomei was convicted of organizing others into prostitution, and sentenced to death with a two year suspension, deprival of political rights for life, and confiscation of personal property.
3. Defendant Liao Kangying was convicted of assisting in organizing others into prostitution, and was sentenced with five years of imprisonment and 1,000 yuan in fines.

Summary of the second trial court

After the announcement of the first court ruling, Gong and Xu appealed to the Superior Court of Hubei Province. Liao accepted the first court ruling and did not appeal. Gong and Xu provided similar arguments and defense in the appeals as in the first trial. They argued that their behavior did not constitute organizing others into prostitution, but instead provided shelter for women to engage in prostitution. They also argued that the sentence was too severe and requested for leniency.

Legal reasoning by the second trial court

The Superior Court of Hubei Province upon receiving the appeal, reviewed the court documents, and investigated the case carefully. It concluded that the facts of the case presented by the first trial court were truthful, and evidence was sufficient. The decision was based on the following evidence:

1. Prostitutes Nie, Liao, Chen, Wu, Li, Peng, Xie, Ding's testimonies;
2. Pimps' testimonies;
3. Accounting books of three months confiscated from Gong and Xu;
4. Administrative sanctions and Party sanctions of sixty-one pimps involving governmental officials;
5. Gong and Xu's testimonies.

The Superior Court of Hubei Province concluded that defendants Gong and Xu recruited, induced and provided shelter for twenty-one young women to engage in prostitution. Their behaviors constituted organizing others into prostitution. Their crime was extremely severe and circumstances were grave, and they should be severely punished. Gong played a major role in the crime. He was the organizer and the main conspirator, and should be sentenced to death. Xu was also a main conspirator, and his crime deserves to be punished with the death penalty. However, his involvement in the crime was not as extensive as Gong, thus immediate execution is not necessary. The Court rejected Gong and Xu's appeals on the ground that they did not commit the crime of organizing others into prostitution and deserved leniency. Liao actively assisted Gong and Xu to organize others into prostitution. Her behavior constituted assisting in organizing others into prostitution. The first court's rulings were appropriate and the procedure was legal. However, the first court's ruling of confiscating Gong and Xu's property did not specify the amount, thus deemed inappropriate and should be reversed. According to the resolution of the NPC and related articles of Criminal Law and Criminal Procedure law, this court modified parts of the first court's ruling on this case.

Sentences by the second trial court

After thorough investigation, on September 24, 1996, the Superior Court of Hubei Province ruled based on Article one of the Resolution of Prohibiting Prostitution issued by the NPC, and Articles 22, 23, 24, and the first item of Article 53 of the Criminal Law, and the first and second items of Article 136 of the Criminal Procedure Law. Its ruling included the following:

1. Reject the appeal, and sustain the first trial's rulings by sentencing Gong Liangchao with the death penalty and deprival of political rights for life; Xu Xiaomei death with a two year suspension and deprival of political rights for life for organizing others into prostitution; and Liao Kangying with five years of imprisonment with 1,000 yuan fines for committing the crime of assisting in organizing others into prostitution.
2. Overturn the first trial court's ruling of confiscating Gong Liangchao and Xu Xiaomei's property.

This ruling is final.

According to the Supreme Court's decision authorizing superior courts to conduct final review and approve some death penalty cases, this ruling also serves as the final review and approval for Gong Liangchao's death sentence.

Source: Mingshan Zhu. *Selected Chinese Criminal Court Cases — 1997.* Beijing: Chinese People's University Publishing House, 1998, 433–7.

Notes

CHAPTER 1

1. Only a few Western studies have been done on China's death penalty. For example, Michael Palmer, "The People's Republic of China." In *Capital Punishment Global Issues and Prospects*, eds. Peter Hodgkinson and Andrew Rutherford. (UK: Waterside Press, 1996). Alan W. Lepp, "Note: The Death Penalty in Late Imperial, Modern, and Post-Tiananmen China," *Michigan Journal of International Law* 11 (1990): 987–1038. Andrew Scobell, "Strung Up or Shot Down?: The Death Penalty in Hong Kong and China and Implications for Post-1997," *Case West Reserve Journal of International Law* 20 (1988):147–67. Stephen B. Davis, "The Death Penalty and Legal Reform in the PRC," *Journal of Chinese Law* 1 (1987): 303–34. Most of these studies were published before the major revision of the Criminal Law and Criminal Procedure Law in 1997 and 1996. While providing valuable review of historical and legal issues surrounding the death penalty practices in China, most studies failed to examine the complex procedural requirements of the death sentence.
2. Xingya Fang, Limin Bao, and Xin Wen. "Murder by Four Peasants in Hebei," *Xinhuan News* at http://news.xinhuanet.com/legal/2004-03/31/content_1392842.htm.
3. Wenbin Fei, Zuocai Yu, and Yuncai Tang. "Death Row Convict Allowed to Meet with Family Members," the Supreme Court Web site at http://www.chinacourt.org/public/detail.php?id=198612 (3/16/2006).
4. Xiao Ni. "Reforms in Kunming Courts," *Legal Daily* at http://www.legal-daily.com.cn/misc/2006-04/07/content_296220.htm.
5. "Conviction without Confessions," cited from *Today Morning News* (7/27/2001), *China Internet News Center* at http://www.china.org.cn/chinese/LP/46479.htm.
6. Zheng Li. "Rapist's Confession Minutes Prior to Execution," cited from *Beijing Youth Gazette* by *People's Daily* at http://unn.people.com.cn/GB/channel286/287/696/200112/04/133416.html.
7. "Legal Aid Exonerated a Death Row Inmate," Justice Ministry of Anhui Province Web site at http://www.ahsft.gov.cn/oldver/flyz/fyxx/20030702/2003070202.htm.
8. Amnesty International. *China Death Penalty Logs* (1996–2004).
9. See Piers Beirne, 1983. "Generalization and Its Discontents — the Comparative Study of Crime." In *Comparative Criminology*, eds. Israel L. Barak-Glantz and Elmer H. Johnson (Sage Publications, 1983), 29.

10. William A. Schabas, "International Legal Aspects." In *Capital Punishment — Global Issues and Prospects,* eds. Peter Hodgkinson and Andrew Rutherford. (U.K.: Waterside Press, 1966), 17–44.
11. Schabas, 1996, 17–44.
12. The *Safeguards* were drafted by the Committee on Crime Prevention and Control in 1984. It was endorsed by the Economic and Social Council, the General Assembly, and the Seventh United Nations Congress on the Prevention of Crime and the Treatment of Offenders in 1985 (Schabas 1996, 27).
13. The United Nations has passed several resolutions related to the death penalty since the birth of its organization. For example, the Universal Declaration of Human Rights, the International Covenant on Civil and Political Rights, along with several failed attempts (e.g., the resolution containing the proposal of a moratorium on the death penalty in 1990 failed to obtain a two-thirds majority support) (Schabas 1996, 26–27).
14. See Economic and Social Council Resolution 1984/50, Annex. General Assembly Resolution 29/118, 1984. See also Schabas, 1996, 27.
15. For a more complete discussion on the European movement, see Roger Hood. *The Death Penalty: A Worldwide Perspective,* third edition. (Oxford University Press, 2002), 16–18.
16. For subsequent developments in the Organization of American States on the issues of the death penalty, see Hood, 2002, 15.
17. See Schabas, 1966, 18–20 for the description of these developments. The particular types of crime and persons who were excluded from the imposition of the death penalty by the Arab charter included political crimes and nonserious crimes, children (under the age of eighteen), pregnant women, nursing mothers for a period of up to two years following childbirth (Schabas 1996, 20).
18. International criminal court has jurisdiction over cases that seriously violated humanitarian law such as genocide, and certain narcotics crimes and terrorism (Schabas 1996, 29).
19. See Schabas, 1996, 29–30.
20. Amnesty International. *Facts and Figures on the Death Penalty* (June, 2005).
21. See *Amnesty International Annual Reports.* 2005: Africa, Americas, Asia and the Pacific, Europe and Central Asia, Middle East and North Africa.
22. Hood, 2002, 75.
23. Hood, 2002, 75–77.
24. As of 2002, 77 retentionist countries made crimes against state capital offenses. Crimes against the state have been variously interpreted as espionage, treason, counter-revolutionary activities, evading military service, sabotage and corruption on earth, planning to detonate bombs and assassinate governmental officials. By the end of 2002, at least fourteen nations imposed the death penalty on offenses against public order, which was variously defined as terrorism (e.g., hijacking), commission of the crime with firearms and explosives, attempted to murder a police officer, illegal arms trade, and numerous military offenses (Hood 2002, 78–79).
25. By the end of 1998, thirty-four countries were known to impose the death penalty on drug offenses. Several countries have even made the death penalty mandatory for drug trafficking (particularly recidivist drug offenders) such as Iran, Singapore, Malaysia (Hood 2002, 80–82).
26. By the end of 2002, at least twenty-five countries penalize economic (e.g., bribery, embezzlement, currency or security counterfeiting, profiteering,

fraud, smuggling) and property offense (e.g., banditry, aggravated robbery, theft) with the death penalty (Hood 2002, 82–83).

27. At least thirty countries impose the death penalty on sexual offenses including rape, abduction and rape, rape and incest, raping a minor, unlawful sexual intercourse with a prisoner, adultery, sodomy, homosexual acts with violence, recidivist prostitution, and pimping (Hood 2002, 83–84).
28. In some Islamic countries, religious dissent such as blasphemy or apostasy may be punished to death (Hood 2002, 85).
29. According to *Amnesty International Death Sentences and Executions,* in 1995, 4,165 death sentences in seventy-nine countries and 2,931 executions from forty-one countries were imposed; the 1985 report revealed 1,437 death sentences from sixty-one countries and 1,125 executions from forty-four countries.
30. For a review of these methods and previous studies, see Terance D. Miethe and Hong Lu, *Punishment—A Comparative Historical Perspective* (Cambridge: Cambridge University Press, 2005). See also Rita Simon and Dagny A. Blaskovich, *A Comparative Analysis of Capital Punishment: Statues, Policies, Frequencies, and Public Attitudes the World Over* (New York: Lexington Books, 2002).
31. Many Islamic countries use stoning and beheading (e.g., Sudan, Iran, Saudi Arabia, Yemen). Before the introduction of lethal injection, the primary methods of execution in the United States were electrocution, gas chamber (Miethe and Lu 2005, 37–44 and 167).
32. Lethal injection was first introduced in Oklahoma in 1977. Currently, thirty-three states in the United States use lethal injection as one of the execution methods. See John H. Culver, "Capital Punishment Politics and Policies in the States, 1977–1997." *Crime, Law & Social Change* 32(1999):287–300.
33. See Austin Sarat and Boulanger, *The Cultural Lives of Capital Punishment: Comparative Perspectives* (CA: Stanford University Press, 2005). M. Costanzo, *Just Revenge: Costs and Consequences of the Death Penalty* (New York: St. Martin's Press, 1997). D. C. Baldus, G. Woodworth, and C. A. Palaski, *Equal Justice and the Death Penalty: A Legal and Empirical Analysis* (Boston: Northwestern University Press, 1990). H. H. Haines and H. Haines, *Against Capital Punishment: The Anti-Death Penalty Movement in America, 1972–1994* (Oxford University Press, 1996).
34. For examples, juveniles under eighteen years old were sentenced to death and executed in the United States in recent decades. Empirical studies found that juvenile offenders receiving the death sentence tended to experience a long history of abuse, had unusually high incidence of neurological impairment, psychiatric disorders, and low IQ. See D. O. Lewis, M. Feldman, L. Jackson, and B. Bard, "Psychiatric, Neurological, and Psycho-educational Characteristics of 15 Death Row Inmates in the United States." *American Journal of Psychiatry* 143(1986): 838–45. For arbitrary, selective, and discriminatory imposition of the death penalty, see J. A. Acker, R. M. Rohm, and C. S. Lanier, *America's Experiment with Capital Punishment — Reflections on the Past, Present, and the Future of the Ultimate Penal Sanction* (Durham, NC: Carolina Academic Press, 1998). For the erroneous sentence and execution, see James S. Liebman, Jeffrey Fagan, Valerie West, and Jonathan Lloyd, "Capital Attrition: Error Rates in Capital Cases, 1973–1995." *Texas Law Review* 78(2000):1771–1803.
35. For example, both the United Kingdom and Canada abolished the death penalty. However, recent public opinion surveys showed that citizens in both countries had a favorable attitude toward the death penalty in instances of

murder. See Lindsay Brook and E. Cape, "Libertarianism in Retreat," in *British Social Attitudes: The 12th Report,* eds. R. Jowell, J. Curtis, A. Park, L. Brook, and D. Ahrendt (Aldershot: Dartmouth Publishing, 1995), 191–209.

36. Lord Windlesham, *Responses to Crime: Penal Policy in the Making.* Volume 1 (Oxford : Clarendon Press, 1987).
37. For example, in 2004, out of the 3,797 recorded executions, China accounted for 3,400. In 1995, it was recorded that China had 2,190 executions. The total number of executions that year was 2,931 (see *Amnesty International Death Sentences and Execution,* 1995, 2004).
38. See Miethe and Lu, 2005, 115–44.
39. Cambodia and Costa Rica abolished the death penalty for all crimes in 1989 and 1877, respectively. The last execution in Mexico was in 1947. See Amnesty International, *The Death Penalty: List of Abolitionist and Retentionist Countries,* February 1, 2004.
40. In fact, most European nations, while following the civil law inquisitorial legal system, have long abolished the death penalty.

CHAPTER 2

1. See Max Weber, *Law in Economy and Society,* ed. Max Rheinstein, trans. Edward Shils and Max Rheistein (Cambridge: Harvard University Press, 1954). Also Max Weber, *Economy and Society,* trans. Guenther Roth and Claus Wittich (New York: Bedminster Press, 1968), 5.
2. Donald Black, *The Behavior of Law* (New York: Academic Press, 1976), 2.
3. Steven Vago, *Law and Society,* fourth ed. (Englewood Cliffs, NJ: Prentice Hall, 1994), 13–15.
4. Robert L. Kidder, *Connecting Law and Society — An Introduction to Research and Theory* (Englewood Cliffs, NJ: Prentice-Hall,1983), 4–5.
5. Roscoe Pound, *The Spirit of the Common Law* (Boston: Marshall Jones, 1921). See also Roscoe Pound, "Sociology of law and sociological jurisprudence." *University of Toronto Law Journal* 5(1943): 1–20.
6. Vago, 1994, 47–49.
7. Richard Quinney, *The Critique of Legal Order* (Boston: Little, Brown, 1974), 16. See also William Chambliss and Robert Seidman, *Law, Order, and Power,* second edition (Reading, MA: Addison-Wesley, 1982).
8. Piers Beirne and Alan Hunt, "Law and Constitution of Soviet Society: The Case of Comrade Lenin." *Law & Society Review* 22(1988): 575–615. See also Paul Paolucci, "The Discursive transformation of Marx's Communism into Soviet Diamat." *Critical Sociology* 30(2004): 617–67. See also William C. Jones, "Trying to Understand the Current Chinese Legal System." In *Understanding China's Legal System — Essays in Honor of Jerome A. Cohen,* ed. C. Stephen Hsu, New York: New York University Press, 2003), 22–38.
9. Xingzhong Yu, "Legal Pragmatism in the People's Republic of China." *Journal of Chinese Law* 3(1989): 29–51.
10. For further readings on legal realism, see Jerome Frank, *Courts on Trial: Myth and Reality in American Justice* (Princeton, NJ: Princeton University Press, 1950). O. W. Holmes, *The Common Law* (London: Macmillan, 1968). Karl Llewellyn, *Jurisprudence: Realism in Theory and Practice* (Chicago: University of Chicago Press, 1962).
11. David M. Trubek, "Where the action is: CLS and Empiricism," *Stanford Law Review* 36(1984): 575–622. See also David M. Trubek and John Esser,

"'Critical Empiricism' in American Legal Studies: Parodox, Program, or Pandora's Box?" *Law & Social Inquiry* 14(1989): 3–52.

12. The decade of the 1980s mainly saw reform efforts in the rural sector with privatization of the land and the responsibility system designed to stimulate agricultural productivity. In the 1990s, urban reforms were deepened. Following the promotion of entrepreneurship in the 1980s, the privatization of state-owned enterprises was coupled with a series of urban reform policies dealing with privatization of housing, pension, and medicare.
13. Justin Lin, "Rural Reforms and Agricultural Growth in China." *American Economic Review* 82(1992): 34–51. See also Justin Lin, Fang Cai, and Zhou Li, *The China Miracle — Development Strategy and Economic Reform* (Hong Kong: The Chinese University Press, 2003), 3–18.
14. See Rongji Zhu, "A Brighter Future — Forward." In *China's Century — the Awakening of the Next Economic Powerhouse,* ed. Laurence J. Brahm (New York: John Wiley & Sons, 2001), xi–xv.
15. According to the *World Development Report* released by the World Bank in recent years, China's annual GDP growth rates since 1980 averaged over 10 percent, representing the highest growth rate in the world during the last twenty-five-year period.
16. See Laurence J. Brahm,(ed.) *China's Century — the Awakening of the Next Economic Powerhouse* (New York: John Wiley & Sons, 2001).
17. See Hongwei Zhao, *Political Regime of Contemporary China* (New York: University Press of America, 2002), 46–49.
18. For example, since the Organic Village Committee Law of the People's Republic of China was promulgated in 1998, such local elections were held each year, some with international observers present. See "U.S. Delegation Observes Village Election in China." *People's Daily* (1/08/2000) at http://english.people.com.cn/english/200001/08/eng20000108W110.html. See also Zhao, 2002, 46–49.
19. John McMillan, John Whalley, and Lijing Zhu, "The Impact of China's Economic Reforms on Agricultural Productivity Growth." *Journal of Political Economy* 97(1989):781–807. Also see Xiushi Yang, "Household Registration, Economic Reform and Migration." *International Migration Review* 27(1993):796–818. York W. Bradshaw and Elvis Fraser, "City Size, Economic Development, and Quality of Life in China: New Empirical Evidence." *American Sociological Review* 54(1989): 986–1003.
20. John P. Burns, "The People's Republic of China at 50: National Political Reform." *China Quarterly* 159(1999): 580–94.
21. Martin Ravallion and Shaohua Chen, "When Economic Reform is Faster Than Statistical Reform: Measuring and Explaining Income Inequality in Rural China." *Oxford Bulletin of Economics and Statistics* 61(1999): 33. Also see Yanjie Bian and John R. Logan, "Market Transition and the Persistence of Power: The Changing Stratification System in Urban China." *American Sociological Review* 61(1996): 739–58.
22. The "floating population" is the term applied to the population movement after the weakening of the urban household registration system. With the economic reforms, control over the population movement has been relaxed, resulting in people, primarily rural residents, leaving their native land and migrating to urban areas for employment and opportunities. This transient population is labeled as the "floating population," which has been collectively blamed for crime and disorder in the urban area. See Curran, D. J., "Economic Reform, the Floating Population, and Crime — The Transformation of Social Control in China." *Journal of Contemporary Criminal Justice*

14(1998): 262–80. See also Joseph C.H. Chai and B. Karin Chai, "China's Floating Population and Its Implications." *International Journal of Social Economics* 24(1997):1038–51.

23. Dean G. Rojek, "Chinese Social Control: From Shaming and Reintegration to 'getting rich is glorious." In *Crime and Social Control in a Changing China*, eds. Jianhong Liu, Lening Zhang and Steven Messner (Westport, CT: Greenwood Press, 2001), 89–104.
24. Richard Levy, "Corruption, Economic Crime and Social Transformation since the Reforms: The Debate in China." *Australian Journal of Chinese Affairs* 33 (1995):1–25. See also Barbara N. Sands, "Decentralizing an Economy: The Role of Bureaucratic Corruption in China's Economic Reforms." *Public Choice* 65(1990):85–91. Willard H. Myers III, "The Emerging Threat of Transnational Organized Crime from the East." *Crime, Law and Social Change* 24(1995):181–222.
25. These characteristics of Chinese law were summarized by the Chinese famous legal scholar, Dr. Shilun Li in his various published works, cited from Xuechao Zhang, "Comments on Professor Shilun Li's Legal History and Thoughts." In *On the Front of the Legal Theory*, eds. Lu, Jingsheng, Chibin Fu, and Zhong Gao (Beijing: The Chinese Procuratorate Press, 2004), 87–109.
26. Chen, Jianfu, *Chinese Law — Towards an Understanding of Chinese Law, Its Nature and Development* (London: Kluwer Law International, 1999), 14–7. For Chinese law's instrumentalism and pragmatism, see also Yu, 1989, 29–51. Pitman B. Potter, *The Chinese Legal System — Globalization and Local Legal Culture* (London: Routledge, 2001), 4–15. For discussions on differences between Western law and the Chinese law, see Stanley Lubman, *Bird in a Cage — Legal Reform in China after Mao* (Stanford, CA: Stanford University Press, 1999), 1–10.
27. Zhou Enlai served as the Premier of the People's Republic of China since its establishment in 1949 until his death in 1976 while serving as Foreign Minister from 1949 to 1958. For more detailed discussions about Zhou, see S. Kuo-kang, *Zhou Enlai and the Foundations of Chinese Foreign Policy* (New York: St. Martin's Press, 1996).
27. In the legal arena, there have been many theoretical debates such as rule of law vs. rule of man, party's leadership and the supremacy of law, market economy and law, nature of law, division of private law and public law, democracy and law spirits of modern law, and legal transplant. See Wang, Chengguang, "Introduction: An Emerging Legal System." In *Introduction to Chinese Law*, eds. Chengguang Wang and Xianchu Zhang (Hong Kong: Sweet & Maxwell, 1997), 26–28. Also see Roderick MacFarquhar and Leroy B. Williams, "The Succession to Mao and the End of Maoism." In *The Cambridge History of China: The People's Republic, Part 2: Revolutions within the Chinese Revolution 1966–1982*, eds. Roderick MacFarquhar and John K. Fairbank (Cambridge, Cambridge University Press, 1991), 305–401.
29. Xiaoping Deng, *Selected Works of Deng Xiaoping* (Beijing: People's Publishing House, 1983),173, 217. See also Chen, 1999, 40–48.
30. Xiaoping Deng, *Selected Works of Deng Xiaoping* third edition (Beijing: People's Publishing House, 1993), 325, 379.
31. Xiaoping Deng, *Selected Works of Deng Xiaoping*, second edition (Beijing: People's Publishing House, 1984), 147.
32. Ibid.
33. Deng, 1993, 325, 379.
34. Ibid., 90.
35. Deng, 1984, 189.

36. During the chaotic ten years (1966–1976), lawmaking was completely halted. These first series of laws drafted in the late 1970s and the early 1980s represented the most urgent matters needed to be addressed by law — the maintenance of the political, economic, and social order. See Yang Xiao, "A New Chapter in Constructing China's Legal System." In *China's Century — The Awakening of the Next Economic Powerhouse,* ed. Laurence J. Brahm (New York: John Wiley & Sons, 2001), 218–33.
37. The political overtone of the laws enacted in the late 1970s and the early 1980s was primarily due to the fact that these laws were drafted during the 1950s and the 1970s, which inevitably reflected the sociopolitical conditions of that time period. For example, the criminal law and criminal procedure law were drafted numerous times during the 1950s–1960s and were finally passed in 1979. See Harold Tanner, *Strike Hard!* (Ithaca, NY: Cornell East Asia Series, 1999).
38. Zemin Jiang, "The talk at the Third legal forum held by the Central Committee of the Chinese Communist Party," *People's Daily*, 1996, February 9.
39. Readers should be cautioned that the Chinese conception of "rule of law" is qualitatively different from the Western "rule of law" because of the different political and economic foundations. For example, China insisted upon one party, not multi-party control, which fundamentally violated one of the core ideas of Western "rule of law" — separation of power. Another reason was that the Chinese government accused Western democracy of serving only a small group of capitalist elites' interests. In contrast, the Chinese law was designed to serve the people.
40. Xuechao Zhang, "The Deepening and Innovation of Deng Xiaoping's Thought on Democracy and Law — on Jiang Zeming's Thought on Democracy and Law." In *On the Front of the Legal Theory*, eds. Jingsheng Lu, Chibin Fu, and Zhong Gao (Beijing: the Chinese Procuratory Press, 2004), 444–67.
41. As the economic reforms deepened, more laws were needed to meet the needs of new economic activities and relations such as laws on company, contract, foreign trade, arbitration, and securities (Xiao 2001, 218–33).
42. See Guangzhong Chen, Weiqiu Cheng, and Vincent C. Yang (eds.), *A Study on Issues in Ratifying and Implementing International Covenant on Civil and Political Rights* (Beijing: China Legal System Press, 2002).
43. See *The Collection of Documents Presented at the Fifteenth National Representative Meetings of the Chinese Communist Party* (Beijing: People's Press, 1997), 34–35.
44. See Vincent C. Yang, 2002. "Judicial and Legal Training in China — Current Status of Professional Development and Topics of Human Rights." A background paper for the United Nations Office of the High Commissioner for Human Rights. Availabnle at http://www.icclr.law.ubc.ca/Publications/Reports/Beijing_August_2002.pdf.
45. See "The Second Lecture on Law Held by the Central Committee of the Chinese Communist Party." *People's Daily,* 1995, January 21. Also see Zemin Jiang, "Intensifying the Reform and Open-door Policy." *Action Guide for the Twenty-First Century* (Beijing: Xinhua Press, 1992), 26.
46. As to legal instrumentalism in China's economic reform era, for social engineering in contemporary China as the Communist Party dictates the goals and the roles of law in the context of economic reforms. See Jianfu Chen, *Chinese Law — Towards an Understanding of Chinese Law, Its Nature and Development* (London: Kluwer Law International, 1999), 355–63.
47. For competing definitions for rule of law and discussions of the fundamental purposes and role of law in contemporary China, see Randall Peerenboom,

"Ruling the Country in Accordance with Law: Reflections on the Rule and Role of Law in Contemporary China." *Cultural Dynamics* 11(1999): 315–51. Alford, however, challenged the realization of rule of law in the current Chinese context citing the inferior status of the judiciary to the administrative branch, and more importantly to the Communist Party (William P. Alford, "A Second Great Wall? China's Post-Cultural Revolution Project of Legal Construction." *Cultural Dynamics* 11(1999): 193–213).

48. In the Chinese academic and legal circles, truth-finding in legal process is not only necessary, but also possible. See Congyi Fan, *Opinions on Objective Truth — A Discussion of the Standard of Proof in Criminal Processes* (Beijing: China Law Press, 2000).
49. Other than the primary agency for criminal investigation and evidence gathering, the Chinese procuratorate enjoys special supervisory power in judicial proceedings, following the Soviet socialist legal model. The power manifests in two aspects: (1) the general supervision of activities of the state agencies such as the police, courts, and detention centers; and (2) the supervision of nonstate participants such as defendants, witnesses and defense lawyers. See Wei Luo, *The Amended Criminal Procedure Law and the Criminal Court Rules of the PRC* (Buffalo, NY: William S. Hein & Co., Inc., 2000), Article 8 and Notes 8, 42.
50. The People's Procuratorate plays a dominant role in criminal investigation and trial in an inquisitorial system, which is even more apparent now than before in China as the court reforms started to push a hands-off approach to case adjudication. For example, in many courts, judges have started to remove themselves from criminal investigations, focusing mainly on the review of evidence and the application of the law. See Xu Chen, Kuanming Zhang, and Jian Yang, "A Decade of the Court Reform in the City of Nanjing." *Zhian* 88(2000): 8–11.
51. Judges are now only in charge of reviewing documents presented by both parties and applying laws, which presumably saves money and time. The proposed change also assumes that by not being part of evidence gathering and criminal investigation, judges have little personal investment and ties with the case, and thus are better able to make an impartial decision. See Liming Wang, *Research on Judicial Reform* (Beijing: Law Press, 2001), 366–75.
52. Lubman, 1999, 292–7.
53 For example, the Intermediate People's Court of City of Shenzhen issued a notice prohibiting judges from playing table games with attorneys involved in the case to prevent corruption. See "Attorney: The Lonely Dancer?" *Nanfang Daily* available at http://www.nanfangdaily.com.cn/zm/20031218/xw/fz/200312180805.asp. See also Wang, 2001, 83–131, 169–215.
54. An approximately 90 percent of practicing lawyers have a minimum of college education in China. Prosecutors and judges have been historically appointed/transferred from military and other governmental units, with an emphasis of their political and ideological qualifications, not legal trainings, which is particularly true in western regions and rural areas. In addition, the dramatic rise of lawyers' socioeconomic status in recent years further heightens the professional rivalry between the prosecutor, judge, and the defense attorney, making it no more likely for defense attorney to win the case solely based on the merit of their arguments now than in the past. See Zhimin Wen, "Difficulties Faced by Chinese Defense Attorneys." Chinese National Lawyers Association Web site (6/06/2005) at http://www.xingbian.cn/template/article.jsp?ID=4979&CID=561598174.

55. See Barton L. Ingraham, *The Structure of Criminal Procedure: Laws and Practice of France, the Soviet Union, China, and the United States* (New York: Greenwood Publishing Group, 1987).
56. Bianjian Lin and Jingjing Li, "Seeing the Improvement of the Criminal Trial Structure from China's Criminal Courtroom Arrangements." *Frontiers of Law in China* 1(2006): 164–84.
57. See Hong Lu and Terance D. Miethe, "Confessions and Criminal Case Disposition in China." *Law & Society Review* 37(2003): 549–78.
58. See Xuechao Zhang, "Comments on Professor Shilun Li's Legal History and Thoughts." In *On the Front of the Legal Theory*, eds. Jingsheng Lu, Chibin Fu, and Zhong Gao (Beijing: the Chinese Procuratorate Press, 2004), 87–109.
59. This point can be illustrated by an interview with a former prosecutor of ten years. She said, "well, there must be torture and forced confession (in criminal investigation)... though I do not believe that torture is out of control...I must say that it exists...you have to understand that defendants, if not 'threatened,' they will not tell the truth...sometimes, a little bit of physical torture is necessary for them to confess... ultimately, it is good for social order." The interview was conducted in Las Vegas, December, 2004.
60. Frank Dikotter, "Crime and Punishment in Post-Liberation China: The Prisoners of a Beijing Gaol in the 1950s." *China Quarterly* 149(1997): 147–59.
61. For example, based on surveys conducted by the National Bureau of Statistics of China in 2001 and 2002, over 50 percent of respondents agreed that strike-hard campaign was effective in reducing crimes. In another survey, respondents said that the strike-hard campaign was one of the "real jobs" the government has done for the people and the sentence for these crimes should be very strict to deter criminals. See J. Zhang, et al., "On Campaign against Crime." *Democracy and Legality* 13(1996): 222. See also Dingjian Cai.,"China's Major Reform in Criminal Law." *Columbia Journal of Asian Law* 11(1997): 213–18.
62. Hugo Adam Bedau, "Retribution and the Theory of Punishment." *Journal of Philosophy* 75(1978): 601–20. See also Richard A. Posner, "Retribution and Related Concepts of Punishment." *Journal of Legal Studies* 9(1980): 71–92.
63. Robert F. Meier and Weldon T. Johnson, "Deterrence as Social Control: The Legal and Extralegal Production of Conformity." *American Sociological Review* 42(1977): 292–304. See also Stephen J. Knorr, "Deterrence and the Death Penalty: A Temporal Cross-Sectional Approach." *Journal of Criminal Law and Criminology* 70(1979): 235–54.
64. John M. Darley, Kevin M. Carlsmith, and Paul H. Robinson, "Incapacitation and Just Deserts as Motives for Punishment." *Law and Human Behavior* 24(2000): 659–83. See also Daniel Kessler and Steven D. Levitt, "Using Sentence Enhancements to Distinguish between Deterrence and Incapacitation." *Journal of Law and Economics* 42(1999): 343–63.
65. Samuel L. Myers, Jr., "The Rehabilitation Effect of Punishment." Economic Inquiry XVIII(1980): 353–66. See also J.G. Murphy, *Punishment and Rehabilitation* (Belmont, CA: Wadsworth Pub. Co.,1995).
66. Gary Colwell, "Capital Punishment, Restoration and Moral Rightness." *Journal of Applied Philosophy* 19(2002): 287. See also Kathleen Daly, "Revisiting the Relationship between Retributive and Restorative Justice." In *Restorative Justice: From Philosophy to Practice*, eds. Heather Strang and John Braithwaite (Aldershot: Dartmouth, 2000).
67. Mao, Zedong, *Selected Works of Mao* (Beijing: People's Publishing House, 1986), 184.

68. See Mao, 1986, 184. The two offenders were Liu Qingshan and Zhang Zishan. Both were high ranking public officials at Taijin, who embezzled large sums of funds appropriated for the airport construction and emergency use, and lavishly spent the money for personal pleasure. They were convicted of corruption and executed in 1952.
69. Deng, 1983, 90, 173, 217, & 371.
70. Deng, 1993, 90.
71. See Xinliang Chen, *The New Horizon of Contemporary Criminal Law in China* (Beijing, China: The Chinese University of Politics and Law Press, 2002), 544.
72. Friedman stated that the death penalty may work efficiently in societies "which use it quickly, mercilessly, and frequently. It cannot work well in the United States, where it is bound to be rare, slow, and controversial." See Lawrence M. Friedman, *American Law: An Introduction* (New York: W. W. Norton & Co., 1984), 214.
73. Mao's comments in 1951 marked the establishment of the suspended death sentence system in China, which became one of the hallmarks of the Chinese death penalty system. This system was designed for those who committed a heinous crime and deserved to be sentenced to death, but showed remorse, preformed meritorious service, and may be a valuable member of the society, who should be sentenced to death, but immediate execution is not necessary. While reflecting the humanness and rehabilitative nature of the Chinese penal policy, this practice may also have a practical utility of preventing excessive and erroneous killings. See Zhengxin Zhang, *Theory and Practice of the Suspended Death Penalty System in China* (Wuhang, China: Wuhan University Press, 2004), 13.
74. See Chen, 2002, 544.
75. Ibid, 544–45.

CHAPTER 3

1. For example, in the Tang Dynasty, there was a brief period of roughly ten years that the death penalty was abolished (747–759 AD). Emperor Illustrious August abolished the death penalty because of his strong regard for human life. See Charles Benn, *Daily Life in Traditional China – The Tang Dynasty* (Westport, CT: Greenwood Press, 2002), 209–12. In the Yuan Dynasty, there was a seventy- to eighty-year period during which no execution was carried out. See Paul H. Chen, *Chinese Legal Tradition under the Mongols – The Code of 1291 as Reconstructed* (Princeton, NJ: Princeton University Press, 1979), 45–47.
2. The Confucians in ancient China denounced the role of punishment in order maintenance. Confucius argued that when people are positively motivated by *li* (i.e., a set of ritual propriety) they will obey the rules and be good. If they are intimidated by fear of punishment, they may obey the law to avoid the punishment but their sense of right from wrong will not be developed. Confucius saw no virtue in capital punishment in a good government. See Herrlee G. Creel, "Legal institutions and procedures during the Chou Dynasty." In *Essays on China's Legal Tradition*, ed. J. A. Cohen, R. R. Edwards, and F. C. Chen (Princeton, NJ: Princeton University Press, 1980), 26–55. More recently, arguments in favor of abolishing the death penalty in China were voiced by some legal scholars. See Xinglong Qiu, *Comparative Criminal law.*

Volume 1. Beijing: China's Procuratorate Publishing House, 2001, 13. See also Xinglong Qiu, "Morality of law." *Politics and Law* 2(2002).

3. This period involves several dynasties, including the Shang (16th–11th century BC), Zhou (11th century–771 B.C.), Spring and Autumn (770–476 B.C.), Warring States (403–211BC), Qin (221–206 BC), Han (206 BC–220 AD), Three Kingdoms (220–280), Jin (265–420), Southern and Northern Dynasties (420–589), Sui (581–618), Tang (618–907), Five Dynasties (907–960), Song (960–1279), Yuan (1279–1368), Ming (1368–1644), and Qing (1644–1911). To be sure, this period of the Chinese history has been characterized differently depending on the theoretical framework. For example, the Marxist framework adopted by the Mainland China depicted this period as largely "feudal" — primarily from the Qin dynasty to the Qing dynasty (see Bozan Jian, Xunzheng Shao and Hua Hu, *A Concise History of China*, Beijing: Foreign Language Press, 1981; Albert Hung-yee Chen, *An Introduction to the Legal System of the People's Republic of China* (Hong Kong: Butterworths Asia, 1998), 6–19; also see Chenguang Wang, "Introduction: An Emerging Legal System." In *Introduction to Chinese Law*, ed. Chenguang Wang and Xianchu Zhang, Hong Kong: Sweet & Maxwell, 1997, 1–30). In contrast, writings of Western scholars and other Chinese from Taiwan tended to label this period of the Chinese history as "imperial" (see Geoffrey MacCormack, *The Spirit of Traditional Chinese Law*, Athens: University of Georgia Press, 1996; also see William P. Alford, "Of Arsenic and Old Laws: Looking Anew at Criminal Justice in Late Imperial China." *California Law Review* 72(1984): 1180–1256). Bodde had some discussions about the appropriateness of the term "feudalism" in describing some parts of the Chinese history (Derek Bodde, "The State and Empire of Chin." In *The Cambridge History of China: Volume 1 the Chin and Han Empires, 221 B.C. – A.D. 220*, eds. Denis Twitchett and Michael Loewe, Cambridge, Cambridge University Press, 1986, 22). To be consistent with Western literature, this book adopts the Western framework, referring to the time period of the ancient China until the collapse of the Qing dynasty in 1911 as "Imperial China."
4. This period between 1911 and 1949 was highlighted by the rule of the Nationalist Republic of China.
5. This period between 1949 and 1978 marked the first thirty years of Socialist China when the state-planned economy and the Marxist-Leninist-Maoist continuing revolution dominated the economic and political landscape.
6. See Jian, Shao, and Hu, 1981. Also see Jacques Gernet, *A History of Chinese Civilization*. Second edition. Trans. J. R. Foster and Charles Hartman (New York: Cambridge University Press, 1996).
7. Shang and Zhou, as an archaic monarchy, were ruled by its kings who enjoyed absolute and divine power and ruled through "a complex and highly stratified governmental network" (See Kwang-Chin Chang, *Shang Civilization*, New Haven: Yale University Press, 1980, 158). This network was maintained through patriarchal royal lineage enforced by laws that emphasized authority, intention of universal application, obligation and sanction, and with rituals of worshiping the ancestors that ultimately legitimized and strengthened the political dominance of the kings (Chang 1980, 200–9).
8. See Gernet, 1996, 73–79. To understand the social structural conditions of the Warring State, one must understand that after the conquering of Shang by Zhou, the new rulers allocated the conquered lands to families, relatives, allies, and descendants of the former Shang rulers, and allowed the locals to keep their lands, which resulted in numerous small kingdoms that over time fought each other for monopolized power (Bodde 1986, 21–23).

9. Shi Huangdi tried to unify China in numerous areas such as political-economic structure, culture, law, and infrastructure. Legalism became the dominant ideology governing the state. While a Marxist perspective would attribute the collapse of the Qin dynasty to particular social institutions and class struggles, other factors such as moral, intellectual, social, and overextension of resources have also caused the fall of the first imperial dynasty (Bodde 1986, 53–90). Some of the most well known artifacts of Chinese history in the Western world were part of the legacy of Shi Huangdi. These include large building projects like the "Great Wall" and Shi Huangdi's burial tomb of a life-size clay army of "Terra Cotta Warriors". The majority of the labor force who built these structures were convicts and other disliked groups whose deaths would not be noted. See Alasdair Clayre, *The Heart of the Dragon* (Boston, MA: Houghton Mifflin Co., 1984).
10. Emperors during these dynasties had to fend off several kinds of threats to keep China unified, including raids and incursions into Chinese territory by foreign peoples; uprisings of foreign peoples within Chinese territory; revolts among Chinese; and religious rebellions (B. J. Mansvelt Beck, "The Fall of Han," in *The Cambridge History of China: Volume 1 the Chin and Han Empires, 221 B.C. – A.D. 220*, eds Denis Twitchett and Michael Loewe, Cambridge, Cambridge University Press, 1986, 334–40).
11. See Jian, et al., 1981, 47–50.
12. For detailed discussions of the military, diplomatic and cultural expansions of the Tang dynasty, see Denis Twitchett, "Introduction." In *The Cambridge History of China: Volume 3 Sui and Tang China, 589–906, Part I*, ed. Denis Twitchett (Cambridge: Cambridge University Press, 1979), 32–38.
13. See Robert M. Somers, "The End of the Tang." In *The Cambridge History of China: Volume 3 Sui and Tang China, 589–906, Part I*, ed. Denis Twitchett (Cambridge: Cambridge University Press, 1979), 682–99. See also Jian et al., 55–84.
14. China's economy relied on the traditional, mechanical technology that could no longer sustain the pressure from population increases. See Albert Feuerwerker, "Economic Trends in the Late Ching Empire, 1870–1911." In *The Cambridge History of China: Volume II Late Ching, 1800–1911, Part 2*, eds. John K. Fairbank and Kwang-Ching Liu (Cambridge: Cambridge University Press, 1980), 58–69.
15. Kwang-Ching Liu, "The Military Challenge: The North-West and the Coast." In *The Cambridge History of China: Volume II Late Ching, 1800–1911, Part 2*, ed. John K. Fairbank and Kwang-Ching Liu (Cambridge: Cambridge University Press, 1980), 202–42.
16. Immanuel C. Y. Hsu, "Late Ching Foreign Relations, 1866–1905." In *The Cambridge History of China: Volume II Late Ching, 1800–1911, Part 2*, eds. John K. Fairbank and Kwang-Ching Liu (Cambridge: Cambridge University Press, 1980), 116–27.
17. Kwang-Ching Liu, 1980, 251–73.
18. David Curtis Wright, *The History of China* (Westport, CT: Greenwood Press, 2001), 102–5. See also Michael Gasster, "The Republican Revolutionary Movement." In *The Cambridge History of China: Volume II Late Ching, 1800–1911, Part 2*, eds. John K. Fairbank and Kwang-Ching Liu (Cambridge: Cambridge University Press, 1980), 506–7.
19. For a more complete treatment of Confucianism, its development, and relation with other schools of thought, see Robert P. Kramers, "The Development of the Confucian Schools." In *The Cambridge of History of China: Volume 1 The Chin and Han Empires, 221 B.C. – A.D. 220*, eds. Denis Twitchett and Michael Loewe, 1986, 747–65; see also Chiyun Chen, "Confucian, Legalist, and Taoist Thought in Later Han." *The Cambridge of History*

of China: Volume 1 The Chin and Han Empires, 221 B.C. – A.D. 220, eds. Denis Twitchett and Michael Loewe, 1986, 766–807. Jianfu Chen, *Chinese Law: Towards an Understanding of Chinese Law, Its Nature and Development* (London: Kluwer Law International, 1999), 7–10.

20. An example of being filial is that "the father conceals the crime of his son and the son conceals the crime of his father." See Leon Stover, *Imperial China and the State Cult of Confucius* (Kefferson, North Carolina: McFarland & Company, Inc. Publishers, 2005), 128–40. See also Heiner Roetz, *Confucian Ethics of the Axial Age* (Albany: State University of New York, 1993), 43–52.
21. Yongping Liu, *Origins of Chinese Law — Penal and Administrative Law in Its Early Development* (Oxford, NY: Oxford University Press, 1998), 91–106.
22. Liu, 1998, 92.
23. Roetz, 1993, 123–45. See also Liu, 1998, 93.
24. Derek Bodde and Clarence Morris, *Law in Imperial China* (Philadelphia: University of Pennsylvania Press, 1973), 21–2. See also Stover, 2005, 131.
25. For example, Confucius said "If good men governed a state for a century, it would then be possible to eliminate violence and do away with capital punishment." Cited in Herrlee Glessner Creel, "Legal Institutions and Procedures during the Chou Dynasty." In *Essays on China's Legal Tradition*, eds. J. A. Cohen, R. R. Edwards, and F. C. Chen (Princeton, NJ: Princeton University Press, 1980), 40.
26. Geoffrey MacCormack, *Traditional Chinese Penal Law* (Edinburgh, England: Edinburgh University Press, 1990), 100.
27. Charles Benn, *Daily Life in Traditional China – The Tang Dynasty* (Westport, CT: Greenwood Press, 2002), 209. As another indication of a more benevolent period, the death penalty was actually abolished in an approximately ten year period of the Tang Dynasty. Emperor Illustrious August abolished the death penalty due to his strong regard for human life. Instead, he instructed his officials to refer to the most similar regulation in dispensing justice (Benn 2002, 209–12).
28. Some authors have even considered the application of the death penalty to be thermostat of a particular imperial dynasty's rise and fall. See Zhengxin Zhang, *The Theory and Practice of the Suspended Death Sentence in China* (Wuhang, China: Wuhan University Press, 2004), 10.
29. Yu-Ning Li, *Shang Yang's Reforms and State Control in China* (White Plains, NY: M. E. Sharpe, 1977), liii. See also Chen, 1999, 10–12.
30. Stover, 2005, 131, 130.
31. Creel, 1980, 45. Also see Stover, 2005, 130.
32. Severe and cruel punishments were manifested by methods of execution, including boiling in a cauldron, cutting in two at the waist, and tearing apart by chariots after bodily mutilations used in the Qin dynasty (Bodde 1986, 58–59).
33. For example, a rebellion broke out when Chen Sheng, a former hired farm laborer, in charge of transporting nine hundred convicts to a penitentiary settlement and was caught by the heavy rain, declared to rebel, knowing that the legal penalty for tardiness was death (Bodde 1986, 83).
34. James Clark, *China* (Evanston, IL: McDougal Little and Co., 1982). In fact, the overextension of resources along with other social and moral factors were attributed to as the cause of the fall of Qin (Bodde 1986, 85–89).
35. Massive executions were conducted after the defeat of the *Taiping Rebellion* in the late Ming Dynasty. During its fourteen-year history, over thirty million people were reported killed in this revolt (Bodde and Morris 1973, 104–12).

36. See R. Randle Edwards, "Chinese Legal Jurisdiction over Foreigners." In *Essays on China's Legal Tradition*, eds. Jerome A. Cohen, R. Randle Edwards, and Fu-mei Chang Chen (Princeton, NJ: Princeton University Press, 1980), 222–69.
37. For example, the old *Five Punishments* (face tattooing, nose amputation, feet amputation, castration, and the death penalty) is said not to be applied to the noble class. The execution of a sailor who incited a strike for better wages with his decapitated head left exposed on the bank of the Grand Canal was an example of law as a mechanism of social control of low class people (Bodde and Morris 1973, 186).
38. See Creel, 1980, 46. Being aware that the indulgence of alcohol of the Shang people led to the fall of Shang, King Wu of Zhou Dynasty imposed severe punishment and even the death penalty on those who drank alcohol (Charles Benn, *Daily Life in Traditional China — The Tang Dynasty*, Westport, CT: Greenwood Press), 2002, 196).
39. Benn, 2002, 196.
40. Hao Chang, "Intellectual Change and the Reform Movement." In The Cambridge History of China" Volume II Late Ching, 1800–1911, Part 2. eds. John K. Fairbank and Kwang-Ching Liu (Cambridge: Cambridge University Press, 1980), 328–9.
41. Kwang-Chih Chang suggests that archaeological evidence revealed that legal records may have existed in as early as the Shang dynasty (1766 –1122 BC) (Chang, 1980, 2001; Liu, 1988, 114), despite other accounts that legal system developed during a later time, such as Western Zhou (1122–771) (H. Creel, *The Origins of Statecraft in China: The Western Zhou Empire*, 1970, 161–95).
42. As an indication of this variability over time, the only punishments mentioned in the record of Kang Kao of the Zhou dynasty involved death, nose amputation, and leg amputation (MacCormack 1990, 3). However, in Western Zhou, persons of noble class often could use their privileged status to avoid death sentences. Instead, they were punished by flogging, banishment and fines for their offenses (Liu 1998, 135).
43. Since the Sui dynasty (581), punishment in Imperial China gradually moved away from bodily amputation to physical punishment with beatings. Fines became more widespread in redeeming the punishment in the later dynasties, although economic sanctions were not recognized as a separate measure of punishment. See Terance D. Miethe and Hong Lu, *Punishment: A Comparative Historical Perspective* (London, England: Cambridge University Press, 2005), 121–3.
44. In addition, three hundred offenses were punishable by castration, five hundred offenses by leg amputation, one thousand offenses by nose amputation, and branding applied to one thousand offenses (MacCormack, 1990, 8).
45. Bodde and Morris, 1973,102–4.
46. Yuan Code was the first that codified death by slicing as a method of execution. Nine capital offenses were subject to this kind of execution. This sharp decline corresponds to the period of Mongol rule (e.g., Genghus Khan) and Mongolian preference of customary law to the formal legal code. See Paul H. Chen, *Chinese Legal tradition under the Mongols — the Code of 1291 as Reconstructed* (Princeton, NJ: Princeton University Press, 1979), 42–43.
47. See Bodde and Morris,1973, 115.
48. The unfilial and unbrotherly conduct typically referred to disrespect of an elderly family member by a younger member of the family (Creel 1980, 30).
49. Filial piety, *xiao,* was considered the "fundamental power on account of which the Chinese nation managed to persist continuously." It was the basic social duty and primary virtue in the Chinese society. Filial piety generally

refers to "a respectful and obliging attitude towards the elders of the family." More specifically, filial piety required respectful care of elderly family members (e.g., not making a long journey when the parents are alive, caring for parents' physical and emotional well-being), obedience to parents and superiors (e.g., submission to the will of the elder family members), and moral vigilance when a son fulfills the wishes of the parents (e.g., be observant of the laws rather than unconditionally following the instruction of the parents) (Roetz 1993, 43–52).

50. In the late Tang and early Song period, for example, to ensure exclusive production and selling of tea and salt by the government, one hundred blows from heavy bamboo was applied for offenders who sold a single pound of illegal tea and the death penalty was imposed on offenders who manufactured or sold twenty or more pounds of tea. See Brian E. McKnight, *Law and Order in Sung China* (Cambridge: Cambridge University Press, 1992), 94–95.
51. Witchcraft was perhaps the most serious and feared crime under the Western Han law and was sometimes conveniently used by political rivals to destroy their foes. It was recorded that two large-scale witch hunts in Western Han resulted in death of more than three hundred people. See Bret Hinsch, *Women in Early Imperial China* (New York: Rowman & Littlefield Publishers, Inc., 2002).
52. *Gu* poison was extracted from venomous creatures such as snakes, toads, scorpions, spiders. It was believed that the *gu* poison was extremely lethal, causing it victim to deteriorate, vomit blood, and die (Benn 2002, 197, 221).
53. Other black magic includes cursing to cause misfortune and death and stabbing the hearts or nailing the eyes in a doll to inflict harm on the intended victims (Benn, 2002, 197).
54. Bodde, 1986, 72-81; Chen, 1999, 12–14.
55. Under the same principle of *xiao,* slaves may be executed by decapitation for attacking their masters, but a master attacking a slave would suffer no punishment unless the injury led to death. See Wallace Johnson. *The Tang Code* (Princeton, NJ: Princeton University Press, 1979), 9–13, 23–33.
56. See Thomas B. Stephens, *Order and Discipline in China: The Shanghai Mixed Court 1911–27* (Seattle, Washington: University of Washington Press, 1992), 24–26.
57. For example, officials who violated the sumptuary regulations were punished by one hunded blows of the heavy bamboo whereas commoners would only received fifty blows for the same offense. Similarly, officials who frequented prostitutes were subject to punishment, but not commoners, according to the Qing Code. See Bodde and Morris, *Law in Imperial China* (Philadelphia: University of Pennsylvania Press, 1973), 35.
58. Under Qin, the law of mutual responsibility was created so that one man's crime could result in execution of kindred to the third degree including parents, brothers, spouse and children (Bodde 1986, 74). This practice of collective responsibility was in use throughout China's history until the fall of the Qing dynasty (Stephens 1992, 23–24).
59. Women were allowed to redeem most of their crimes with monetary payment. For example, it was common for masters to mistreat their household slave girls. When found guilty, the head of the household usually blamed the offense on the wife, who could redeem the punishment. See Marinus J. Meijer, "Slavery at the End of the Ch'ing Dynasty." In *Essays on China's Legal tradition,* eds. Jerome A. Cohen, R. Randle Edwards and Fu-mei Chang Chen (Princeton, NJ: Princeton University Press, 1980), 327–58.

    Similarly, monetary redemption was also widely permitted to the old, the young and the infirm. Bodde argued that special treatment for these groups of people in ancient China was due to both the pragmatic and moralistic reasons

(Derek Bodde, "Age, Youth, and Infirmity in the Law of Ch'ing China." In *Essays on China's Legal tradition,* eds. Jerome A. Cohen, R. Randle Edwards, and Fu-mei Chang Chen, Princeton, NJ: Princeton University Press, 1980, 137–69).

60. Using disciplinary theory, Stephens explains that the importance of obtaining a criminal confession in the Chinese courts was based on its Confucian ideas of filial piety that subjected individuals of a lower status (e.g., a criminal) to a subordinated position. See Thomas B. Stephens, *Order and Discipline in China: The Shanghai Mixed Court 1911–27* (Seattle: University of Washington Press, 1992), 40–43.
61. See Bodde and Morris, 1973, 39–43.
62. The feature of the lack of the separation of powers at the magistrate level during imperial China was frequently commented and criticized in Western writings (Alford, 1984, 1180–256; Cohen, 1968, 5–7; Stanley Lubman, "Mao and Mediation: Politics and Dispute Resolution in Communist China." *California Law Review* 55(1969): 1292). Nevertheless, as documented by Alford (1984, 1180–256) and by Ocko (Johnathan K. Ocko, "I'll Take it All the Way to Beijing: Capital Appeals in the Qing." *The Journal of Asian Studies* 47(1988): 291–315), despite the typically presumed association between the lack of separation of powers and the lack of checks and balances by Westerners, the Chinese imperial system appeared to have instigated an elaborated appellate system to ensure that the local magistrates' powers in criminal investigation and trial were properly checked. Whether or not these checks performed adequate functions to stop abuse remained questionable as numerous mechanisms such as forced confessions and the presumption of guilt tended to work against the criminal defendant.
63. A witness could also bring a criminal in the process of crime commission to the court for reward. In addition, police and military officials had the power to arrest anyone who was suspected of a crime. See Ichisada Miyazaki, 1980. "The Administration of Justice during the Sung Dynasty." In *Essays on China's Legal tradition,* eds. Jerome A. Cohen, R. Randle Edwards, and Fu-mei Chang Chen (Princeton, NJ: Princeton University Press, 1980), 59.
64. The police were not present at the trial for two reasons: (1) their sole power rested on making an arrest, not on acting as a prosecutor or a witness; (2) the concern that their presence would add undue pressure to the defendant (Miyazaki, 1980, 61; see also William C. Jones, "Trying to Understand the Current Chinese Legal System." In *Understanding China's Legal System — Essays in Honor of Jerome A. Cohen*, ed. C. Stephen Hsu, New York: New York University Press, 2003, 15–18).
65. See Miyazaki 1980, 61.
66. Not only the defendant, but also the plaintiff and witness were subject to legalized physical beatings during interrogation in the ancient Chinese court. As a result, certain types of individuals were prohibited to appear in court. In the Song Dynasty, for example, men older than seventy and pregnant women were not allowed to appear in court as a plaintiff because they could not withstand beating (if plaintiffs were suspected of falsely accusing the defendant, they were subject to beating during interrogation). Instead, their kinsmen were ordered to appear in court on their behalf (Miyazaki, 1980, 60). See also Alison W. Conner, "True Confessions? Chinese Confessions Then and Now." In *The Limits of the Rule of Law in China* (Seattle: University of Washington Press, 2000), 132–62.
67. Miyazaki noted that based on records in a Song court, officials used tactics such as "stuffing rags into the accused's mouth, or reading the confession

quickly and unintelligibly" to prevent the defendant from repudiating the confession (Miyazaki 1980, 64).

68. The above description was largely based on a Song court (Miyazaki 1980, 56–75).
69. See detailed descriptions of the complicated review and ratification process for capital cases in the Qing Dynasty in Bodde and Morris, 1973, 111–43.
70. Emperors could also change a less serious sentence to the death penalty to set an example for the rest community members. For example, Emperor Kangxi in the Qing Dynasty ordered an execution for a corrupt official and his entire family to be carried out in his native place to show other gentry class the consequences of official misconduct (Stephens 1992, 22).
71. More specifically, ninety-eight offenses were eligible for decapitation after assizes, and eighty-seven strangulation after assizes. Other capital offenses included thirteen deaths by slicing, thirty-eight immediate decapitations, thirteen immediate strangulation, and twenty other capital offenses stipulated in other sub-statutes (Bodde and Morris 1973, 102–3).

    The assizes system as a formalized legal system did not exist until the Ming Dynasty. It was designed as a safeguard for the death penalty cases. All capital cases labeled as "after the assizes" needed to be reviewed by the Board of Punishments, consisted of a mixed panel of officials such as jurists and chief ministries, in the capital city of Beijing. The session was open to public. The decision could be made to place a capital case in one of the following four categories: (1) deferred execution; (2) worthy of compassion; (3) remaining at home caring for parents; and (4) execution (Bodde and Morris 1973, 134–43).
72. Wallace Johnson, *The Tang Code* (Princeton, NJ: Princeton University Press, 1979), 9–13 and 23–33.
73. Bodde and Morris, 1973,102.
74. Miyazaka, 1980, 56–75.
75. Miyazaki, 1980, 69–72; Alford, 1996, 26–27; Philip Huang, "Codified Law and Magisterial Adjudication in the Qing." In *Civil Law in Qing and Republican China*, ed. Philip Huang and Kathryn Bernhart (Stanford, CA: Stanford University Press, 1994).
76. For example, in the Song Dynasty, there was a brief period of time when popularization of the law was tolerated by the government (Miyazaki 1980, 71). However, in the Qing Dynasty, law specifically prohibited inciting litigation. If one prepared legal documents for another person who was not a close relative, he may be punishable by three years penal servitude. One court case indicates as few as six or seven legal petitions prepared for a nonrelative by an individual qualified that individual as a "professional litigation trickster" and may subject him to the punishment (Bodde and Morris 1973, 413–23).
77. See Miyazaki, 1980, 71.
78. Melisa MaCauley, *Social Power and Legal Culture: Litigation Masters in Late Imperial China* (Stanford, CA: Stanford University Press, 1998), 17.
79. See Bodde and Morrison, 1973, 189, & 198.
80. See Jerome Cohen, *The Criminal Process in the People's Republic of China 1949–1963* (Cambridge, Massachusetts: Harvard University Press, 1968), 5.
81. In the Tang Dynasty, scourging to death with the heavy bamboo was, though not legal, often used in cases of gross corruption. The emperor's brother-in-law in 716 was beaten to death in front of his officials for having assaulted a man in the capital (Benn 2002, 210).
82. Other unusual execution methods were also documented. For example, in the Yuan Dynasty, three men were sentenced to death for murder and were executed by having their flesh pickled (Chen 1979, 46).

83. The Tang and Song codes stipulated strangulation and decapitation as methods of execution. In Yuan Dynasty, death by slicing was codified to replace strangulation (Chen 1979, 41–68). The Ming and Qing Codes codified all three as legal methods of execution (Bodde and Morris 1973, 91–95).
84. See McKnight, 1992, 447–9.
85. It was recorded that a thief may be sentenced to decapitation if upon discovery of the crime the thief resisted capture and wounded the property owner (Bodde and Morris 1973, 475–6).
86. Strangulation became was a formal method of execution at the end of the sixth century. See A. F. P. Hulsewe, "Chin and Han Law." In *The Cambridge History of China*, eds. Dennis Twitchett and Michael Loewe, Volume 1 (Cambridge: Cambridge University Press, 1986), 520–44. See McKnight, 1992, 448–9.
87. See Benn, 2002, 207–9.
88. See Chen, 1979, 42–44.
89. Slicing was also applied to murder of multiple victims. For example, in 1828, the principle offender in a looting and killing of thirteen French sailors was sentenced to death by slicing (Edwards 1980, 222–69; Bodde and Morris 1973, 78, and 93–95).
90. McKnight, 1992, 469.
91. Bodde and Morris,1973, 104–12.
92. It has been argued that traditional Chinese governments were extremely hostile to the transmitters of many popular religious/quasi-religious beliefs. Individuals who teach and/or practice black magic sorcery and adopted heretical beliefs were subject to severe sanctions. In the eleventh century, cult leaders who practiced human sacrifice were often executed (McKnight 1992, 75–79).
93. For example, it is possible that the decline in the number of death sentences given in the late Song dynasty may be attributed to Southern Song's selective counting of only death sentences affirmed by review and excluding from those executions conducted immediately without court or state review. Similarly, Yuan's low number of death sentences could be partially attributed to Yuan ruler's cautious attitude about the death penalty, as illustrated by Emperor Shigtsu's statement in 1287 after reviewing 190 death penalty cases that "prisoners are not a mere flock of sheep. How can they be suddenly executed?" (Chen 1979, 46). Alternatively, the low number of recorded executions may simply reflect the inadequacies of existing records.
94. McKnight, 1992, 464–9.
95. McKnight, 1992, 464–9
96 Miyazaki, 1980, 56–75.
97. McKnight, 1992, 463–9
98. Benn, 2002, 209–12.
99. Chen, 1979, 41–47.
100. The *Taiping Rebellion* represented one of the most destructive civil wars in Chinese history, killing twenty million or more people, and nearly overthrowing the Qing government (Bodde and Morris 1973, 104–12).
101. Cited in Bodde and Morris, 1973, 110.
102. China was punctuated with numerous civil wars among the warlords during the 1910s and the 1920s. See Ernest P. Young, "Politics in the Aftermath of Revolution: The Era of Yuan Shih-kai, 1912–16." In *The Cambridge History of China: Volume 12 Republican China 1912–1949, Part I*, ed. John K. Fairbank (Cambridge: Cambridge University Press, 1983), 209–58. See also James E. Sheridan, "The Warlord Era: Politics and Militarism under the Peking Government, 1916–28." In *The Cambridge History of China: Vol-*

ume 12 Republican China 1912–1949, Part I, ed. John K. Fairbank (Cambridge: Cambridge University Press, 1983), 284–321.

103. This brief Republican era was also marked with great intellectual change including nationalism, evolutionism, the future of Confucianism, social utopia, and introduction of Marxism-Leninism. See Charlotte Furth, "Intellectual Change: From the Reform Movement to the May Fourth Movement, 1895–1920." In *The Cambridge History of China: Volume 12 Republican China 1912–1949, Part I*, ed. John K. Fairbank (Cambridge: Cambridge University Press, 1983), 322–405. Also see Benjamin I. Schwartz, "Themes in Intellectual History: May Fourth and After." In *The Cambridge History of China: Volume 12 Republican China 1912–1949, Part I*, ed. John K. Fairbank (Cambridge: Cambridge University Press, 1983), 406–51.
104. The revolutionary movement, Northern Expedition, aimed at reuniting China, overcoming foreign privilege, and reforming social inequalities. It was one of the rare coalitions among the Nationalists, Communists, and the Russians that fought from the southern region of China, Guangdong (Canton) to the northern region, Beijing (Peking) to defeat the warlord. See C. Martin Wilbur, "The Nationalist Revolution: From Canton to Nanking, 1923–28." In *The Cambridge History of China: Volume 12 Republican China 1912–1949, Part I*, ed. John K. Fairbank (Cambridge: Cambridge University Press, 1983), 527–721.
105. See Lloyd E. Eastman, "Nationalist China during the Sino-Japanese War 1937–1945." In *The Cambridge History of China: Volume 13 Republican China 1912–1949, Part 2*. ed. John K. Fairbank and Albert Feuerwerker (Cambridge: Cambridge University Press, 1986), 547–608. See also Lyman Van Slyke, "The Chinese Communist Movement during the Sino-Japanese War 1937-1945." In *The Cambridge History of China: Volume 13 Republican China 1912–1949, Part 2*, eds. John K. Fairbank and Albert Feuerwerker (Cambridge: Cambridge University Press, 1986), 609–722.
106. Furth, 1983, 350–73.
107. Furth, 1983, 322–49, 374–405.
108. Schwartz, 1983, 406–51. See also Jerome Chen, 1983. "Chinese Communist Movement to 1927." In *The Cambridge History of China: Volume 12 Republican China 1912–1949, Part I*, ed. John K. Fairbank (Cambridge: Cambridge University Press, 1983), 505–27.
109. Slyke. 1986, 609–722. See also Suzanne Pepper, "The KMT – CCP Conflict 1945–1949." In *The Cambridge History of China: Volume 13 Republican China 1912–1949, Part 2*, eds. John K. Fairbank and Albert Feuerwerker (Cambridge: Cambridge University Press, 1986), 723–88.
110. Physical amputation was legally abolished in 1905. Beatings with sticks were replaced with fines during this Republic era. See Frank Dikotter, "The Promise of Repentance — Prison Reform in Modern China." *British Journal of Criminology* 42 (2002): 240–9.
111. See Frank Dikotter, *Crime, Punishment and the Prison in Modern China* (NY: Columbia University Press, 2002), 43–52, 141–81.
112. See Dikotter, 2002, 42: 240–9.
113. Alan W. Lepp, "Note: the Death Penalty in Late Imperial, Modern, and Post-Tiananmen China." *Michigan Journal of International Law* 11(1990): 987–1038.
114. See Dikotter, 2002, 178–81.
115. During these early years, the Communist Party was under several independent leaderships. The headquarters in Shanghai was led by Qu Qiubai and Li Lishan who continued with military uprisings against the Nationalist government in urban areas. The remote countryside territorial base (e.g., Jing

Gang Mountains of Jiangxi province) was established and secured by Mao Zedong and Zhu De. They used guerrilla and rural revolutionary tactics to fight against the warlords and the Nationalist army. See Patricia E. Griffin, *The Chinese Communist treatment of Counterrevolutionaries: 1924–1949* (Princeton, NJ: Princeton University Press, 1976), 11–26.

In later years, special committees such as *Weed-Out Traitors Committees*, comprised of voluntary mass groups, were created to assist the police in identifying and apprehending counterrevolutionaries (Griffin 1976, 71). In addition, based on a record of cases tried in 1939, 1940, and 1941, opium possession, gambling, interfering with marriage and family, banditry, larceny, and corruption replaced counterrevolutionary offenses (e.g., traitor) to become major concerns for the Communist Party during that period of time (Griffin 1976, 5).

116. Hard labor appeared to be frequently given to a large number of offenders. For example, in Jiangxi province in six months of 1932, an estimated 1,108 people were sentenced to hard labor at the local level. Some were sentenced to hard labor indefinitely (Griffin 1976, 36–37).
117. In later years (1934–1944) when the Communist Party was able to reinforce its control at the territorial base, education and criticisms were included as an additional punishment in dispensing justice (Griffin 1976, 87).
118. See Griffin, 1976, 14–17.
119. Ibib., 40.
120. Stuart Schram, "Mao Tse-tung's Thought to 1949." In *The Cambridge History of China: Volume 13 Republican China 1912–1949, Part 2,* eds. John K. Fairbank and Albert Feuerwerker (Cambridge: Cambridge University Press, 1986), 789–870.
121. See Stephen B. Davis, "The Death Penalty and Legal Reform in the PRC." *Journal of Chinese Law* 1(1987):303–34. Also see Chen, 1999, 23–24.
122. See Dikotter, 2002, 230–5.
123. Unfortunately, specific laws and statutes could not be found to discern legal stipulations of capital offenses. However, based on Dikotter, capital punishment was at least applied to counterrevolutionaries (Dikotter 2002, 364–8).
124. See Stephens, 1992, 23–24.
125. Counterrevolutionaries included three categories: (1) the class enemies based on individuals' socioeconomic background; (2) the political enemies based on ideological concerns; and (3) the militant enemies (Griffin 1976, 26–2).
126. These stipulations can be found in the "Draft Statute of the Chinese Soviet Republic Governing Punishment of Counterrevolutionaries" and the revised document (Griffin 1976, 50–52).
127. See Appendix J, Appendix K, and Appendix L in Griffin, 1976, 191–9.
128. See Dikotter, 2002, 230–1.
129. Departing from the traditional practice of confession for its probative and moral value, during the Republican era, both the Nationalists and the Communists required that some redemptive action must be present to show proof of the criminals' repentance in order for them to receive lenient punishment. It is in this regard that "confession" requirements lost its moral appeal and became more pragmatic (Griffin 1976, 73–88).
130. See Griffin, 1976, 36, 51–52, & 181–90.
131. See Stephens, 1992, 48–65.
132. For example, after being held for two months without a trial, a suspect was then quickly sentenced and executed because of the criticism that it was a waste to have to feed the criminal while there was a food shortage (Griffin 1976, 42).

133. See Griffin, 1976, 47–50.
134. Ibid., 73–74.
135. See Jerome Cohen, *The Criminal Process in the People's Republic of China 1949–1963* (Cambridge: Harvard University Press, 1968), 4.
136. A trial conducted in 1933 on four criminals, two labeled as "Social Democratic counterrevolutionaries" charged with spreading rumors among the masses, plotting to kill revolutionary workers, helping organize secret armed forces, and deserting the army, and the other two charged with deserting the Red Army, may serve as a good example of a mass trial in the Communist territory during the Republican era. Upon the starting of the rally, the crowd repeatedly yelled out in a high voice "oppose deserting," "deserting is the biggest shame," "eliminate the Social Democratic Party and all kinds of counterrevolutionaries." The evidence was then read by the Public Security Bureau's representative followed by the trial of each of the offenders. All four criminals confessed to their crime. Afterwards, representatives of more than thirty districts took turns speaking, pointing out the shame and danger of deserting. Upon the crowd's demand, the two counterrevolutionaries were sentenced to death by method of a firing squad, and the other two received a long-term hard labor and one year of hard labor, respectively. Immediately after the trial, the two criminals sentenced to death were paraded through the streets with large crowd following and yelling slogans. They were then executed in front of the crowd (Griffin 1976, 60–62).
137. Dikotter, 2002, 136–8.
138. Hanging was the only legal method of execution under the Nationalist rule since 1927 (Dikotter 2002, 178).
139. Public display of the head of executed Communist leaders was particularly common during this period as the Nationalist regime used it as a means to terrorize those who join and continue working for the Communist cause (Dikotter 2002, 137–8).
140. Dikotter, 2002, 77.
141. Ibid., 231.
142. Ibid., 137.
143. It was recorded that during the period of 1924–1927, some two thousand landlords were executed within a few months in the communist jurisdiction. See Shao-chuan Leng, *Justice in Communist China* (Dobbs Ferry, NY: Oceana Publications, 1967), 3.
144. The Judicial Committee handled litigation and trial of counterrevolutionaries. At the mass trials, landlords and counterrevolutionaries upon being sentenced to death were often killed on the spot before the cheering crowd (Griffin 1976, 13–14).
145. See Griffin, 1976, 36.
146. Ibid., 39.
147. Ibid.
148. A series of social reforms and movements were launched during the 1950s to transform the basic social and political structures in the newly established PRC, for example the Land Reform (1950–1952), the Movement of Suppression of Counter-revolutionaries (1950–1953), the Movement against the Three Evils (corruption, waste and bureaucracy) in 1952 and the Movement of Judicial Reform starting from 1952 that resulted in the promulgation of the Constitution in 1954 (Wang 1997, 9–11).
149. Other political and economic campaigns such as the Great Leap Forward, the Anti-Rightist Movement, and the Cultural Revolution led to disastrous economic and social consequences. See Kenneth Lieberthal, "The Great Leap

Forward and the Split in the Yenan Leadership." In *Cambridge History of China, Volume 15 The People's Republic, Part 2: Revolutions within the Chinese Revolution 1966–1982*, eds. Roderick MacFaruhar and John K. Fairbank (Cambridge: Cambridge University Press, 1991), 293–359. Dwight H. Perkins, "China's Economic Policy and Performance." In *Cambridge History of China, Volume 15 The People's Republic, Part 2: Revolutions within the Chinese Revolution 1966–1982*, eds. Roderick MacFaruhar and John K. Fairbank (Cambridge: Cambridge University Press, 1991), 475–539. Suzanne Pepper, "Education." In *Cambridge History of China, Volume 15 The People's Republic, Part 2: Revolutions within the Chinese Revolution 1966–1982*, eds. Roderick MacFaruhar and John K. Fairbank (Cambridge: Cambridge University Press, 1991), 540–93. Douwe Fokkema, "Creativity and Politics." In *Cambridge History of China, Volume 15 The People's Republic, Part 2: Revolutions within the Chinese Revolution 1966–1982*, eds. Roderick MacFaruhar and John K. Fairbank (Cambridge: Cambridge University Press, 1991), 594–618.

150. In the *Decision Concerning the Differentiation of Class Status in the Countryside* adopted by the Government Administration Council of the Central People's Government on August 4, 1950, a rich peasant who participated in serious counterrevolutionary activities such as leading the militia in the massacre of workers and peasants before, during, and after the Communist liberation was classified as a "reactionary rich peasant" and the property "shall be confiscated." See Albert P. Blaustein (ed.), *Fundamental Legal Documents of Communist China* (South Hackensack, NJ: Fred B. Rothman & Co., 1962), 307.
151. Stuart R. Schram, "Mao Tse-tung's Thought from 1949–1976." In *Cambridge History of China: Volume 15 The People's Republic of China, Part 2*, eds. Roderick MacFarquhar and John K. Fairbank (Cambridge: Cambridge University Press, 1991), 1–106.
152. The *Labor-Capital Consultative Councils in Private Enterprises* issued by the Ministry of Labor in 1950 offers some glimpse on the highly regulated private enterprises during that time. The Directive required that any privately owned business or factories employing fifty or more persons must establish a labor-capital consultative council where the leadership should be alternated between a capitalist and a laborer, and issues with regard to "collective agreement" and other production issues must be discussed at regularly scheduled meetings. This directive indicated the Chinese Communist Party's concerns of workers' rights and equal participation, even in private sectors (Blaustein 1962, 495–500). See also Natalie G. Lichtenstein, "Law in China's Economic Development — An Essay from Afar." In *Understanding China's Legal System — Essays in Honor of Jerome A. Cohen*, ed. C. Stephen Hsu. (New York: New York University Press, 2003), 275.
153. Richard Madsen, "The Countryside under Communism." In *Cambridge History of China, Volume 15 The People's Republic, Part 2: Revolutions within the Chinese Revolution 1966–1982*, eds. Roderick MacFaruhar and john K. Fairbank (Cambridge: Cambridge University Press, 1991), 619–81. See also Martin King Whyte, "Urban Life in the People's Republic." *Cambridge History of China, Volume 15 The People's Republic, Part 2: Revolutions within the Chinese Revolution 1966–1982*, eds. Roderick MacFaruhar and John K. Fairbank (Cambridge: Cambridge University Press, 1991), 682–742.
154. Mao's theory on law was deeply influenced by Confucians, Marxist-Leninist Communist legal ideology and his own revolutionary experiences. Mao insisted upon continuing revolution, class struggle, and the mass-line, which

applied to the justice system requiring that the law be flexible and changing. One way of making the law keep up with the continuous revolution is through popular participation. Mao believed that lay people should be the subject rather than the object of law and be encouraged to participate in every aspect of the legal work, including in criminal investigation, prosecution, and in a trial. Additional to their involvement in the legal sphere, Mao's massline called for popular justice at the community level, encouraging greater involvement and mobilization for masses to manage their own affairs, resolve their own conflicts, and achieve self-control through mutual policing (Chen 1999, 32–40; Schram, 1991, 1–106).

155. When interpreting Mao's speech on how to handle contradictions of different nature, in the context of criminal justice system, punishment would be oppressive and stern for crimes committed for counterrevolutionary purposes (contradiction between us and the enemy), and punishment would emphasize rehabilitation and education for crimes committed for non-counterrevolutionary purposes, particularly without evil intent (contradiction among the people). See Jerome A. Cohen, *The Criminal Process in the People's Republic of China 1949–1963* (Cambridge: Harvard University Press, 1968), 22–23.
156. There were only regulations and decrees of various kinds promulgated by a variety of legislative and administrative bodies.
157. William P. Alford, "Tasselled Loafers for Barefoot Lawyers: Transformation and Tension in the World of Chinese Legal Workers." In *China's Legal Reforms*, ed. Stanley Lubman (Oxford University Press, 1996), 22–39. See also Henry Zheng, "The Evolving Role of Lawyers and Legal Practice in China." *American Journal of Comparative Law* 36(1988): 473.
158. Michael Palmer, "The People's Republic of China." In Peter Hodgkinson and Andrew Rutherford (eds.) *Capital Punishment — Global Issues and Prospects* (Waterside Press Criminal Policy Series Volume II, 1996), 105–41.
159. Harold Tanner, *Strike Hard!* (Ithaca, NY: Cornell East Asia Series, 1999).
160. Chengguang Wang, "Introduction: An Emerging Legal System." In Introduction to Chinese Law, eds. Chengguang Wang and Xianchu Zhang (Hong Kong: Sweet & Maxwell, 1997), 1–30.
161. Cohen (1968) called the period between 1953–1957 the "golden age" of law in the PRC because of the codification movement in formalizing the Chinese legal system under the socialist government. See Jerome A. Cohen, *The Criminal Process in the People's Republic of China 1949–1963 (*Cambridge, Massachusetts: Harvard University Press, 1968), 10–12.
162. For example, during the 1950s and the 1970s, several short periods of time (e.g., 1949-56, 1961–62, 1972–74) were marked by legal construction of promulgation of laws. However, during this period of time, numerous political and economic campaigns disrupted the legal construction efforts. Particularly, during the Cultural Revolution (1966–76), the entire legal system was halted and destroyed with legal professionals struggled and replaced by revolutionaries. The emphasis of informal, popular justice seemed to have been persistent at the community level with little interference of ideological struggles, where community rules and norms superseded the laws, formal procedures were simplified and by-passed, and professionals were out favored by common folks during that period of time. See Jianfu Chen, *Chinese Law — Towards an Understanding of Chinese Law, Its Nature and Development* (London: Kluwer Law Interrnational, 1999), 34--39. See also Wang, 1997, 1–30.
163. See Cohen, 1968, 7–8.

164. For details of the statues enacted during this period of time, see Blaustein, 1962, 215–65. The statues included: Statute on Punishment for Counter-Revolutionary Activity, 1951; Temporary Regulations for the Surveillance of Counter-Revolutionary Elements, 1952; Statue on Penalties for Corruption, 1952; Provisional Statute on Penalties for Undermining the State Monetary System, 1951; Order of the State Administrative Council Concerning the Strict Prohibition of Opium and Other Narcotics, 1950; Statute on Labor Re-education.

     In addition, discussions of these statutes along with the 1951 Provisional Law on Guarding State Secrets can be found in Stephen B. Davis, "The Death Penalty and Legal Reform in the PRC." *Journal of Chinese Law* 1(1987):303–34 and Palmer, 1996, 126–30.
165. See the 1951 Statute on Punishment for Counter-Revolutionary Activity in Blaustein, 1962, 215–21.
166. See the 1952 Statute on Corruption in Blaustein, 1962, 227–33.
167. See the 1952 Statute on Corruption in Blaustein, 1962, 227–33.
168. See the 1951 Provisional Statute on Penalties for Undermining the State Monetary System in Blaustein, 1962, 233–36.
169. These crimes were stipulated in the 1950 General Rules for the Organization of People's Tribunals. See Cohen, 1968, 536.
170. Cohen (1968) called the period between 1953–1957 the "golden age" of law in the PRC because of the codification movement in formalizing the Chinese legal system under the socialist government (Cohen 1968, 10–12).
171. See Blaustein, 1962, 96–171.
172. These legal stipulations of the formality and procedure the police and the courts must adhere to occurred mostly during the 1953--1957 period, when attempts were made to build a Soviet-style legal system in China (Cohen 1968, 10–14).
173. Cohen argued that the Chinese criminal justice system in the early socialist period differed from the European inquisitorial system because it did not follow the principles of "directness" and "orality" that essentially required those who hear the case deciding the case. This was not followed by the Chinese practice at the time because judicial decisions were typically made by the chief judge of the criminal division of the court, and some were transferred to the local Party leader for final decisions (Cohen 1968, 15–16).
174. For example, the police frequently conducted large scale roundups of the socially "undesirables" such as petty thieves, gamblers, opium addicts, prostitutes, and vagrants (Cohen 1968, 10).

CHAPTER 4

1. These broad crime categories included counterrevolution, endangering public security, undermining the socialist economic order, infringing upon the rights of the person and the democratic rights of citizens, property violation, obstructing the administration of public order, disrupting marriage and the family, dereliction of duty. See *1979 Criminal Law of the People's Republic of China*. Web site of *Zhongguo Falu Fagui Jiansuo (Index of Chinese Law and Regulation)* at http://202.99.23.199/home/begin.cbs.
2. In the original PRC's Criminal Law (1979), five possible punishments were available: surveillance, short-term detention, fixed-term sentence, life imprisonment, and the death penalty. Additional supplementary punishments of fines, deprival of political rights, and confiscation of property are also

included (*1979 Criminal Law of the People's Republic of China, Articles 28 & 29*. Web site of *Zhongguo Falu Fagui Jiansuo (Searching Index of Chinese Law and Regulation)* at http://202.99.23.199/home/begin.cbs).

When counting the number of capital offenses in law, different standards may generate different results. To be consistent with the literature, we follow Chen's (2002) classification. See Xingliang Chen. *The New Horizon of Contemporary Criminal Law in China* (Beijing: The Chinese University of Politics and Law Publishing House, 2002), 540-57.

3. See Hong Lu and Lening Zhang, "Death Penalty in China: The Law and the Practice." *Journal of Criminal Justice* 33(2005): 367–76. See also *1979 Criminal Law of the People's Republic of China*. Web site of Zhongguo Falu Fagui Jiansuo (Searching Index of Chinese Law and Regulation) at http://202.99.23.199/home/begin.cbs.
4. See Wei Luo, *The 1997 Criminal Code of the People's Republic of China* (Buffalo, NY: William S. Hein & Co., Inc., 1998).
5. Dean G. Rojek, "Chinese Social Control: From Shaming and Reintegration to 'Getting Rich is Glorious." In *Crime and Social Control in a Changing China*, eds. Jianhong Liu, Lening Zhang and Steven Messner (Westport, CT: Greenwood Press, 2001).
6. Mingshan Zhu, *Collection of Criminal Court Cases in 1998* (Beijing, China: China People's University Publishing House, 1999), 125-32.
7. To respond to the potential epidemic of SARS, the People's Supreme Court and People's Supreme Procuratorate jointly issued *The Interpretation of Laws in Criminal Cases Regarding Obstruction of the Prevention and Control of the Outbreak of Infectious Diseases*, effective May 13, 2003. Article 1 of the *Interpretation* states "Whoever intentionally spreads pathogens, which cause an outbreak of infectious disease, and thereby endangers public security, shall be punished under Articles 114 and 115 (1) of the Criminal Law for crimes of endangering public security through the use of dangerous means." (Chenglin Liu, *Chinese Law on SARS* (Buffalo, New York: William S. Hein & Co., Inc. 2004, Appendix 4, 143–8). Article 115 (1) of the Criminal Law (1997) stipulated "Anyone who sets fires, breaches dike, causes explosions, spreads poison, or employs other dangerous means that lead to serious bodily injuries or death, or causes a great loss to public or private property shall be sentenced to fixed-term imprisonment of not less than ten years, life imprisonment or death." (Luo 1998, 77). Thus, the *Interpretation* makes intentionally spreading SARS another crime punishable by death.
8. For more detailed discussions on economic reforms and anomie in China, see Cheng Chen, "A Typological Analysis of Anomie in Current China." *Society* 12(2002): 12–4. Jianghong Liu and Steven F. Messner, "Modernization and Crime Trends in China's Reform Era." In *Crime and Social Control in a Changing China*, eds. Jianhong Liu, Lening Zhang, and Steven F. Messner (Westport, CT.: Greenwood Press, 2001), 3–22. Gordon White, "Democratization and Economic Reform in China." *Australian Journal of Chinese Affairs* 31(1994): 73–92. Raymond W. K. Lau, "Socio-Political Control in Urban China: Changes and Crisis." *British Journal of Sociology* 52(2001): 605–20. Gary Jensen, "Institutional Anomie and Societal Variations in Crime: A Critical Appraisal." *International Journal of Sociology and Social Policy* 22(2002): 45–74.
9. See Bin Liang, Hong Lu, Terance D. Miethe, and Lening Zhang, "Sources of Variation in Pro-Death Attitudes in China: An Exploratory Study of Chinese Students at Home and Abroad." *British Journal of Criminology* 46(2006): 119–30. Terance D. Miethe and Hong Lu, *Punishment: A Comparative Historical Perspective*. London: Cambridge University Press, 2005.

10. See Liming Wang, *Research on Judicial Reform* (Beijing: Law Press, 2001).
11. Article 152 of Criminal Procedure Law of 1996 stipulates cases involving the following circumstances shall not be tried publicly: (1) the state's secrets, (2) personal privacies, (3) juvenile criminals aged fourteen years or more but under the age of sixteen. The Article also indicates that juvenile criminals aged sixteen years or more but under the age of eighteen generally shall not be tried publicly (Luo 2000, 96). The Supreme People's Court's *Interpretation* of the CPL further specifies that a trial shall not be held publicly if a party requests a closed door hearing and it truly involves business secrets (Article 121). In addition, the *Interpretation* specifies that when a closed trial is conducted, only close relatives and family members shall be allowed in the courtroom to audit the hearing of the case and no other citizens, including the functionaries of the court, who have nothing to do with the adjudication of the case, are allowed in the courtroom (Article 122) (Luo 2000, 186–7).
12. While it was cautious not to interpret the procedure law "on the book" as the law "in action," the Lawyers Committee for Human Rights seemed to also acknowledge the major transformation in the criminal process in China (*Opening to Reform? An Analysis of China's Revised Criminal Procedural Law*, Lawyers Committee for Human Rights, 1996, i–ii).
13. Systematic comparisons of the 1979 and 1996 Criminal Procedure Laws were made by Luo (2000, 11–23).
14. Article 12 of the CPL states "no one shall be found guilty without a judgment rendered by a people's court according to law" (Luo 2000, 11–12, 43).
15. Article 174 of the CPL states that courts may apply the simplified procedure and have a single judge conduct adjudication when (1) the accused may be sentenced to a fixed-tem imprisonment of less than three years or other lesser punishments (e.g., a fine, detention), the facts of crime are clear and the evidence is sufficient, and the procuratorate recommends or agrees to the procedure; (2) a petty criminal cases filed by the victim with supporting evidence (Luo 2000, 12–13, 103–4).
16. Article 34 of the CPL states that "in cases where the accused may be sentenced to capital punishment and he does not retain any defenders, the people's court shall appoint a lawyer, who voluntarily is undertaking legal aid obligation, to defend him." (Luo 2000, 13–15, 53).
17. Luo, 2000, 15–16.
18. Ibid., 16–17.
19. Both the 1979 and 1997 Criminal Procedure Law (Article 183) stipulated a ten day appeal time after conviction. However, based on the 1983 Decision issued by the NPC, the appeal time was limited to three days to expedite the adjudication of capital cases due to the strike-hard campaigns. See Steven Davis, "The Death Penalty and Legal Reform in the PRC." *Journal of Chinese Law* 1(1987):303–34.
20. The Supreme Court's *Interpretation Concerning Several Issues in the Implementation of the Criminal Procedure Law of the People's Republic of China* further stipulates detailed review procedure for capital punishment. See Table Endnote 4.1.
21. Chen, 2002, 554–6.
22. Ibid., 555.
23. Whether the Supreme Court's final review and approval authority of the death penalty cases should be waived or not has been at the center of the debate of the death penalty system in recent years in China. A review of the temporary decrees and criminal procedure laws passed in the past twenty years or so suggests that while the waiver of the Supreme Court's final review

Table Endnote 4.1 Selected review procedure for capital punishment amended in the interpretations by the Supreme People's Court

Article 274

If a death sentence is imposed by a people's court which changes an original sentence to a death sentence according to the procedure of the second instance upon a protest filed by a people's procuratorate, the death sentence shall be submitted to the Supreme People's Court for verification and approval.

Article 275

Cases of capital punishment to be submitted to the Supreme People's Court for verification and approval shall be handled according to the following respective circumstances:

1. In a case of the first instance where an intermediate people's court sentences the defendant to death, if the defendant does not appeal and the people's procuratorate does not protest, within three days after the time limit to appeal or protest expires the court shall submit the case to the higher people's court for review. If the higher people's court assents to the capital punishment, it shall make such a ruling according to law and submit the case to the Supreme People's Court for verification and approval. If the higher people's court does not assent to the imposition of capital punishment, it shall bring the case up for adjudication or return the case to the intermediate people's court for a new trial.
2. If the defendant appeals or the people's procuratorate protests a case, … the higher court makes a final ruling to sustain the death sentence, the case shall be submitted to the Supreme Court for verification and approval.
3. If the defendant does not appeal and the peoples' procuratorate does not protest a case of the first instance in which a higher court sentences the defendant to death, the case, within three days after the time limit to appeal or protest expires, shall be submitted to the Supreme Court for verification and approval.
4. If an offender is sentenced to death with a two-year suspension of execution in a capital punishment case which must be submitted to the Supreme People's Court for verification and approval, if he intentionally commits a new crime during the period of suspension of executing the death sentence, such new offense is confirmed after investigation, and the death sentence should be carried out, the higher people's court shall submit the case to the Supreme Court for verification and approval.

Article 278

When verifying and approving a death sentence with a two-year suspension of execution, a higher court shall not impose a heavier punishment on a defendant simply because the case was raised to a higher level for review.

Article 279

If one of the offenses which causes a defendant to be sentenced to death shall be submitted to the Supreme Court for verification and approval, or if the offenses that cause some of the defendants in a case of criminal conspiracy to be sentenced to death shall be submitted to the Supreme Court for verification and approval, the whole case shall be submitted to the Supreme Court for verification and approval.

Source: "Interpretation Concerning Several Issues in the Implementation of the Criminal Procedure Law of the People's Republic of China." In *The Amended Criminal Procedure Law and the Criminal Court Rules of the People's Republic of China: with English Translation, Introduction and Annotation*, ed. and trans. Wei Luo (Buffalo, New York: William S Hein & Co., Inc., 2000) 229–34.

and approval authority in certain capital offenses is a temporary demand of current sociopolitical conditions, in the long run, the Supreme Court will take back its authority to review and approve all death penalty cases (Chen 2002, 554–6).

24. See the *1996 Criminal Procedure Law, Articles 203 & 204* (Luo 2000, 112).
25. According to the Criminal Procedure Law, Article 205, if the courts of various levels discover the erroneous rulings that have already become effective, the case should be reviewed by the adjudicative committees of the court. If the Supreme Court or courts of a higher level discover the erroneous rulings by lower courts, the higher court shall have the right to bring the case up to adjudicate it or to order the lower court to retry it. If the Supreme Procuratorate or procuratorates at a higher level discover the erroneous rulings by lower courts, they shall have the right to lodge protests to the court at the same levels (Luo 2000, 112–3).
26. See Criminal procedure law, Article 206 & 207 (Luo 2000, 113–4).
27. See the *1996 Criminal Procedure Law, Article 203 & 211* (Luo 2000, 112–4 and 238–42).
28. *Xin fang,* refers to citizens' reporting of problems, provision of information and suggestions, and the appeal of mistreatment and illegal treatment by governmental officials to various administrative agencies through the means of letters, phone calls, and personal visits. See Yongqing Wang and Xiwei Lu, *The Interpretation of the Act on Xin Fang* (Beijing: Chinese Legal System Publishing House, 2005), 179–90. For detailed descriptions of *xin fang* and its functions, see Kangtai Cao and Xuejun Wang, *Decrees of Xin Fang* (Beijing: China Law Publishing House, 2005).
29. Luo, 2000, 116–8.
30. See Luo, 2000, 116–8.
31. See the *1997 Criminal Law Articles 33 & 34* (Luo 1998, 45–6).
32. See Chen, 2002, 545 & 552.
33. See the *Interpretation* on the Criminal Law, Article 313 by the *Standing Committee* of the *National People's Congress*, issued on August 29, 2002. Available at Web site of *Zhongguo Falu Fagui Jiansuo* (Searching Index of Chinese Law and Regulation) at http://202.99.23.199/home/begin.cbs
34. See *1979 Criminal Law, Article 44.* Web site of *Zhongguo Falu Fagui Jiansuo* (Searching Index of Chinese Law and Regulation) at http://202.99.23.199/home/begin.cbs.
35. See Luo, 1998, 50. A UN resolution stipulated that no young person under eighteen should be subject to the death penalty.
36. See Luo, 1998, 50.
37. See Luo, 1998, 38–39.
38. See Mingli Gong, "On confession," in *Criminal Law*, ed. Y. Gan (Beijing: Beijing University Press, 1989).
39. See Wallace Johnson, *The Tang Code* (Princeton, NJ: Princeton University Press, 1979), 3–8.
40. See Albert P. Blaustein, *Fundamental Legal Documents of Communist China* (South Hackensack, NJ: Fred B. Rothman & Co., 1962), 229.
41. See Luo, 1998, 56–57.
42. See Hong Lu and Terance D. Miethe, "Confessions and Criminal Case Disposition in China." *Law & Society Review* 37(2003):549–78.
43. See 1996 Criminal Procedure, Article 34 (Luo 2000, 53).
44. Legal training is now provided at universities, special centers, continued legal education institutions, and secondary vocational law schools. By the end of

2002, the number of professional lawyers reached a total of 136,684, and the number of law offices increased to a total of 10,873. See *Law Yearbook of China*. Beijing: Law Yearbook Publishing House, 2003, 1335.

45. Legal aid programs have increased markedly since their inception in 1994. By the end of 2004, the number of legal aid programs reached approximately three thousand and the number of legal aid professional workers in legal aid offices increased to approximately ten thousand. See "Ordinary Chinese Citizens Access More Legal Aid." China *Daily* Web site: http://www.chinadaily.com.cn/english/doc/2004-10/01/content_379261.htm (10/01/2004).
46. See Zhengxin Zhang, *The Theory and Practice of the Chinese Suspended Death Sentence* (Wuchang, China: Wuhan University Press, 2003). Michael Palmer. "The People's Republic of China." In *Capital Punishment — Global Issues and Prospects*, ed. Peter Hodgkinson and Andrew Rutherford (Waterside Press Criminal Policy Series Volume II., 1996). Also Andrew Scobell, "The Death Penalty under Socialism, 1917–90: China, the Soviet Union, Cuba, and the German Democratic Republic." *Criminal Justice History: An International Annual* (Westport, CT: Greenwood Press, 1993, Volume 12).
47. See Luo, 1998, 50.
48. See Chen, 2002, 546–7.
49. See Zhang, 2004, 1. In other countries, amnesty and gubernatorial/presidential pardon was common in sparing death roll inmates' lives.
50. Based on the *1951 Notice of the Standard for Meting Out Sentences* issued by the Public Ministry, offenders who commit offenses such as robbery, abduction, use of firearms, and seriously threatening socialist construction, when serious, must be sentenced to death. However, if they had done meritorious services, the sentence could be suspended for two years for labor reform and observation (Zhang 2004, 126–7).
51. Based on the *1951 Interpretation on how to carry out the Suspended Death Sentence for Counterrevolutionary Offense* issued by the Judicial Committee, upon satisfactory performance by the death roll inmate after two years, the original sentence was to be reduced to life imprisonment. However, further reduction to a lighter sentence was possible if the offender's performance was exceptional (Zhang 2004, 127–8).
52. See *1979 Criminal Law*. Articles 43 & 46. Web site of *Zhongguo Falu Fagui Jiansuo* (Index of Chinese Law and Regulation) at http://202.99.23.199/home/begin.cbs.
55. See Luo, 1998, 50–51.

CHAPTER 5

1. See Amnesty International Web site at http://www.amnesty.org/uk/amnesty/vision/index.shtml.
2. See Amnesty International Web site at http://web.amnesty.org/library/Index/ENGASA170351997?open&of=ENG-2S2.
3. See Amnesty International Web site at http://web.amnesty.org/library/Index/ENGASA170351997?open&of=ENG-2S2.
4. See "Editorial Comments," *Law Yearbook of China* (Beijing: Law Yearbook of China Press, 2004).
5. These fifteen parts included (1) the overview of national law promulgation, law enforcement, law supervision, and arbitration activities; (2) the PRC laws; (3) the PRC administrative laws; (4) an index of regional and local administrative rules; (5) international or multi-lateral/ bilateral treaties signed by

the PRC; (6) Judicial documents and notices; (7) legal development of the various organizations of the central government; (8) legal development of the various organizations of the local governments; (9) selected cases; (10) an overview of the development of various aspects of legal studies; (11) an index of law schools, legal study institutions, and law books; (12) statistics; (13) administrative tracts; (14) major events of law development; (15) appendix. See "The Table of Contents," *Law Yearbook of China* (Beijing: Law Yearbook of China Press, 2004).

The coverage varied by issues, particularly in earlier issues where fewer parts were included and a great deal of information was missing in the statistics section.

6. Additional judicial judgment documents were obtained from the following list of criminal case collections.

   List of Case Collections

   Yang Xiao, *Selected Chinese Criminal Court Cases — 2003* (Beijing: People's Court Publishing House and China People University Publishing House, 2004).

   Mingshan Zhu, *Selected Chinese Criminal Court Cases —1998* (Beijing: Chinese People's University Publishing House, 2003).

   Peiyou Li, *Judicial Document Selections of the People's Court — Jiangsu 2000* (Beijing: Law Press, 2001).

   Zhengan Qin, *Judicial Document Selections of the People's Court — Beijing 2000* (Beijing: Law Press, 2001).

   Sichuan Superior People's Court, *Judicial Document of Selection of the People's Court — Sichuan 2000* (Beijing: Law Press, 2001).

   Qimei Zhang, *Judicial Document Selections of the People's Court — Zhejiang 2000* (Beijing: Law Press, 2001).

   Mingshan Zhu, *Selected Chinese Criminal Court Cases — 1998* (Beijing: Chinese People's University Publishing House, 2001).

   Jianming Cao, *Selected Cases from the People's Courts —1992–1999* (Beijing: China Law Publishing House, 2000).

   Mingshan Zhu, *Selected Chinese Criminal Court Cases — 1998* (Beijing: Chinese People's University Publishing House, 1999).

   Mingshan Zhu, *Selected Chinese Criminal Court Cases — 1997* (Beijing: Chinese People's University Publishing House, 1998).

   Mingshan Zhu, *Selected Chinese Criminal Court Cases — 1994* (Beijing: Chinese University of People's Public Security Publishing House, 1995).

   Mingshan Zhu, *Selected Chinese Criminal Court Cases — 1993* (Beijing: Chinese University of People's Public Security Publishing House, 1994).

7. See, for example, Zhengan Qin, *Judicial Document Selections of the People's Court - Beijing 2000* (Beijing: Law Press, 2001), 1. Mingshan Zhu, *Selected Chinese Criminal Court Cases — 1998 (*Beijing:Chinese People's University Publishing House, 1999), 1.
8. See Qin (2001, 1) and Zhu (1999, 1).
9. For example, various Web sites (e.g., a Southwestern University of Political and Law professor's personal Web site, and a couple of English language Web sites) reported Wang Binyu's execution ruling by Ningxia Superior Court on October 20, 2005. However, none of the reputable news outlets (e.g., *Xinhua News Agency*, *Legal Daily*, *People's Daily* and the *Supreme Court* Web site) carried the news. To be cautious, this study did not conclude that Wang had been executed (see chapter 7 of this book).
10. Ruihua Chen, Professor of Law at Beijing University, pointed out that under the current conditions, case studies (studying individual criminal cases) seemed

the best and most fruitful approach in investigating legal issues because of the lack of systematic data collection capabilities and funding in China. See Xingliang Chen (ed.), *An Examination of the Death Penalty System in China* (Beijing: China Procuratorial Publishing House, 2003), 29–31.

11.See *Law Yearbook of China*, 2003, 1320.

12.See *Law Yearbook of China*, 2004, 1054.

13.See Weidong Chen and Lei Chen, "Not Just Taking Back — Comments on the Strategies of the Supreme Court Taking Back the Final Review and Approval Authority for the Death Penalty Cases." *Legal Studies of China and the Abroad* 5(2005).

14.More specifically, in 2003, 22 percent of death penalty cases were reduced to suspended death sentence or life imprisonment and 7 percent of death penalty cases were returned for a retrial by the Supreme Court. See "The Supreme Court Spared More than 20 Percent of Death Penalty Cases since 2003." Wang Yi Web site at http://news.163.com/05/1026/15/210GQ5ID0001124T.html (11/07/2005).

These statistics are consistent with data presented by the *Law Yearbook of China* on the reversion rate in the appellate court and the Supreme Court on all criminal cases in 2002 and 2003.

Table Endnote 5.1 Reversion rate in the appellate court and the Supreme Court

Sustained	Modified	Returned	Withdrawn	Mediation	Other	For a Retry
2003	71,788	12,401	6,633	4,611	690	674
2002	65,459	11,879	6,114	4,502	806	680

15. Amnesty International, 1994–2004.
16. For example, 72 percent of those who were sentenced to death were actually executed in 1996; discounting 424 cases that received a death sentence with suspended execution, the execution rate becomes 77 percent.
17. For example, based on our analysis of the 520 death penalty cases, in only 32 cases (6 percent), did the high court change the lower court's decision by mostly reducing the death sentence to suspended death sentence or life imprisonment, or increase the suspended death sentence to death sentence. We would expect low rates of appeals in China because of the inquisitorial legal system in which the facts have been examined before trial and in complex cases, opinions of high courts have been sought before the rulings are made in the trial of first instance. Additionally, strike-hard campaigns demanded the criminal justice system to impose stiff and swift sanctions on criminal offenders. The reversal of legal rulings seemed incompatible with the "tough on crime" climate that is currently in operation in China.
18. Alternatively, data sources that rely on newspaper accounts may also seriously undercount the number of capital convictions because the reporting of the actual executions is often considered a more newsworthy event. Under this condition, the gap between capital convictions and executions may even be wider than reported based on available data.
19. Suspended death was classified into the same group with life imprisonment for the following reasons. First, technically speaking, almost all suspended death sentences are commuted to life imprisonment after the two year observation period. Second, because the sample size for suspended death sentence cases and cases of life imprisonment were relatively small compared to other samples (e.g., death sentence with immediate execution), combining the two groups into one will aid the analysis.

20. A total of 1,010 serious criminal cases were included in the analysis. Among them, 544 cases received the death penalty with immediate execution (e.g., 73 corruption cases, 189 violent crimes, 145 property crimes, 38 economic crimes, 26 crimes against public safety, and 73 crimes against public order); 224 cases received suspended death sentence (128 cases) and life imprisonment (96 cases) (e.g., 34 corruption, 64 violent, 61 property, 21 economic, 10 public safety and 34 public order offenses); 242 cases received fix prison sentences greater than 10 years (e.g., 30 corruption, 48 violent, 107 property, 22 economic, 16 public safety and 19 public order offenses).
21. See "Capital Punishment Statistics." *Bureau of Justice Statistics* Web site at http://www.ojp.usdoj.gov/bjs/cp.htm.
22. See Palmer, 1996, 126–30.
23. An offender, who received the death sentence with immediate execution for robbery committed when he was seventeen years old, was tried and sentenced to death in 1992, prior to the 1997 law that banned the execution of offenders younger than eighteen years old.
24. This offender was a retired worker, who conspired with others to commit graft and was sentenced to death with immediate execution in 2000.
25. This finding was consistent with the findings of a study using samples of lethal murder and robbery cases from two jurisdictions (Beijing and Shenzhen) between 1995–2000. It found that young people were disproportionately more likely to commit murder and robbery. For example, offenders twenty-five years of age and younger committed nearly 70 percent of murders and robberies in the two cities. See Guoling Zhao, "An Analysis of Murder and Robbery." *Journal of Huadong University of Political Science and Law* 38(2005): 58–66.
26. Studies found that only about 1.5 percent of all death row inmates in the United States were women. See Hugo Adam Bedau, "The United States." In Peter Hodgkinson and Andrew Rutherford (eds.) *Capital Punishment — Global issues and Prospects*. Winchester, UK: Waterside Press Criminal Policy Series, Volume II, 1996).
27. If only violent crimes were considered, the gap between the Chinese and the U.S. female death row offenders is at 9–1.5 percent.
28. Supplemental analysis indicated that women committed corruption mostly in the capacity of being a manager of a company or a clerk rather than as a governmental official. An opposite pattern is found among men convicted of corruption.
29. Zhao (2005) found that among 684 offenders involved in murder and robbery between 1995–2000 in the city of Beijing and Shenzhen, 232 were rural residents, 247 were unemployed, 75 were worker, 22 were students, 9 were self-employed, 14 were employed in other capacities (nonworkers), 5 were governmental employees, 15 were escaped criminals, 2 were retired, and 63 were unknown of their employment status (Zhao 2005, 38: 58–66).
30. Hong Lu and Kriss A. Drass, "Transience and the Disposition of Theft Cases in China." *Justice Quarterly* 19(2002): 401–34.
31. See Lening Zhang and Steven F. Messner, "Bonds to the Work Unit and Official Offense Status in Urban China." *International Journal of Offender Therapy and Comparative Criminology* 43(1999): 375–90.
32. Lu and Drass, 9(2002): 401–34.
33. See Palmer, 1996, 126–30.
34. Lu and Drass, 19(2002): 401–34
35. For example, if the listed place of origin is the same with the place of jurisdiction, the offender is coded as "local resident". However, if the place of origin

is different from the place of jurisdiction, depending on whether and what kind of the employment the offender held, he/she is either coded as "local resident" (e.g., if the current employment is long-term) or "transient" (e.g., if without an employment, or the current employment is short-term [e.g., construction worker]).

36. See Xiaogang Deng, Lening Zhang, and Ann Cordila, "Social Control and Recidivism in China." *Journal of Contemporary Criminal Justice* 14(1998): 281–95.
37. This first and only national study on recidivism rate in China used samples from most of the thirty provinces and autonomous regions except Tibet, Guang Zi, and Hainan provinces. Data used in this study involved a three year follow-up of 159,177 adult offenders who were released form prison from 1982 to 1986. It defined the recidivism rate as offenders rearrested within a three year period for a new offense, which is punishable according to the criminal law. See J. Li. (ed.), *China's Recidivism Study* (Beijing: Law Publishing House, 1992).
38. For example, in our sample of analysis, 20 percent of offenders who were convicted of manufacturing and trafficking narcotics had been arrested at least once before and all of the offenders who were convicted of escaping from prison had been arrested at least once had prior to the current conviction.
39. For example, in out sample of analysis, 21 percent of offenders who were convicted of robbery had been arrested at lest once in the past and 29 percent of offenders convicted of theft had criminal records.
40. Hong Lu and Terance D. Miethe, "Confessions and Criminal Case Disposition in China." *Law & Society Review* 37(2003): 549–78.
41. According to Lu and Miethe (2003), legal disposition is theoretically in accordance with the degree of confession. For nonconfessors who refuse to admit their guilt, it is likely to result in more severe punishment within the legal limit. For offenders who confessed, but their confession was deemed incomplete or nonspontaneous, insincere, or instrumental, it may not affect the final disposition. Offenders who completely confessed to their crime and showed remorse, but confessed only after their crime was detected by the law enforcement authority, may be treated with leniency even though this is neither written nor guaranteed in law. The last category of voluntary submission refers the highest degree of confessions. That is, the offender voluntarily turned him/herself in before the crime was detected. This may result in reduced sentences according to the criminal law. See Lu and Miethe, 37(2003): 549–578.
42. Lu and Miethe, 37(2003): 549–78.
43. For example, in capital cases, offenders merely showing good attitude by admitting to the crime are unlikely to receive a sentencing reduction. Only in circumstances where they voluntarily surrendered to the police authority before their crime was detected would a sentencing reduction be considered. In some cases, however, voluntary surrender may not be sufficient to spare an offender the death penalty (e.g., in Wang Binyu's case to be discussed in chapter 7, he was sentenced to death with immediate execution by an intermediate court for murdering four people and severely wounding one person in the heat of passion, despite that he turned himself in and confessed to the crime).
44. In other cases where offenders' attitudes may also be noted by the court, but were not included in this analysis, these offenders' attitudes could be classified into one of the following categories: (1) the refusal to admit quilt, (2) good attitude (e.g., offenders admitted to the crime); and (3) no comments on the offenders' attitude by the court.

45. See Dao Wen, "Brutally Raping and Murdering a High School Student, a Capital Murderer's Sentence Caused Controversial." *Heilongjiang TV and Broadcasting Newspaper*, cited by Ying Jing Web site at http://news.163.com/05/1222/10/25INJ76U0001122E.html (12/22/2005).
46. See Palmer, 1996,126–30. See also *Beijing Review*, 19–24, April, 1988; Shaochuan Leng and Hangda Chiu, *Criminal Justice in Post-Mao China* (Albany: State University of New York Press, 1985). Even though the death penalty is disproportionately less likely to be applied to economic crimes, overall a significant number of crimes were imposed with the death penalty where there was no loss of human lives in China.
47. *Law Yearbook of China* (Beijing: Law Yearbook of China Publishing House, 1987–2001).
48. Amnesty International China death penalty log (1996, 2000) is the compilation of death sentence reports from various news outlets.
49. Other major crime categories included thefts (487 cases), prostitution and pimping (43 cases), and hooliganism (64 cases).
50. Offenses against the public security include cases of stealing and illegal trading of guns or ammunition, setting fires and causes explosions in public, and sabotaging electric power.
51. Economic offenses include producing and distributing fake and shoddy goods, smuggling, and obstructing tax collection and enforcement.
52. Violent offenses include murder, assault, rape, kidnapping, and human smuggling.
53. Property offenses include robbery, theft, fraud, and blackmailing.
54. Crimes against public order include smuggling, trafficking, transporting and manufacturing narcotics, organizing and forcing prostitution, organized jailbreak or prison riot.
55. Corruption cases include graft, bribe taking, and misappropriate public funds.
56. While no cases of endangering the national defense interest and violating duties by military servicemen were included in these publications, several cases of endangering national security (e.g., espionage) were reported in these case collection. However, in none of the espionage cases did offenders receive the death penalty.
57. Zhengxin Zhang, *The Theory and Practice of the Chinese Suspended Death Sentence* (Wuchang, China: Wuhan University Press, 2004), 130–2.
58. See Chen, 2002.

CHAPTER 6

1. "Simplified procedure" was stipulated in the 1996 Criminal Procedure Law Article 174. According to the new stipulation, cases under these conditions may follow the simplified procedure and have a single judge conducting adjudication: (1) the accused may be sentenced to a fixed-term imprisonment of less than three years; (2) the facts are clear; (3) the evidence is sufficient; and (4) the procuratorate recommends or agrees with the process. See Wei Luo, *The Amended Criminal Procedural Law and the Criminal Court Rule of the People's Republic of China* (Buffalo, NY: William S. Hein & Co., Inc., 2000), 19.
2. For detailed procedural requirements for the trial of first instance, see Luo, 2000, 93–102.

3. An additional month may be extended if approved by the Higher Court. In cases tried by the Supreme Court, the time limit of adjudication is decided by the Supreme Court. For detailed legal requirements for the time limit of the second trial, see Luo, 2000, 109–10.
4. See Luo, 2000, 107–8.
5. See "The Case of Intentional Assault and Rape by Sun Aijun." In *Selected Chinese Criminal Court Cases — 2002,* ed. Mingshan Zhu (Beijing: Chinese People's University Publishing House, 2003), 242–6.
6. See "The Case of Graft by Fang Yong." In *Judicial Document Selections of the People's Court — Zhejing, 2000,* ed. Qimei Zhang (Beijing: Law Publishing House, 2001), 161–3.
7. See "The Case of Selling Narcotics by Xiang Yanrong." In *Selected Chinese Criminal Court Cases — 2002,* Mingshan Zhu (Beijing: Chinese People's University Publishing House, 2003), 480-4.
8. This judicial judgment document was obtained from the Supreme Court's Web site at http://www.court.gov.cn/study/penal/200401120019.htm (1/12/2004).
9. This judicial judgment document was obtained from the Supreme Court's Web site at http://www.court.gov.cn/study/penal/200401120020.htm (1/12/2004).
10. See Liming Wang. *Research on Judicial Reform* (Beijing: Law Press, 2001), 3–168
11. According to the first author's observations of courts of various jurisdictions, defendants were brought into the courtroom sometimes with handcuffs, yet other times without.
12. Xingliang Chen (ed.) *An Examination of the Death Penalty System in China* (Beijing: China Procuratorial Publishing House, 2003), 34–35.
13. Case observed in a Chinese district court in September, 2005 by the first author.
14. Case observed in a Chinese intermediate court in July, 2005 by the first author.
15. In an unusual interview, *China Youth Daily* reported the following of Chen's account of torture that he endured during police interrogation: "At the first interrogation, they used electric batons to give shocks to my face and neck. The second time, I was fastened to a "cross" fetter, my feet were cuffed and they put the telephone leads round my big toes and rang the telephone making me jump again and again. To stop the jumping, they put me on a stool and pressed the stool's legs on my feet. They rang the phone again and my legs involuntarily jumped. After this, my memory got worse, and my brain was poorer." *China Youth Daily*, 12/27/2000.
16. See "Why Did Governmental Officials Overturn Their Confessions?" *Beijing Morning News,* cited on the Web site at http://cn.news.yahoo.com/040916/84/25r4s_1.html (9/16/2004).
17. For example, in the case of Liu Yong, the defendant and his attorney raised police torture and forced confessions again in the retrial conducted by the Supreme Court. The Court, based on evidence presented by the procuratorate (e.g., the affidavit of police offenders and jail guards involved in the case, and the defendant's medical records from August 5, 2000 to July 9, 2001) ruled that it could not conclude that torture and coerced confessions were present during the preliminary investigation by the police, thus rejecting the defense's claims. See Lan Liu, "Why was Liu Yong Sentenced to Death?" *Xin Lang* Web site at http://news.sina.com.cn/c/2003-12-24/10542456318.shtml (12/24/2003).

18. Popular national and regional television programs including “Live Court,” “Law and Morality,” “Society & Law,” “Investigative Report” are among a few that cover actual criminal investigation and trials in China.
19. See Susan Trevaskes, “Propaganda Work in Chinese Courts.” *Punishment & Society* 6(2005):5–21.
20. A public parade of convicted offenders after a sentencing rally was still done frequently in the reform era despite that the recent Supreme Court’s Interpretation of Specific Questions on the Implementation of the Criminal Procedure Law (1998) stating that “Parading in public or other actions which humiliate the person being executed are forbidden” (Luo, 2000).
21. Prior to the reform era, sentencing rallies were more commonly viewed as an expression of “the unmediated relationship between the masses and the criminal.” See Trevaskes, 2005, 5–21.
22. See the Supreme Court’s Web site at http://www.chinacourt.org/public/detail.php?id=133167 (9/28/2004). Also see Yi Sheng, 2004. “A Promise Unfulfilled; The Impact of China’s 1996 Criminal Procedure Reform on China’s Criminal Defense Lawyers’ Role at the Pretrial Stage.” *Perspectives* 5:1–27.
23. See Hongxiang Xiong, “Sentencing Rally in Guangzhou — A Group of Offenders Were Sentenced to Death.” On the Web site of Xinhua News at http://news.xinhuanet.com/legal/2005-06/23/content_3123272.htm (6/23/2005).
24. See Jiayue Sun, “Shanghai Held Sentencing Rally for Drug Offenders.” On the Web site of Xinhua News at http://news.xinhuanet.com/photo/2004-06/26/content_1548818.htm (06/26/2005).
25. Han (2005) argued that it is important for legal rulings to have enforcement power and to be definitive. Otherwise, it will not help resolve problems, may cause further conflicts to arise. However, in reality, judicial errors do occur. Laws thus must establish procedures to deal with such errors. Retrial is one of the ways the Chinese criminal procedure law resorts to correct the problem. See Yang Han, “An Exploration of Reasons for a Retrial in Criminal Cases.” *Research in Law* 27(2005):88–98.
26. See “Supreme Court Retries Shenyang Gang Leader.” On the Web site of People’s Daily (English edition) at http://english.people.com.cn/200312/19/eng20031219_130753.shtml (12/19/2003).
27. See “Supreme Court to Retry High-Profile Murder Case.” on the Web site of People’s Daily (English edition) at http://english.people.com.cn/200312/18/eng20031218_130682.shtml (12/18/2003).
28. See Zhaowei Nie, On the Formalization of Legal Experts’ Opinions in Criminal Litigations in China. *Legal Studies* 2(2005):110–116.
29. The 1996 Criminal Procedure Law stipulated in Article 205 that “if the Supreme People’s Court discovers that there are mistakes in the judgments or rulings of the people’s courts at various levels that already have become legally effective, ...the court shall have the right to bring the cases up and adjudicate them or to order the people’s courts at lower levels to retry them” (Luo, 2000).
30. See “Supreme Court Retries Shenyang Gang Leader.” On the Web site of People’s Daily (English edition) at http://english.people.com.cn/200312/19/eng20031219_130753.shtml (12/19/2003).
31. See “The Judicial Judgment Document of the Case of Dong Wei.” In *An Examination of the Death Penalty System in China*, ed. Xingliang Chen (Beijing: China Procuratorial Publishing House, 2003), 308–11.
32. See Chen, 2003, 308–11.
33. Ibid., 312–21.

34. Ibid., 2003, 322–23.
35. Ibid., 275–01.
36. It was not unusual for courts of appeals to hold a "closed hearing." In fact, statistics showed that only 8 percent of all cases tried by the appeals court were open to the public. See Rong Zhang, "Reflections on Several Issues regarding the Improvement of Criminal Procedure." *Chinese Legal Studies* 4(2005):142–52.
37. See Chen, 2003, 324–30.
38. For a detailed review of the case and commentaries related to the case, see Chen, 2003.
39. See "A Perplex Case of Death Sentence with a Two Year Suspension." Xinhua News Web site at http://news.xinhuanet.com/legal/2005-07/11/content_3202716.htm (7/11/2005).
40. See "A Perplex Case of Death Sentence with a Two Year Suspension." Xinhua News Web site at http://news.xinhuanet.com/legal/2005-07/11/content_3202716.htm (7/11/2005).
41. See "Innocent Man Sentenced to Death Five Times and the Real Criminal Emerged Ten Years Later." *Legal Morning News* cited on the Web site of Xin Lang at http://news.sina.com.cn/s/2005-03-31/12416251935.shtml (3/31/2005).
42. See Xiaozheng Guo, "Judicial Local Protectionism and Its Effect on Judicial Authority and Credibility." The Supreme Court's Web site at http://www.chinacourt.org/public/detail.php?id=207891 (6/09/2006).
43. Starting from 1992, courts of various levels in China began to implement the responsibility system in the judiciary. Presiding judges are held responsible for intentional or major errors in either substantive or procedural legal rulings. The possible punishments included (1) deprival of one's qualification to try a case; (2) no merit raise; (3) no promotion. Li (2005) commented that judges, particularly those at the lower level courts, felt tremendous pressure in trying a case because of the increasing new laws and complex cases. One of the major ways to check judicial mistakes is the returned cases and/or modified rulings by a higher court. To reduce "judicial mistakes," lower courts tried to (1) persuade the litigants to mediate; (2) establish internal mechanisms to correct a ruling before the case goes to an appeal; and (3) rely on judicial committee so that it becomes a collective responsibility rather than a single judge's responsibility is a judicial mistake was found. See Fujin Li, "On the Judicial Reform of the Lower Level Courts." *Journal of Huadoing University of Political Science and Law* 38(2005): 47–57.

    Liao (1999) called the judicial responsibility system a product of "crisis" in the trust of the judiciary in China. See Yongan Liao, "A Reflection on the Judicial Responsibility System." *Jiangsu Social Sciences* 3(1999).
44. Chen commented that the media may have killed Dong Wei. He said that by the point when the national media focused on Dong Wei's case, Shaanxi Superior Court had no choice but to sustain its original ruling and immediately carry out the execution as the judges had to weigh the costs and benefits of changing their decisions (Chen 2003, 45–49).
45. It becomes extremely difficult to achieve judicial independence in the current political, economic and social context of China because of the concerns for judicial corruption. Many oversight agencies (e.g., adjudicative committee as an internal quality control mechanism, procuratorate agency, higher courts, and the National People's Congress) were established to ensure that judicial decisions are not influenced by external forces. Unfortunately, the mecha-

nism itself violates judicial independence and making it unlikely to improve judicial efficiency. See Li, 2005, 47–57.

46. For criminals who should be arrested yet lacked sufficient evidence, the criminal may be released on bail or put under house surveillance. But the time period for bail shall not exceed twelve months and house surveillance shall not exceed six months (1996 CPL Article 58) (Luo, 2000).
47. With special circumstances, the time limit on submitting the application for review and approval of an arrest can be extended for one to four more days. See CPL Article 69 (Luo, 2000). In addition, for those criminal suspects who do not need to be arrest, the procuratorates or the police may summon them to a designated place for interrogation. The time of such an interrogation shall not exceed twelve hours (CPL, Article 92, Luo, 2000).
48. The interrogation shall be conducted by the police, the procuratorate or the court on suspects the agency decided to arrest on its own. When it is found that the person should not have been arrested, the individual shall be released immediately and be issued a release certificate (CPL, Article 72, Luo, 2000).
49. Under one of the following conditions, the time limit for an investigation may be further extended by two months: (1) a major and complicated case in a remote area with very poor transportation facilities; (2) a major criminal case involving gangs; (3) a major and complicated case involving the suspect moving from one place to another to commit crimes; (4) a major and complicated case involving a broad spectrum of crimes for which evidence is difficult to collect; and (5) if a criminal suspect may be sentenced to ten years imprisonment or more (CPL Article 126 & 127). In addition, if a criminal suspect is discovered to have committed another serious crime during investigation, or refuses to disclose his/her real name and residential address or if his/her identity cannot be verified, the time limit of detaining the criminal suspect shall start from the day of the new discovery (of the crime or identity) (CPL Article 128, Luo, 2000).
50. The following circumstances may postpone the trial: (1) there is a need to notify a new witness to appear in the court, to obtain new physical evidence, or to conduct a new evaluation or inspection; (2) if the public prosecutor discovers there is a need to conduct a supplementary investigation and requests to conduct a supplementary investigator for the case in which a public prosecution has been initiated; and (3) if the trial of the case cannot proceed because the parties have filed the application for disqualification (CPL Article 165, Luo, 2000).
51. Taking a step further, Jin argued about the importance of statute of limitation and defendants' rights not to be tried twice for the same offense (double jeopardy), all in the spirit of the timing of criminal investigation and trial. Jin called this type of stipulations reflecting "law's humility." See Zegang Jin, "Amended Prosecution, Amended Trial, and Amended Sentence." *Legal Studies* 7(2005):72–76.
52. It was estimated that more than 90 percent of criminal defendants were arrested and detained while waiting for prosecution and trial. Many more individuals were detained without an arrest warrant, and/or were arrested but never prosecuted. See Changyong Sun, "A Comparative Analysis of Coercive Measures in the Criminal Justice System." *Research in Law* 1(2005):111–25.
53. The judicial judgment document, in its standard format, records the defendant's arrest date, the close date of a first trial, the close date of a second trial (if any), and the close date of a retrial (if any) and the final review and approval by the Supreme Court (if any). In cases where the judicial judgment document of the first trial was available, yet its subsequent legal dispositions

were not, only the first time period from arrest and announcement of first trial was included in this analysis.

54. This case involved nine offenders, who were convicted for murder, rape and robbery in 1995. All of the offenders were young male, with the youngest nineteen years old and the oldest twenty-two. All of them were given the death sentence with immediate execution.
55. This case involved a forty-one-year-old female offender who was convicted of financial fraud and received the death sentence with immediate execution by the Yanbian Chaoxian Autonomous Region Intermediate Court of Jilin Province, and had her sentence sustained by Jilin Superior Court and finally reviewed and approved by the Supreme Court between 1994 and 1997. This case involved extremely large amount of money and severely impacted the financial order, according to the judicial judgment document. The crime involved three offenders. Besides the defendant, the main offender in this case who received the death sentence, the other two offenders received a suspended death sentence and fifteen years of imprisonment, respectively. See Mingshan Zhu (ed.), *Selected Chinese Criminal Court Cases — 1998* (Beijing: Chinese People University Publishing House, 1999), 173–83.
56. The case had a total of eight offenders. Other offenders received the suspended death sentence (three offenders), life imprisonment (one offender), twelve years of incarceration, and eight years of incarceration, respectively. See Mingshan Zhu (ed.), *Selected Chinese Criminal Court Cases Court Cases – 2001* (Beijing: China People's University Press, 2002), 31–38.
57. This case was the one with the longest first trial that involved financial fraud. In its judicial judgment document, it indicated that the trial was extended according to the legal procedure. See Mingshan Zhu, *Selected Chinese Criminal Court Cases — 1998* (Beijing: Chinese People University Publishing House, 1999), 173–83.
58. Some of the cases reported in these case collections may not include information on the final review and approval process by the Supreme Court. Thus the category of "cases without Supreme Court's review" may include cases that actually went through the Supreme Court's review but were not reported.
59. See Gaofeng Ye, *Research on the Strategies towards Violent Crimes in China* (Beijing: Law Press, 1998), 270–3. Yi Mao and Xiaoming Wang, *Research on Public Security Cases in China* (Wuchang, China: Hubei Science and Technology Publishing House, 2002), 93–97, 133–38, 184–86, 580–99.
60. See Ping Yu, "Problems of the Death Penalty System in China." *Legal Studies* 5(2005): 88–90.
61. This is especially true in this study where cases were coded with the final legal ruling, not the original ones (e.g., for a case that received a death penalty with immediate execution in the first and second trial, but was modified to death sentence with a two year reprieve in the final review and approval process by the Supreme Court, it was coded as suspended death in this study). When a change of legal rulings was involved, it typically required more time.
62. See "Liu Yong's final 84 hours." *Shenyang Today News*, cited on the Web site of Xin Lang at http://news.sina.com.cn/c/2003-12-24/02082450393.shtml (12/14/2003).
63. For example, in June, 2005, sentencing rallies that announced sentences for a group of drug offenders were held in various cities to mark the World Anti-Drugs Day. See Hongxiang Xiong. "Sentencing Rally in Guangzhou – A Group of Offenders were Sentenced to Death." On the Web site of Xinhua News at http://news.xinhuanet.com/legal/2005-06/23/content_3123272.htm (6/23/2005). Also see Jiayue Sun. "Shanghai Held Sentencing Rally for

Drug Offenders." On the Web site of Xinhua News at http://news.xinhuanet.com/photo/2004-06/26/content_1548818.htm (6/26/2005).

64. For example, it was reported that defendant Sun Kaihong was detained in Wuhan No. 2 Detention Center for the charge of murder in early 2004. When he first came to the detention center, Sun was mentally unstable, imitating dog's barking, eating very little, and speaking no words all day long. At one time, Sun caught a cold, officer He took him to the hospital. Since then, Sun's most spoken words were "Officer He was very good!" The officer often approached Sun asking him what he wanted to say to his family. Sun's answer was always that his missed his mother the most. On December 3, 2004, Sun was sentenced to death and was transferred to the special unit in the detention center. On December 21, Officer He took two packs of cigarettes, two drinks, crackers, and a pair of sneakers to Sun's cell. Officer He started to ask: "Do you have any regrets?" "Do you have any repentance that you want to make to the victim's family?" "Do you have any last words to say to your mother and sister?" Though Sun did not say a word, his tears said a lot.

    It was also reported that condemned offender Chen Qiaohua, convicted of murder, robbery and rape, wrote that with the officer's caring and encouragement, he realized the wrongs that he had done to society. He was willing to donate his organs (e.g., heart, liver, kidney) to repay the society. See "The Last Night of the Condemned." On the Web site of Wang Niao at http://news.netbirds.com/zhenqingshike/2005-04-23/1114243200,62772.html (4/23/2005).

65. Since September 1, 2003, Beijing Superior Court issued a notice to improve the judicial service to the people. Among the services provided was to allow the death row inmates a final chance to meet with their family. In 2004, Beijing No. 1 Intermediate Court approved 7 condemned offenders to meet with the family. See Zheng Li, "Beijing Allows Death Row Inmates to Meet with Family." *Beijing Youth Newspaper*, cited on the Web site of People Daily at http://legal.people.com.cn/GB/42735/3123784.html (12/15/2005).

    Other jurisdictions quickly followed the Beijing reform, allowing condemned offenders to meet with family, such as in Huaibei Intermediate Court of Anhui province (see "Humanitarian Measures in the Judiciary." *Jianghuai Morning News*, cited on the Web site at http://www.hf365.com/epublish/gb/paper32/1/class003200003/hwz566603.htm (4/01/2005).

66. See Haiqi Liu, "Humanitarian Enforcement of Law." Web site of *Legal Daily* at http://www.legaldaily.com.cn/bm/2003-12/31/content_68057.htm (12/31/2003).
67. See "Kidnaper Wu Executed Today," *Legal Daily*, cited on the Web site of MSN at http://msn.ynet.com/view.jsp?oid=6336709 (7/14/2005).
68. See "Kidnaper Wu Executed Today," *Legal Daily*, cited on the Web site of MSN at http://msn.ynet.com/view.jsp?oid=6336709 (7/14/2005).
69. See "Disclosing the Secrecy of Execution in China." Cited on the Web site of *China Affairs* at http://www.chinaaffairs.org/gb/detail.asp?id=57416 (10/23/2005).
70. See "The Last Night of the Condemned." Cited on the Web site of Wang Niao at http://news.netbirds.com/zhenqingshike/2005-04-23/1114243200,62772.html (4/23/2005).
71. For example, three kidnappers, Wu, Wang, and Wang of Beijing, right before their execution told the executioners of their last words to ask their parents to take care of themselves. "Kidnaper Wu was Executed Today," *Legal Daily* cited on the Web site of MSN at http://msn.ynet.com/view.jsp?oid=6336709 (9/14/2005).

72. For example, it was reported that on November 12, 2003, Li, convicted of graft, knowing that he was to be executed the next day, spent a sleepless night at the Tangshan Detention Center. At 7:00 a.m. of November 13, officials of Hebei Superior Court came to the detention center, announcing to Li the Supreme Court's decision on finally approving the superior court's death sentence and immediate execution ruling. Between 7:40 and 8:10 a.m., the court left half an hour for Li to meet with his mother, three brothers and a sister. He was then escorted into an execution van to be given lethal injection. At 8:17a.m., the lethal injection started. Two minutes later, the forensic doctor pronounced his death. See "Exclusive Report: The Day of the Execution for Offender Li." *Metropolitan News*, cited http://www.yzdsb.com.cn/20031130/ca303659.htm (12/01/2003).
73. See "Disclosing the Secrecy of Execution in China." Cited on the Web site of *China Affairs* at http://www.chinaaffairs.org/gb/detail.asp?id=57416 (10/23/2005).
74. See "Disclosing the Secrecy of Execution in China." Cited on the Web site of *China Affairs* at http://www.chinaaffairs.org/gb/detail.asp?id=57416 (10/23/2005).
75. See "Disclosing the Secrecy of Execution in China." Cited on the Web site of *China Affairs* at http://www.chinaaffairs.org/gb/detail.asp?id=57416 (10/23/2005).
76. See Renwen Liu, "Reforming Execution Methods and Improving Humanitarianism." Web site of *Xihu Law Library* at http://www.law-lib.com/lw/lw_view.asp?no=264 (1/05/2001).
77. See Yun Chen, "Lethal Injection Faces Obstacles." Beijing Nightly News cited on the Web site of *People's Daily* at http://www.people.com.cn/GB/shehui/46/20030320/948571.html (3/20/2003).
78. Yunnan province invested in mobile execution vans in 2003, claiming that it will rely on lethal injection as an exclusive means of execution throughout the province.
79. See "The Condemned also Deserves Humanitarian Treatment." *Sanqin Metropolitan News*, cited on the Web site of *Xinhua News* at http://news.xinhuanet.com/legal/2005-07/29/content_3281796.htm (7/29/2005).
80. See "The Condemned also Deserves Humanitarian Treatment." *Sanqin Metropolitan News*, cited on the Web site of *Xinhua News* at http://news.xinhuanet.com/legal/2005-07/29/content_3281796.htm (7/29/2005).
81. See "Exposing an Execution Van." Tainfu Morning News, cited on the Web site of *Xinghua News* at http://news.xinhuanet.com/newmedia/2004-02/26/content_1332545.htm (2/26/2004).
82. See "Exposing an Execution Van." *Tainfu Morning News*, cited on the Web site of Xinhua News at http://news.xinhuanet.com/newmedia/2004-02/26/content_1332545.htm (2/26/2004).
83. See "Exposing an Execution Van." *Tainfu Morning News*, cited on the Web site of Xinhua News at http://news.xinhuanet.com/newmedia/2004-02/26/content_1332545.htm (2/26/2004).
84. See "Exposing an Execution Van." *Tainfu Morning News*, cited on the Web site of Xinhua News at http://news.xinhuanet.com/newmedia/2004-02/26/content_1332545.htm (2/26/2004).
85. See "Eleven Criminals Executed by Lethal Injection Yesterday in Lanzhou, Witnessing the Execution Process", available (in Chinese) at: www.jcrb.com, cited by *Amnesty International*. "People's Republic of China Executed `According to Law'? — The Death Penalty in China" at http://web.amnesty.org/library/Index/ENGASA170032004?open&of=ENG-375 (3/22/2004).

86. It was reported that the execution was carried out on July 28, 2005, at 9:50 a.m. A total of four condemned offenders were escorted to the execution chamber awaiting execution. The execution was carried out one by one, in less than one and one-half minutes for each of the offenders. See "The Condemned also Deserves Humanitarian Treatment." *Sanqin Metropolitan News*, cited on the Web site of Xinhua News at http://news.xinhuanet.com/legal/2005-07/29/content_3281796.htm (7/29/2005).
87. It was reported that on July 9, 2002, a convicted offender was executed with lethal injection under one minute, with no sign of painful expression on his face during execution. See Jinwu Hu and Yunfeng Wang, "Execution with Humanity." At http://cnm21.com/xinwen/yyxw_754.htm (7/09/2002).
88. These accounts of Liu Yong's final moments leading to execution were reported by Wei Wen. "Liu Yong's Last 84 Hours of His Life." In *Shenyang Today Newspaper* cited on the Web site of Xin Lang at http://news.sina.com.cn/c/2003-12-24/02082450393.shtml (12/24/2003) and Yehui Lu. "120 Minutes Eyewitnesses of the Criminal Gang Leader Liu Yong's Death in Jinzhou." In *Shenyang Today Newspaper*, cited on the Web site of Xin Lang at http://news.sina.com.cn/c/2003-12-23/13242448081.shtml (12/23/2003).
89. See Wen, 12/24/2003.
90. Liu was reportedly said: "there is no need for that [band aid]. There are only three days left." See Wen, 12/24/2003.
91. Liu reportedly said to an officer that "I have earned enough money for the entire family to live for several lifetimes." See Wen, 12/24/2003.
92. The foods served to Liu included soymilk, fried sticks, and steamed buns. See Wen, 12/24/2003.
93. It was reported that the detention chief official went to Liu's cell to persuade Liu to cooperate with the authority. The officer told Liu that the Supreme Court's unprecedented decision of retrial proved that the government cared about Liu's rights. If not, the nation would not spend the vast amount of resources to retry the case. The officer continued that as a man, Liu should have enough courage to face whatever fate that lies ahead of him, instead of giving up on life. See Wen, 12/24/2003.
94. It was reported that about half an hour later, Liu's family cars arrived. When asked about the prediction of the outcome of the trial, a male family relative with large built said that there was 50 percent chance that the original sentence (suspended death) would be sustained. This relative knew that another offender's family was notified to prepare a new set of clothes by the court prior to the announcement of death sentence with immediate execution. "Until now, we have not been notified by the court to prepare for new clothes." He said, "That is a good sign." See Wen, 12/24/2003.
95. One commented that "the Supreme Court should be fair and firm in ridding off the bad elements in our society." See Wen, 12/24/2003.
96. See Wen, 12/24/2003.
97. Ibid.
98. See Wen, 12/24/2003 and Lu, 12/23/2003.
99. See Lu, 12/23/2003.

CHAPTER 7

1. See Bingzhi Zhao, "Guidelines for the Gradual Abolition of the Death Penalty in China." *Legal Studies* 1(2005):55–62. See also Xinglinag Chen (ed.), *An Examination of the Death Penalty System in China* (Beijing: China Procuratorial Press, 2003), 18, 43–48.

2. For example, see Robert M. Somers, "The End of the Tang." In *The Cambridge History of China: Volume 3 Sui and Tang China, 589–906, Part I*, eds. Denis Twitchett (Cambridge: Cambridge University Press, 1979), 682–789.
3. For example, in the early 1980s, when speaking about the surging crime rates, particularly regarding crimes of declined morality (e.g., corruption, prostitution, banditry), Deng commented that the speedy and certain imposition of the death penalty would not only rid off the bad elements of the society, deter like criminals, but appease the general public. Xiaoping Deng, *Selected Works of Deng Xiaoping,* third edition (Beijing: People's Publishing House, 1993), 33–34.
4. For example, Tian argued that the death penalty has existed in China for thousands of years and become part of the Chinese culture. Values such as "a life for a life" and "paying back the debt" are as natural as sunset and sunrise. He wrote that if a national survey on the death penalty was conducted, the answer should be obvious (implying that the majority of the Chinese people would support the death penalty.) See He Tian, "On the Conditions of Abolishing the Death Penalty." *Research in Law* 2(2005): 66–74.
5. See Tian, 2(2005):66–74. Qiyuan Wu, *Public Policy* (Taiwan Shangwu Printing House, 1985), 7. See also Xinliang Chen, 2002. *The New Horizon of Contemporary Criminal Law in China* (Beijing: The Chinese University of Politics and Law Press, 2002), 544–45.
6. Public opinion surveys have emerged since the economic reforms even though these surveys are limited when compared with their Western counterparts. The limited development of public opinion surveys may be largely attributed to a variety of reasons including censorship, a long history of totalitarian and bureaucratic control, and political sensitivity on topics such as the death penalty, even though discussion of capital punishment is no longer a taboo in the current Chinese social context. See Bin Liang, Hong Lu, Terance D. Miethe, and Lening Zhang, "Sources of Variation in Pro-Death Penalty Attitudes in China: An Exploratory Study of Chinese Students at Home and Abroad." *British Journal of Criminology* 46(2006): 119–30.
7. The only national survey regarding crime and punishment was conducted by the National Bureau of Statistics of China (NBSC) between 2001 and 2003. During this three year period of time, three surveys on public security and safety were conducted, and more than 100,000 respondents were polled. The survey results showed that 70 percent of respondents felt safe walking along at night in their district, whereas one third of the respondents rated crime as the most troubling public issues in recent years. These survey results were posted on the official Web site of the *National Bureau of Statistic of China* in Chinese at http://www.stats.gov.cn.
8. The first empirical study on the death penalty opinion in China was conducted by Cao and Cullen (Liqun Cao and Francis T. Cullen, "Thinking about Crime and Control: A Comparative Study of Chinese and American Ideology." *International Criminal Justice Review* 11(2001): 58–81). Aother study analyzed survey data on the death penalty opinions collected from two small student samples from two university campuses — one was in China and the other was in the U.S. See Liang, et al., 2006, 119–30. Various Chinese internets sites have conducted surveys on the death penalty in the past. These Web sites included Xin lang (http://wwwsina.com.cn), *People's Daily* (http:www.people.com), Xinhua News (http://www.news.xinhuanet.com), Souhu (http://www.sohu.com), and Wang Yi (http://www.163.com).
9. See R. M. Bohm, "American Death Penalty Attitudes: A Critical Examination of Recent Research." *Criminal Justice and Behavior* 14(1987):380–96. See also R. M. Bohm and R. E. Vogel, "A Comparison of Factors Associated

with Uniformed and Informed Death Penalty Opinions." *Journal of Criminal Justice* 22(1994): 125–43.

10. See Liang, et al. 2006, 119–30.
11. The homepage of the Web site of Xin lang at http://sina.com.cn.
12. See Cao and Cullen, 2001, 58–81.
13. See Liang, et al., 2006, 119–30.
14. The survey results were obtained from the homepage of Xin lang Web site at http://sina.com.cn.
15. The survey results were posted immediately after the close of the poll at the homepage of Xin lang Web site at http://sina.com.cn. However, the results are no longer available on the site at this writing.
16. Available on the Web site of *Hunan Television Station* at http://www.hunantv.com/newspaper/20050126/news.htm (1/26/2005).
17. Cited by Zhi Zhenfeng, "Can the Death Sentence be Sentenced to Death?" On the Web site of *Legal Morning Newspaper* at http://www/chinalegalnews.com.cn/legaltimes/20050419/0801.htm (4/19/2005).
18. This most recent execution in Singapore sparked international attention and controversy because of the drastic positions on the death penalty issued by two governments involved. The Singapore government has been a steadfast believer in the death penalty, particularly in its imposition on drug offenders. Its law requires that those who carry heroine in the amount of 15 grams or more will be subject to the death penalty. Offender Ruan carried a total of 397 grams of heroin when stopping at the Singapore airport to catch a connecting flight from Cambodia to Australia. In contrast, the Australian government has long abolished the death penalty, calling it inhuman and cruel. The Australian government officials repeatedly called to spare Ruan the death penalty. When it failed, it requested on the family's behalf to allow the offender to meet with his mother prior to execution. That request was denied. On December 2, 2005, Ruan was hanged. See "Hanging of a Drug Trafficker Causing Debates in Singapore and Australia." *Yangcheng Nightly News*. Cited on the Web site of Wang Yi at http://talk.163.com/05/10.241QRI2700301JAK.html (12/03/2005).
19. See the homepage of the Web site Wangyi at http://talk.163.com/. Last retrieved on December 5, 2005.
20. See Phoebe Ellsworth and Samuel R. Gross, "Hardening of the Attitudes: Americans' Views on the Death Penalty." In *The Death Penalty in America*, ed. Hugo Adam Bedau (Oxford University Press, 1997), 90–115. See also H. Zeisel and A. M. Gallup. "Death Penalty Sentiment in the United States." *Journal of Quantitative Criminology* 5(1989): 285–97.
21. See R. Hood, *The Death Penalty: A World-Wide Perspective*, third edition (Oxford: Clarendon Press, 2002), 234. See also Lindsay Brook and Ed Cape, "Liberalism in Retreat." In *British Social Attitudes: The 12th Report*, eds. Roger Jowell, J. Curtice, A. Park, L. Brook, D. Ahrendt, and K. Thomson (Aldershot: Dartmouth Publishing Co. 1995), 194.
22. See A. F. P. Hulsewe, "Chin and Han Law." In *The Cambridge History of China Volume 1: The Chin and Han Empires 221B.C. – A.D.220*, eds. Denis Twitchett and Michael Loewe (Cambridge: Cambridge University Press, 1986), 52-44. See also Bohm, 1987, 380–96; Ellsworth and Gross, 1997; Zeisel and Gallup, 1989, 285–97.
23. See Bohm and Vogel, 1994, 22:125--143. See also R. M. Bohm and R. E. Vogel, "More than Ten Years Later: The Long-Term Stability of Informed Death Penalty Opinions." *Journal of Criminal Justice* 32(2004): 307–27.

24. Even though more scholars tended to voice the need to abolish the death penalty than not at a recent scholarly meeting on the death penalty held in Xiangtan, Hunan province in 2002, the main argument for the abolition of the death penalty in China was due to humanitarian concerns and the global trend, rather than the concerns of special political social conditions in China. See He Tian, "On the Conditions of Abolishing the Death Penalty." *Legal Studies* 2(2005): 66–74.
25. The abolitionist movement in China only started in the 1990s with several high profile cases involving offenders wrongfully convicted and executed first appearing on the internet and quickly sparked the public and scholarly debate about the death penalty. Historically, there has been a lack of debate on the death penalty in China. Few scholars voiced their opinions on the death penalty.
26. See Xinglong Qiu, *Comparative Criminal law.* Volume 1. (Beijing: China's Procuratorate Publishing House, 2001), 13. See also Xinglong Qiu, "Morality of law." *Politics and Law* 2(2002).
27. See Qiu. 2001.
28. Other legal scholars such as Xinjiu Qu, law professor of Chinese University of Politics and Law have also been an abolitionist. See "Law Professors' Comments on Wang Binyu's Case." *Procuratorial Daily* cited on the Web site of Legal Daily at http://legal.people.com.cn/GB/42731/3694947.html (9/14/2005).
29. See Xingliang Chen, *The Purpose of Rule of Law* (Beijing: Law Press, 2003), 218-21.

    This view was severely criticized by Qiu. In particular, Qiu argued that if the Chinese scholars are satisfied with the position that "the death penalty should be abolished eventually in China," the abolition of the death penalty will perhaps only exist in the dreams (Qiu 2001, 13).

    Other scholars, such as He Tian, argued that the current social conditions (e.g., instability and social conflicts caused by unemployment, layoffs, large influx of migrants, polarization of the population, corruption), lack of rights consciousness, and high illiteracy rate may prevent China from abolishing the death penalty against the overwhelming support for such a legal practice for centuries (Tian 2005, 2: 66–74).
30. See Chen, 2003, 37–38.
31. See the Web site of *China Daily* at http://www.chinadaily.com.cn/english/doc/2005-07/23/content_462667.htm (7/23/2005).
32. See Bingzhi Zhao, "The Gradual Abolition of the Death Penalty for Non-Violent Crimes in China." *Journal of China University of Political Science and Law* 23(2005):92–99. See also Bingzhi Zhao, "Guidelines for the Gradual Abolition of the Death Penalty in China." *Legal Studies* 1(2005): 55–62. Bingzhi Zhao, *An Exploration of the Abolitionist Movement in China* (Beijing: Chinese University of People's Public Security University Press, 2004), 6.
33. See Jianhua Zhu, "On the Conflict of Law Regarding the Stipulation of the Final Approval of the Death Penalty." *Contemporary Legal Studies* 1(1999). Genlin Liang and Wen Zhang, "Discussions on the Imposition of the Death Penalty on Economic Offenses." *Legal Studies* 1(1997). Bingzhi Zhao, "Issues Involving the Revision of the Criminal Law." *Legal Studies* 5(1996). Huizhi Chu, "Modernizing Punishment." *Legal Studies* 1(1997). Genlin Liang and Wen Zhang, *An Examination of the Current Economic Crime* (Beijing: Beijing University Press, 1996). Mingkai Zhang, *Criminal Law,* second edition (Beijing: Law Press, 2003). Weidong Chen (ed.), *Jurisdictional*

Justice and Innovation (Beijing: China Procuratorate Press, 2002). Dingjian Cai, *Supervision and Judicial Fairness* (Beijing: Law Press, 2005).

34. See "President Xiao Yang Claimed that Abolition of the Death Penalty Does Not Fit the Current Social Conditions of China." On the Web site of Yi Jing at http://news.163.com/06/0311/19/2BV5ARO50001124T.html (3/11/2006).
35. See Z. Zhi, "Can the Death Penalty be Sentenced to Death?" on the Web site of *Legal Daily* at http://www.chinalegalnews.com.cn/legaltimes/20050419/0801.htm (04/19/2005).
36. See "The Central Government Signaled Campaigns against Commercial Bribery." Web site of Tom Group at http://news.tom.com/2006-02-28/0016/09818805.html.
37. See "President Xiao Yang Claimed that Abolition of the Death Penalty Does Not Fit the Current Social Conditions of China." On the Web site of Yi Jing at http://news.163.com/06/0311/19/2BV5ARO50001124T.html (3/11/2006).
38. See Zhuqing Jiang, "Meeting Hears Calls for Death Penalty Reform." Web site of *China Daily* at http://www.chinadaily.com.cn/english/doc/2005-07/23/content_462667.htm (7/23/2005).
39. See Zhuqing Jiang, "Meeting Hears Calls for Death Penalty Reform." Web site of *China Daily* at http://www.chinadaily.com.cn/english/doc/2005-07/23/content_462667.htm (7/23/2005).
40. See Xingliang Chen (ed.), *An Examination of the Death Penalty System in China* (Beijing: China Procuratorate Publishing House, 2003), 1–7.
41. See Furong Zhang, "A Revisit of the Death Penalty in China." Web site of the *Supreme Court* at http://www.chinacourt.org/public/detail.php?id=180534 (10/10/2005).
42. See Chen, 2003, 15–17. Several capital offense categories were rarely used in practice. For example, one study found that in one year after the new 1997 law was passed, only one offender was sentenced to death for theft. See Zuojin Zhao, *On the Restriction of the Death Penalty* (Wuchang: Wuhan University Press, 2001), 209.
43. For example, on the recent online discussion on the death penalty, many online participants expressed strong support for the death penalty, citing most frequently the reason of governmental corruption. See the online special topics discussion posted on the homepage of Wang Yi at http://talk.163.com/, last retrieved on December 5, 2005.
44. See Zhao, 2001, 232–37. Bingzhi Zhao. *Reforms of the Criminal Law* (Beijing: China Legal System Press, 1996), 232.
45. See "China Cracks Down on Torture and Forced Confessions." Web site of Xinhua News at http://english.sina.com/china/1/2005/0517/31270.html (5/17/2005).
46. See Lei Bi, Hongwu Liao and Qianfeng Tian, "An Innocent Young Man was Executed." Web site of People's Daily at http://www.people.com.cn/GB/channel2/13/200503/18/6602.html (6/23/2005).
47. See Guili Chen and Chun Tao, *A Survey of Chinese Peasants* (Beijing: People's Literature Publishing House, 2004).
48. In some cases, there are more incentives for police officers to use coercive means to extract confessions. For example, police officers' performance evaluation is largely based on outcome (e.g., case clearance rate) rather than on means. See Jianming Li, "Research on Mistakes in Death Penalty Cases." *Litigation Law and Justice System* 4(2005): 58–65.
49. See Xianquan Liu, "Reflections on the Traditional Criminal Justice Rationality." *Legal Studies* 5(2005): 81–83. Weidong Chen, "Physical Evidence Key to Avoidance of Wrongful Conviction." *Legal Studies* 5(2005): 84–85. Yuop-

ing Xie, "Improving the Judicial Process to Prevent Wrongful Convictions." *Legal Studies* 5(2005): 85–86. Junmin Wang, "Enforcing the Law by Law to Avoid Wrongful Convictions." *Legal Studies* 5(2005): 87–88. Chunying Zhuang, "Improvement of the Rights Guarantee of the Criminal Suspect and the Defendant in China's Criminal Proceedings and the Existing Problems." *Justice of China* 68(2005): 23–27.

50. See "China Cracks Down on Torture and Forced Confessions." Xinhua News cited on the Web site of Xinglang at http://english.sina.com/china/1/2005/0517/31270.html (5/17/2005).
51. See Victor, "Tighter Rein on Police, Prosecutors Urged." Web site of the Supreme Court at http://en.chinacourt.org/public/detail.php?id=3840 (3/15/2005).
52. See "China Cracks Down on Torture and Forced Confessions." Xinhua News cited on the Web site of Xin Lang at http://english.sina.com/china/1/2005/0517/31270.html (5/17/2005).
53. See "Extended Detention, Forced Confession Still Salient in Chinese Judiciary: Report." Web site of *People Daily* (English edition) at http://english.people.com.cn/english/20001228/eng20001228_59073.html (12/28/2000).
54. See "China Cracks Down on Torture and Forced Confessions." Xinhua News cited on the Web site of Xin Lang at http://english.sina.com/china/1/2005/0517/31270.html (5/17/2005).
55. The report indicated that even though this process is predicted to be longer than desired due to regional developmental disparities, the measure is likely to be implemented first in more developed regions such as Shanghai, Zhejiang, Guangdong, and Jiangsu provinces. See "China to Adopt Live Voice Recording of the Entire Police Interrogation to Curb Police Brutality." Web site of Xinhua News at http://news.xinhuanet.com/legal/2006-05/16/content_4553645.htm (5/16/2006).
56. See Ziliu Jun, "Misjudged Cases Reflecting the Flaws in the Judicial System." *Justice of China* 67 (2005): 97–99.
57. Difference judicial and police departments have adopted different strategies to curb coercion and torture in police interrogation. For example, courts in Beijing have now focused more on physical evidence than on defendants' confessions, making confessions by torture less useful ("Confession Evidence Downplayed in Beijing Courts." Web site of Xinhua News at http://news.xinhuanet.com/legal/2006-02/14/content_4176924.htm, 2/14/2006). The exclusionary rule is applied to confession evidence obtained by torture in Chongqing ("Confession Evidence Obtained by Torture to be Excluded in Chongqing." Web site of Xinhua News at http://news3.xinhuanet.com/legal/2006-03/22/content_4332583.htm, 3/22/2006). Zhejiang Department of Public Security issued a Measure on Punishing Police Officers Involved in Interrogative Torture in September 2003, stating that police officers involved in interrogative torture to extract confessions, and their supervisors who ordered and directed the interrogation and torture must be fired from their job if causing suspects minor or major injuries. Other higher ranking officers who have direct supervisory responsibilities of the officers must be given administrative warning and sanctions ("Police Officers to be Fired from Their Job When Involving in Interrogative Torture." Web site of Xinhua News at http://news.xinhuanet.com/legal/2003-09/22/content_1093365.htm, 9/22/2003).
58. In the past ten years since the passage of the State Compensation Law, very few cases involving state compensation for wrongful convictions in criminal cases received financial compensation. In addition, the amount paid by the state to the victim was minimal only dealing with actual economic losses

(e.g., loss of wages), rather than emotional distress and suffering. See Ziliu Jun, "Misjudged Cases Reflecting the Flaws in the Judicial System." *Justice of China* 67(2005): 97–99.

59. Weidong Chen and Lei Chen, "Not Just Taking Back — Comments on the Strategies of the Supreme Court Taking Back the Final Review and Approval Authority for the Death Penalty Cases." *Legal Studies of China and the Abroad* 5(2005).
60. Chen and Chen, 2005, 5.
61. For example, representatives from Beijing and Shanxi province proposed that the Supreme Court take back its final review and approval authority on the death penalty cases and was endorsed by forty-one representatives at the second meeting of the 10th National People's Congress in 2004. In the same year, dozens of Chinese legal scholars and President of the Chinese Society of Criminology, supported the call. See Shaoqian Zhang, "Ten Problems Associated with the Death Penalty Process in China." *Litigation Process and Judicial System* 5(2005): 46--52. See also Rong Zhang, "Reflections on Several Issues Regarding the Improvement of Criminal Procedure." *Chinese Legal Studies* 4(2005): 142–52.
62. The debate over the final review and approval authority on the death penalty discussed in this section was primarily drawn from the following studies: Weidong Chen, *Research on Procedure for Criminal Trial Supervision* (Beijing: Law Press, 2001). Guoqing Chen and Binqun He, *China's Litigation System and its Reform* (Beijing: The People's Public Security University of China Press, 2001). Liming Wang, *Research on Judicial Reform* (Beijing: Law Press, 2001). Weidong Chen and Lei Chen, 2005, 5.

    Other scholars also considered a further appeals process. Specifically, even after a death sentence is finally approved, if the defendant appeals, the system of suspended execution should be available for the defendant to seek further redress. See Chen, 2003, 213–53.
63. Chen and Chen argued that the Supreme Court in its final review and approval of the death sentences must serve to prevent erroneous killing because under the current conditions, courts for trial of first instance and appeals do not provide sufficient mechanisms to correct and prevent possible wrongful convictions and sentencing. The Supreme Court's returning and reversal rate in the past was no less than 25 percent of all cases it reviewed, indicating a need for the Court to be judicious about its final review process. However, they argued that given the current conditions of the Chinese judicial system, neither the administrative process nor the adjudicative process should be strictly or mechanically followed. Combined use of both procedures (e.g., when certain facts and evidence arouse little disputes between the procuratorate and the defense, testimony and hearings on the parts may not be necessary) may be most efficient and effective in the actual practice (See Chen and Chen 2005, 5).
64. See "The Supreme Court to Set Up Three Criminal Courts to Assume Authority of Final Review and Approval of Death Penalty Cases." Web site of Xinhua News http://news.xinhuanet.com/legal/2005-09/27/content_3548779.htm (9/27/2005).
65. See "Death Row Inmate Wang Binyu's Confession." Web site of Xinhua News at http://news.xinhuanet.com/newscenter/2005-09/04/content_3440619.htm (9/04/2005)
66. See Zhenghua Wang. "Convicted Migrant Work Killer Waits for Final Verdict." Web site of China Daily at http://www.chinadaily.com.cn/english/doc/2005-09/21/content_479492.htm (9/21/2005).

Other reports suggested that Wang Binyu was sentenced to death by Ningxia Superior Court and executed on October 20, 2005. See Zeyuan Zhou's (professor of Southwestern University of Politics and Law) personal Web site at http://www.juristical.com/view/php?tid=372 and other English language Web sites. However, further searches on major Web sites in China (e.g., http://www.chinacourt.org, http://www.xinhuanet.com, http://www.legaldaily.com, http://www.chinadaily.com, http://www.sina.com) did not yield any reports on Wang's execution.

67. See Cuixiao Liu, "Issues on Social Protections for Rural Migrant Workers." *Legal Studies* 2(2005):109–125. See also Tiankui Jing, *Theory and Policy on Social Justice (*Social Sciences Documentation Publishing House, 2004), 124.
68. A project on "san nong issues" (countryside, agriculture and peasant) found that almost all construction companies in Beijing delayed payments to rural migrant workers in 2001, in the total amount of 4 billion yuan. See Zhonghan Economic Research Institute. *A Survey Report from the Grass-roots in China,* (Chinese Social Sciences Publishing House, 2004), 329.
69. See Cuixiao Liu, "Issues on Social Protections for Rural Migrant Workers." *Legal Studies* 2(2005):109–25. Tiankui Jing, *Theory and Policy on Social Justice.* (Social Sciences Documentation Publishing House, 2004), 136. Zhonghan Economic Research Institute, *A Survey Report from the Grass-roots in China* (Chinese Social Sciences Publishing House, 2004), 84. Qing Zhang, "An analysis of peasant class." *China Legal Studies* 2(2005): 24–33.
70. Zhaoli Meng, Jiaqian Liu and Xiaoli Liu, "Do Not Ignore Rural Migrant Workers' Basic Rights." Web site of Xinhua News at http://news.xinhuanet.com/newscenter/2005-09/04/content_3440619_1.htm (9/04/2005).
71. See Xin Kuaibao, "Should Migrant Worker Wang's Life be Spared?" Web site of China Law at http://www.law.cn/zhuanti/wby/pinglun/2005921134912.htm (9/21/2005).
72. According to the judicial judgment document prepared by Ningxia Shizuishan Intermediate Court and published on the Web site of *Procuratorial Daily* at http://jcrb.com.n1/jcrb842/ca415495.htm (11/25/2005).
73. According to the judicial judgment document prepared by Ningxia Shizuishan Intermediate Court and published on the Web site of *Procuratorial Daily* at http://jcrb.com.n1/jcrb842/ca415495.htm (11/25/2005)
74. See Dunping Wang, "Comments on Wang Binyu's case." Web site of *CCTV* at http://bbs.cctv.com.cn/forumthread.jsp?id=7021940 (9/08/2005).
75. Xi Shi, "Legal Scholar's Comments on Wang Binyu's Case." Web site of *Legal Daily* at http://legal.people/cpm.cn/GB/42731/3694947.html (9/14/2005).
76. Cited Hanzhang Dou, 9/21/2005. "Legal Experts' Opinions were Questioned." Web site of *China Law* at http://www.law.cn/zhuanti/wby/pinglun/2005921135054.htm (9/21/2005).

    For discussions on the intertwined relations between emotion and rationality, and community norms and law in China, see Yingzi Wu, "Strategies in Channeling the Gap between Emotion and Rationality by Rural Judges in China." *Litigation Process and Judicial System* 6(2005):2–11. Zhongxin Fan, *Emotion, Rationality and Law* (Beijing: China People University Press, 1992).
77. These opinions were posted by online users of various Web sites such as Xin Liang (http://www.xinlang.com), Wang Yi (http://www.163.com), and Sohu (http://www.sohu.com).
78. Xi Shi, "Legal Scholar's Comments on Wang Binyu's Case." Web site of *Legal Daily* at http://legal.people/cpm.cn/GB/42731/3694947.html (9/14/2005).

79. Chen, 2003, 49.
80. For example, Nie argued that legal scholars should be able to exert their legal opinions on particular criminal cases to influence the final judicial decision so long that their opinions are introduced in a formal and standard manner so that neither the prosecutor nor the defense is unfairly treated. See Zhaowei Nie, "On the Formalization of Legal Experts' Opinions in Criminal Litigations in China." *Legal Studies* 2(2005):110–16.
81. See Hanzhang Dou, 9/21/2005. "Legal Experts' Opinions were Questioned." Web site of *China Law* at http://www.law.cn/zhuanti/wby/pinglun/2005921135054.htm (9/21/2005).
82. For example, Liu Yong's case finally broke when a Shanghai-based newspaper carried an article questioning the modified judgment from death to death with a two-year reprieve in August after Liu's second trial. The author, Shuming Li, argued that the sentence modification was on poor legal grounds. He challenged the legality of the court's judgment and urged the Supreme Court and the Supreme Procuratorate to stand out and defend the sanctity of law. The article sparked the national media's attention on Liu's case. Consequentially, the Supreme Court decided to retry the case in October 2003 and executed Liu in December that year. See "Media doubts the final sentence of notorious criminal." Web site of *People's Daily* (English edition) at http://english.people.com.cn/200308/25/eng20030825_123040.shtml (8/25/2005).
83. For example, offenders younger than 18 years old are no longer subject to the death penalty in China (since 1997) and in the United States (since 2005).
84. As a retentionist country, China has increasingly met the difficulties in seeking international judicial cooperation from countries such as Canada that has abolished the death penalty, such as in the context of requesting an extradition of a corrupt offender. In this regard, it may be imperative for the Chinese government to reevaluate its death penalty law and policy to become more effective in crime fighting.
85. See Yong Xia, Guangxing Zhang, Jun Feng, Minyuan Wang, Yuzhang Wu, and Hailin Zou, *Blue Book of Rule of Law —The Development Report of Rule of Law in China (*Beijing: Social Sciences Documentation Publishing House, 2003), 1–48.
86. See Yunteng Hu, *General Discussions on the Death Penalty* (Beijing: China University of Political Science and Law Publishing House, 1995), 304. Bingzhi Zhao, "Guidelines for the Gradual Abolition of the Death Penalty in China." *Legal Studies* 1(2005): 55–62.
87. See Mingkai Zhang, "The Harmonized Society in the Eyes of Legal Scholars." *Legal Studies* 5(2005): 17–20.

Bibliography

Acker, James A., R. M. Rohm, and C. S. Lanier. *America's Experiment with Capital Punishment — Reflections on the Past, Present, and the Future of the Ultimate Penal Sanction*. Durham, NC: Carolina Academic Press, 1998.

Alford, William P. "Of Arsenic and Old Laws: Looking Anew at Criminal Justice in Late Imperial China." *California Law Review* 72(1984): 1180–1256.

———. "Tasselled Loafers for Barefoot Lawyers: Transformation and Tension in the World of Chinese Legal Workers." In *China's Legal Reforms*, ed. Stanley Lubman. Oxford University Press, 1996.

———. "A Second Great Wall? China's Post-Cultural Revolution Project of Legal Construction." *Cultural Dynamics* 11(1999): 193–213.

Amnesty International Annual Reports. Africa, Americas, Asia and the Pacific, Europe and Central Asia, Middle East and North Africa, 2005.

Amnesty International, The Death Penalty: List of Abolitionist and Retentionist Countries, February 1, 2004.

Baldus, D. C., G. Woodworth, and C. A. Palaski. *Equal Justice and the Death Penalty: A Legal and Empirical Analysis*. Boston: Northwestern University Press, 1990.

Beck, B. J. Mansvelt. "The Fall of Han." In *The Cambridge History of China: Volume 1 the Chin and Han Empires, 221 B.C. – A.D. 220*, eds. Denis Twitchett and Michael Loewe. Cambridge, Cambridge University Press, 1986.

Bedau, Hugo Adam. "Retribution and the Theory of Punishment." *Journal of Philosophy* 75(1978): 601–620.

Bedau, Hugo Adam. "The United States." In *Capital Punishment — Global Issues and Prospects,* eds. Peter Hodgkinson and Andrew Rutherford. Winchester, UK: Waterside Press Criminal Policy Series, Volume II, 1996.

Beirne, Piers. 1983. "Generalization and Its Discontents — the Comparative Study of Crime." In *Comparative Criminology,* eds. Israel L. Barak-Glantz and Elmer H. Johnson. Sage Publications, 1983.

Beirne, Piers and Alan Hunt. "Law and Constitution of Soviet Society: The Case of Comrade Lenin." *Law & Society Review* 22(1988): 575–615.

Benn, Charles. *Daily Life in Traditional China — The Tang Dynasty*. Westport, CT: Greenwood Press, 2002.

Bian, Yanjie, and John R. Logan. "Market Transition and the Persistence of Power: The Changing Stratification System in Urban China." *American Sociological Review* 61(1996): 739–58.

Black, Donald. *The Behavior of Law*. New York: Academic Press, 1976.

Blaustein, Albert P. (ed.) *Fundamental Legal Documents of Communist China*. South Hackensack, NJ: Fred B. Rothman & Co., 1962.

Bodde, Derek. "Age, Youth, and Infirmity in the Law of Ch'ing China." In *Essays on China's Legal Tradition*, eds. Jerome A. Cohen, R. Randle Edwards and Fu-mei Chang Chen. Princeton, NJ: Princeton University Press, 1980.

———. "The State and Empire of Chin." In *The Cambridge History of China: Volume 1 the Chin and Han Empires, 221 B.C. – A.D. 220*, eds. Denis Twitchett and Michael Loewe. Cambridge, Cambridge University Press, 1986.

Bodde, Derek, and Clarence Morris. *Law in Imperial China*. Philadelphia: University of Pennsylvania Press, 1973.

Bohm, R. M. "American Death Penalty Attitudes: A Critical Examination of Recent Research." *Criminal Justice and Behavior* 14(1987): 380–96.

Bohm, R. M., and R. E. Vogel. "A Comparison of Factors Associated with Uniformed and Informed Death Penalty Opinions." *Journal of Criminal Justice* 22(1994): 125–43.

Bohm, R.M., and R. E. Vogel. "More than Ten Years Later: The Long-Term Stability of Informed Death Penalty Opinions." *Journal of Criminal Justice* 32(2004): 307–27.

Bradshaw, York W., and Elvis Fraser. "City Size, Economic Development, and Quality of Life in China: New Empirical Evidence." *American Sociological Review* 54(1989): 986–1003.

Brahm, Laurence J. *China's Century — The Awakening of the Next Economic Powerhouse*. New York: John Wiley & Sons, 2001.

Brook, Lindsay, and Ed Cape. 1995. "Libertarianism in Retreat." In *British Social Attitudes: The 12th Report*, eds. R. Jowell, J. Curtis, A. Park, L. Brook, and D. Ahrendt. Aldershot: Dartmouth Publishing, 1995.

Burns, John P. "The People's Republic of China at 50: National Political Reform." *China Quarterly* 159(1999): 580–94.

Cai, Dingjian. "China's Major Reform in Criminal Law." *Columbia Journal of Asian Law* 11 (1997): 213–18.

Cai, Dingjian. *Supervision and Judicial Fairness*. Beijing: Law Press, 2005.

Cao, Liqun, and Francis T. Cullen. "Thinking about Crime and Control: A Comparative Study of Chinese and American Ideology." *International Criminal Justice Review* 11(2001): 58–81.

Cao, Kangtai, and Xuejun Wang. *Decrees of Xin Fang*. Beijing: China Law Publishing House, 2005.

Chai, Joseph C. H., and B. Karin Chai. "China's Floating Population and Its Implications." *International Journal of Social Economics* 24(1997): 1038--51.

Chambliss, William and Robert Seidman. *Law, Order, and Power*. Second edition. Reading, MA: Addison-Wesley, 1982.

Chang, Hao. "Intellectual Change and the Reform Movement." In *The Cambridge History of China" Volume II Late Ching, 1800–1911, Part 2*, eds. John K. Fairbank and Kwang-Ching Liu. Cambridge: Cambridge University Press, 1980.

Chang, Kwang-Chin. *Shang Civilization*. New Haven: Yale University Press, 1980.

Chen, Albert Hung-yee. *An Introduction to the Legal System of the People's Republic of China*. Hong Kong: Butterworths Asia, 1998.

Chen, Cheng. "A Typological Analysis of Anomie in Current China." *Society* 12(2002): 12–4.

Chen, Chiyun. "Confucian, Legalist, and Taoist Thought in Later Han." In *The Cambridge of History of China: Volume 1 The Chin and Han Empires, 221 B.C. – A.D. 220*, eds. Denis Twitchett and Michael Loewe. Cambridge: Cambridge University Press, 1986.

Chen, Guangzhong, Weiqiu Cheng, and Vincent C. Yang (eds.). *A Study on Issues in Ratifying and Implementing International Covenant on Civil and Political Rights*. Beijing: China Legal System Press, 2002.

Chen, Guili, and Chun Tao. *A Survey of Chinese Peasants.* Beijing: People's Literature Publishing House, 2004.

Chen, Guoqing, and Binqun He. *China's Litigation System and its Reform.* Beijing: The People's Public Security University of China Press, 2001.

Chen, Jerome. 1983. "Chinese Communist Movement to 1927." In *The Cambridge History of China: Volume 12 Republican China 1912–1949, Part I*, ed. John K. Fairbank. Cambridge: Cambridge University Press, 1983.

Chen, Jianfu. *Chinese Law — Towards an Understanding of Chinese Law, Its Nature and Development.* London: Kluwer Law International, 1999.

Chen, Paul H. *Chinese Legal Tradition under the Mongols — the Code of 1291 as Reconstructed.* Princeton, NJ: Princeton University Press, 1979.

Chen, Weidong. *Research on Procedure for Criminal Trial Supervision.* Beijing: Law Press, 2001.

———. *Jurisdictional Justice and Innovation.* Beijing: China Procuratorate Press, 2002.

———. "Physical Evidence Key to Avoidance of Wrongful Conviction." *Legal Studies* 5(2005): 84–85.

Chen, Weidong, and Lei Chen. "Not Just Taking Back — Comments on the Strategies of the Supreme Court Taking Back the Final Review and Approval Authority for the Death Penalty Cases." *Legal Studies of China and the Abroad* 5(2005).

Chen, Xingliang. *The New Horizon of Contemporary Criminal Law in China.* Beijing, China: The Chinese University of Politics and Law Press, 2002.

———. *An Examination of the Death Penalty System in China.* Beijing: China Procuratorial Publishing House, 2003a.

———. *The Purpose of Rule of Law.* Beijing: Law Press, 2003b.

Chen, Xu, Kuanming Zhang, and Jian Yang. "A Decade of the Court Reform in the City of Nanjing." *Zhian* 88 (2000): 8–11.

Chu, Huizhi. "Modernizing Punishment." *Legal Studies* 1(1997).

Clark, James. *China.* Evanston, IL: McDougal Little and Co., 1982.

Clayre, Alasdair Clayre. *The Heart of the Dragon.* Boston: Houghton Mifflin Co., 1984.

Cohen, Jerome A. *The Criminal Process in the People's Republic of China 1949–1963.* Cambridge: Harvard University Press, 1968.

Colwell, Gary. "Capital Punishment, Restoration and Moral Rightness." *Journal of Applied Philosophy* 19(2002): 287.

Conner, Alison W. "True Confessions? Chinese Confessions Then and Now." In *The Limits of the Rule of Law in China,* eds. K.G. Turner, J.V. Feineman, and R. K. Guy. Seattle: University of Washington Press, 2000.

Costanzo, M. *Just Revenge: Costs and Consequences of the Death Penalty.* New York: St. Martin's Press, 1997.

Creel, Herrlee G. *The Origins of Statecraft in China: The Western Zhou Empire.* Chicago, IL: University of Chicago Press, 1970.

———. "Legal Institutions and Procedures during the Chou Dynasty." In *Essays on China's Legal Tradition*, eds. J.A. Cohen, R.R. Edwards, and F.C. Chen. Princeton, NJ: Princeton University Press, 1980.

Culver, John H. "Capital Punishment Politics and Policies in the States, 1977–1997." *Crime, Law & Social Change* 32 (1999): 287–300.

Curran, D. J. "Economic Reform, the Floating Population, and Crime — The Transformation of Social Control in China." *Journal of Contemporary Criminal Justice* 14(1998): 262–80.

Daly, Kathleen. "Revisiting the Relationship between Retributive and Restorative Justice." In *Restorative Justice: From Philosophy to Practice*, eds. Heather Strang and John Braithwaite. Aldershot: Dartmouth, 2000.

Darley, John M., Kevin M. Carlsmith, and Paul H. Robinson. "Incapacitation and Just Deserts as Motives for Punishment." *Law and Human Behavior* 24(2000): 659–83.

Davis, Stephen B. "The Death Penalty and Legal Reform in the PRC." *Journal of Chinese Law* 1 (1987): 303–334.

Deng, Xiaogang, Lening Zhang and Ann Cordila. "Social Control and Recidivism in China." *Journal of Contemporary Criminal Justice* 14(1998): 281–95.

Deng, Xiaoping. *Selected Works of Deng Xiaoping.* Beijing: People's Publishing House, 1983.

———. *Selected Works of Deng Xiaoping.* Second edition. Beijing: People's Publishing House, 1984.

———. *Selected Works of Deng Xiaoping.* Third edition. Beijing: People's Publishing House, 1993.

Dikotter, Frank. "Crime and Punishment in Post-Liberation China: The Prisoners of a Beijing Gaol in the 1950s." *China Quarterly* 149(1997): 147–59.

———. "The Promise of Repentance — Prison Reform in Modern China." *British Journal of Criminology* 42 (2002): 240–9.

———. *Crime, Punishment and the Prison in Modern China.* New York: Columbia University Press, 2002.

Eastman, Lloyd E. "Nationalist China during the Sino-Japanese War 1937–1945." In *The Cambridge History of China: Volume 13 Republican China 1912–1949, Part 2,* eds. John K. Fairbank and Albert Feuerwerker. Cambridge: Cambridge University Press, 1986.

Edwards, R. Randle. "Chinese Legal Jurisdiction over Foreigners." In *Essays on China's Legal Tradition*, eds. Jerome A. Cohen, R. Randle Edwards, and Fu-mei Chang Chen. Princeton, NJ: Princeton University Press, 1980.

Ellsworth, Phoebe, and Samuel R. Gross. "Hardening of the Attitudes: Americans' Views on the Death Penalty." In *The Death Penalty in America,* ed. Hugo Adam Bedau. Oxford University Press, 1997.

Fan, Congyi. *Opinions on Objective Truth – A Discussion of the Standard of Proof in Criminal Processes*. Beijing: China Law Press, 2000.

Fan, Zhongxin. *Emotion, Rationality and Law.* Beijing: China People University Press, 1992.

Feuerwerker, Albert. "Economic Trends in the Late Ching Empire, 1970–1911." In *The Cambridge History of China: Volume II Late Ching, 1800–1911, Part 2*, eds. John K. Fairbank and Kwang-Ching Liu. Cambridge: Cambridge University Press, 1980.

Fokkema, Douwe. "Creativity and Politics." In *Cambridge History of China, Volume 15 The People's Republic, Part 2: Revolutions within the Chinese Revolution 1966–1982*, eds. Roderick MacFaruhar and john K. Fairbank. Cambridge: Cambridge University Press, 1991.

Frank, Jerome. *Courts on Trial: Myth and Reality in American Justice.* Princeton, NJ: Princeton University Press, 1950.

Friedman, Lawrence M. *American Law: An Introduction.* New York: W. W. Norton & Co., 1984.

Furth, Charlotte. "Intellectual Change: From the Reform Movement to the May Fourth Movement, 1895–1920." In *The Cambridge History of China: Volume 12 Republican China 1912–1949, Part I*, ed. John K. Fairbank. Cambridge: Cambridge University Press, 1983.

Gasster, Michael. "The Republican Revolutionary Movement." In *The Cambridge History of China: Volume II Late Ching, 1800–1911, Part 2*, eds. John K. Fairbank and Kwang-Ching Liu. Cambridge: Cambridge University Press, 1980.

Gernet, Jacques. *A History of Chinese Civilization*. Second edition. Trans. J. R. Foster and Charles Hartman. New York: Cambridge University Press, 1996.

Gong, Mingli. "On confession." In *Criminal Law*, ed. Y. Gan. Beijing: Beijing University Press, 1989.

Griffin, Patricia E. *The Chinese Communist Ttreatment of Counterrevolutionaries: 1924–1949*. Princeton, NJ: Princeton University Press, 1976.

Haines, H. H., and H. Haines. *Against Capital Punishment: The Anti-Death Penalty Movement in America, 1972–1994*. Oxford: Oxford University Press, 1996.

Han, Yang. "An Exploration of Reasons for a Retrial in Criminal Cases." *Research in Law* 27(2005): 88–98.

Hinsch, Bret. *Women in Early Imperial China*. New York: Rowman & Littlefield Publishers, Inc., 2002.

Holmes, O. W. *The Common Law*. London: Macmillan, 1968.

Hood, Roger. *The Death Penalty A Worldwide Perspective*. Third edition. Oxford: Oxford University Press, 2002.

Hsu, Immanuel C. Y. "Late Ching Foreign Relations, 1866–1905." In *The Cambridge History of China: Volume II Late Ching, 1800–1911, Part 2*, eds. John K. Fairbank and Kwang-Ching Liu. Cambridge: Cambridge University Press, 1980.

Hu, Yunteng. *General Discussions on the Death Penalty*. Beijing: China University of Political Science and Law Publishing House, 1995.

Huang, Philip. "Codified Law and Magisterial Adjudication in the Qing." In *Civil Law in Qing and Republican China*, eds. Philip Huang and Kathryn Bernhart. Stanford, CA: Stanford University Press, 1994.

Hulsewe, A. F. P. "Chin and Han Law." In *The Cambridge History of China: Volume 1*, eds. Dennis Twitchett and Michael Loewe. Cambridge Cambridge University Press, 1986.

Ingraham, Barton L. *The Structure of Criminal Procedure: Laws and Practice of France, the Soviet Union, China, and the United States*. New York: Greenwood Publishing Group, 1987.

Jensen, Gary. "Institutional Anomie and Societal Variations in Crime: A Critical Appraisal." *International Journal of Sociology and Social Policy* 22(2002): 45–74.

Jian, Bozan, Xunzheng Shao, and Hua Hu. *A Concise History of China*. Beijing: Foreign Language Press, 1981.

Jiang, Zemin. "Intensifying the Reform and Open-Door Policy." *Action Guide for the Twenty-First Century*. Beijing: Xinhua Press, 1992.

Jiang, Zemin. "The Talk at the Third Legal Forum Held by the Central Committee of the Chinese Communist Party," *People's Daily*, 1996, February 9.

Jin, Zegang. "Amended Prosecution, Amended Trial, and Amended Sentence." *Legal Studies* 7(2005): 72–76.

Jing, Tiankui. *Theory and Policy on Social Justice*. Social Sciences Documentation Publishing House, 2004.

Johnson, Wallace. *The Tang Code*. Princeton, NJ: Princeton University Press, 1979.

Jones, William C. "Trying to Understand the Current Chinese Legal System." In *Understanding China's Legal System — Essays in Honor of Jerome A. Cohen*, ed. C. Stephen Hsu, New York: New York University Press, 2003.

Jun, Ziliu. "Misjudged Cases Reflecting the Flaws in the Judicial System." *Justice of China* 67(2005): 97–99.

Kessler, Daniel, and Steven D. Levitt. "Using Sentence Enhancements to Distinguish between Deterrence and Incapacitation." *Journal of Law and Economics* 42(1999): 343–63.

Kidder, Robert L. *Connecting Law and Society — An Introduction to Research and Theory*. Englewood Cliffs, NJ: Prentice-Hall, Inc., 1983.

Knorr, Stephen J. "Deterrence and the Death Penalty: A Temporal Cross-Sectional Approach." *Journal of Criminal Law and Criminology* 70(1979): 235–54.

Kramers, Robert P. "The Development of the Confucian Schools." In *The Cambridge of History of China: Volume 1 The Chin and Han Empires, 221 B.C. – A.D. 220*, eds. Denis Twitchett and Michael Loewe. Cambridge: Cambridge University Press, 1986.

Kuo-kang, S. *Zhou Enlai and the Foundations of Chinese Foreign Policy*. New York: St. Martin's Press, 1996.

Lau, Raymond W. K. "Socio-Political Control in Urban China: Changes and Crisis." *British Journal of Sociology* 52(2001): 605–20.

Law Yearbook of China. Beijing: Law Yearbook of China Publishing House, 1987–2001.

Leng, Shao-chuan. *Justice in Communist China*. Dobbs Ferry, NY: Oceana Publications, 1967.

Leng, Shaochuan, and Hangda Chiu. *Criminal Justice in Post-Mao China*. Albany, NY: State University of New York Press, 1985.

Lepp, Alan W. "Note: The Death Penalty in Late Imperial, Modern, and Post-Tiananmen China." *Michigan Journal of International Law* 11 (1990): 987–1038.

Levy, Richard. "Corruption, Economic Crime and Social Transformation since the Reforms: The Debate in China." *Australian Journal of Chinese Affairs* 33 (1995): 1–25.

Lewis, D. O., M. Feldman, L. Jackson, and B. Bard. 1986. "Psychiatric, Neurological, and Psycho-educational Characteristics of 15 Death Row Inmates in the United States." *American Journal of Psychiatry* 143 (1986): 838–45.

Li, Fujin. "On the Judicial Reform of the Lower Level Courts." *Journal of Huadoing University of Political Science and Law* 38(2005): 47–57.

Li, J. (ed.) *China's Recidivism Study*. Beijing: Law Publishing House, 1992.

Li, Jianming. "Research on Mistakes in Death Penalty Cases." *Litigation Law and Justice System* 4(2005): 58–65.

Li, Yu-Ning. *Shang Yang's Reforms and State Control in China*. White Plains, NY: M. E. Sharpe, 1977.

Liang, Bin, Hong Lu, Terance D. Miethe and Lening Zhang. "Sources of Variation in Pro-Death Penalty Attitudes in China: An Exploratory Study of Chinese Students at Home and Abroad." *British Journal of Criminology* 46(2006): 119–30.

Liang, Genlin, and Wen Zhang. *An Examination of the Current Economic Crime* Beijing: Beijing University Press, 1996.

———. "Discussions on the Imposition of the Death Penalty on Economic Offenses." *Legal Studies* 1(1997).

Liao, Yongan. "A Reflection on the Judicial Responsibility System." *Jiansu Social Sciences* 3(1999).

Lichtenstein, Natalie G. "Law in China's Economic Development — An Essay from Afar." In *Understanding China's Legal System — Essays in Honor of Jerome A. Cohen*, ed. C. Stephen Hsu, New York: New York University Press, 2003.

Lieberthal, Kenneth. "The Great Leap Forward and the Split in the Yenan Leadership." In *Cambridge History of China, Volume 15 The People's Republic, Part 2: Revolutions within the Chinese Revolution 1966–1982*. eds. Roderick MacFaruhar and John K. Fairbank. Cambridge: Cambridge University Press, 1991.

Liebman, James S., Jeffrey Fagan, Valerie West, and Jonathan Lloyd. "Capital Attrition: Error Rates in Capital Cases, 1973–1995." *Texas Law Review* 78 (2000): 1771–1803.

Lin, Bianjian, and Jingjing Li. "Seeing the Improvement of the Criminal Trial Structure from China's Criminal Courtroom Arrangements." *Frontiers of Law in China* 1(2006): 164–84.

Lin, Justin. "Rural Reforms and Agricultural Growth in China." *American Economic Review* 82 (1992): 34–51.

Lin, Justin, Fang Cai, and Zhou Li. *The China Miracle – Development Strategy and Economic Reform.* Hong Kong: The Chinese University Press, 2003.

Liu, Chenglin. *Chinese Law on SARS.* Buffalo, New York: William S. Hein & Co., Inc. 2004.

Liu, Cuixiao. "Issues on Social Protections for Rural Migrant Workers." *Legal Studies* 2(2005): 109–125.

Liu, Jianghong, and Steven F. Messner. "Modernization and Crime Trends in China's Reform Era." In *Crime and Social Control in a Changing China*, eds. Jianhong Liu, Lening Zhang, and Steven F. Messner. Westport, CT: Greenwood Press, 2001.

Liu, Kwang-Ching. "The Military Challenge: The North-West and the Coast." In *The Cambridge History of China: Volume II Late Ching, 1800–1911, Part 2*, eds. John K. Fairbank and Kwang-Ching Liu. Cambridge: Cambridge University Press, 1980.

Liu, Xianquan. "Reflections on the Traditional Criminal Justice Rationality." *Legal Studies* 5(2005): 81–83.

Liu, Yongping. *Origins of Chinese Law — Penal and Administrative Law in Its Early Development.* New York: Oxford University Press, 1998.

Llewellyn, Karl. *Jurisprudence: Realism in Theory and Practice.* Chicago: University of Chicago Press, 1962.

Lu, Hong, and Kriss A. Drass. "Transience and the Disposition of Theft Cases in China." *Justice Quarterly* 19(2002): 401–34.

Lu, Hong, and Terance D. Miethe. "Confessions and Criminal Case Disposition in China." *Law & Society Review* 37 (2003): 549–78.

Lu, Hong, and Lening Zhang. "Death Penalty in China: The Theory and the Practice." *Journal of Criminal Justice* 33(2005): 367–76.

Lubman, Stanley. "Mao and Mediation: Politics and Dispute Resolution in Communist China." *California Law Review* 55(1969): 1292.

———. *Bird in a Cage — Legal Reform in China after Mao.* Stanford, CA: Stanford University Press, 1999.

Luo, Wei. *The 1997 Criminal Code of the People's Republic of China.* Buffalo, NY: William S. Hein & Co., Inc., 1988.

———. *The Amended Criminal Procedure Law and the Criminal Court Rules of the People's Republic of China: with English Translation, Introduction and Annotation.* Buffalo, New York: William S Hein & Co., Inc., 2000.

MaCauley, Melisa. *Social Power and Legal Culture: Litigation Masters in Late Imperial China.* Stanford, CA: Stanford University Press, 1998.

MacCormack, Geoffrey. *Traditional Chinese Penal Law.* Edinburgh, England: Edinburgh University Press, 1990.

———. *The Spirit of Traditional Chinese Law.* Athens: University of Georgia Press, 1996.

MacFarquhar, Roderick and Leroy B. Williams. "The Succession to Mao and the End of Maoism." In *The Cambridge History of China: The People's Republic, Part 2: Revolutions within the Chinese Revolution 1966–1982*, eds. Roderick MacFarquhar and John K. Fairbank. Cambridge, Cambridge University Press, 1991.

Madsen, Richard. "The Countryside under Communism." In *Cambridge History of China, Volume 15 The People's Republic, Part 2: Revolutions within the Chinese Revolution 1966–1982,* eds. Roderick MacFaruhar and John K. Fairbank. Cambridge: Cambridge University Press, 1991.
Mao, Yi, and Xiaoming Wang. *Research on Public Security Cases in China.* Wuchang: Hubei Science and Technology Publishing House, 2002.
Mao, Zedong. *Selected Works of Mao.* Beijing: People's Publishing House, 1986.
McKnight, Brian E. McKnight. *Law and Order in Sung China.* Cambridge: Cambridge University Press, 1992.
McMillan, John, John Whalley, and Lijing Zhu. "The Impact of China's Economic Reforms on Agricultural Productivity Growth." *Journal of Political Economy* 97(1989): 781–807.
Meier, Robert F., and Weldon T. Johnson. "Deterrence as Social Control: The Legal and Extralegal Production of Conformity." *American Sociological Review* 42(1977): 292–304.
Meijer, Marinus J. "Slavery at the End of the Ch'ing Dynasty." In *Essays on China's Legal tradition*, eds. Jerome A. Cohen, R. Randle Edwards, and Fu-mei Chang Chen. Princeton, NJ: Princeton University Press, 1980.
Miethe, Terance D., and Hong Lu. *Punishment: A Comparative Historical Perspective.* London: Cambridge University Press, 2005.
Miyazaki, Ichisada. "The Administration of Justice During the Sung Dynasty." In *Essays on China's Legal tradition*, eds. Jerome A. Cohen, R. Randle Edwards, and Fu-mei Chang Chen. Princeton, NJ: Princeton University Press, 1980.
Murphy, J. G. *Punishment and Rehabilitation.* Belmont, CA: Wadsworth Pub. Co., 1995.
Myers, Samuel L. Jr. "The Rehabilitation Effect of Punishment." *Economic Inquiry* XVIII(1980): 353–66.
Myers, Willard H. III. "The Emerging Threat of Transnational Organized Crime from the East." *Crime, Law and Social Change* 24(1995): 181–222.
Nie, Zhaowei. "On the Formalization of Legal Experts' Opinions in Criminal Litigations in China." *Legal Studies* 2(2005): 110–116.
Ocko, Johnathan K. "I'll Take it All the Way to Beijing: Capital Appeals in the Qing." *The Journal of Asian Studies* 47(1988): 291–315
Opening to Reform? An Analysis of China's Revised Criminal Procedural Law. Lawyers Committee for Human Rights, 1996.
Palmer, Michael. "The People's Republic of China." In *Capital Punishment Global Issues and Prospects*, eds. Peter Hodgkinson and Andrew Rutherford. U.K.: Waterside Press, 1996.
Paolucci, Paul. "The Discursive Transformation of Marx's Communism into Soviet Diamat." *Critical Sociology* 30(2004): 617–67.
Peerenboom, Randall. "Ruling the Country in Accordance with Law: Reflections on the Rule and Role of Law in Contemporary China." *Cultural Dynamics* 11(1999): 315–51.
Pepper, Suzanne. "The KMT — CCP Conflict 194501949." In *The Cambridge History of China: Volume 13 Republican China 1912–1949, Part 2,* eds. John K. Fairbank and Albert Feuerwerker. Cambridge: Cambridge University Press, 1986.
———. "Education." In *Cambridge History of China, Volume 15 The People's Republic, Part 2: Revolutions within the Chinese Revolution 1966–1982,* eds. Roderick MacFaruhar and John K. Fairbank. Cambridge: Cambridge University Press, 1991.
Perkins, Dwight H. "China's Economic Policy and Performance." In *Cambridge History of China, Volume 15 The People's Republic, Part 2: Revolutions*

within the Chinese Revolution 1966–1982, eds. Roderick MacFaruhar and John K. Fairbank. Cambridge: Cambridge University Press, 1991.

Posner, Richard A. "Retribution and Related Concepts of Punishment." *Journal of Legal Studies* 9(1980): 71–92.

Potter, Pitman B. *The Chinese Legal System – Globalization and Local Legal Culture*. London: Routledge, 2001.

Pound, Roscoe. *The Spirit of the Common Law*. Boston: Marshall Jones, 1921.

———. "Sociology of Law and Sociological Jurisprudence." *University of Toronto Law Journal* 5(1943): 1–20.

Qin, Zhengan. *Judicial Document Selections of the People's Court — Beijing 2000*. Beijing: Law Press, 2001.

Qiu, Xinglong. *Comparative Criminal Law*. Volume 1. Beijing: China's Procuratorate Publishing House, 2001.

———. "Morality of Law." *Politics and Law* 2(2002).

Quinney, Richard. *The Critique of Legal Order*. Boston: Little, Brown, 1974.

Ravallion, Martin, and Shaohua Chen. "When Economic Reform is Faster than Statistical Reform: Measuring and Explaining Income Inequality in Rural China." *Oxford Bulletin of Economics and Statistics* 61(1999): 33.

Rojek, Dean G. "Chinese Social Control: From Shaming and Reintegration to 'Getting Rich is Glorious." In *Crime and Social Control in a Changing China*, eds. Jianhong Liu, Lening Zhang, and Steven Messner. Westport, CT: Greenwood Press, 2001.

Roetz, Heiner. *Confucian Ethics of the Axial Age — A Reconstruction under the Aspect of the Breakthrough towards Postconventional Thinking*. Albany, NY: State University of New York Press, 1993.

Sands, Barbara N. "Decentralizing an Economy: The Role of Bureaucratic Corruption in China's Economic Reforms." *Public Choice* 65(1990): 85–91.

Sarat, Austin, and Boulanger. *The Cultural Lives of Capital Punishment: Comparative Perspectives*. Stanford, CA: Stanford University Press, 2005.

Schabas, William A. "International Legal Aspects." In *Capital Punishment — Global Issues and Prospects*, eds. Peter Hodgkinson and Andrew Rutherford. U.K.: Waterside Press, 1966.

Schram, Stuart. "Mao Tse-tung's Thought to 1949." In *The Cambridge History of China: Volume 13 Republican China 1912–1949, Part 2*, eds. John K. Fairbank and Albert Feuerwerker. Cambridge: Cambridge University Press, 1986.

———. "Mao Tse-tung's Thought from 1949–1976." In *Cambridge History of China: Volume 15 The People's Republic of China, Part 2*, eds. Roderick MacFarquhar and John K. Fairbank. Cambridge: Cambridge University Press, 1991.

Schwartz, Benjamin I. "Themes in Intellectual History: May Fourth and After." In *The Cambridge History of China: Volume 12 Republican China 1912–1949, Part I*, ed. John K. Fairbank. Cambridge: Cambridge University Press, 1983.

Scobell, Andrew. "Strung Up or Shot Down?: The Death Penalty in Hong Kong and China and Implications for Post-1997." *Case West Reserve Journal of International Law* 20 (1988):147–67.

———. "The Death Penalty under Socialism, 1917–90: China, the Soviet Union, Cuba, and the German Democratic Republic." *Criminal Justice History: An International Annual*. Westport, CT: Greenwood Press, 1993, Volume 12.

Sheng, Yi. "A Promise Unfulfilled; The Impact of China's 1996 Criminal Procedure Reform on China's Criminal Defense Lawyers' Role at the Pretrial Stage." *Perspectives* 5(2004): 1–27.

Sheridan, James E. "The Warlord Era: Politics and Militarism under the Peking Government, 1916–28." In *The Cambridge History of China: Volume 12 Republican China 1912–1949, Part I*, ed. John K. Fairbank. Cambridge: Cambridge University Press, 1983.

Simon, Rita, and Dagny A. Blaskovich. *A Comparative Analysis of Capital Punishment: Statues, Policies, Frequencies, and Public Attitudes the World Over.* New York: Lexington Books, 2002.

Slyke, Lyman Van. "The Chinese Communist Movement during the Sino-Japanese War 1937–1945." In *The Cambridge History of China: Volume 13 Republican China 1912–1949, Part 2,* eds. John K. Fairbank and Albert Feuerwerker. Cambridge: Cambridge University Press, 1986.

Somers, Robert M. "The End of the Tang." In *The Cambridge History of China: Volume 3 Sui and Tang China, 589–906, Part I*, ed. Denis Twitchett. Cambridge: Cambridge University Press, 1979.

Stephens, Thomas B. *Order and Discipline in China: The Shanghai Mixed Court 1911–27.* Seattle: University of Washington Press, 1992.

Stover, Leon. *Imperial China and the State Cult of Confucius.* Kefferson, NC: McFarland & Company, Inc. Publishers, 2005,

Sun, Changyong. "A Comparative Analysis of Coercive Measures in the Criminal Justice System." *Research in Law* 1(2005): 111–25.

Tanner, Harold. *Strike Hard!* Ithaca, NY: Cornell East Asia Series, 1999.

Tian, He. "On the Conditions of Abolishing the Death Penalty." *Research in Law* 2(2005): 66–74.

Trevaskes, Susan. "Propaganda Work in Chinese Courts." *Punishment & Society* 6(2005): 5–21.

Trubek, David M. "Where the Action is: CLS and Empiricism," *Stanford Law Review* 36(1984): 575–622.

Trubek, David M., and John Esser. "`Critical Empiricism' in American Legal Studies: Parodox, Program, or Pandora's Box?" *Law & Social Inquiry* 14(1989): 3–52.

Twitchett, Denis. "Introduction." In *The Cambridge History of China: Volume 3 Sui and Tang China, 589–906, Part I*, ed. Denis Twitchett. Cambridge: Cambridge University Press, 1979.

Vago, Steven. *Law and Society.* Fourth edition. Englewood Cliffs, NJ: Prentice Hall, 1994.

Wang, Chengguang. "Introduction: An Emerging Legal System." In *Introduction to Chinese Law*, eds. Chengguang Wang and Xianchu Zhang. Hong Kong: Sweet & Maxwell, 1997.

Wang, Junmin. "Enforcing the Law by Law to Avoid Wrongful Convictions." *Legal Studies* 5(2005): 87–8.

Wang, Liming. *Research on Judicial Reform.* Beijing: Law Press, 2001.

Wang, Yongqing, and Xiwei Lu. *The Interpretation of the Act on Xin Fang.* Beijing: Chinese Legal System Publishing House, 2005.

Weber, Max. *Law in Economy and Society.* Edited by Max Rheinstein and translated by Edward Shils and Max Rheistein. Cambridge: Harvard University Press, 1954.

———.*Economy and Society.* Translated by Guenther Roth and Claus Wittich. New York: Bedminster Press, 1968.

White, Gordon. "Democratization and Economic Reform in China." *Australian Journal of Chinese Affairs* 31(1994): 73–92.

Whyte, Martin King. "Urban Life in the People's Republic." *Cambridge History of China, Volume 15 The People's Republic, Part 2: Revolutions within the Chinese Revolution 1966–1982,* eds. Roderick MacFaruhar and John K. Fairbank. Cambridge: Cambridge University Press, 1991.

Wilbur, C. Martin. "The Nationalist Revolution: From Canton to Nanking, 1923–28." In *The Cambridge History of China: Volume 12 Republican China 1912–1949, Part I*, ed. John K. Fairbank. Cambridge: Cambridge University Press, 1983.

Windlesham, Lord. *Responses to Crime: Penal Policy in the Making*. Volume 1. Oxford: Clarendon Press, 1987.

Wright, David Curtis Wright. *The History of China*. Westport, CT: Greenwood Press, 2001.

Wu, Qiyuan. *Public Policy*. Taiwan Shangwu Printing House, 1985.

Wu, Yingzi. "Strategies in Channeling the Gap between Emotion and Rationality by Rural Judges in China." *Litigation Process and Judicial System* 6(2005): 2–11.

Xia, Yong, Guangxing Zhang, Jun Feng, Minyuan Wang, Yuzhang Wu, and Hailin Zou. *Blue Book of Rule of Law — The Development Report of Rule of Law in China*. Beijing: Social Sciences Documentation Publishing House, 2003.

Xiao, Yang. "A New Chapter in Constructing China's Legal System." In *China's Century — The Awakening of the Next Economic Powerhouse,* ed. Laurence J. Brahm. New York: John Wiley & Sons, 2001.

Xie, Yuoping. "Improving the Judicial Process to Prevent Wrongful Convictions." *Legal Studies* 5(2005): 85–86.

Yang, Xiushi. "Household Registration, Economic Reform and Migration." *International Migration Review* 27(1993): 796–818.

Ye, Gaofeng. *Research on the Strategies towards Violent Crimes in China*. Beijing: Law Press, 1998.

Yong, Ernest P. "Politics in the Aftermath of Revolution: The Era of Yuan Shih-kai, 1912–16." In *The Cambridge History of China: Volume 12 Republican China 1912–1949, Part I*, ed. John K. Fairbank. Cambridge: Cambridge University Press, 1983.

Yu, Ping. "Problems of the Death Penalty System in China." *Legal Studies* 5(2005): 88–90.

Yu, Xingzhong. "Legal Pragmatism in the People's Republic of China." *Journal of Chinese Law* 3(1989): 29–51.

Zeisel, H. and A. M. Gallup. "Death Penalty Sentiment in the United States." *Journal of Quantitative Criminology* 5(1989): 285–297.

Zhang, J. et.al. "On Campaign against Crime." *Democracy and Legality* 13 (1996): 222.

Zhang, Lening and Steven F. Messner. "Bonds to the Work Unit and Official Offense Status in Urban China." *International Journal of Offender Therapy and Comparative Criminology* 43(1999): 375–90.

Zhang, Mingkai. "The Harmonized Society in the Eyes of Legal Scholars." *Legal Studies* 5(2005): 17–20.

Zhang, Mingkai. *Criminal Law*. Second edition. Beijing: Law Press, 2003.

Zhang, Qimei (editor). *Judicial Document Selections of the People's Court — Zhejing, 2000*. Beijing: Law Publishing House, 2001.

Zhang, Qing. "An Analysis of Peasant Class." *China Legal Studies* 2(2005):24–33.

Zhang, Rong. "Reflections on Several Issues Regarding the Improvement of Criminal Procedure." *Chinese Legal Studies* 4(2005): 142–52.

Zhang, Shaoqian. "Ten Problems Associated with the Death Penalty Process in China." *Litigation Process and Judicial System* 5(2005): 46–52.

Zhang, Xuechao. "Comments on Professor Shilun Li's Legal History and Thoughts." In *On the Front of the Legal Theory*, eds. Lu, Jingsheng, Chibin Fu and Zhong Gao. Beijing: the Chinese Procuratorate Press, 2004.

Zhang, Xuechao. "The Deepening and Innovation of Deng Xiaoping's Thought on Democracy and Law — on Jiang Zeming's Thought on Democracy and Law." In *On the Front of the Legal Theory*, eds. Lu, Jingsheng, Chibin Fu, and Zhong Gao. Beijing: The Chinese Procuratory Press, 2004.

Zhang, Zhengxin. *The Theory and Practice of the Chinese Suspended Death Sentence*. Wuchang, China: Wuhan University Press, 2004.

Zhao, Bingzhi Zhao. "Guidelines for the Gradual Abolition of the Death Penalty in China." *Legal Studies* 1(2005): 55–62.

Zhao, Bingzhi. "The Gradual Abolition of the Death Penalty for Non-Violent Crimes in China." *Journal of China University of Political Science and Law* 23(2005): 92–99.

Zhao, Bingzhi. *An Exploration of the Abolitionist Movement in China*. Beijing: Chinese University of People's Public Security University Press, 2004.

Zhao, Bingzhi. "Issues Involving the Revision of the Criminal Law." *Legal Studies* 5(1996).

Zhao, Bingzhi. *Reforms of the Criminal Law*. Beijing: China Legal System Press, 1996.

Zhao, Guoling. "An Analysis of Murder and Robbery." *Journal of Huadong University of Political Science and Law* 38(2005): 58–66.

Zhao, Hongwei. *Political Regime of Contemporary China*. New York: University Press of America, 2002.

Zhao, Zuojin. *On the Restriction of the Death Penalty*. Wuchang: Wuhan University Press, 2001.

Zheng, Henry. "The Evolving Role of Lawyers and Legal Practice in China." *American Journal of Comparative Law* 36(1988): 473.

Zhonghan Economic Research Institute. *A Survey Report from the Grass-roots in China*, Chinese Social Sciences Publishing House, 2004.

Zhu, Jianhua. "On the Conflict of Law Regarding the Stipulation of the Final Approval of the Death Penalty." *Contemporary Legal Studies* 1(1999).

Zhu, Mingshan (ed.). *Selected Chinese Criminal Court Cases — 1998*. Beijing: Chinese People University Publishing House, 1999.

———. *Selected Chinese Criminal Court Cases Court Cases — 2001*. Beijing: China People's University Press, 2002.

———. *Selected Chinese Criminal Court Cases — 2002 (*Beijing: Chinese People's University Publishing House, 2003.

Zhu, Rongji. "A Brighter Future — Forward." In *China's Century — the Awakening of the Next Economic Powerhouse*, ed. Laurence J. Brahm. New York: John Wiley & Sons, 2001.

Zhuang, Chunying. "Improvement of the Rights Guarantee of the Criminal Suspect and the Defendant in China's Criminal Proceedings and the Existing Problems." *Justice of China* 68(2005): 23–27.

Index

A life for a life, 24, 229n *see also* retribution
Abduction of women 53, 62, 66, 85,
Abolition movement 4–5, 26, 40, 87, 124–25, 138, 140, 231n
  obstacles for 128
Abolitionist countries
  by region 5–7
  retentionist countries, comparison 6–7, 124, 138–39, 190n, 236n
  status of death penalty 5–6, 8, 13
Accusation rally, see sentencing rally
Administrative avenues to appeal, *see xin fang*
Administrative Litigation Law 138, 199n, 215n
Administrative Procedure Law 18
Administrative review 131, *see also* Supreme People's Court
Administrative warning 233n
Adversarial system 20–21, 23, 42, 47
  semi-adversarial, semi-inquisitorial system 21, 57
  inquisitorial system, comparison 20–21, 57, 65, 95
Adultery 41, 189n
Africa 6, 188n
African Charter of Human and People's Rights 5, *see also* international organization
Age, *see* offender characteristics, *see* minor
Agrarian society 8, 28
America 6, 188n–91n, 196n, 229n–30n
  American Convention on Human Rights 5–6, *see also* international organization 4–6
  Amnesty 215n, *see also* exemption for punishment
Amnesty International, 5, 72–76, 117, 215n, 217n, 227n *see also* data
  annual reports 6–7, 69–70, 188–90
  death penalty log 2, 69–70, 76, 85, 187n, 220n
Anglo-American law 4
Anhui province 2, 187n, 226n
Anti-Rightist movement 207n
Appeal 2, 9, 18, 47, 71, 76, 84, 91–93, 101–03, 126–27, 135, 202n, 206n, 214n, 217n, 223n, 234n
  time limit 106–07, 110, 212–13
  process 58–60, 89–90, 213
  authority for the death penalty, 57 *see also* judicial review; death sentence, process
Approval authority for the death penalty, *see* death sentence, process
Apostasy 6, 189n
Arab Charter of Human Rights, 5, 188n, *see also* international organization
Arbitrary imposition of punishment, *see* discriminatory treatment in punishment
Arrest warrant 106, 224n
Arson 33, 50, 54, 58, 77, 109–10
Asia 6, 28, 188n, 193n
Assault, 220n
Assizes system 35, 203n
Attitude of defendant, *see* confession; Offender Characteristics, attitude and confessions

Bail, 18, 21, 65, 224n, *see also* detention
Banditry 29, 31, 36–37, 44, 189n, 206n, 229n
Banishment 40, 200n

Beating with sticks, *see* five punishments
Beijing municipality 43, 60, 79, 102, 113, 115, 131, 203n, 205n, 218n
Blackmailing 220n
Blasphemy 189n
Bombing 51–52, 118, 188n
Boxer Rebellion 29
Bribery 18, 46, 52–55, 58–59, 61, 77, 96, 99, 188n, 220n, 232n

Cambodia 8, 190n, 230n
Canada 189–90n, 236n
Capital offense, *see* death sentence, scope
Cao Jianmin, 126, 216n *see also* opinion, public officials and legal practitioners'
Car-jacking 103
Checks and balances 15, 17, 202n
Chen Guoqing, 96,103–05, 234n *see also* death sentence, high profile cases
Chen Xingliang, 53, 101, 124–25, 211n, 217n, 221n–22n, 231n–32n *see also* opinion, scholars'
Cheng Kejie, 96, *see also* death sentences, high profile cases
China-Foreign Equity Joint Venture Law 17, 49
Civil law 4, 17, 21, 40, 188n, 190n, 193n, 203n
Clan law, *see* customary law
Class struggle, *see* Maoism
Closed hearing 101–03, 105, 212n, 223n
Collectivism 8, 16, 22, 56, 139
Collegiate bench 59, 89, 102
Common law 21, 137, 190n
Communist Era, *see* communist movement
Communist Party 14–20, 24–25, 38–47, 105, 192n–94n, 205n–06n, 208n, 210n
Communist movement
  socio-political context 44–45
  view of punishment and the death penalty 8, 39–40, 45–46
  substantive criminal law on the death penalty 40–41, 46–47
  procedural criminal law on the death penalty 41–42, 46–47
  execution practices 42–43
Communitarianism 15, 56
Comparative research 3, 11, 139–40, 187n, 189n, 200n, 211n, 224n, 229n
  Methodological relativism 3
Confession 2, 9–10, 21, 34, 46, 48, 65, 67, 71, 83–84, 88, 90, 127, 129, 187n, 195n, 202n, 206n, 214n, 219n, 221n, 234n,
  forced confessions 1, 21, 34, 39, 42, 96–97, 100, 103–104, 127–29, 131, 195n, 202n–203n, 221n, 232n–33n
  judicial investigation of coerced confession 221n
  reforms to curb forced confessions 125, 129, 233n
Confiscation of property 46, 61, 63–64, 93–94, 208n, 210n
Conflict approach 12
Confucianism 16, 29–31, 198n, 205n
  confucianization of law 33
  filial piety 199–01n
  legalism, comparison 16, 29, 31
  ren 29–30, 33–34
  xiao 29, 33, 200n–201n
  zhong 29–30, 33
Consensus approach 12–13
Constitution 17–18, 40, 190n, 207n
Continuing revolution, *see* Maoism
Counterfeiting financial instrument 53–54
  currency counterfeiting 47, 91, 188n
Counter-revolutionary 46, 85, 188n, 210n
Corruption, 6, 9, 15, 17–18, 20, 24, 29, 33, 40, 44, 46, 50, 56, 58–60, 65–66, 72, 76–83, 85–88, 100, 105, 108–11, 121, 125–28, 131, 139, 188n, 192n, 194n, 196n, 203n, 206n–207n, 210n, 218n, 220n, 223n, 229n, 231n–32n *see also* death sentence, scope
Costa Rica 8, 190n
Court appointed attorney, *see* defense attorney
Court of second instance, *see* appeal
Court Structure 20
Courtroom dynamics 9, 94
Courtroom structure 21–22, 57–58, 94–98
Credit card fraud 18, 53–55, 77
Crime trends 15, 211

Criminal Case Collections, 72, 216n, *see* also Data
Critical legal studies movement 13
Critical perspective 11
Cross-examination, 18, 21, 57–58, 68, *see also* evidence
Customary law 11, 200n
state law, comparison 11
Criminal Code, 1979 18, 49–52, 56–58, 61, 64–66, 193n, 210n–12n, 214n–15n
capital offenses, 50–52 *see also* death sentence, scope
crime types 49
Criminal Code, 1997 18
capital offenses, 54 *see also* death sentence, scope
crime types 50–56
1979 criminal code, comparison 18, 50
Criminal Procedure Code, 1979 56
trial process 56
Criminal Procedure Code, 1996 56
major improvements 57–58
trial process 56–58
Culture Revolution 15, 194, 208–209

Data 69–73
case collections 69, 72, 77, 85, 107, 216n, 225n
court records 38, 70–72
fieldwork 3
limited access to 2
national data 2, 43, 69, 87
on the website 2–3, 69, 72–73
Death penalty
Debate 4, 7, 48, 100, 121–33, 212n, 231n
Justification 11, 23–24, 26, 121, 124
deterrence 23–26, 37, 84, 115, 122–24, 195n
retribution 23–26, 115, 124–25, 195n
policy 25–26, see also kill fewer, kill carefully
Death row 35, 66, 79, 103, 113–114, 187, 189, 218
counseling programs 113, 118
final meeting with family 114, 187, 226
time on 113
Death sentence
exemplified cases
bombing 118, 174–77
bribery 86, 99, 168–74
currency counterfeiting 91, 163–68
drug trafficking 92, 123, 177–81
forcing women into prostitution 181–86
graft 91–92
intentional assault 90, 100–01, 150–56, 221n
murder 1–2, 24, 31, 33, 84, 96, 99–101, 103–04, 109–10, 113, 128, 132–34, 141–50, 203n, 219n–20n, 225n–26n
rape 1, 84, 90, 128, 150–53, 221n, 225n–26n
theft 99, 157–63
high profile cases
Chen Guoqing 96, 103–05, 234
Cheng Kejie 96
Dong Wei 96, 100–105, 113, 126, 137, 168–74, 217n, 222n, 223n, 231n–32n, 234n
Liu Yong 99–100, 105, 113, 117–19, 122–23, 136, 221n, 225n, 228n, 235n–36n
Wang Binyu 132–134, 136, 216n, 219n, 231n, 234n–35n
Prevalence 8–9, 43, 72
China 8–9, 43, 70, 72, 74–76
Global 7, 73–74, 189
process
time limit 106–07, 224n
involving complex cases 98
scope 4, 6, 9, 46, 50, 53–55, 58, 75, 85–86, 125, 127–8, 130–31, 137–8 *see also* United Nations
China
corruption 6, 9, 15, 17–18, 20, 24, 29, 33, 40, 46, 58–60, 66, 72, 76–88, 100, 105, 108–11, 121, 125–28, 131, 139, 192n, 196n, 203n, 206n, 210n, 218n, 220n, 223n, 232n
economic crimes 24, 41, 46, 50, 78–83, 88, 110, 220n
property crimes 15, 33, 41, 78–83, 86, 88, 108, 110–11, 218n
public order crimes 50, 72, 78–83, 88
public safety crimes 9, 72, 77–83, 85, 87–88, 108–09, 127, 218n
violent crimes 15, 41, 47, 78–83, 88, 101, 109, 218n, 225n
United Nations 4–6, 188n, 193n

China (*continued*)
  reform to limit capital offenses 127–28, 188n
Decision Concerning the Differentiation of Class Status in the Countryside 208n
Decision regarding the Approval of Cases Involving Death Sentences 58
Declaration of Independence, 4 *see also* human rights
Decree on Severely Punishing Those Who Disturb the Economic Order 50
Decree on Severely Punishing Those Who Threaten Public Security 50
Decree on Prohibiting Narcotics 50
Decree on Punishing Military Personnel Who Derelicts Military Duty 52
Decree on Punishing Those Who Hijack an Aircraft 51, 54
Defendants' rights, see also human rights 57, 67, 107, 128–30, 224n
Defense attorney, *see also* legal representation
  court-appointed 91
  in death penalty cases 20–21, 47, 57–58, 91, 95, 100–02, 105, 129, 194n
  rights under 1979 criminal procedure law 18
  rights under 1996 criminal procedure law 18
  obstacles faced by 21
Democratic Republic of Congo 74
Deng Xiaoping 14
  view on law 16–20, 229n
Deprival of political rights 61, 90–94, 101, 210n
Detention, see also bail
  length of 43, 71, 106–07
  pretrial detention 106–07
  police discretionary power 61–64
Deterrence, 23–26, 37, 84, 98, 115, 122, 124, 128, 140; *see also* death penalty, justification
Discriminatory treatment in punishment
  in death penalty 7, 189n
Deserting the army 44, 52, 207n
Dispute resolution 11–12
Disrupting public services 99
Dong Wei, 96, 100–105, 113, 117, 126, 137, 217n, 222n, 223n, 231n–32n, 234n *see also* death sentence, high profile cases
Drug–related offense 6
  Drug trafficking, 6, 18, 52–55, 58–59, 63–64, 76–77, 85, 87, 98, 110, 123, 188n, 219n, 220n, 230n, *see also* death sentence, exemplified cases

Economic crimes 6, 24, 41, 46, 50–55, 72, 77–88, 108–11, 188–89n, 220n, *see also* death sentence, scope
Economic reforms 2, 14–16, 49–50, 56, 94, 112, 133, 138–39, 191n, 193n
  benefits 14–15
  household registration system 14–15, 45, 134, 191n–93n, 211n, 229n
  impact on crime 15, 50, 56
Economic superpower 3
Education program for lawyers and judges, *see* training program for lawyers and judges
Embezzlement 18, 40, 85, 94, 188n
Emperor Gaozu 30
Emperor Wen 30
Empress Wu 30
England (United Kingdom) 21, 189–90n
English Bill of Rights, 4 *see also* human rights
Errors in death sentences 125, 128, 196n
Espionage 41, 46, 51, 54, 85, 188n, 220n
Europe 5–6, 124, 188n, 190n, 210n
European Union, 5 *see also* international organization
Evading military service 6, 188n
Evidence 21, 34, 42, 46, 57–58, 71, 131, 194n, 212n, 224n, 232n, 234n
  as stipulated in 1996 criminal procedure law 220n
  confession 129, 233n, *see also* confession
  DNA 2
  United Nations' standards 5
Exclusionary rule, 129, 233n *see also* confession

Execution
  methods
    beating to death 36
    beheading 7, 36, 39, 43, 189n
    boiling 199n
  burning 33, 36
  decapitation 31, 36, 38, 43, 201n, 203n–04n
  disemboweling 4
  draw and quartering 4
  drowning 36
  electrocution 7, 189n
  garroting 25
  gas chambers 7, 189n
  hanging and strangulations 7, 36, 43, 207n, 230n
  lethal injection 1, 7, 112, 115–117, 189n
  debate 115
  process 116–17
    shooting and firing squads 7, 10, 43, 60, 112, 114–15, 189n
    slicing 25, 36–39, 200n, 203n–04n
    stoning 7, 189n
  prevalence
  China 6–8, 43, 70, 74–76, 190n
  Global 5–7, 73–74, 189n
  process
    time between the death sentence and execution 110
Exempt population 9, 49, 64, 67, 138, *see also* mentally ill; minor; pregnant women
  International standards 5
Extradition, 5, 236n *see also* international organization
Extra-legal factors 88
Extra-legal punishment 4, 36
Exoneration 2, 7, 187n
Extortion 46, 53, 99, 104, 129
Eyewitnesses' testimony, 90, 101 *see also* evidence

Feudal society 27, 197n
Filial piety, *see* Confucianism
Fines 44, 200n
Five Dynasty and Ten States 29, 197n
Five punishments 32, 200n
Firearm related offenses 6, 82, 99, 188n, 215n
Floating population, 15, 81, 191–92n, *see also* transient population
Forensic evidence 90, 95, *see also* evidence
Four-tiered court system 20
France 21, 70, 123, 195
Fraud 18, 44, 53–56, 77, 85, 91–92, 109–110, 139, 189n, 220n, 225n
Full trial process 89
Functions of law 11–12, 15, 18, 137
Functionalism 12

Gambling 40, 41, 44, 99, 206n
Gansu province 117, 132, 134
Gender, *see* Offender Characteristics
General Rules for the Organization of People's Tribunals 210n
Germany 21, 123
Globalization 4, 15, 192n
Graft 18, 51, 53, 55, 63–64, 77, 91–94, 110, 128, 218n, 220n–21n, 227n,
Great Leap Forward 207n–08n
Gu poison 201n
Guangdong province 59, 98, 205n, 233n

Han dynasty 28, 30, 32, 66, 197–99n, 201n, 204n, 230n
Harmonious society 139
Hard labor, *see* physical labor
Hebei province 1, 103–04, 128, 187n, 227n
Homosexual acts with violence 189n
Hooliganism 220n
Household registration system, *see* economic reforms
Hu Jintao, 121, 126, *see also* opinion, public officials and legal practitioners'
Human rights 4–6, 26, 40, 57, 69–70, 138, 188n, 193n, 212n
House surveillance 210n, 224n
Hunan province 124, 231n

Imperial China 27–38
  socio-political context 28–29
  view of punishment and the death penalty 29–32
  substantive criminal law on the death penalty 32–34
  procedural criminal law on the death penalty 34–36
  execution practices 36–38

Imposition of the death penalty, *see* discriminatory treatment in punishment
Incapacitation 23–24, 26, 84, 124, 195n
Incarceration 39, 128, 140
Incest 33, 189n
Individualism 16, 56
Individual rights 22–23, 125, 138, *see also* human rights
Informal social control 11, 82
Inquisitorial system 20–21
  adversarial system, comparison 20, 57–58, 65, 95
  principles of "directness" and "orality" 210n
Inspection system 19
Instrumentalism, *see* critical perspective
Intentional assault 52, 86, 90, 100–101, 221n
Interpretation Concerning Several Issues in the Implementation of the Criminal Procedure Law of the People's Republic of China 212n–13n
Interpretation on how to carry out the Suspended Death Sentence for Counterrevolutionary Offense 215n
Interpretation of Laws in Criminal Cases Regarding Obstruction of the Prevention and Control of the Outbreak of Infectious Diseases 211n
Interfering with marriage and family 44, 206n
International Covenant on Civil and Political Rights, 4, 188n, 193n *see also* United Nations
Interrogation, *see* police
International judicial cooperation, 5, 236n *see also* international organization
International organization 4–5
International Covenant on Civil and Political Rights 4, 6, 74, 188–89n, 193n, *see also* United Nations
Iran 6, 74, 188n–89n

Jilin province 225n
Jiangsu province 90–91, 127, 216n, 233n
Jiangxi province 206n
Jiang Zemin
  view on law 18–19
  view on the death penalty 19
Judge's Law 18
Judicial accountability 19
Judicial committee 20, 207n, 215n, 223n
Judicial efficiency 94
Judicial exam, *see* State Judicial Exam
Judicial fairness 94
Judicial independence 17, 19–20, 94, 104–05, 114, 137, 223n–24n
Judicial judgment documents 71–73, 77, 81–82, 85–86, 90–94, 97, 99, 101, 104, 106–08, 137, 194n, 216n, 221n–22n, 224n–25n, 235n *see also* data, case collections
Judicial oversight 19–20, 60, 129, 223n
Judicial protectionism 20, 60, 104–05, 131, 137, 223n
Judicial responsibility system 105, 191n, 223n
Judicial review 9–10, 18, 20, 22, 34–35, 38, 42, 56, 58–60, 72, 75, 89–93, 96, 98–113, 119, 125–27, 130–33, 194n, 203n–04n, 212n–14n, 217n, 224n–25n, 234n
Judicial uniform 94–95
Just deserts, *see* retribution
Justice model, see restoration
Justification for the death penalty, *see* death penalty, justification
Juvenile offender, *see* minor

Kidnapping 220n
Kill fewer, kill carefully, *see* death penalty, policy
Killing a chicken before a monkey, 24 *see also* deterrence
Killing one to warn a hundred, 24 *see also* deterrence
Korea 28

Labor-Capital Consultative Councils in Private Enterprises 208n
Land reform 207n
Law Enforcement 18–19
Law in Action 9, 69
Law on the books 9
Law on Public Security Organ 18

Law Yearbook of China, 69–74, 75, 77, 215n–217n, 220n *see also* data
Law's objectivity 10, 134–36
Law's relativity 134
Law's supremacy 10, 18–19, 94
Lawyer, *see* legal representation
Lawyer's Law 18
Lawmaking activities 12–13, 17–18, 70, 193n
Lay judge, *see* people's assessor
Legal aid 2, 19–20, 58, 65, 135, 187n, 212n, 215n
Legal consciousness 19, 96
Legal culture 22–23, 192n, 203n
Legal formalism 9, 11–13, 26, 127
Legal promulgation 12, 22, 207n, 209n, 215n
Legal realism 9, 11, 13, 19, 26, 132, 190
Legal reforms 2, 16, 18, 20, 48, 57, 65, 114, 121, 125–32, 137
Legal representation 10, 18, 20, 47–48, 65, 127–29
  Problems 21, 65
  reforms to enhance the effectiveness of 20–21, 58, 65, 125
Legal structure 19–22
Legal system, organizational structure, 20–25, 39–40, 42, 45, 57, 94, 126–28, 138, 190n, 197n, 200n, 202n–03n, 209n–10n, 214n, 217n
Legal training, *see* training program for lawyers and judges
Legalism 31, 198n
  Confucianism, comparison 16
Leninism, *see* critical perspective
Lethal injection, *see* execution methods
Li Lishan 205n
Liaoning province 99, 117–18
Life imprisonment 5, 46, 56, 61–64, 66, 71, 75–84, 86, 91–92, 98, 103–04, 108–12, 122, 126, 210n–11n, 215n, 217n–18n, 225n
Litigation trickster 35–36, 203n, *see also* defense attorney
Liu Shaoqi 45
Liu Yong 99–100, 113, 117–19, 122–23, 136, 221n, 225n, 228n, 235–36n *see also* death sentence, process
Living law, *see* Maoism
Local protectionism, *see* judicial protectionism

Magistrate, *see* inquisitorial system
Malaysia 188n
Mandatory legal representation 18, 21*see also* defense attorney
Manchuria 28
Mass trial 42, 207n
Mass-line justice, *see* popular justice
Mao era 15, 17–18, 49–50, 98
Mao Zedong 14–19, 24–25, 38–40, 43–46, 49–50, 98, 121, 192n, 195n–97n, 202n, 206n, 208n–209n, 220n
Maoism 16–17, 192n
Mass struggle meeting 40
Materialism 15
Market economy, *see* economic reforms
Marxism, see critical perspective
Marxist, Leninist and Maoist thought 12, 16, 19, 197n, 208n
May Fourth Movement 39, 205n
Media censorship 15, 229n
Media reports of death penalty 1–2
Medical model, *see* rehabilitation
Mentally ill, *see* death sentence, exempt population
Meritorious service 2, 60, 66, 90–91, 136, 196n, 215n *see also* evidence, confession
Methodological relativism 3, *see also* comparative research
Mexico 8, 190n
Migrant population, *see* transient population
Ming Dynasty 22, 33, 199n, 203n
Minority threat 1
Minor 51, 62–64, 91, 189n, 236n, *see also* Offender Characteristics; *see* exempt population
Misappropriation 41, 92, 220n
Monetary redemption, *see* redeeming punishment
Moral education 11, 24–25, 113
Movement of suppression of counter-revolutionaries 25, 40–47, 50–52, 58–59, 66, 85, 88, 188n, 206n–10n, 215n
Movement against the Three Evils 207n
Movement of judicial reform 100, 105, 207n, 223n

Multi–party cooperation 17, 193n *see also* Deng Xiaoping, view on law
Murder 218n, 220n
Muslim Rebellion 29
Mutual responsibility 201n

Narcotics trafficking, *see* drug-related offense, drug trafficking
Nationalist 38–44, 197n, 205n–07n
Nien War 29
Ningxia Autonomous Region 133–34, 216n, 234n–35n
Northern Expedition 38–39, 205n
Notice on Using Lethal Injection in Executions 115
Notice of the Standard for Meting Out Sentences 215n

Objectivity of Law 134–37
Oceania 6
Offender characteristics 71, 77–84
  age 35, 41, 62–64, 77–78, 87, 202n, 212n, *see also* minor
  attitude and confessions 83–84, *see also* confession
  gender 78–79, 87, *see also* pregnant women
  occupation 79–80, 87
  residency status 80–82, 87, *see also* transient population, floating population
  criminal history 82, 87, *see also* recidivism
Offense characteristics 71, 84–87
One Center and Four Principles 14
Opinion
  public officials and legal practitioners' 126–127
  public's, *see* public opinion
  scholars' 124–26, 231
Opium possession 40–41, 46, 63, 206n
Opium War 29
Organ transplantation 1, *see also* execution
Organization law 17,
Organized crime 37, 99–100, 105, 117–19, 123, 129, 136, 192n
Organizing secret armed forces 207n

People's assessor 47
People's democratic dictatorship, *see* Maoism
People's representative system 17, *see also* Deng Xiaoping, view on law
Pimping 50, 53, 189n, 220n
Physical amputation 32, 39, 200n, 205n, *see also* five punishments
Physical labor 133
Planned economy 14–16, 44, 197n, *see also* economic reforms
Pluralism 4, *see also* globalization
Police
  interrogation, time limit 106, 128–29, 233n
  record 90, *see also* evidence
Political campaign 25
Political reforms 14–15
Popular justice 25, 40, 42, 45, 97, 209n,
Pragmatism, legal 190n, 192n, *see also* instrumentalism
Predictive model, *see* incapacitation
Pregnant women, *see* death sentence, exempt population
Presumption of innocence 128
Presumption of guilt 20, 202n
Pretrial detention, *see* bail
Preventive model, see deterrence
Primitive commune 27
Principle of analogy 46
Prison reform 205n
Profiteering 188n
Procedural safeguards 1, 4, 6, 10, 18, 34, 48, 57, 188n
Procuratorate 129, 194n
  prosecutor's uniform 95
  prosecution time limit 106
Proletariat dictatorship, *see* critical perspective; Maoism
Property crimes, 85–86, 189n, 220n, *see also* death sentence, scope
Prosecutor, *see* procuratorate
Prostitution 15, 18, 41, 50, 52–55, 62–63, 77, 110, 139, 189n, 220n, 229n *see also* public order offenses
Protection against cruel, inhuman and degrading punishment 4, *see also* human rights, international organization
Provisional Law on Guarding State Secrets 210n
Provisional Statute on Penalties for Undermining the State Monetary System 46, 210n

Public's indignation 24–25, 97–98, 121, 135–136
Public opinion
  China 23, 121–23, 136–38, 195n, 229n, 232n
  western 7, 124, 189–90n
Public order crimes, 188n, 220, *see also* death sentence, scope
Public security, *see* police
Public safety crimes, *see* death sentence, scope
Public trial 91
Punishments of *Lu* 32
Punitive attitude, *see* legal culture

Qin dynasty 28, 32, 197n–99n, 201n
Qiu Xinglong 124, 196n–97n, 231n, *see also* opinion, legal scholars'
Qing dynasty 27, 29, 31, 33, 35, 37–38, 197n, 201n, 203n
Qing Code 32, 201n, 204n
Qu Qiubai 205n

Rape, 189n, 220n
Recidivism 82, 87, 219n, *see also* offender characteristics, criminal history
Rehabilitation 23–24, 26, 39, 195n, 209n
Redeeming punishment
  with money 33, 59–60, 200n–01n
  with official rank 33
  in death penalty 33
Reintegrative shaming 11
Relativity of Social Context 134–37
Ren, see Confucianism
Republican era 38–43
  socio-political context 39
  view of punishment and the death penalty 39–40
  substantive criminal law on the death penalty 40–41
  procedural criminal law on the death penalty 41–42
  execution practices 42–43
Religion and punishment 8, 37
Religious offenses 6, 76, 189n, 198n
Resolution on Prohibiting Prostitution and Pimping 50, 53
Resolution on Severely Punishing Those Who Abduct and Sell Women and Children 53
Resolution on Prohibiting Prostitution and Pimping 53
Resolution on Punishing Those Who Produce and Sell Fake and Shoddy Products 53
Resolution on Punishing Those Who Disturb the Financial Order 53
Resolution on Punishing Those Who Issue, Counterfeit or Sell Special Value-Added Tax Invoices 53
Restoration 23, 26, 195n
Retribution 23–24, 26, 115, 124–25, 195n
Retentionist countries 7, 138–39, 188n
  by region 6
Review, *see also* death sentence, process
  authority 58
  in Imperial China 34–35, 38
  involving complex cases 98
  length 106
Right to life, *see* human rights, *see also* international organization
Riot 29, 41, 54–55, 220n
Robbery 218n, 220n
Rule by law 16, 18–19
Rule of law 16, 18–19, 22, 30, 57, 94, 97–98, 132, 193n, 194n, 202n, 231n, 236n
Rule of man 15–16, 18, 22, 192n

Sabotage 41, 51, 188n, 220n
Safeguards Guaranteeing Protection of the Rights of Those Facing the Death Penalty 4, *see also* United Nations
Saudi Arabia 74
Self–defense 100–02, 134–36, *see also* evidence
Semi–adversarial system 21, 57, *see also* adversarial system; inquisitorial system
Sentencing discretion, 61, *see also* discriminatory treatment in punishment
Sentencing rally 9, 97–98, 113, 122, 222n, 225n
Sexual offenses 6, 189n, *see also* death sentence, scope
Shaanxi province 100–02, 104–05, 223n
Shanxi province 234n
Shang Dynasty 32, 197n, 200n
Shanghai municipality 201n–02n, 205n, 222n, 225n, 233n, 235n
Shang Yang, *see* legalism

Shelter and Investigation 138
Shi Huangdi 28, 198n
Sichuan province 1, 109, 216n
Simplified procedure 57, 89, 209n, 212n, 220n
Singapore 123, 188n, 230n
Six Codes 40
Slave society 27
Smuggling 37, 52–55, 58–59, 63, 82, 99, 128, 139, 189n, 220n
Speedy trial 10, 106, *see also* death sentences, process
Spreading rumors among the masses 46, 52, 55, 207n
Spring-Autumn period 28, 197n
Social change 3, 10, 12, 14–15, 45, 138–39
Social engineering 12, 193n
Social norm 10
Social unrest 28–29, 136
Socialism 14, 16, 46, 215n
Socialist China 8–9, 26–27, 43–48, 56, 66
  socio-political context 44–45
  view of punishment and the death penalty 45–46
  substantive criminal law on the death penalty 46–47
  procedural criminal law on the death penalty 47–48
  execution practices 48
Socialist legal system 13, 16, 22, 49, 194n
Sociological jurisprudence 9, 11–14, 19, 26, 132, 190n
Sodomy 189n
Song dynasty 34, 37, 202n–04n
Soviet model, *see* Communist era
State, capital crimes against 6, 188n
State Compensation Law 130, 138, 233–34n
State Judicial Exam 19
State law 3, 11
State punishment 4, *see also* the death penalty
Statute on Punishment for Counter-Revolutionary Activity 210n
Statue of the International Tribunal for the Former Yugoslavia 5, *see also* international organization
Stereotype of the death penalty 1, *see also* media reports of death penalty
Strike-hard campaign 22, 24, 58, 76, 107, 112, 195n, 212n, 217n
Substantive law 8–9, 16, 18, 27, 32–34, 40–41, 46–49, 61, 67, 72, 127, 223n
Sudan 189n
Sui Code 32
Sui dynasty 28, 30, 200n
Sun Aijun, *see* death sentences, Sun Aijun
Supervising adjudication 59–60, *see also* judicial review
Supplementary Regulation on Punishing Illegally Digging and Robbing Ancient Remains or Tombs 53, 55
Supplemental Regulation on Punishing Those Who Leak National Secrets 52, 54
Supreme People's Court 56, 75, 212n–13n, 217n, 222n
  final review and approval authority in the death penalty case 59, 127, 130–32, 234n
  length 112
Suspended death sentence 1–2, 9, 24, 65–67, 75–77, 79, 86, 92–93, 102–04, 108–10, 112, 196n, 199n, 217–18n

Tax evasion 99, 220n
Tianjin 80, 93–94
Taiping Rebellion 22, 31, 38, 199n, 204n
Tang dynasty 28–30, 32, 38, 196n, 198n–200n, 203n
Tang Code 32–34, 36, 65, 201n, 203n, 214n
Terrorism 6, 53–55, 188n
Theft 33, 41, 46, 52, 55, 77, 79, 82, 86, 88, 96, 99, 110, 189n, 218n–20n, 220n, 232n
Torture, *see* confession
Training program for lawyers and judges 19
Transient population 81, 87, 218–19, *see also* offender characteristics, residency status
Treason 30, 33, 37, 188n
Trial
  of first instance 47, 59, 71, 89–91, 98, 107–09, 213n, 217n, 220n, 234n

of second instance 59, 71, 89, 213n, *see also* review
length 90, 106–12

United Kingdom, *see also* England 123–24, 189–90n
United Nations 4–6, 188n, 193n, *see also* international organization
United States 6–7, 11, 20–21, 67, 74, 79, 123, 189n, 195n–96n, 218n, 230n, 236n
Universal Declaration of Human Rights 188n, *see also* United Nations
Utilitarian doctrine 23, 25, *see also* deterrence

Vietnam 6, 28, 74
Violent crimes 15, 41, 47, 83, 85–86, 88, 101, 105, 108–12, 218n, 220n, 225n, *see also* death sentence, scope

Wang Binyu 132–37, 216n, 219n, 231n, 234n–35n, *see also* death sentences, high profile cases
Warring States period 28, 197n
Websites 72–73
Western Zhou Dynasty 28, 32, 197
Witchcraft 33, 37, 201n
World Anti-Drug Day 98
Wu Xing, *see* five punishments

Xiao, see Confucianism
Xiao Yang 126, 130, 136, 232n, *see also* opinion, public officials and legal practitioners'
Xin Fang 60, 214n

Yanan era 24
Yemen 189n
Yuan dynasty 32, 38, 196n, 200n, 203n–04n
Yunnan province 1, 29, 92–93, 115, 227n

Zhang Jun 126, *see also* opinion, public officials and legal practitioners'
Zhejiang province 91
Zhong, *see* Confucianism
Zhou Enlai 16, 192n
Zhu De 206n
Zhu Zhanping 126–27, *see also* opinion, public officials and legal practitioners'

For Product Safety Concerns and Information please contact our EU representative GPSR@taylorandfrancis.com
Taylor & Francis Verlag GmbH, Kaufingerstraße 24, 80331 München, Germany

www.ingramcontent.com/pod-product-compliance
Ingram Content Group UK Ltd.
Pitfield, Milton Keynes, MK11 3LW, UK
UKHW040855180926
475701UK00001B/11

* 9 7 8 0 4 1 5 8 0 3 9 6 0 *